DATE DUE

K

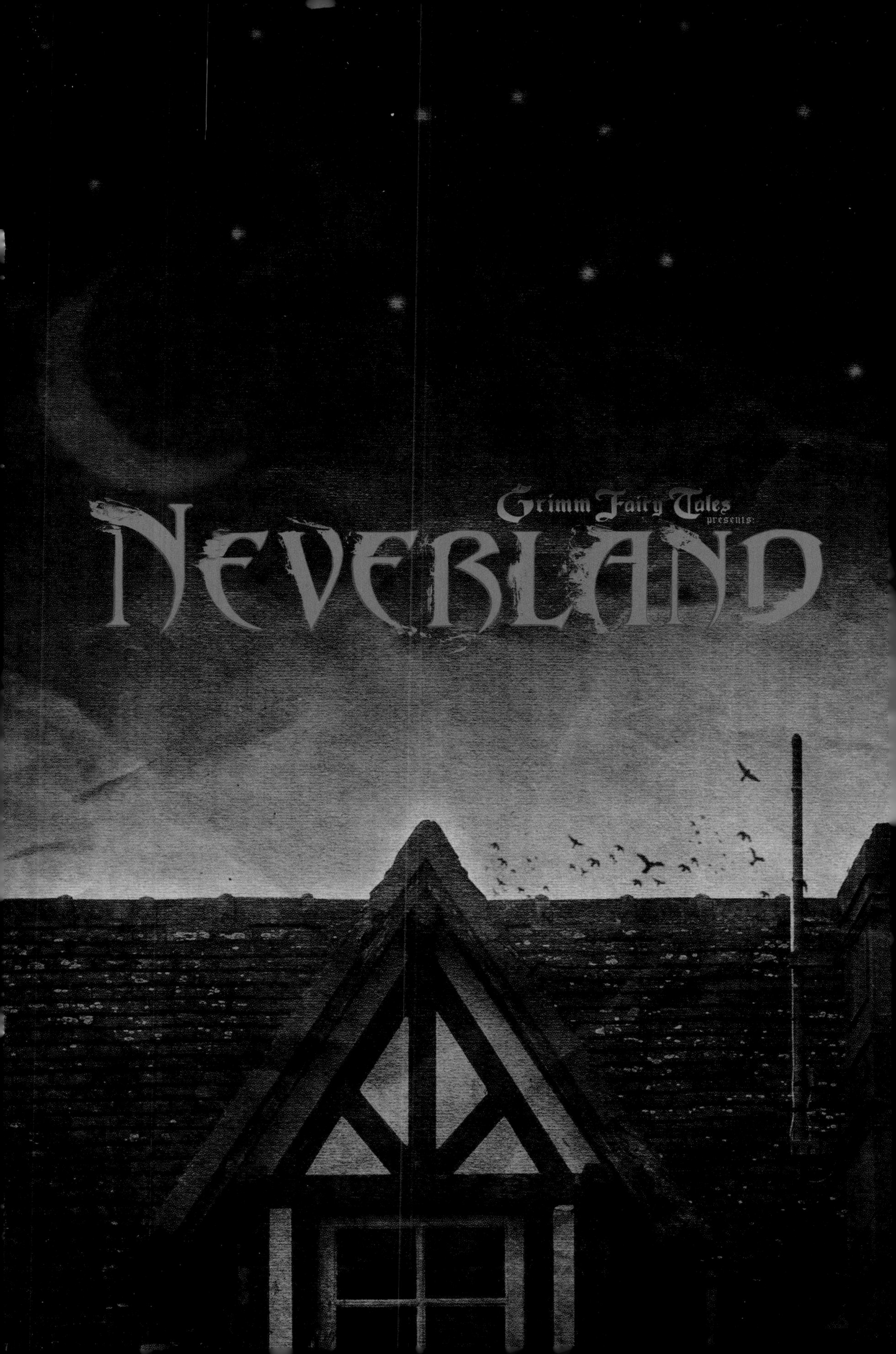
Grimm Fairy Tales
presents:
NEVERLAND

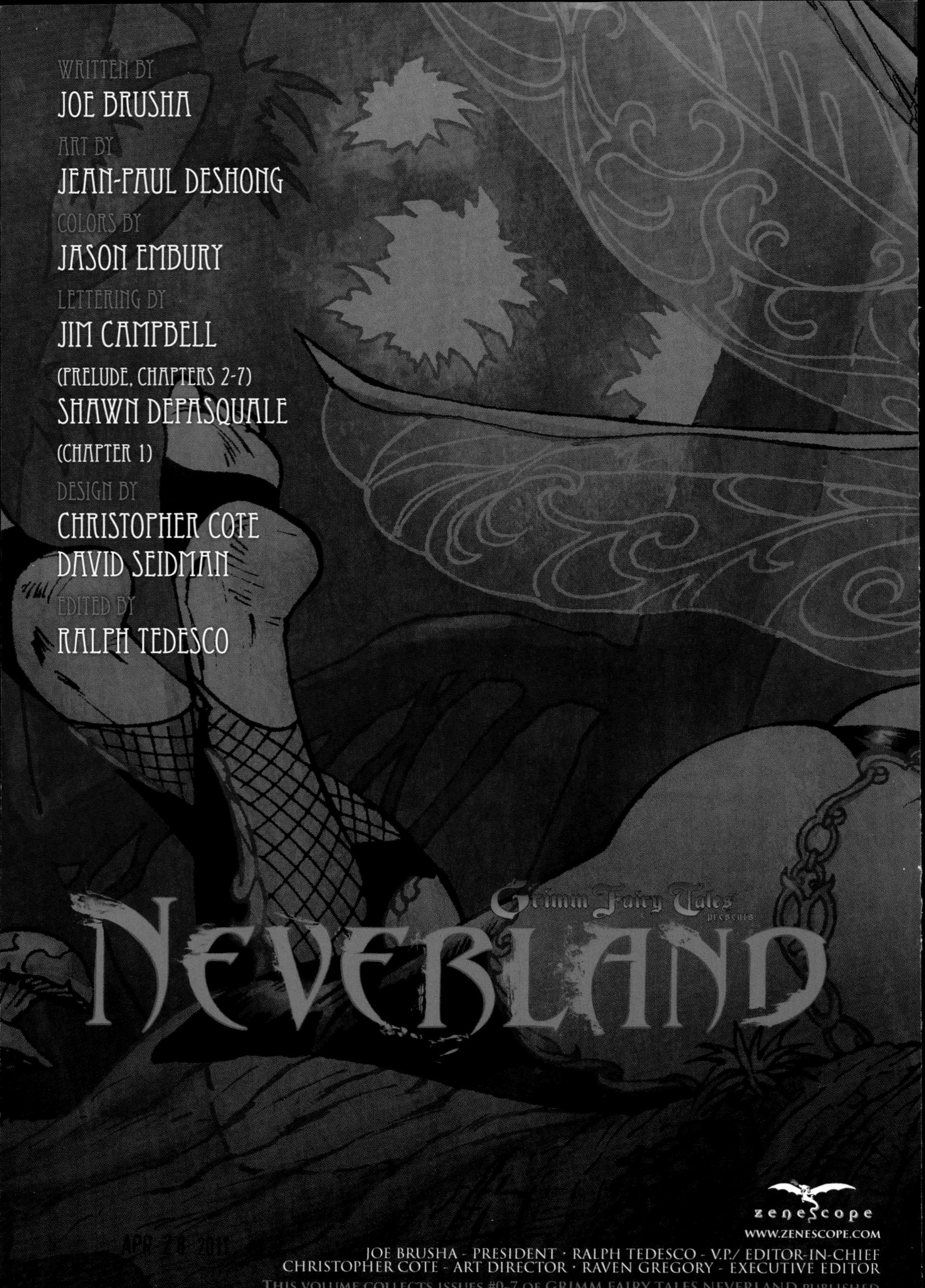
Grimm Fairy Tales presents
NEVERLAND

WRITTEN BY
JOE BRUSHA
ART BY
JEAN-PAUL DESHONG
COLORS BY
JASON EMBURY
LETTERING BY
JIM CAMPBELL
(PRELUDE, CHAPTERS 2-7)
SHAWN DEPASQUALE
(CHAPTER 1)
DESIGN BY
CHRISTOPHER COTE
DAVID SEIDMAN
EDITED BY
RALPH TEDESCO

zenescope
WWW.ZENESCOPE.COM

JOE BRUSHA - PRESIDENT · RALPH TEDESCO - V.P./ EDITOR-IN-CHIEF
CHRISTOPHER COTE - ART DIRECTOR · RAVEN GREGORY - EXECUTIVE EDITOR

THIS VOLUME COLLECTS ISSUES #0-7 OF GRIMM FAIRY TALES NEVERLAND PUBLISHED BY ZENESCOPE ENTERTAINMENT. FIRST EDITION, FEBRUARY 2011 · ISBN: 978-0-9825826-1-9

Grimm Fairy Tales: Neverland Hardcover, February, 2011. First Printing. Published by Zenescope Entertainment Inc.,433 Caredean Drive, Ste. C, Horsham, Pennsylvania 19044.

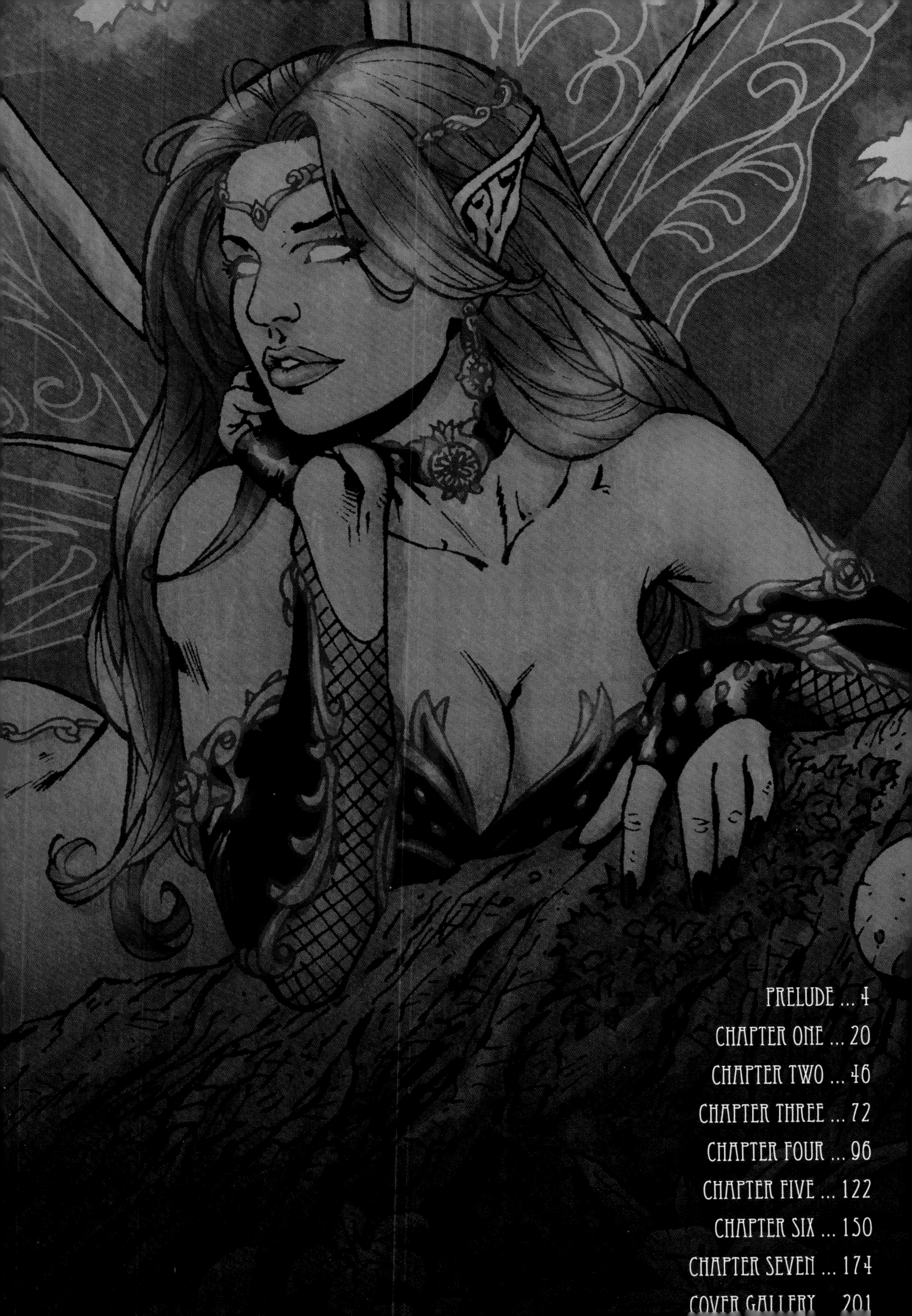

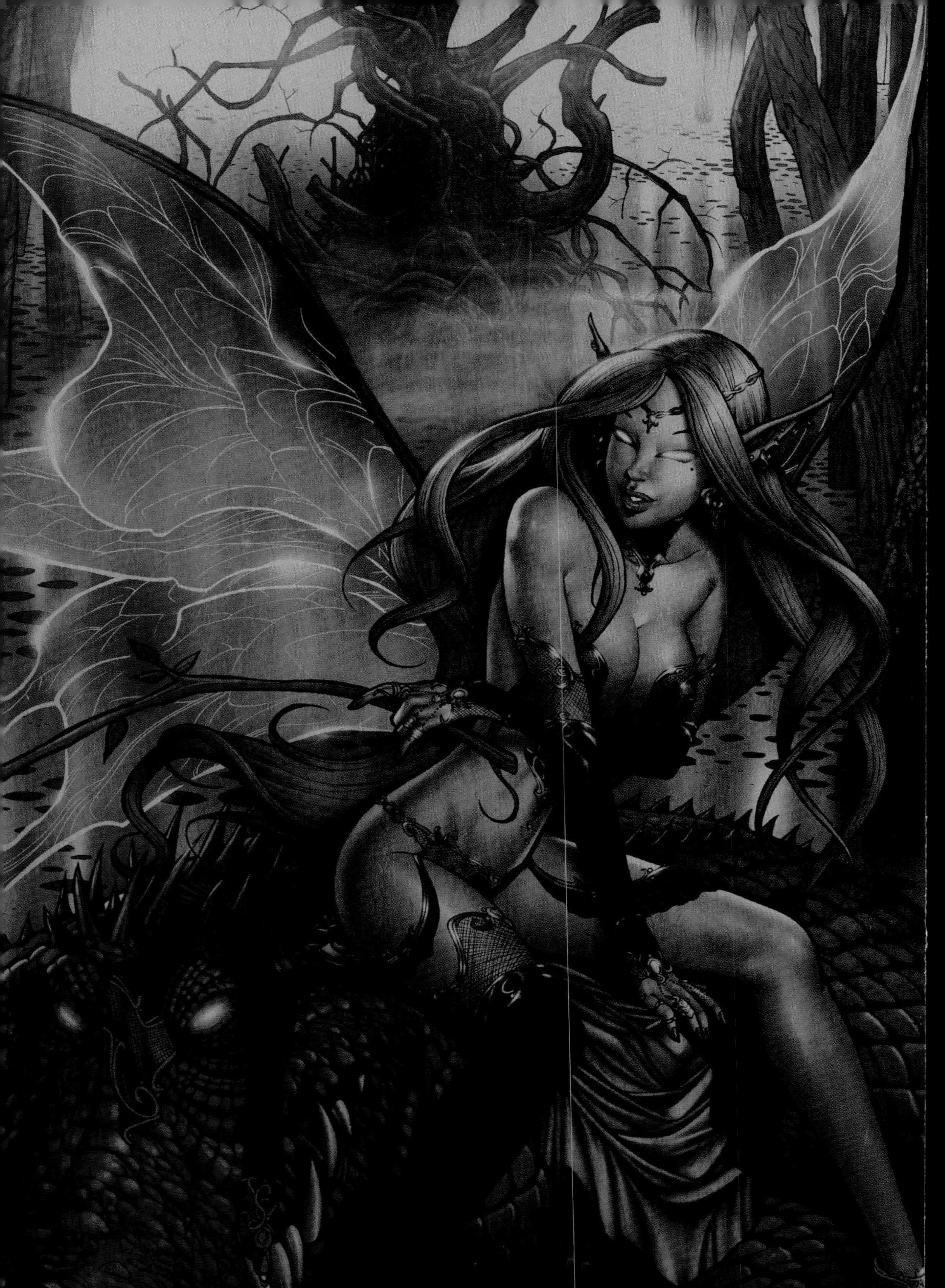

PRELUDE

Zenescope Entertainment
Proudly Presents
Grimm Fairy Tales
NEVERLAND
NEW YORK.
THE CITY THAT
NEVER SLEEPS.
BILLY HITCHCOCK
WISHES THAT WERE
REALLY TRUE.

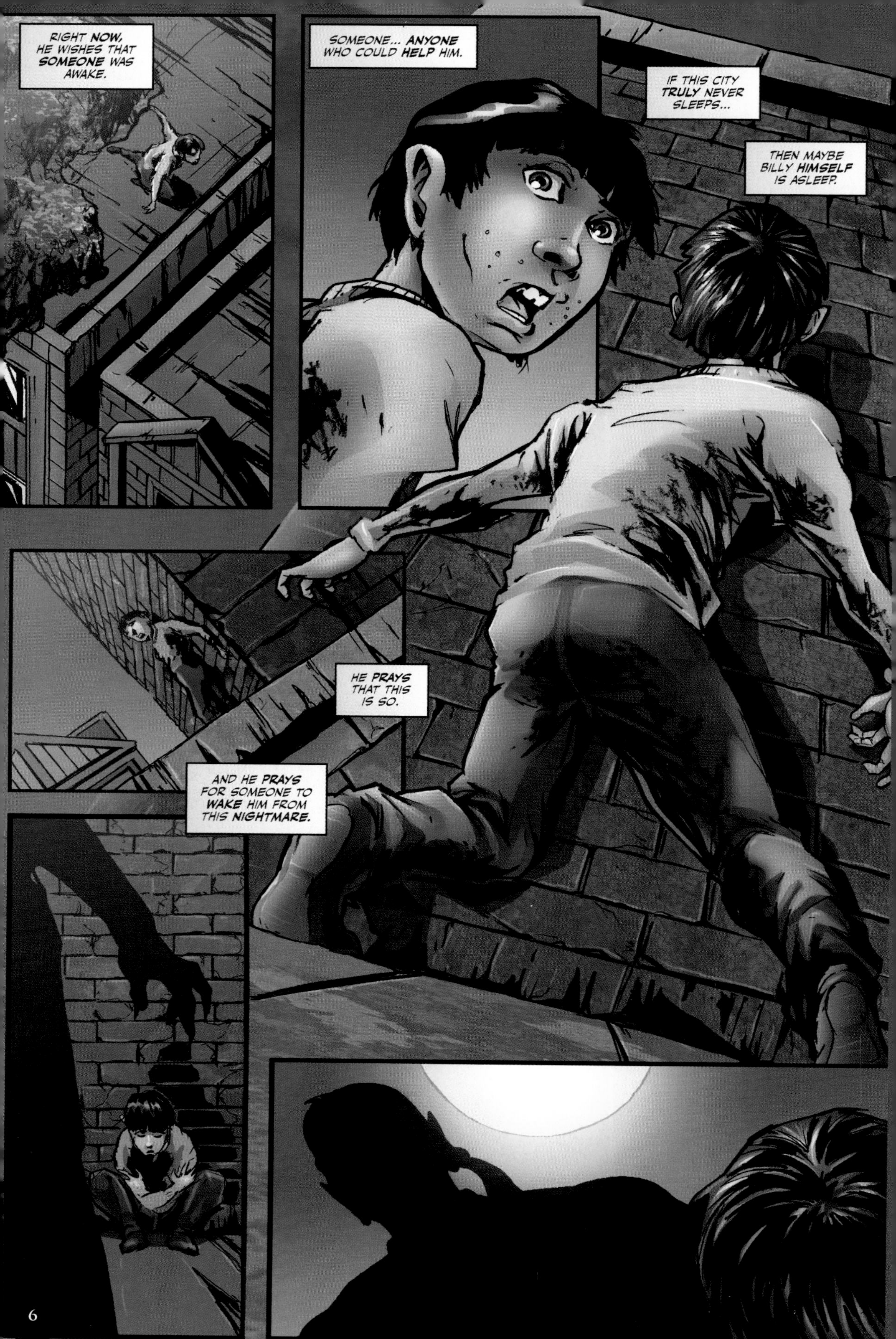
RIGHT NOW, HE WISHES THAT SOMEONE WAS AWAKE.
SOMEONE... ANYONE WHO COULD HELP HIM.
IF THIS CITY TRULY NEVER SLEEPS...
THEN MAYBE BILLY HIMSELF IS ASLEEP.
HE PRAYS THAT THIS IS SO.
AND HE PRAYS FOR SOMEONE TO WAKE HIM FROM THIS NIGHTMARE.

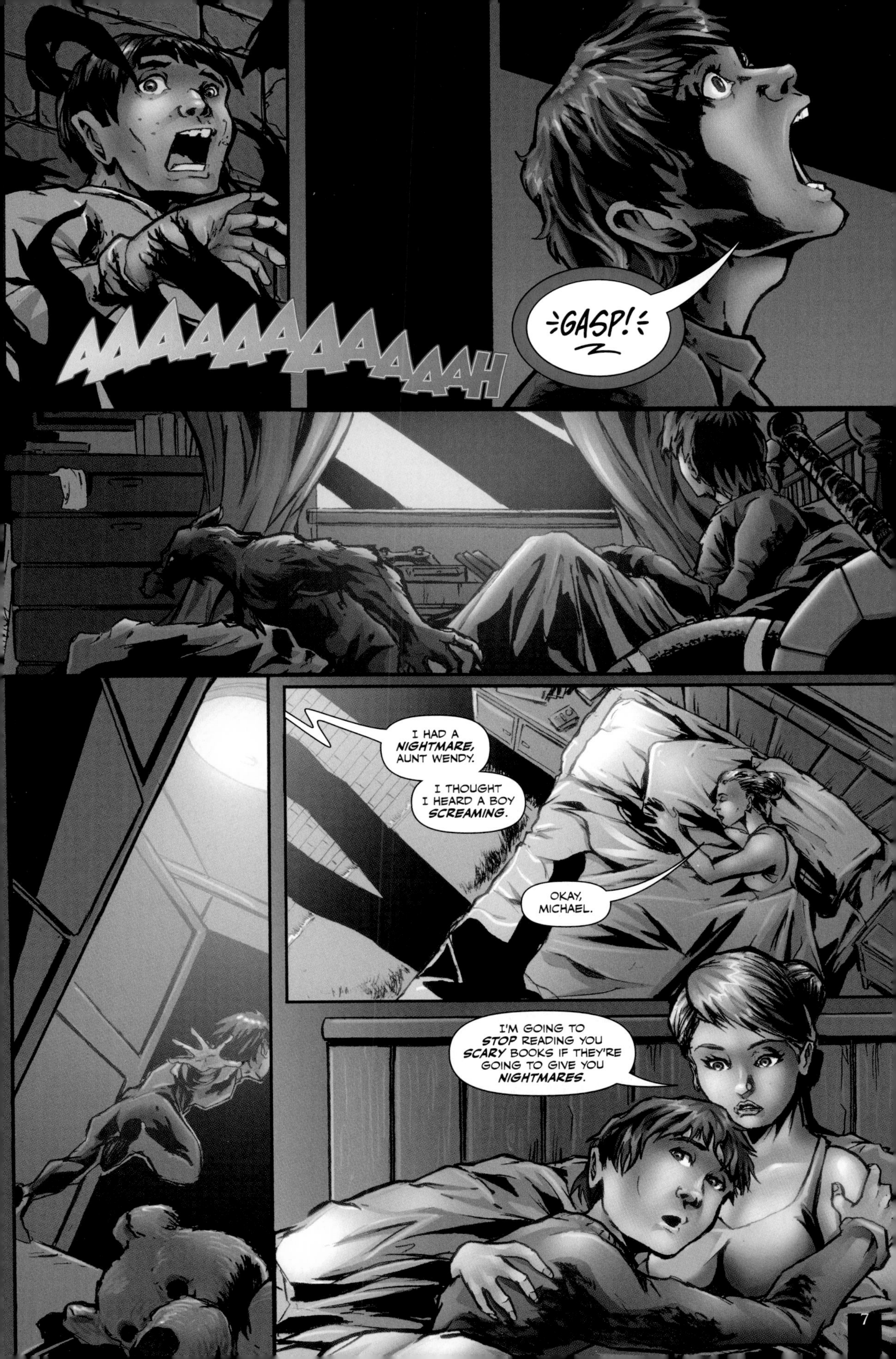
AAAAAAAAAAAAAH
GASP!
I HAD A NIGHTMARE, AUNT WENDY.
I THOUGHT I HEARD A BOY SCREAMING.
OKAY, MICHAEL.
I'M GOING TO STOP READING YOU SCARY BOOKS IF THEY'RE GOING TO GIVE YOU NIGHTMARES.

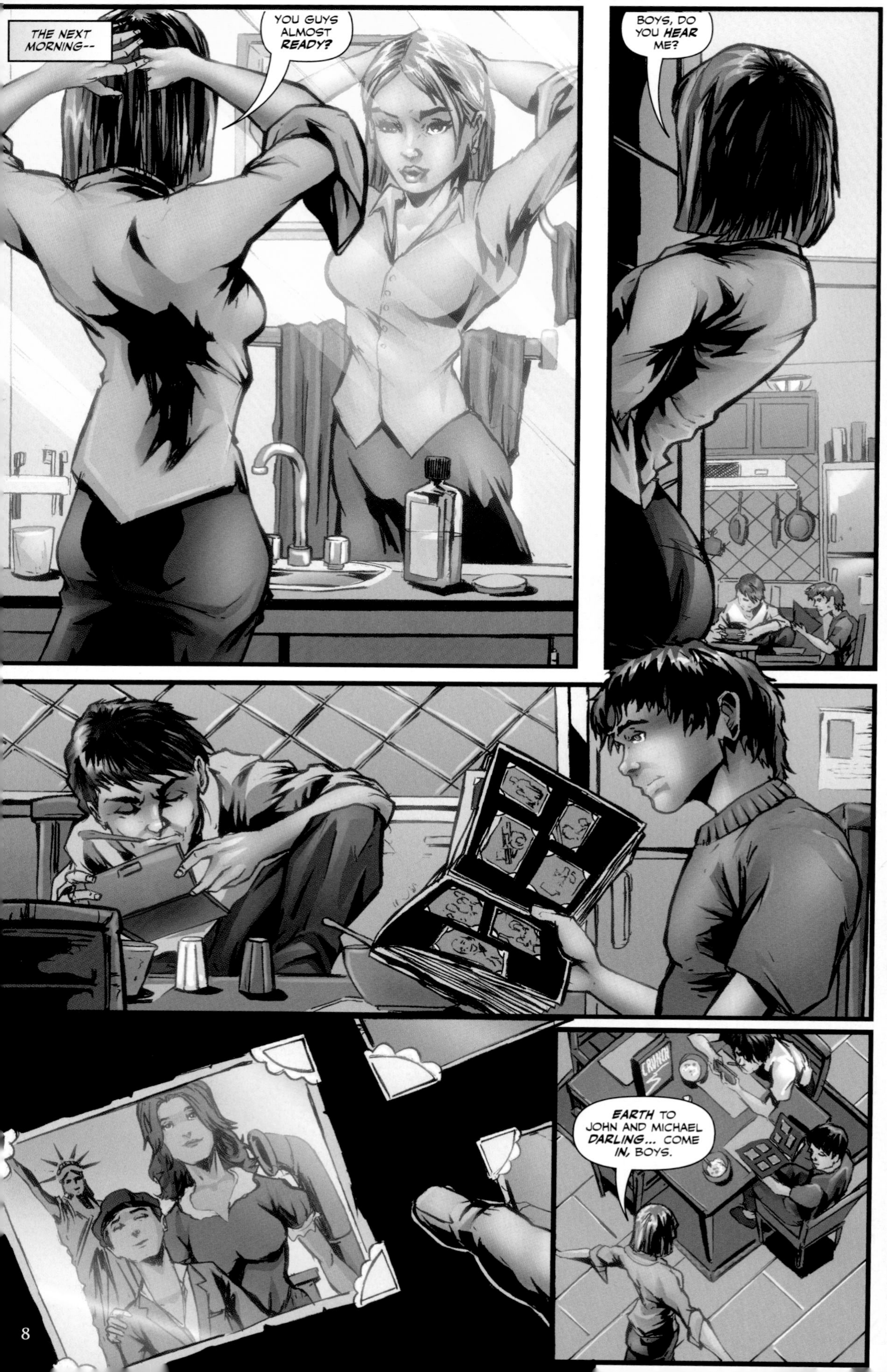
THE NEXT MORNING--
YOU GUYS ALMOST READY?
BOYS, DO YOU HEAR ME?
CRUNCH
EARTH TO JOHN AND MICHAEL DARLING... COME IN, BOYS.

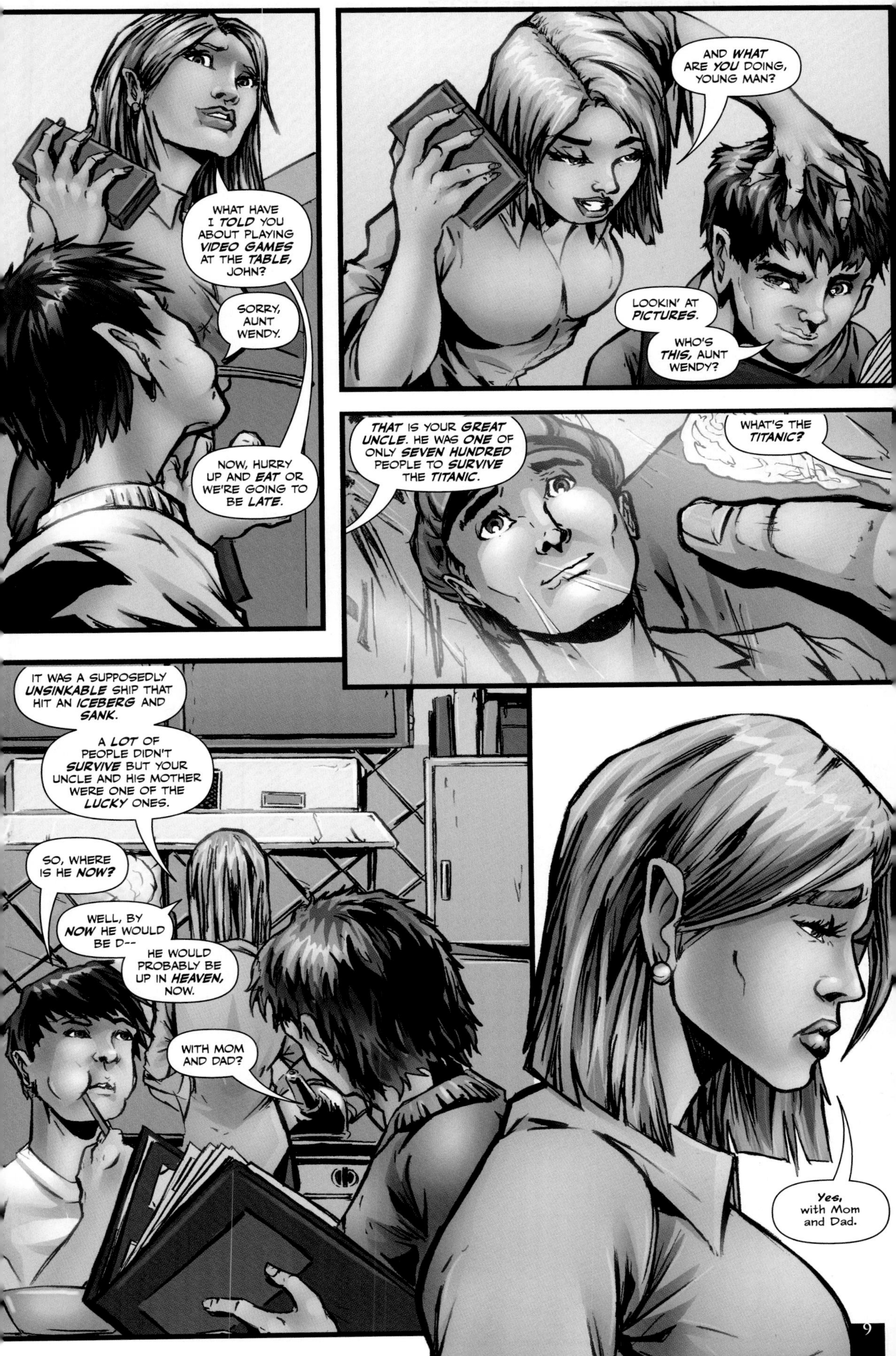

WHAT HAVE I TOLD YOU ABOUT PLAYING VIDEO GAMES AT THE TABLE, JOHN?
SORRY, AUNT WENDY.
NOW, HURRY UP AND EAT OR WE'RE GOING TO BE LATE.
AND WHAT ARE YOU DOING, YOUNG MAN?
LOOKIN' AT PICTURES.
WHO'S THIS, AUNT WENDY?
THAT IS YOUR GREAT UNCLE. HE WAS ONE OF ONLY SEVEN HUNDRED PEOPLE TO SURVIVE THE TITANIC.
WHAT'S THE TITANIC?
IT WAS A SUPPOSEDLY UNSINKABLE SHIP THAT HIT AN ICEBERG AND SANK.
A LOT OF PEOPLE DIDN'T SURVIVE BUT YOUR UNCLE AND HIS MOTHER WERE ONE OF THE LUCKY ONES.
SO, WHERE IS HE NOW?
WELL, BY NOW HE WOULD BE D--
HE WOULD PROBABLY BE UP IN HEAVEN, NOW.
WITH MOM AND DAD?
Yes, with Mom and Dad.

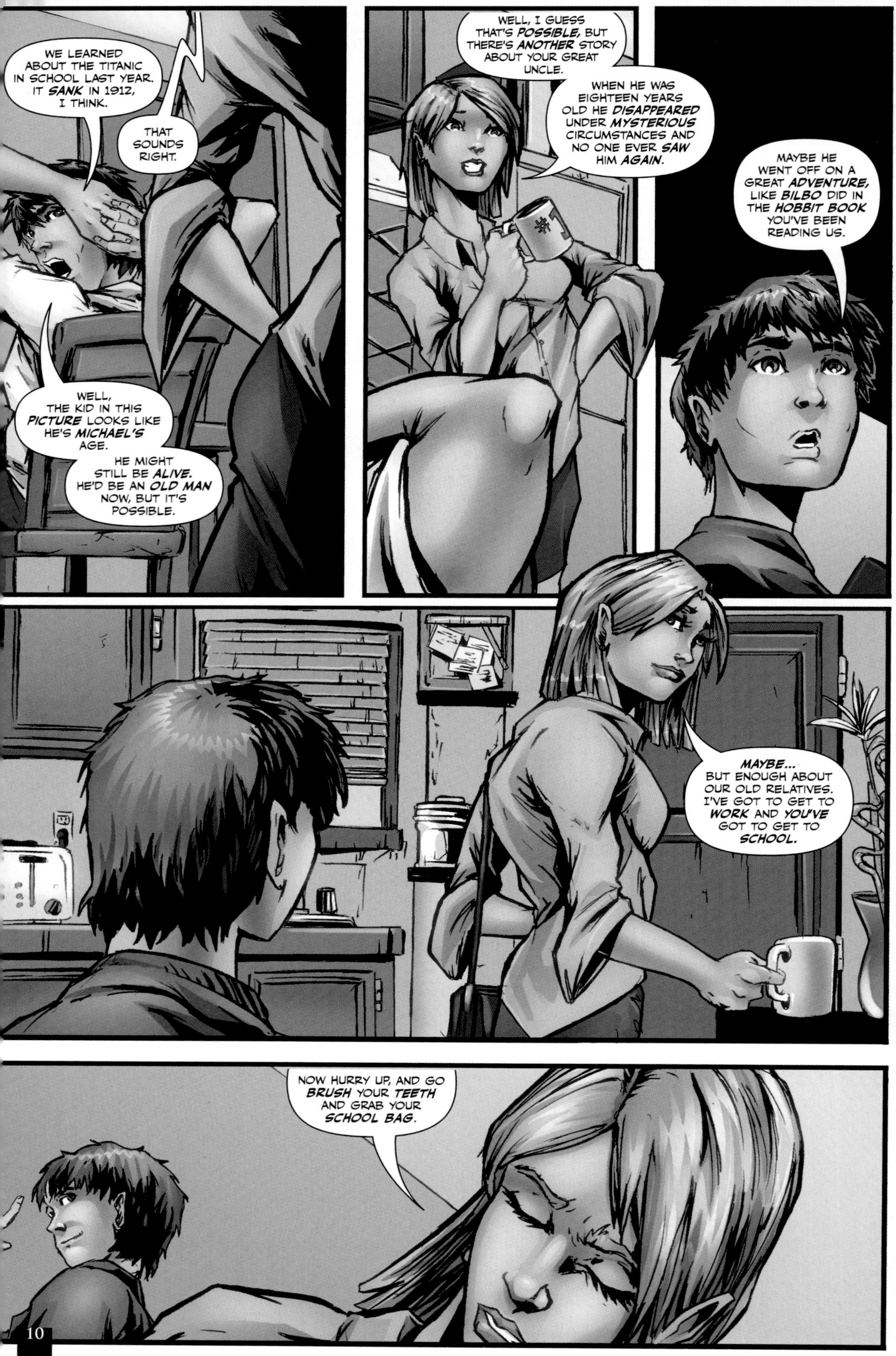

WE LEARNED ABOUT THE TITANIC IN SCHOOL LAST YEAR. IT SANK IN 1912, I THINK.
THAT SOUNDS RIGHT.
WELL, THE KID IN THIS PICTURE LOOKS LIKE HE'S MICHAEL'S AGE.
HE MIGHT STILL BE ALIVE. HE'D BE AN OLD MAN NOW, BUT IT'S POSSIBLE.
WELL, I GUESS THAT'S POSSIBLE, BUT THERE'S ANOTHER STORY ABOUT YOUR GREAT UNCLE.
WHEN HE WAS EIGHTEEN YEARS OLD HE DISAPPEARED UNDER MYSTERIOUS CIRCUMSTANCES AND NO ONE EVER SAW HIM AGAIN.
MAYBE HE WENT OFF ON A GREAT ADVENTURE, LIKE BILBO DID IN THE HOBBIT BOOK YOU'VE BEEN READING US.
MAYBE... BUT ENOUGH ABOUT OUR OLD RELATIVES. I'VE GOT TO GET TO WORK AND YOU'VE GOT TO GET TO SCHOOL.
NOW HURRY UP, AND GO BRUSH YOUR TEETH AND GRAB YOUR SCHOOL BAG.

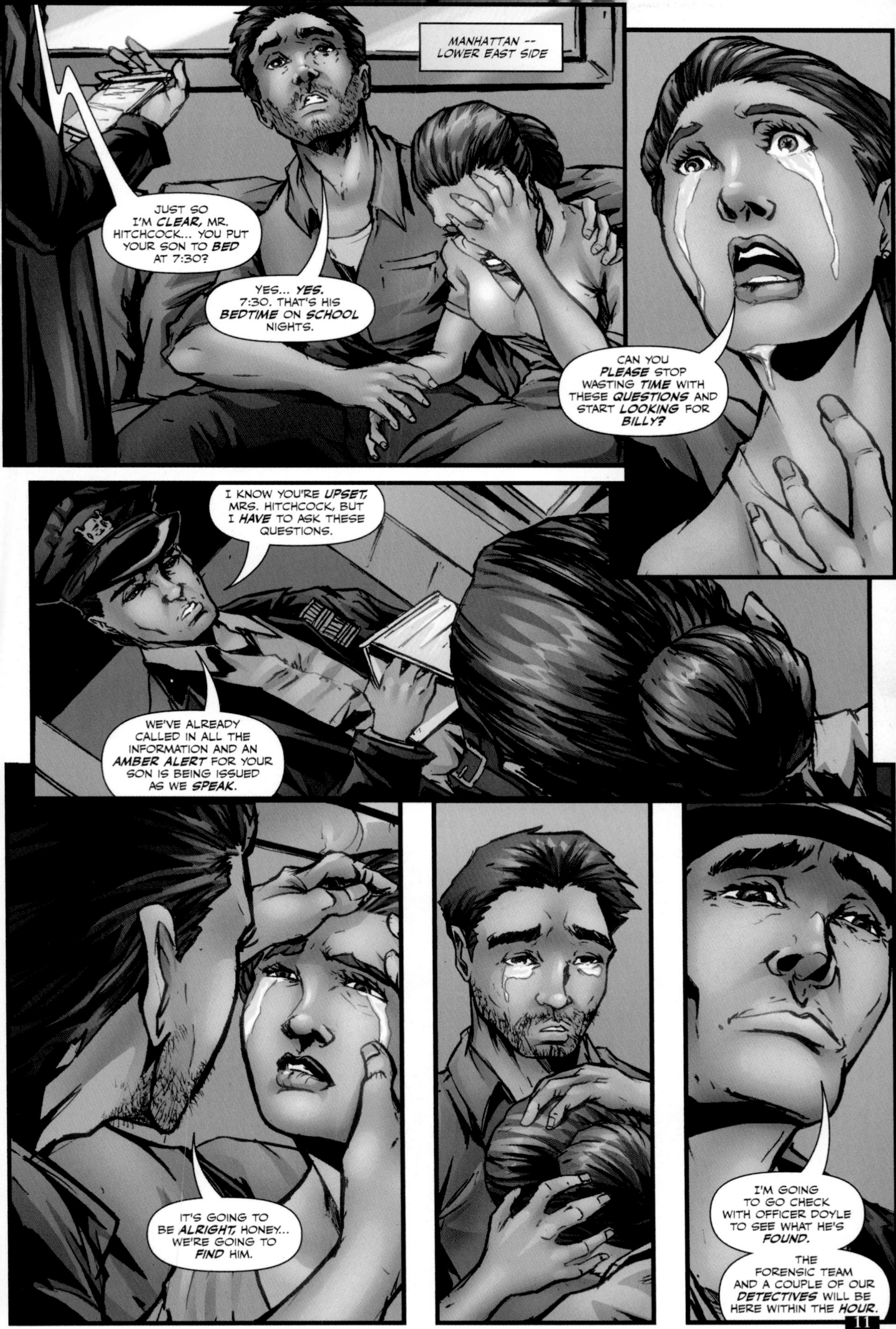
MANHATTAN -- LOWER EAST SIDE
JUST SO I'M CLEAR, MR. HITCHCOCK... YOU PUT YOUR SON TO BED AT 7:30?
YES... YES. 7:30. THAT'S HIS BEDTIME ON SCHOOL NIGHTS.
CAN YOU PLEASE STOP WASTING TIME WITH THESE QUESTIONS AND START LOOKING FOR BILLY?
I KNOW YOU'RE UPSET, MRS. HITCHCOCK, BUT I HAVE TO ASK THESE QUESTIONS.
WE'VE ALREADY CALLED IN ALL THE INFORMATION AND AN AMBER ALERT FOR YOUR SON IS BEING ISSUED AS WE SPEAK.
IT'S GOING TO BE ALRIGHT, HONEY... WE'RE GOING TO FIND HIM.
I'M GOING TO GO CHECK WITH OFFICER DOYLE TO SEE WHAT HE'S FOUND.
THE FORENSIC TEAM AND A COUPLE OF OUR DETECTIVES WILL BE HERE WITHIN THE HOUR.

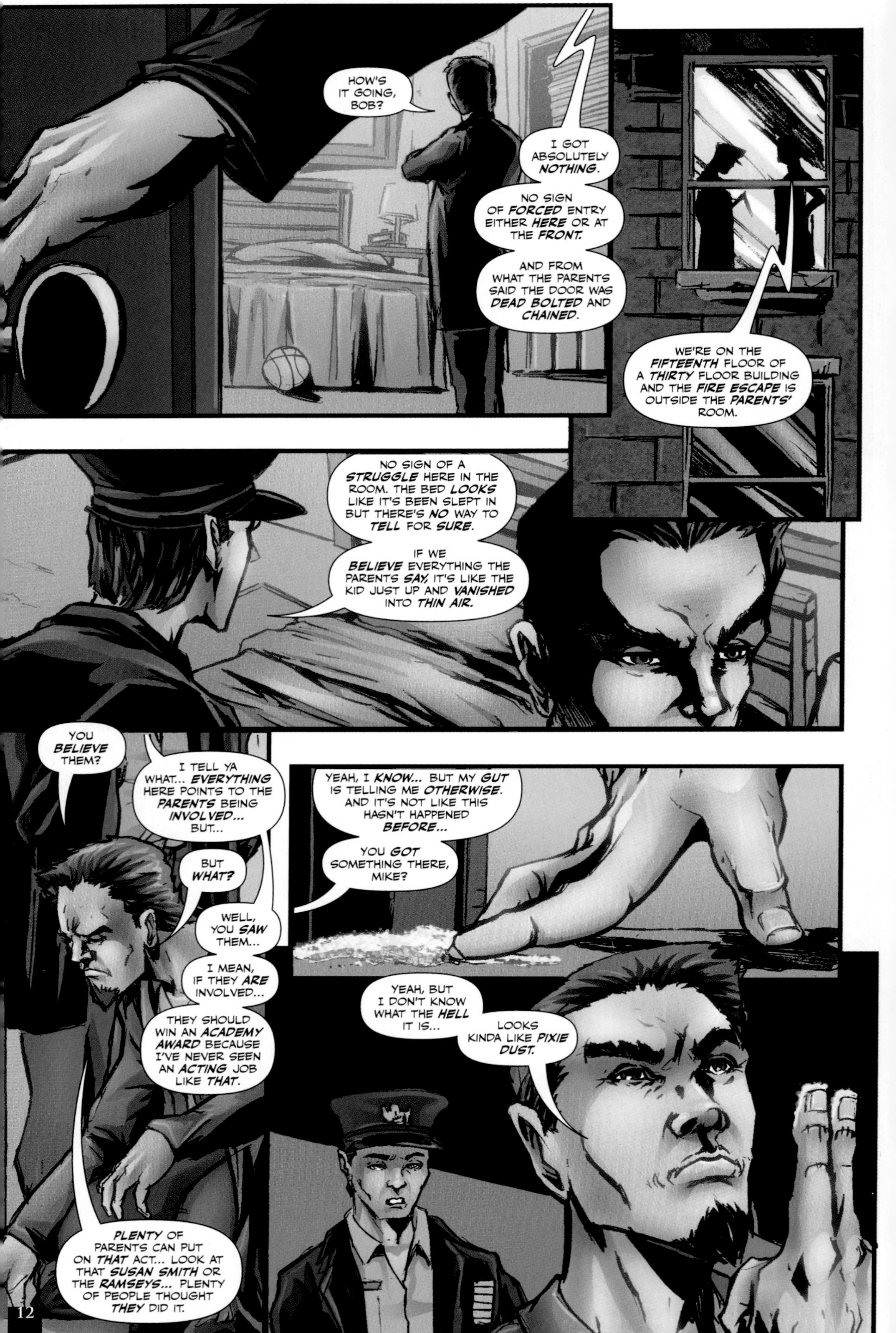
HOW'S IT GOING, BOB?
I GOT ABSOLUTELY NOTHING.
NO SIGN OF FORCED ENTRY EITHER HERE OR AT THE FRONT.
AND FROM WHAT THE PARENTS SAID THE DOOR WAS DEAD BOLTED AND CHAINED.
WE'RE ON THE FIFTEENTH FLOOR OF A THIRTY FLOOR BUILDING AND THE FIRE ESCAPE IS OUTSIDE THE PARENTS' ROOM.
NO SIGN OF A STRUGGLE HERE IN THE ROOM. THE BED LOOKS LIKE IT'S BEEN SLEPT IN BUT THERE'S NO WAY TO TELL FOR SURE.
IF WE BELIEVE EVERYTHING THE PARENTS SAY, IT'S LIKE THE KID JUST UP AND VANISHED INTO THIN AIR.
YOU BELIEVE THEM?
I TELL YA WHAT... EVERYTHING HERE POINTS TO THE PARENTS BEING INVOLVED... BUT...
BUT WHAT?
WELL, YOU SAW THEM...
I MEAN, IF THEY ARE INVOLVED...
THEY SHOULD WIN AN ACADEMY AWARD BECAUSE I'VE NEVER SEEN AN ACTING JOB LIKE THAT.
PLENTY OF PARENTS CAN PUT ON THAT ACT... LOOK AT THAT SUSAN SMITH OR THE RAMSEYS... PLENTY OF PEOPLE THOUGHT THEY DID IT.
YEAH, I KNOW... BUT MY GUT IS TELLING ME OTHERWISE. AND IT'S NOT LIKE THIS HASN'T HAPPENED BEFORE...
YOU GOT SOMETHING THERE, MIKE?
YEAH, BUT I DON'T KNOW WHAT THE HELL IT IS...
LOOKS KINDA LIKE PIXIE DUST.

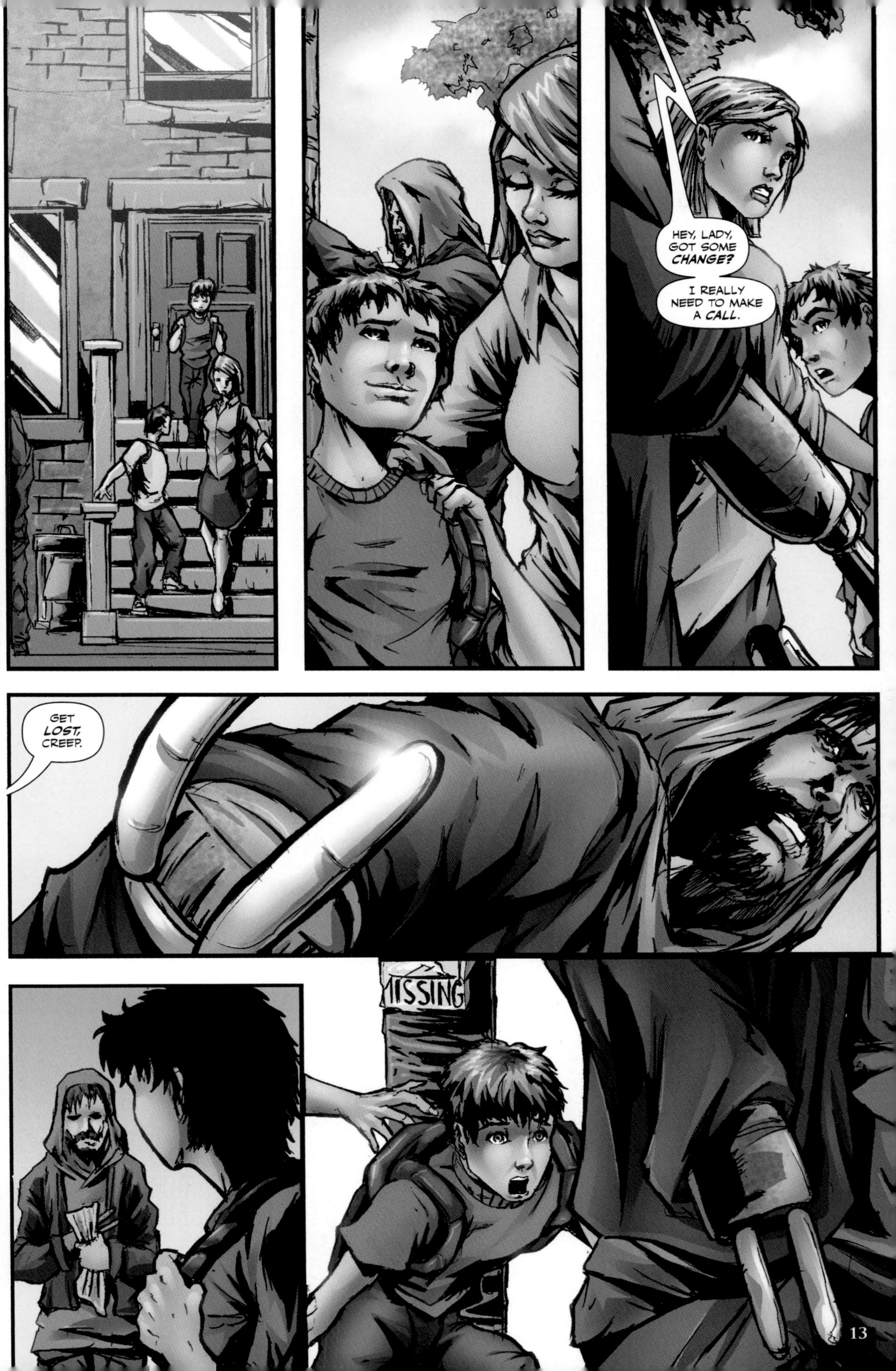
HEY, LADY, GOT SOME CHANGE?
I REALLY NEED TO MAKE A CALL.
GET LOST, CREEP.
MISSING

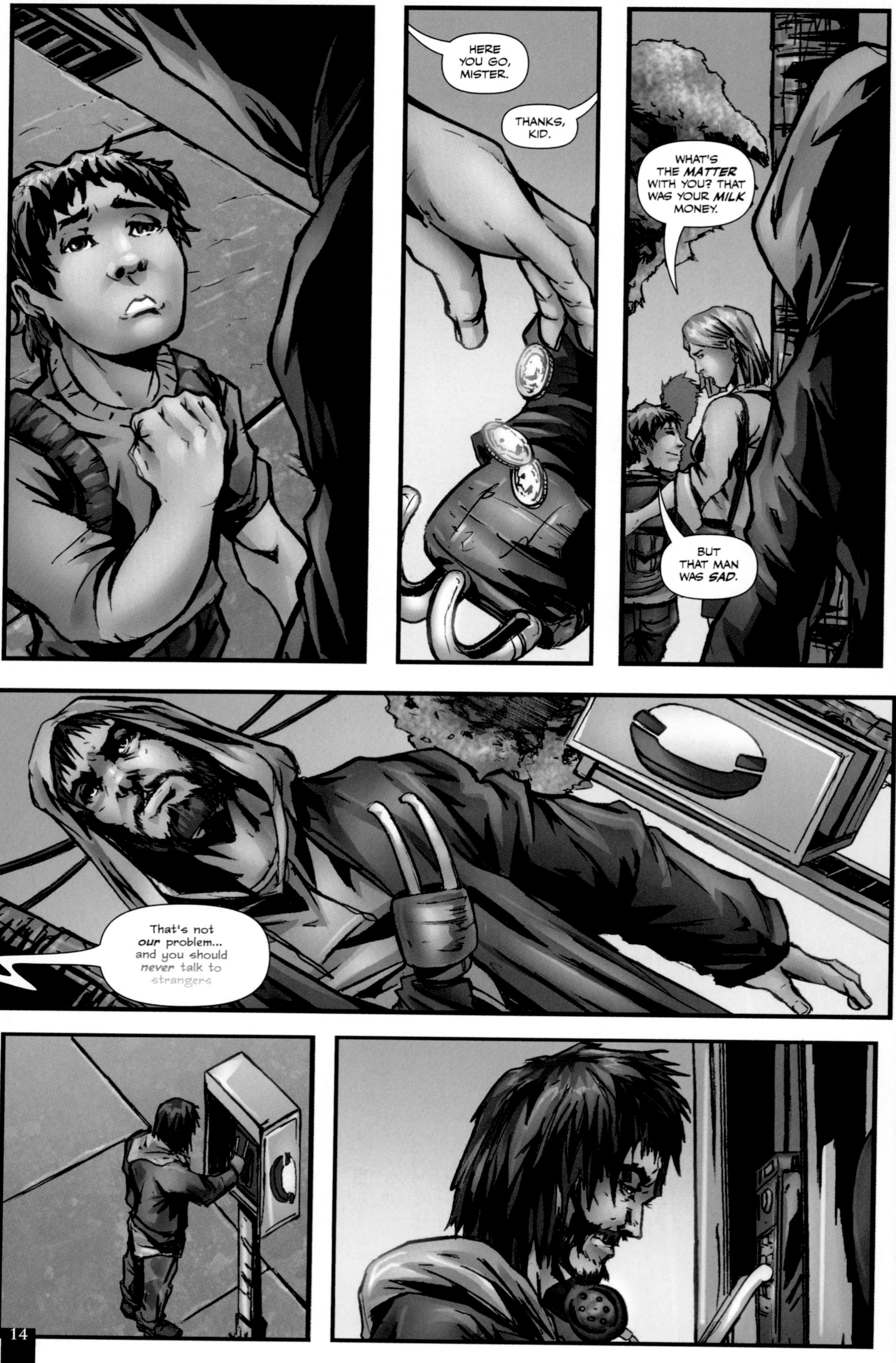
HERE YOU GO, MISTER.
THANKS, KID.
WHAT'S THE MATTER WITH YOU? THAT WAS YOUR MILK MONEY.
BUT THAT MAN WAS SAD.
That's not our problem... and you should never talk to strangers

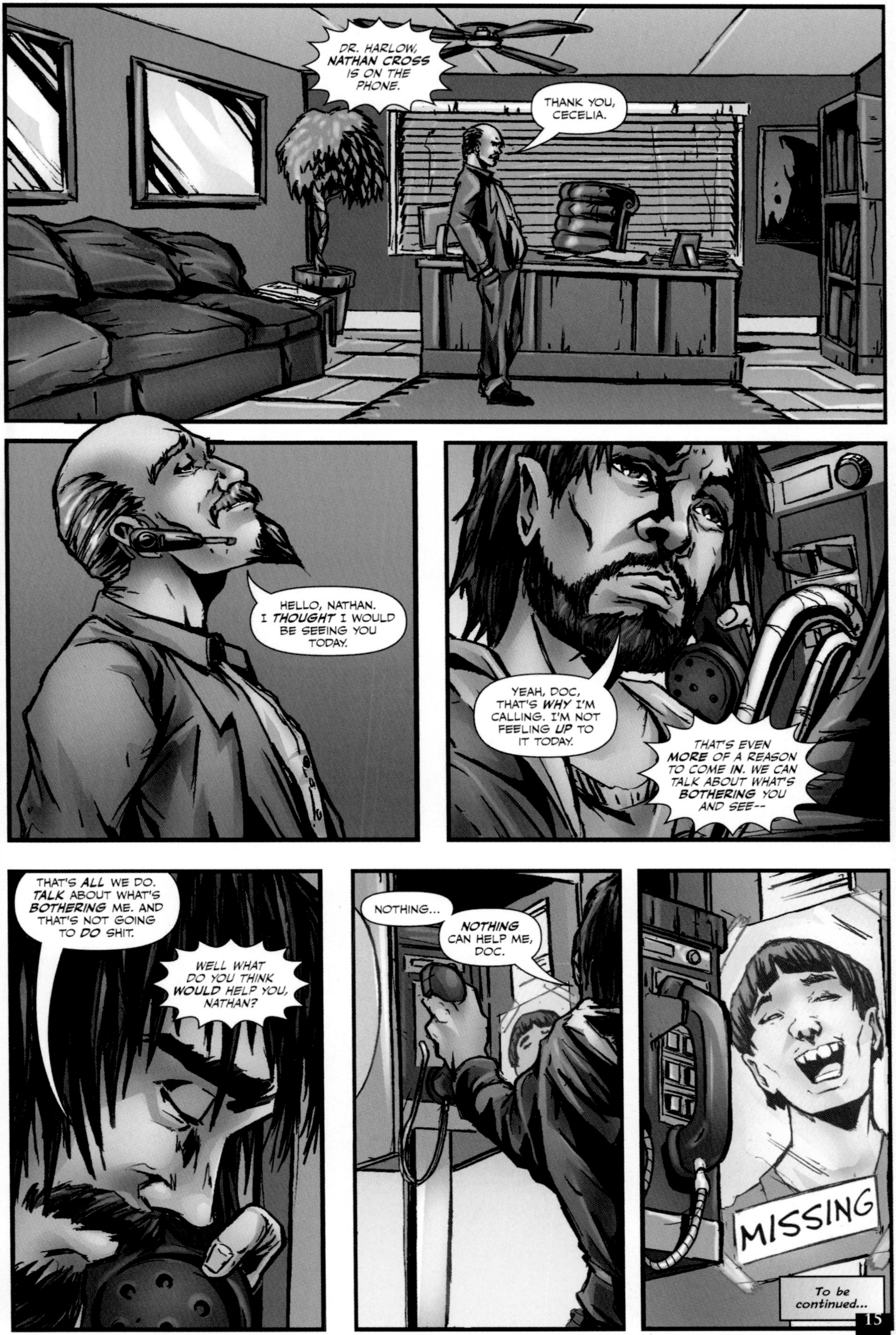
DR. HARLOW, NATHAN CROSS IS ON THE PHONE.
THANK YOU, CECELIA.
HELLO, NATHAN. I THOUGHT I WOULD BE SEEING YOU TODAY.
YEAH, DOC, THAT'S WHY I'M CALLING. I'M NOT FEELING UP TO IT TODAY.
THAT'S EVEN MORE OF A REASON TO COME IN. WE CAN TALK ABOUT WHAT'S BOTHERING YOU AND SEE--
THAT'S ALL WE DO. TALK ABOUT WHAT'S BOTHERING ME. AND THAT'S NOT GOING TO DO SHIT.
WELL WHAT DO YOU THINK WOULD HELP YOU, NATHAN?
NOTHING...
NOTHING CAN HELP ME, DOC.
MISSING
To be continued...

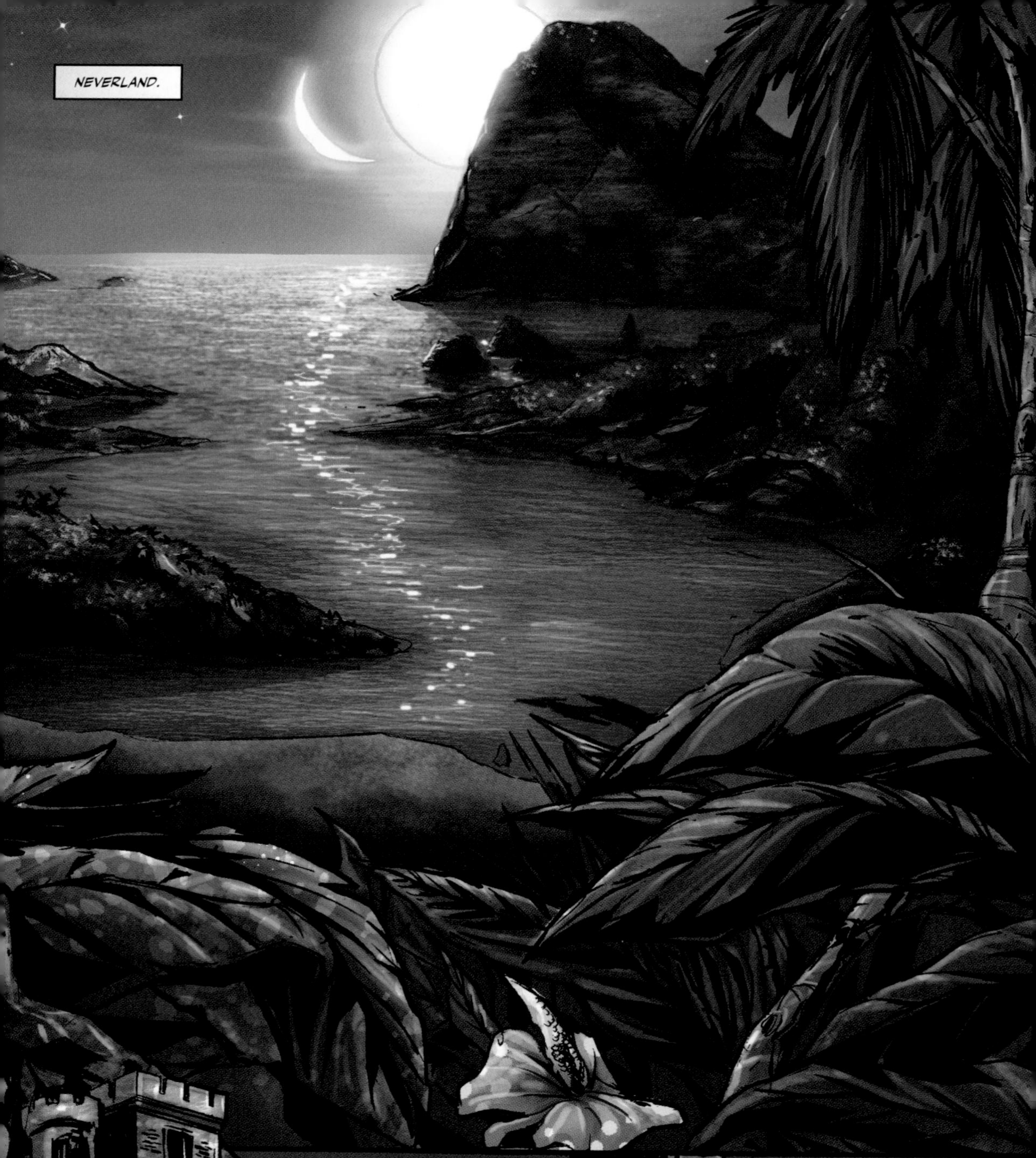
NEVERLAND.
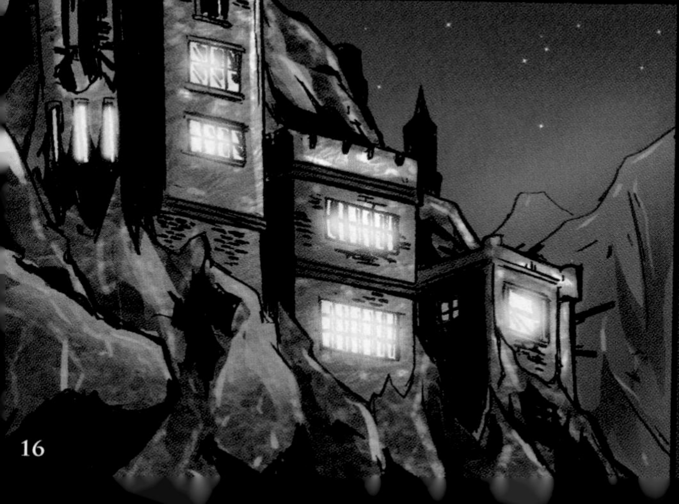
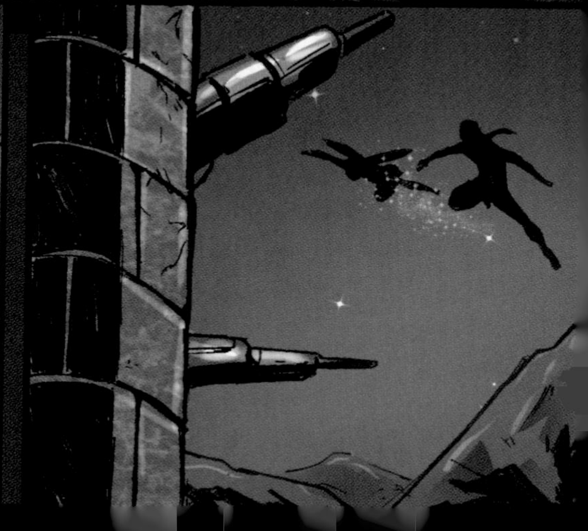

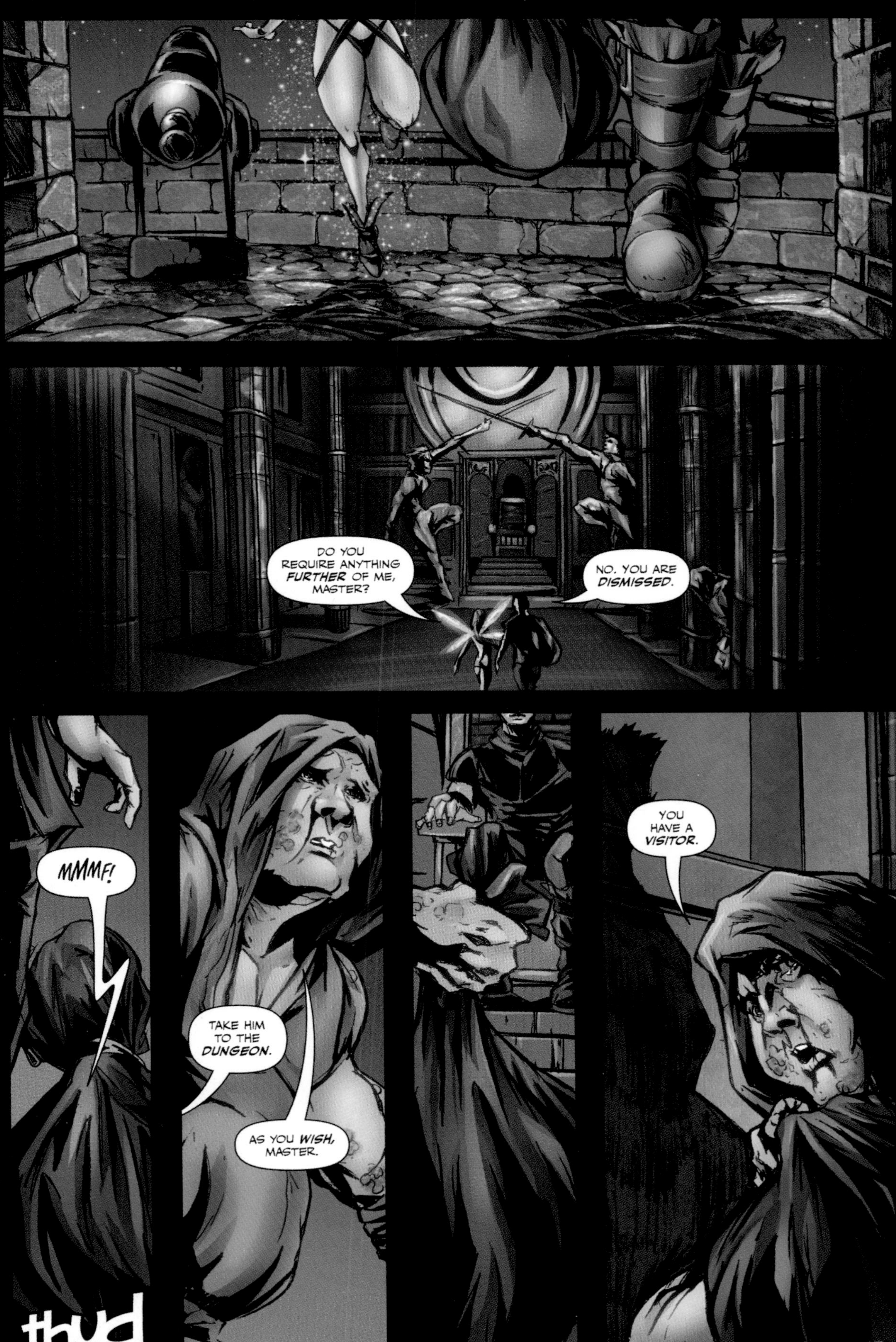
DO YOU REQUIRE ANYTHING *FURTHER* OF ME, MASTER?
NO. YOU ARE *DISMISSED*.
MMMF!
TAKE HIM TO THE *DUNGEON*.
AS YOU *WISH,* MASTER.
YOU HAVE A *VISITOR*.
thud

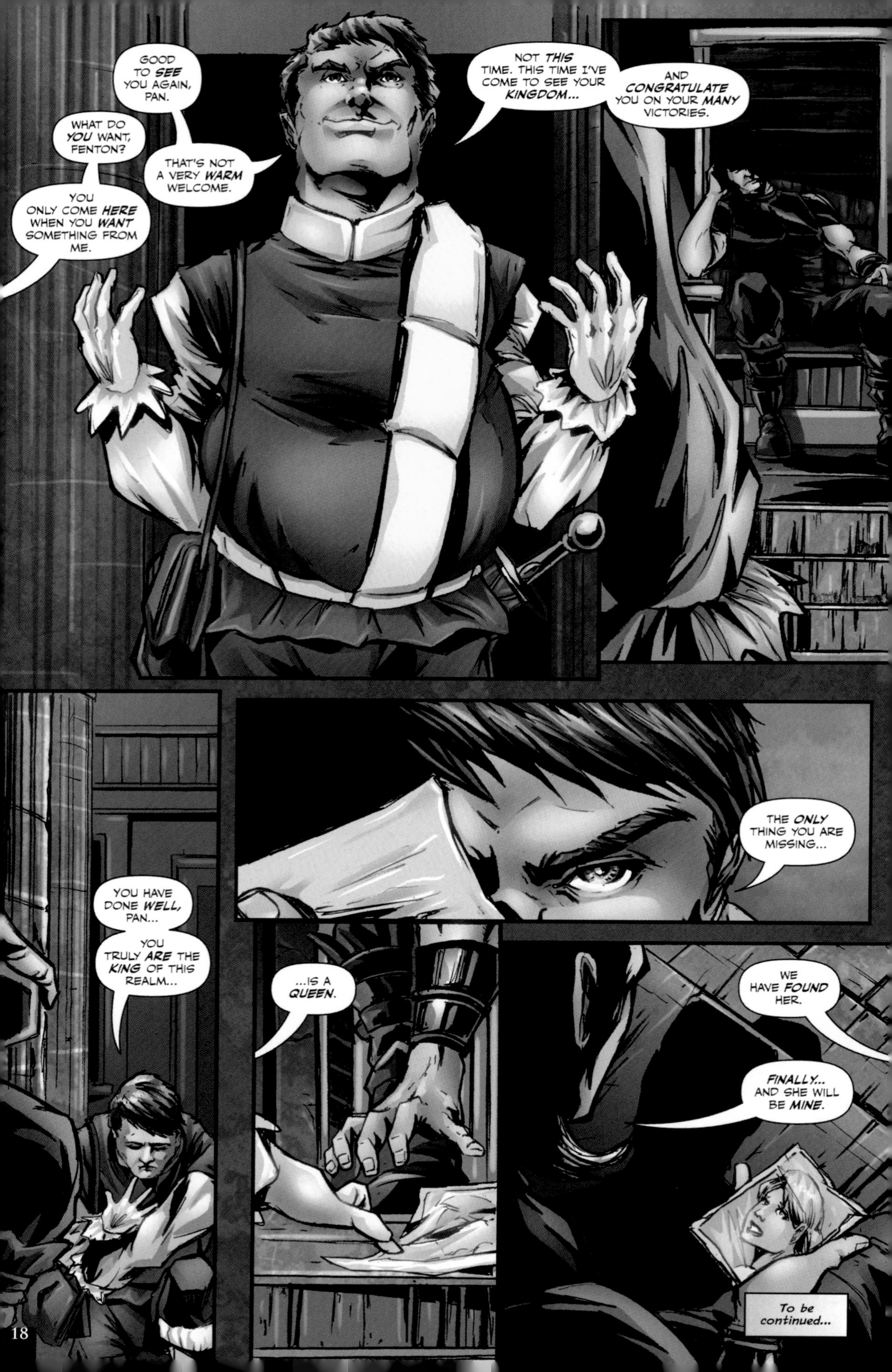
WHAT DO YOU WANT, FENTON?
YOU ONLY COME HERE WHEN YOU WANT SOMETHING FROM ME.
GOOD TO SEE YOU AGAIN, PAN.
THAT'S NOT A VERY WARM WELCOME.
NOT THIS TIME. THIS TIME I'VE COME TO SEE YOUR KINGDOM...
AND CONGRATULATE YOU ON YOUR MANY VICTORIES.
YOU HAVE DONE WELL, PAN...
YOU TRULY ARE THE KING OF THIS REALM...
THE ONLY THING YOU ARE MISSING...
...IS A QUEEN.
WE HAVE FOUND HER.
FINALLY... AND SHE WILL BE MINE.
To be continued...

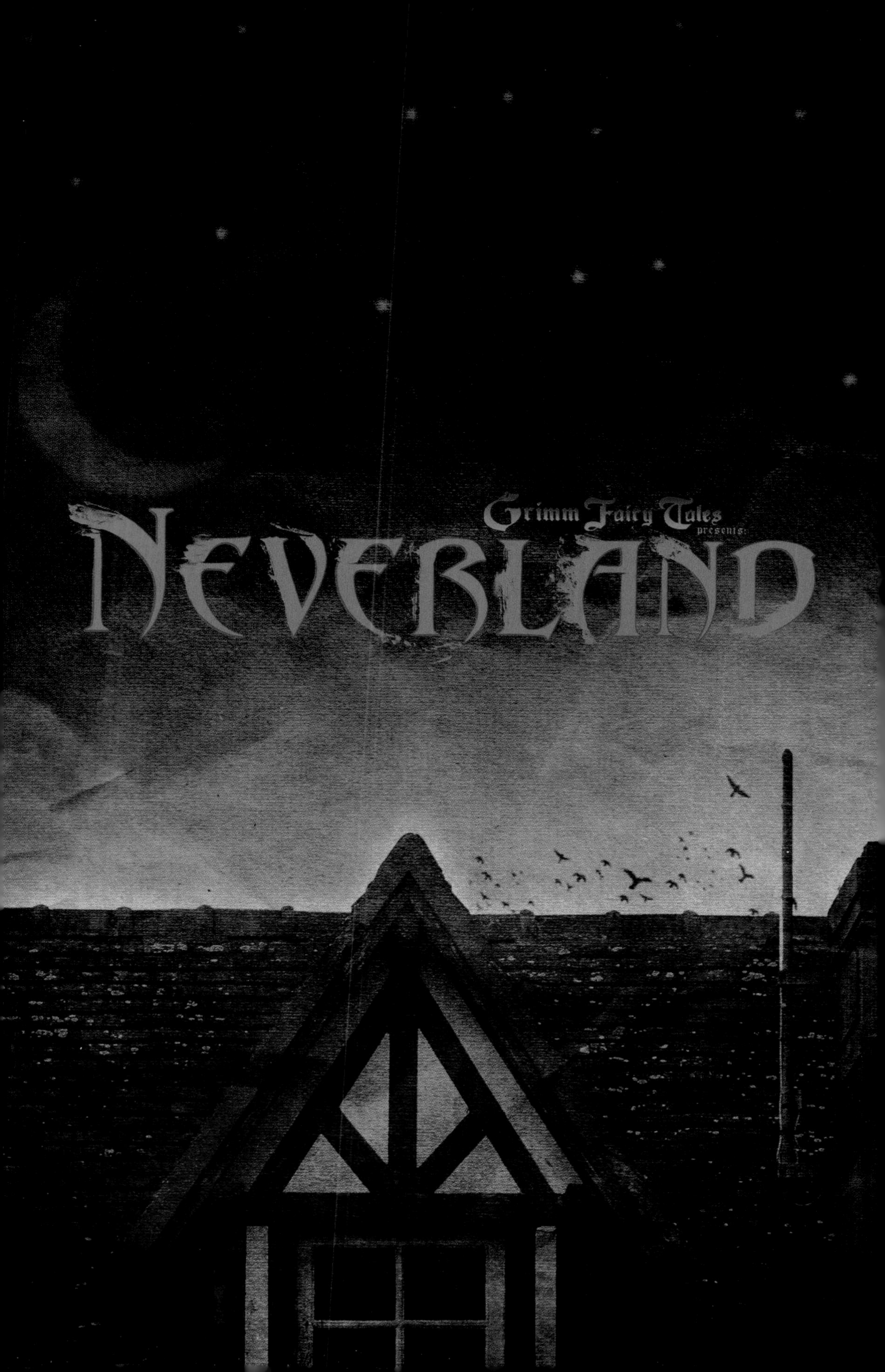
Grimm Fairy Tales
presents:
NEVERLAND

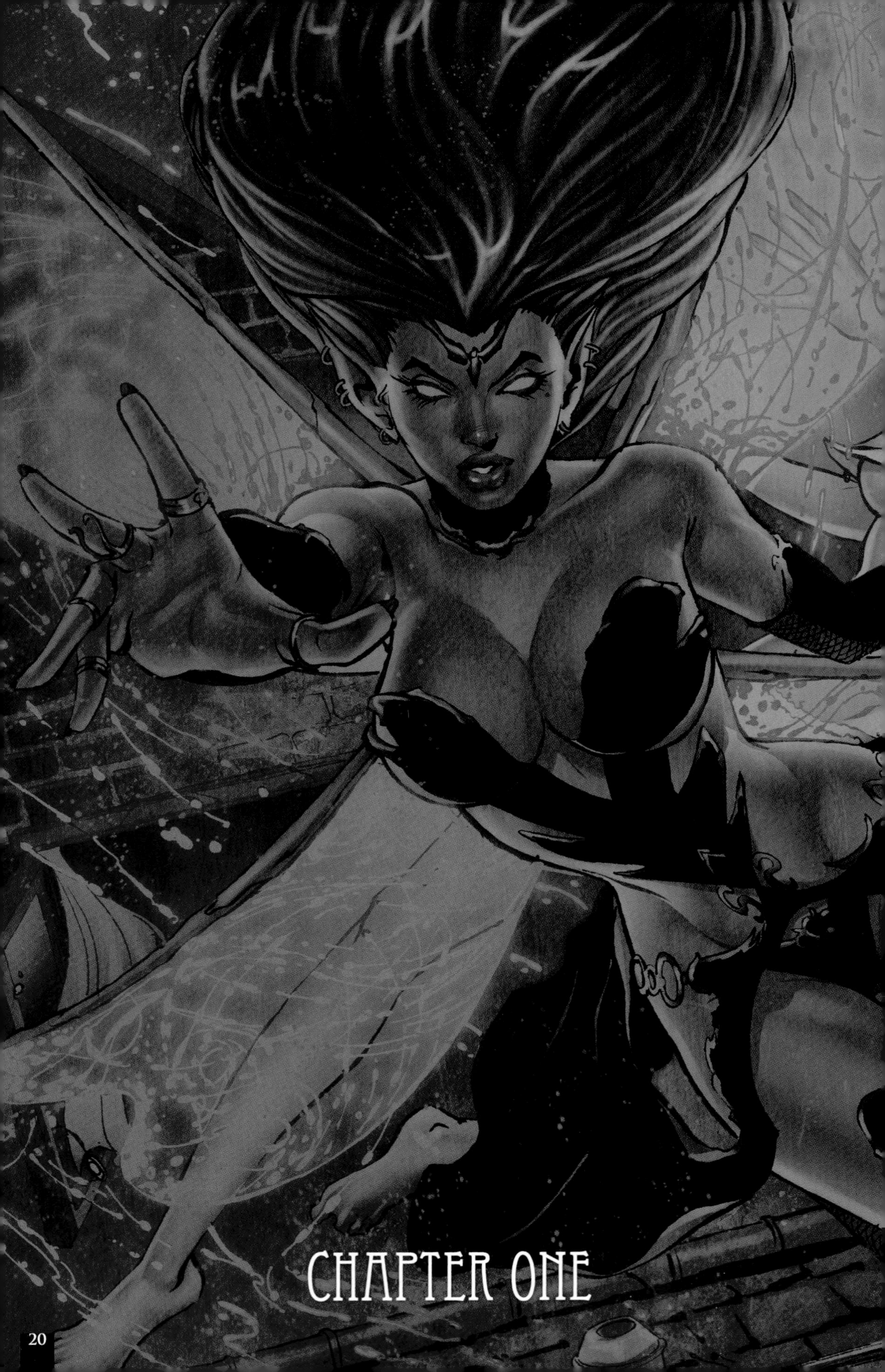

CHAPTER ONE

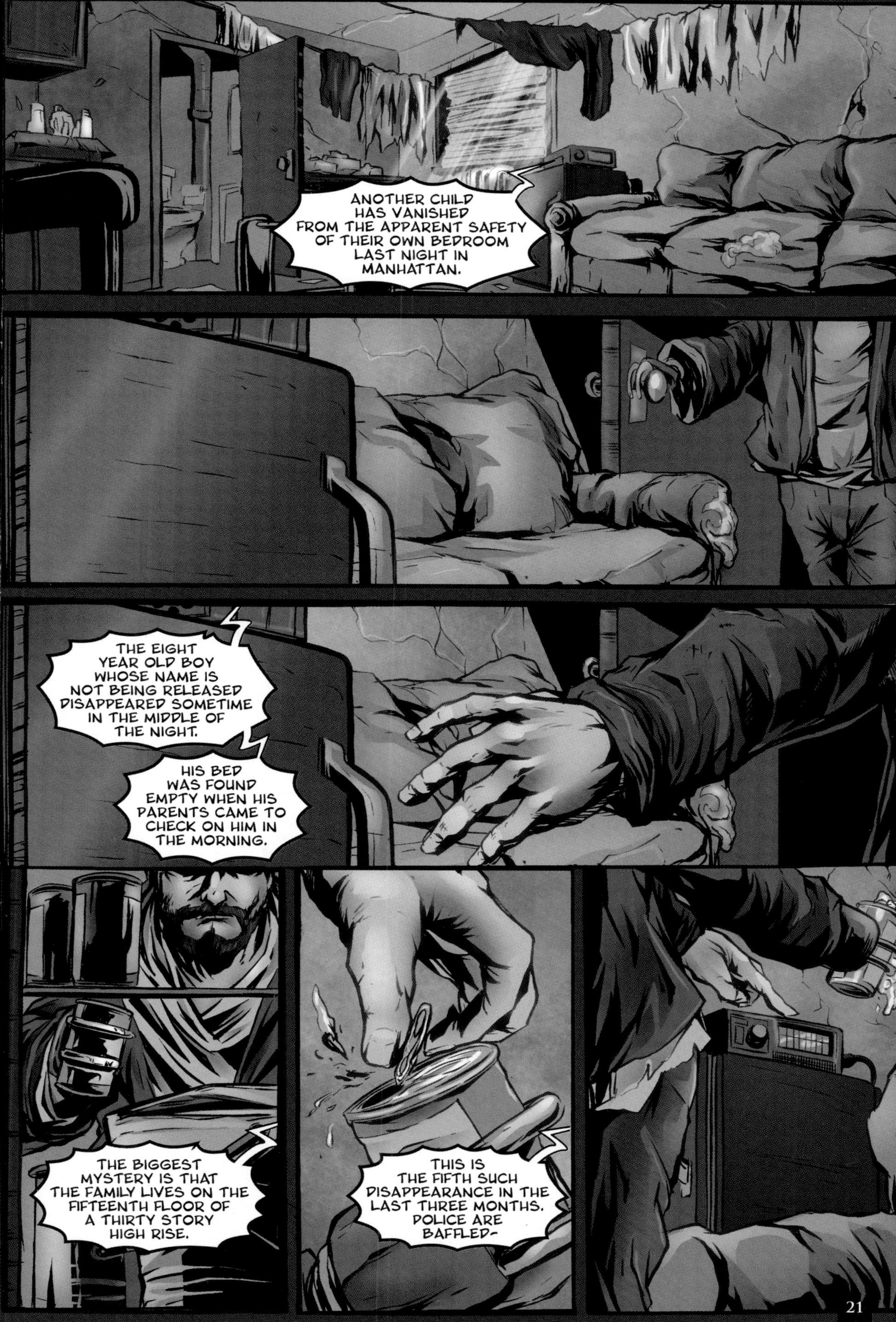
ANOTHER CHILD HAS VANISHED FROM THE APPARENT SAFETY OF THEIR OWN BEDROOM LAST NIGHT IN MANHATTAN.
THE EIGHT YEAR OLD BOY WHOSE NAME IS NOT BEING RELEASED DISAPPEARED SOMETIME IN THE MIDDLE OF THE NIGHT.
HIS BED WAS FOUND EMPTY WHEN HIS PARENTS CAME TO CHECK ON HIM IN THE MORNING.
THE BIGGEST MYSTERY IS THAT THE FAMILY LIVES ON THE FIFTEENTH FLOOR OF A THIRTY STORY HIGH RISE.
THIS IS THE FIFTH SUCH DISAPPEARANCE IN THE LAST THREE MONTHS. POLICE ARE BAFFLED-

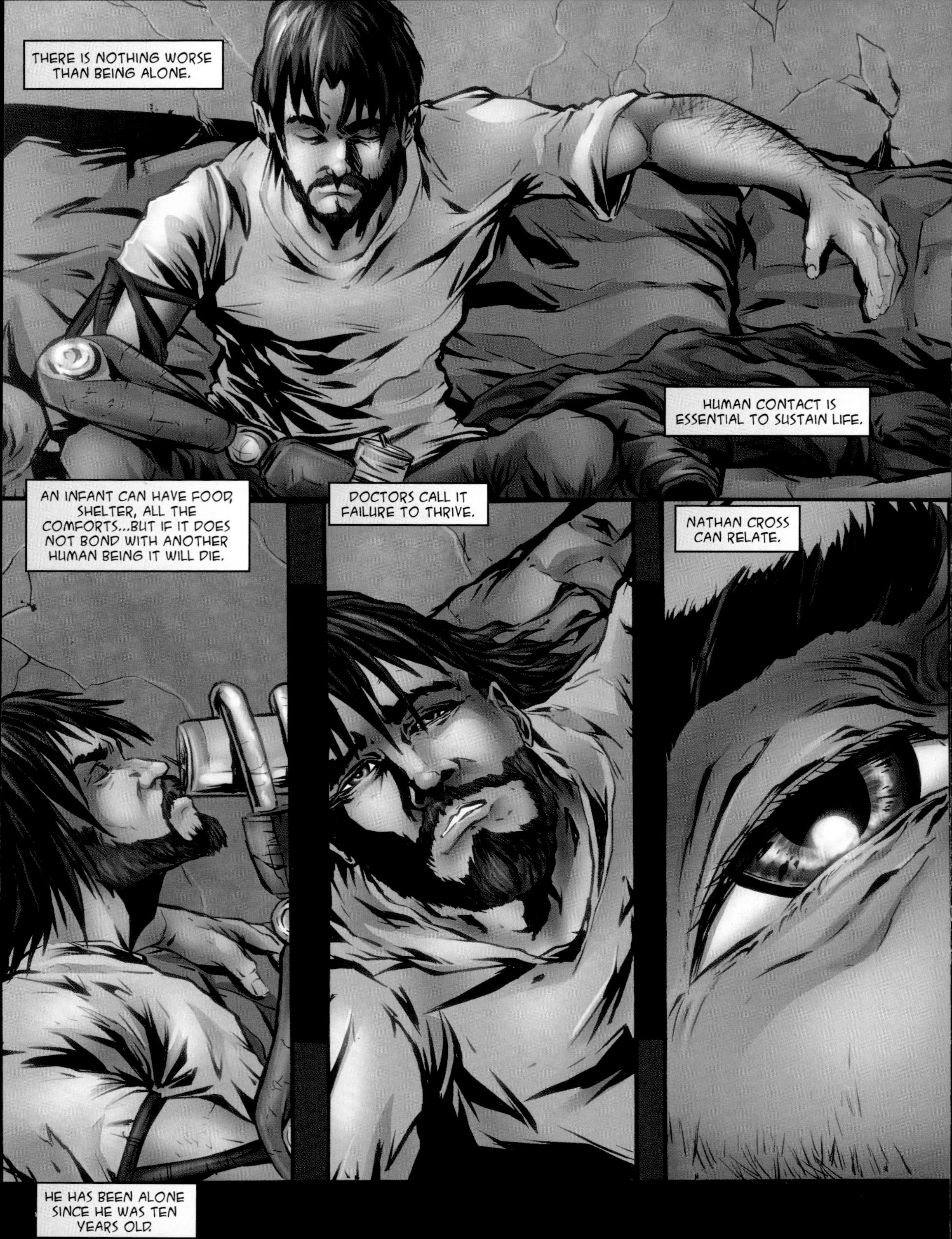
THERE IS NOTHING WORSE THAN BEING ALONE.
HUMAN CONTACT IS ESSENTIAL TO SUSTAIN LIFE.
AN INFANT CAN HAVE FOOD, SHELTER, ALL THE COMFORTS...BUT IF IT DOES NOT BOND WITH ANOTHER HUMAN BEING IT WILL DIE.
DOCTORS CALL IT FAILURE TO THRIVE.
NATHAN CROSS CAN RELATE.
HE HAS BEEN ALONE SINCE HE WAS TEN YEARS OLD.

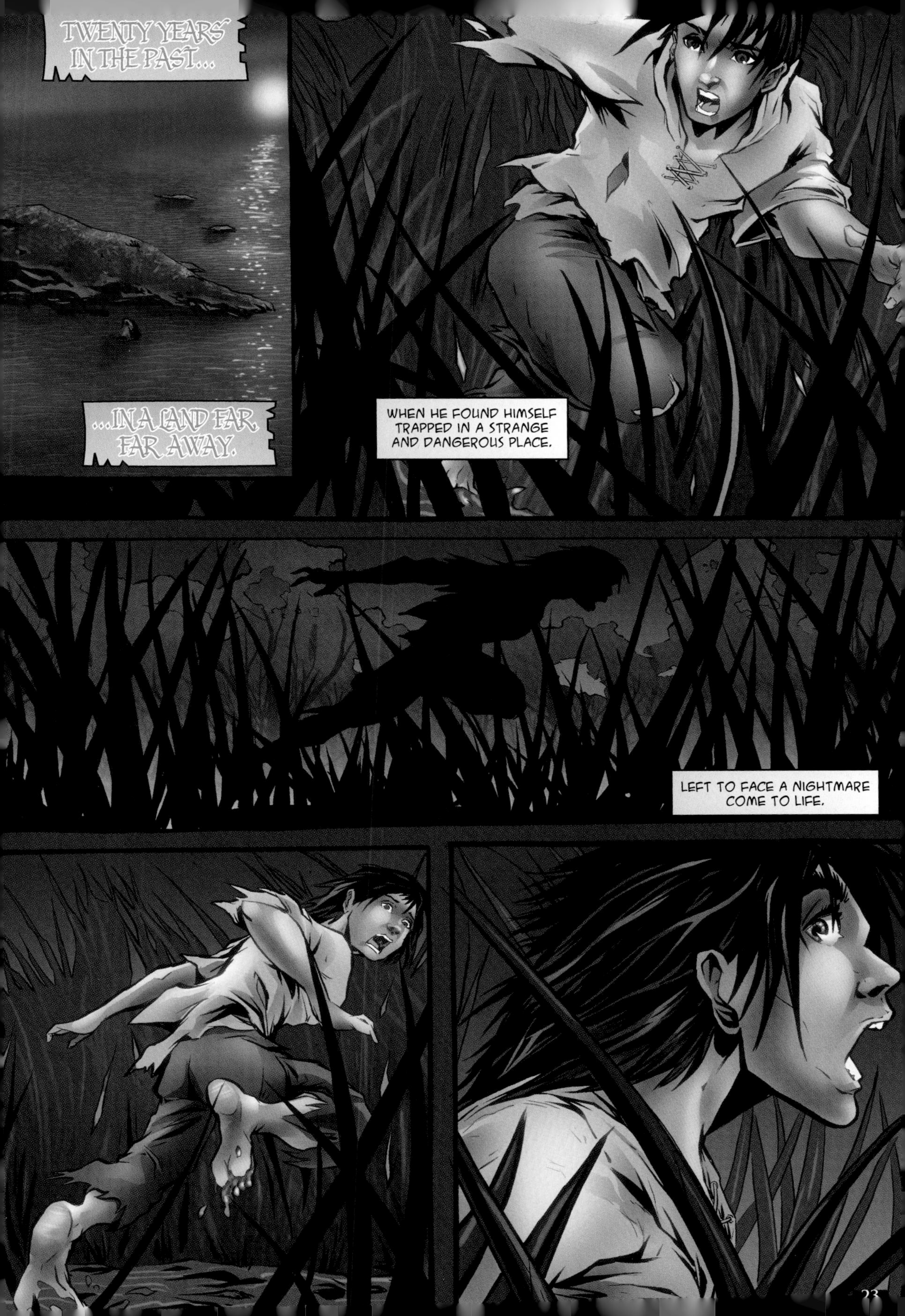
TWENTY YEARS IN THE PAST...
...IN A LAND FAR, FAR AWAY.
WHEN HE FOUND HIMSELF TRAPPED IN A STRANGE AND DANGEROUS PLACE.
LEFT TO FACE A NIGHTMARE COME TO LIFE.

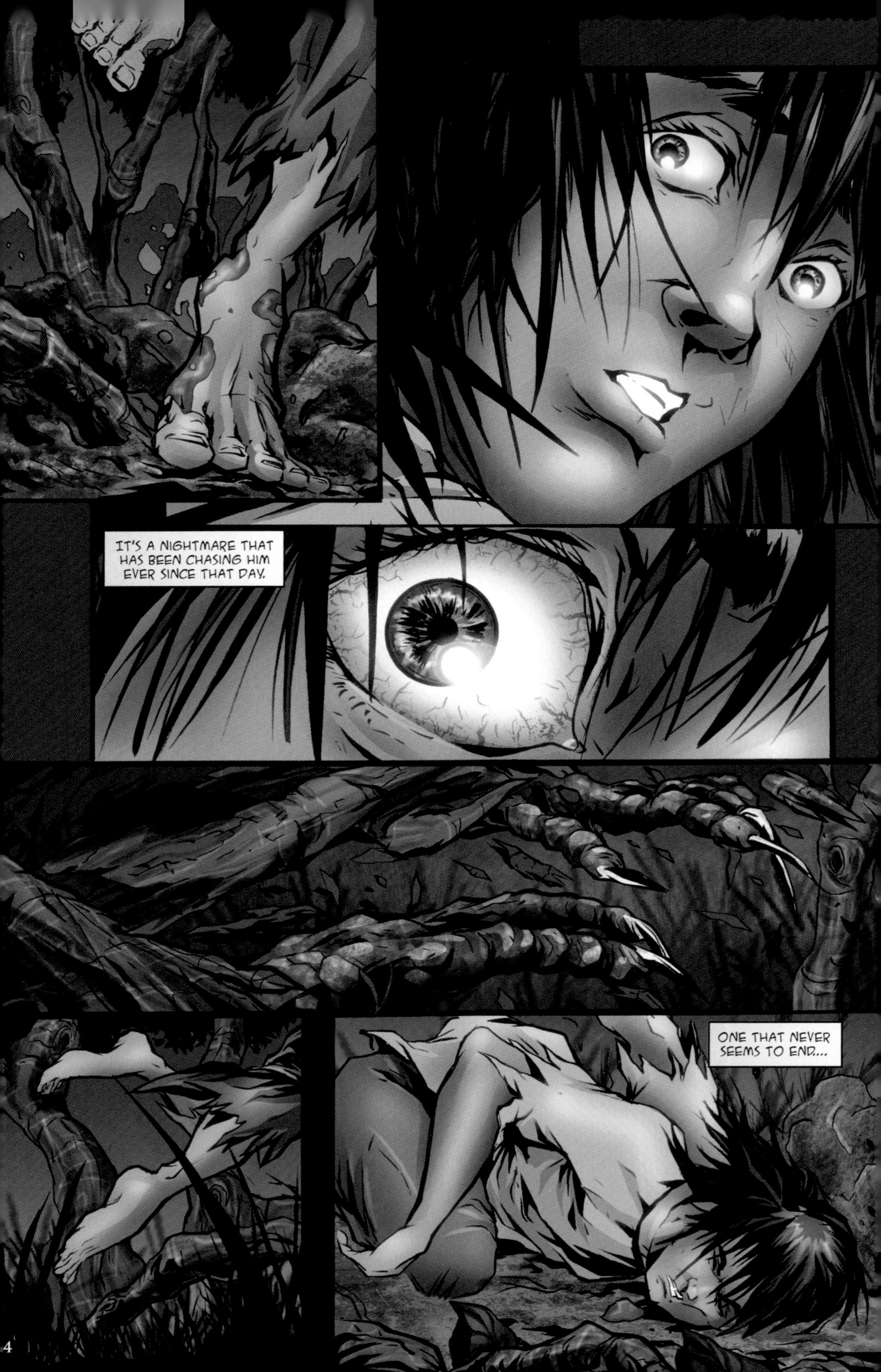
IT'S A NIGHTMARE THAT
HAS BEEN CHASING HIM
EVER SINCE THAT DAY.
ONE THAT NEVER
SEEMS TO END....

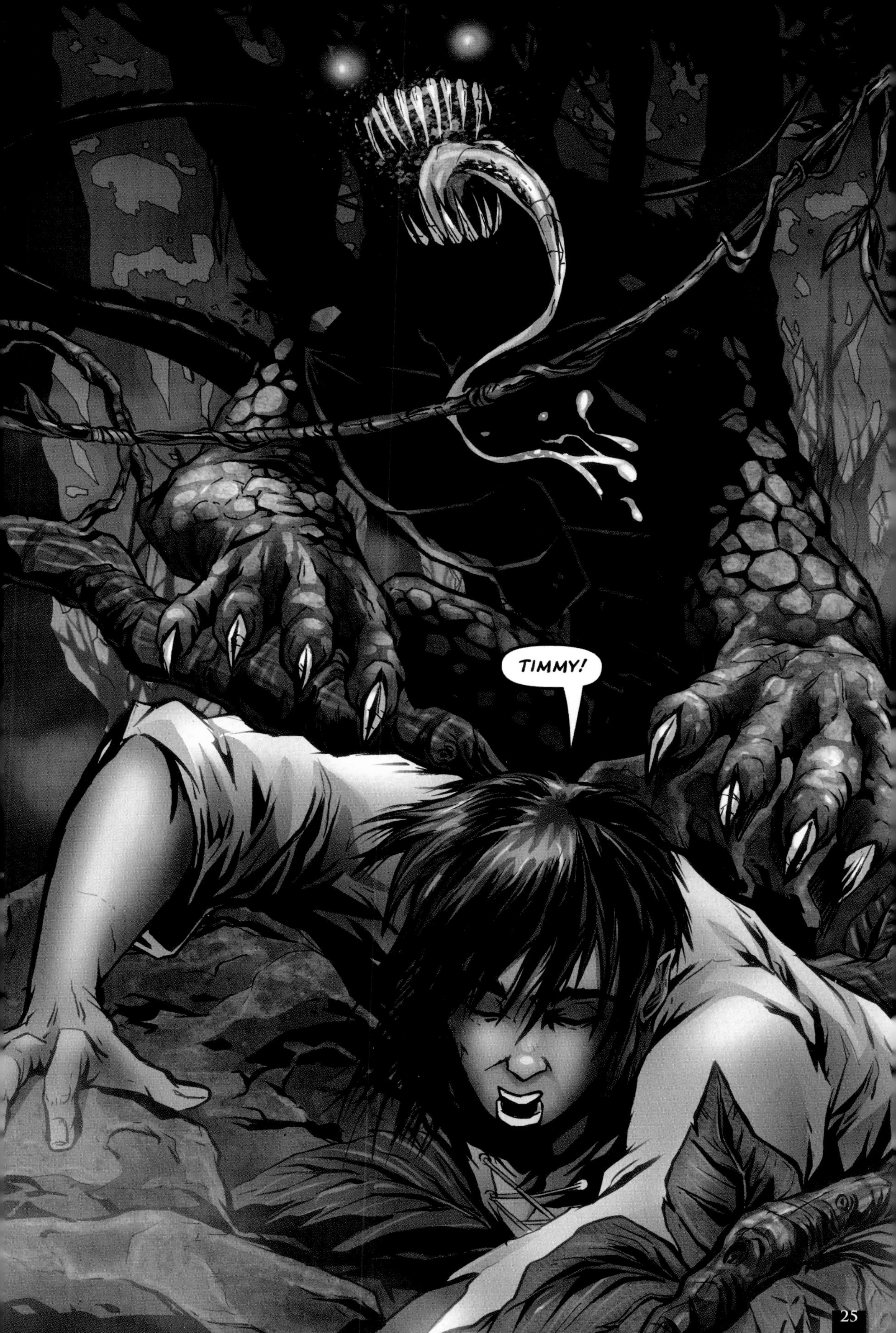
TIMMY!

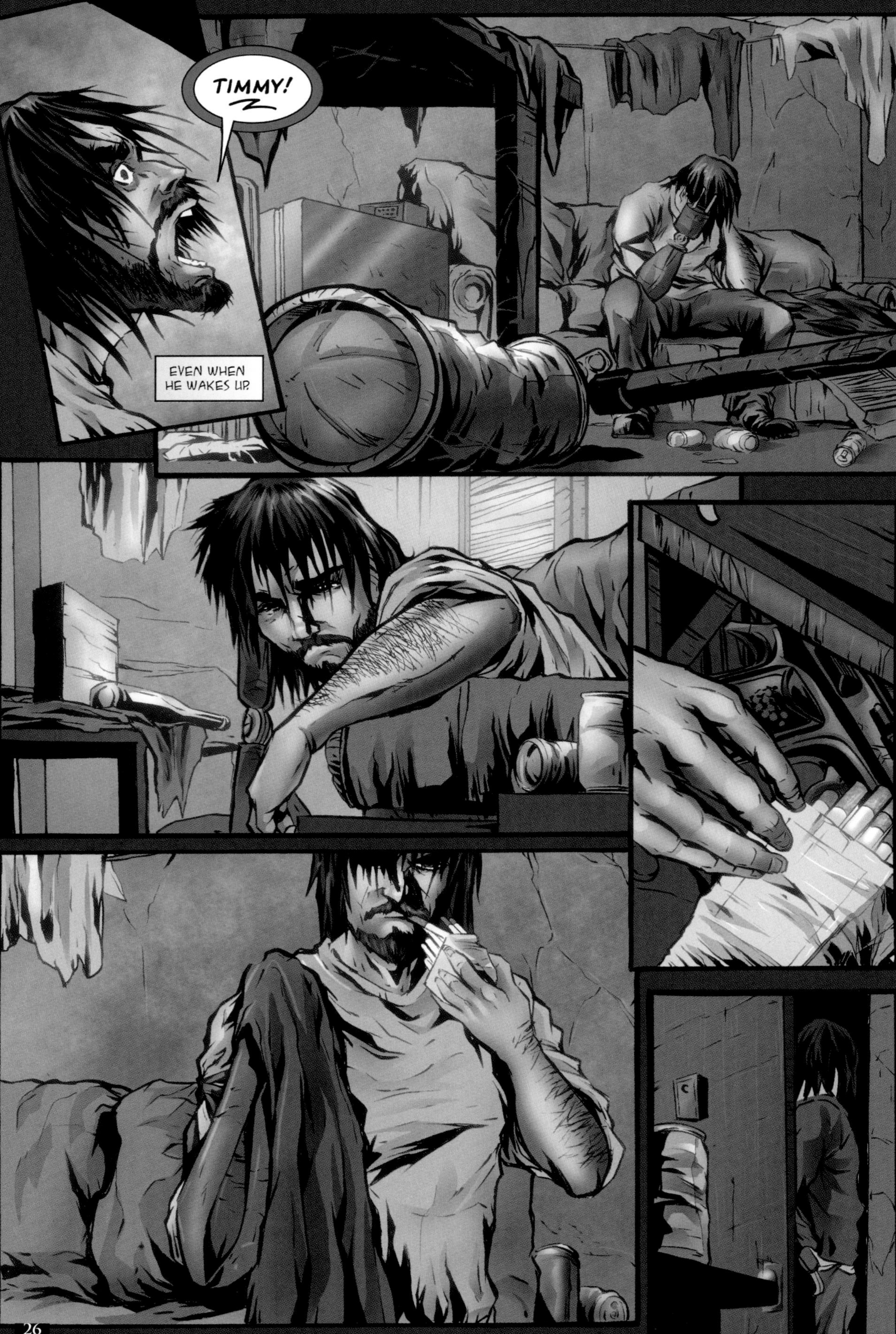
TIMMY!
EVEN WHEN HE WAKES UP.

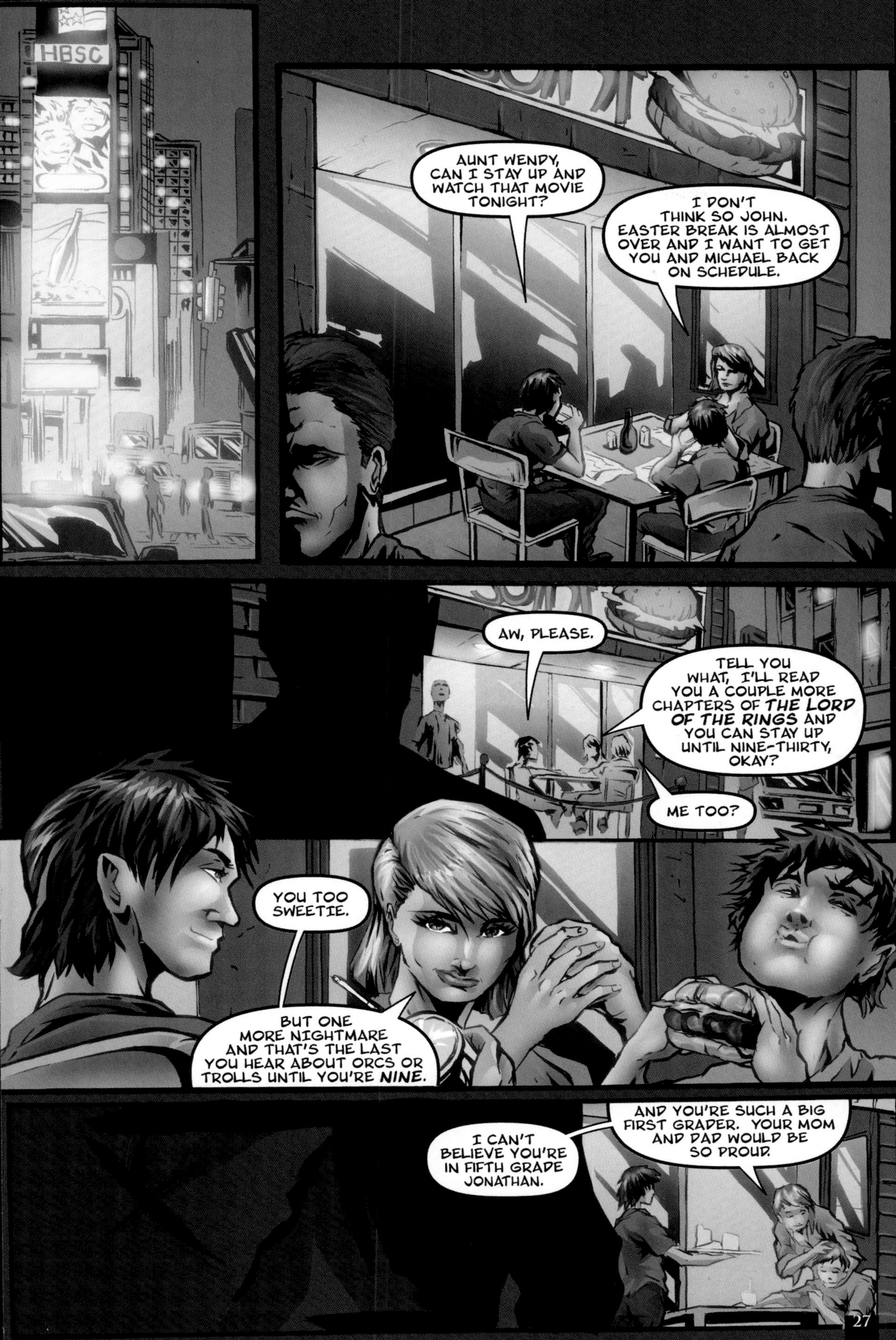

HBSC
AUNT WENDY, CAN I STAY UP AND WATCH THAT MOVIE TONIGHT?
I DON'T THINK SO JOHN. EASTER BREAK IS ALMOST OVER AND I WANT TO GET YOU AND MICHAEL BACK ON SCHEDULE.
AW, PLEASE.
TELL YOU WHAT, I'LL READ YOU A COUPLE MORE CHAPTERS OF ***THE LORD OF THE RINGS*** AND YOU CAN STAY UP UNTIL NINE-THIRTY, OKAY?
ME TOO?
YOU TOO SWEETIE.
BUT ONE MORE NIGHTMARE AND THAT'S THE LAST YOU HEAR ABOUT ORCS OR TROLLS UNTIL YOU'RE ***NINE***.
I CAN'T BELIEVE YOU'RE IN FIFTH GRADE JONATHAN.
AND YOU'RE SUCH A BIG FIRST GRADER. YOUR MOM AND DAD WOULD BE SO PROUD.

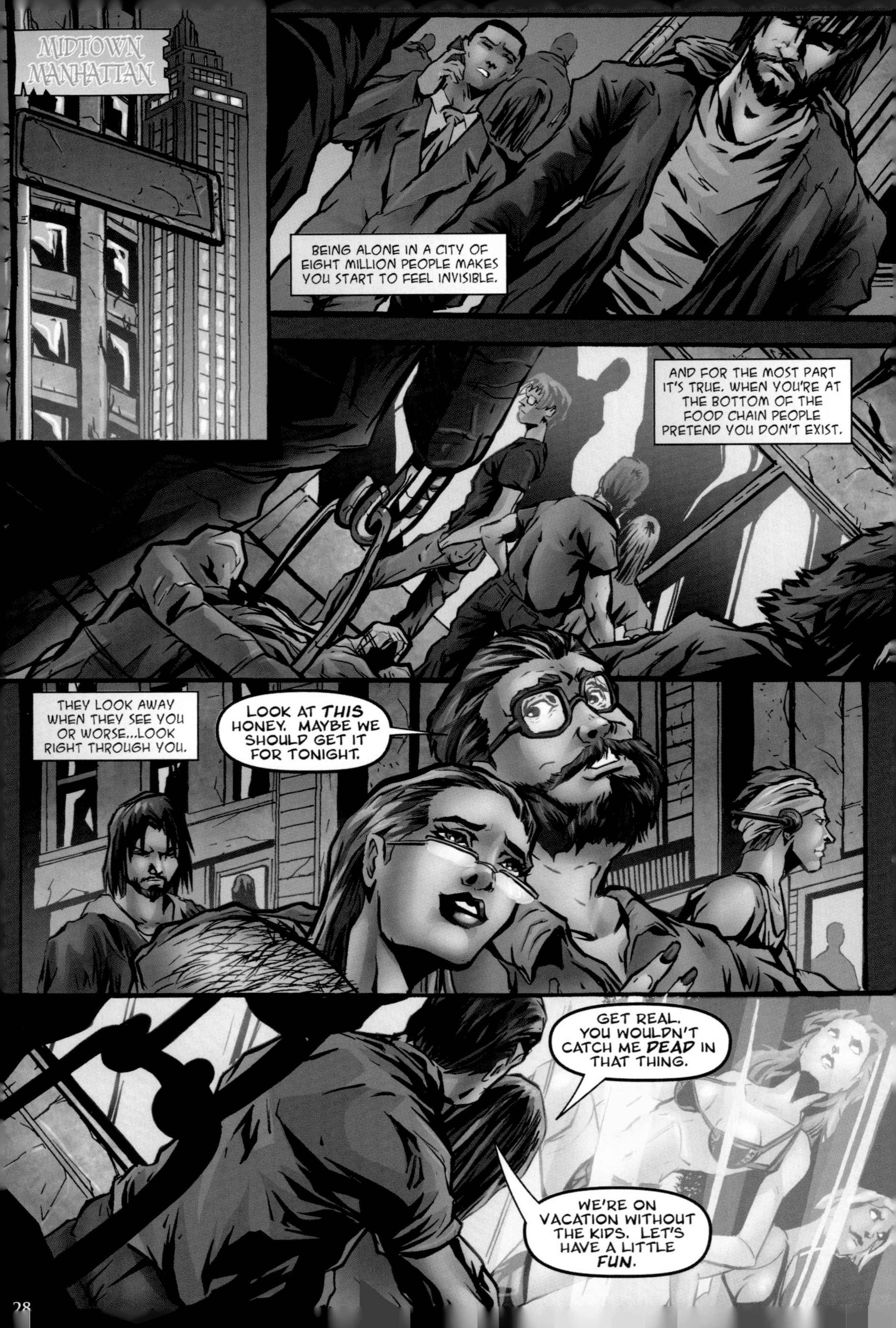
MIDTOWN MANHATTAN
BEING ALONE IN A CITY OF EIGHT MILLION PEOPLE MAKES YOU START TO FEEL INVISIBLE.
AND FOR THE MOST PART IT'S TRUE. WHEN YOU'RE AT THE BOTTOM OF THE FOOD CHAIN PEOPLE PRETEND YOU DON'T EXIST.
THEY LOOK AWAY WHEN THEY SEE YOU OR WORSE...LOOK RIGHT THROUGH YOU.
LOOK AT THIS HONEY. MAYBE WE SHOULD GET IT FOR TONIGHT.
GET REAL. YOU WOULDN'T CATCH ME DEAD IN THAT THING.
WE'RE ON VACATION WITHOUT THE KIDS. LET'S HAVE A LITTLE FUN.

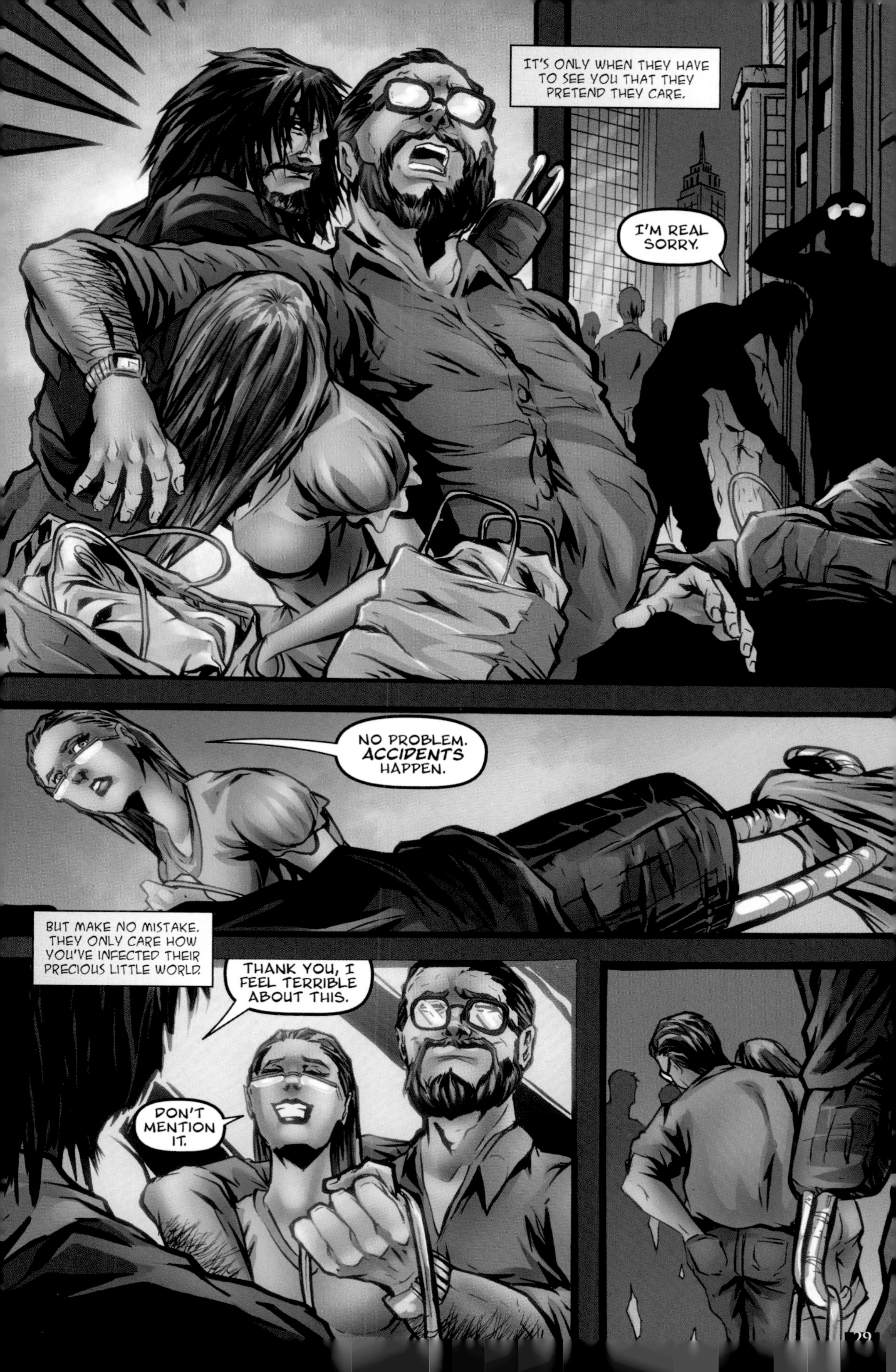
IT'S ONLY WHEN THEY HAVE TO SEE YOU THAT THEY PRETEND THEY CARE.
I'M REAL SORRY.
NO PROBLEM. ACCIDENTS HAPPEN.
BUT MAKE NO MISTAKE. THEY ONLY CARE HOW YOU'VE INFECTED THEIR PRECIOUS LITTLE WORLD.
THANK YOU, I FEEL TERRIBLE ABOUT THIS.
DON'T MENTION IT.

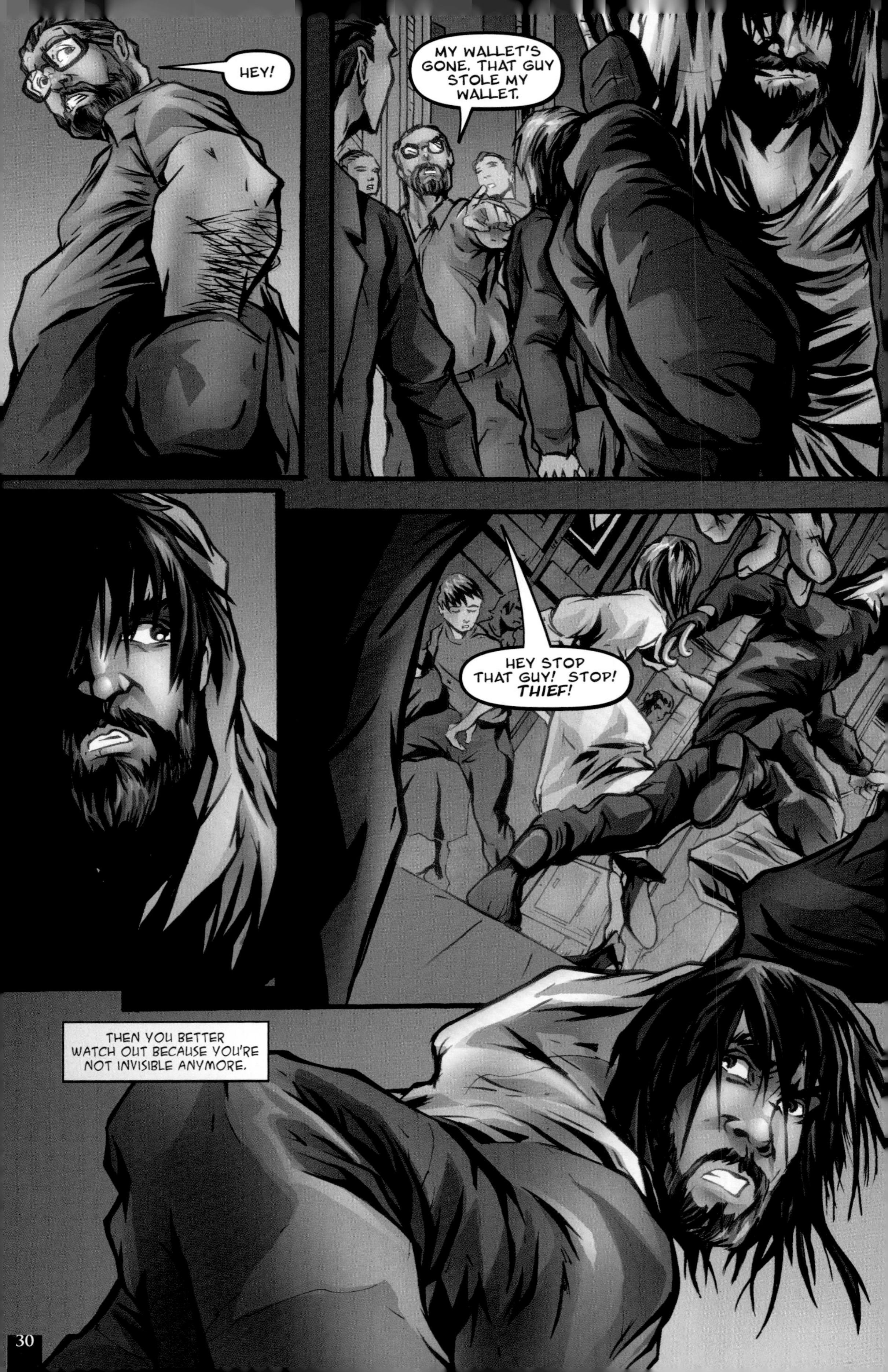
HEY!
MY WALLET'S GONE. THAT GUY STOLE MY WALLET.
HEY STOP THAT GUY! STOP! THIEF!
THEN YOU BETTER WATCH OUT BECAUSE YOU'RE NOT INVISIBLE ANYMORE.

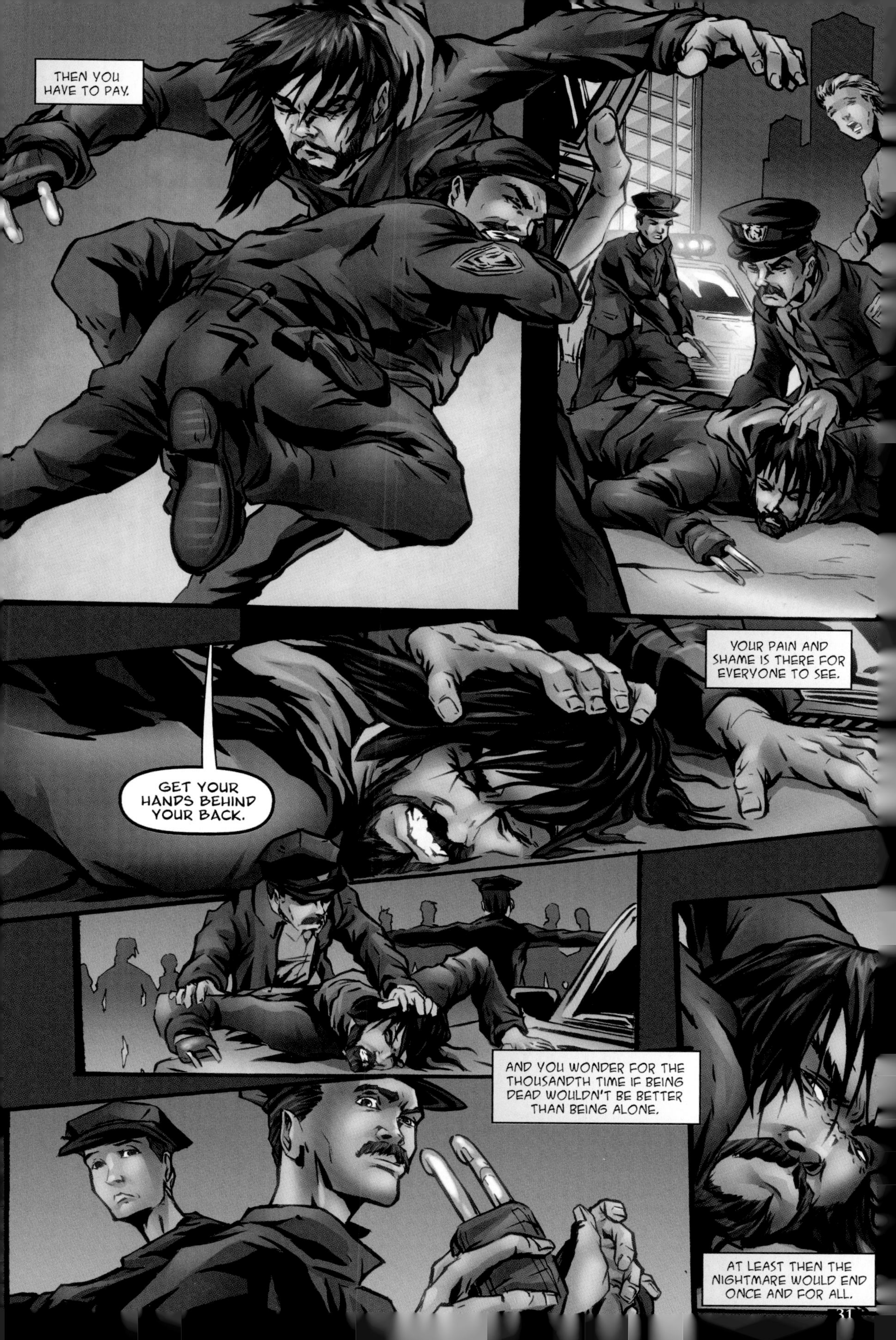

THEN YOU HAVE TO PAY.
YOUR PAIN AND SHAME IS THERE FOR EVERYONE TO SEE.
GET YOUR HANDS BEHIND YOUR BACK.
AND YOU WONDER FOR THE THOUSANDTH TIME IF BEING DEAD WOULDN'T BE BETTER THAN BEING ALONE.
AT LEAST THEN THE NIGHTMARE WOULD END ONCE AND FOR ALL.

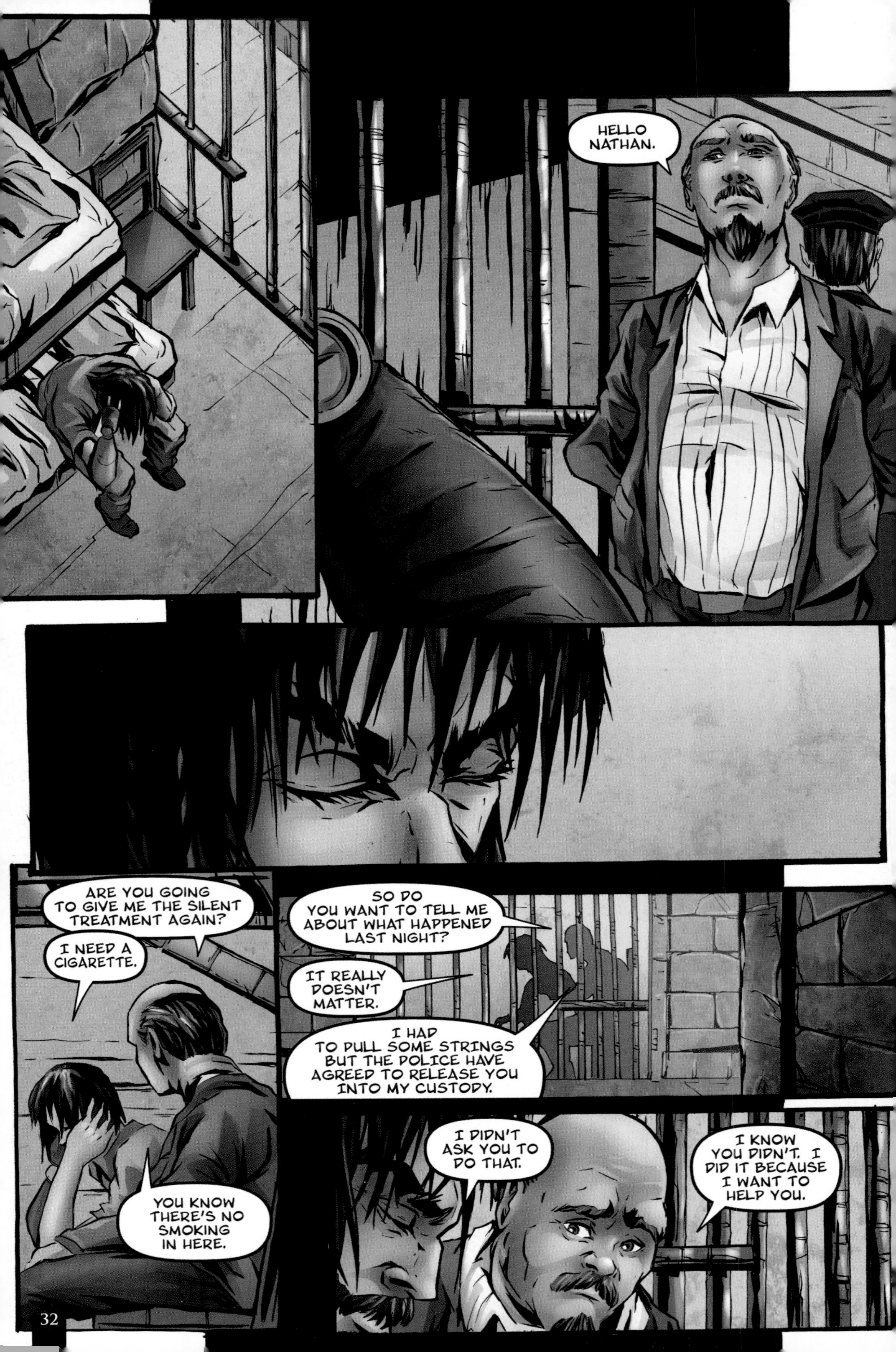
HELLO NATHAN.
ARE YOU GOING TO GIVE ME THE SILENT TREATMENT AGAIN?
I NEED A CIGARETTE.
YOU KNOW THERE'S NO SMOKING IN HERE.
SO DO YOU WANT TO TELL ME ABOUT WHAT HAPPENED LAST NIGHT?
IT REALLY DOESN'T MATTER.
I HAD TO PULL SOME STRINGS BUT THE POLICE HAVE AGREED TO RELEASE YOU INTO MY CUSTODY.
I DIDN'T ASK YOU TO DO THAT.
I KNOW YOU DIDN'T. I DID IT BECAUSE I WANT TO HELP YOU.

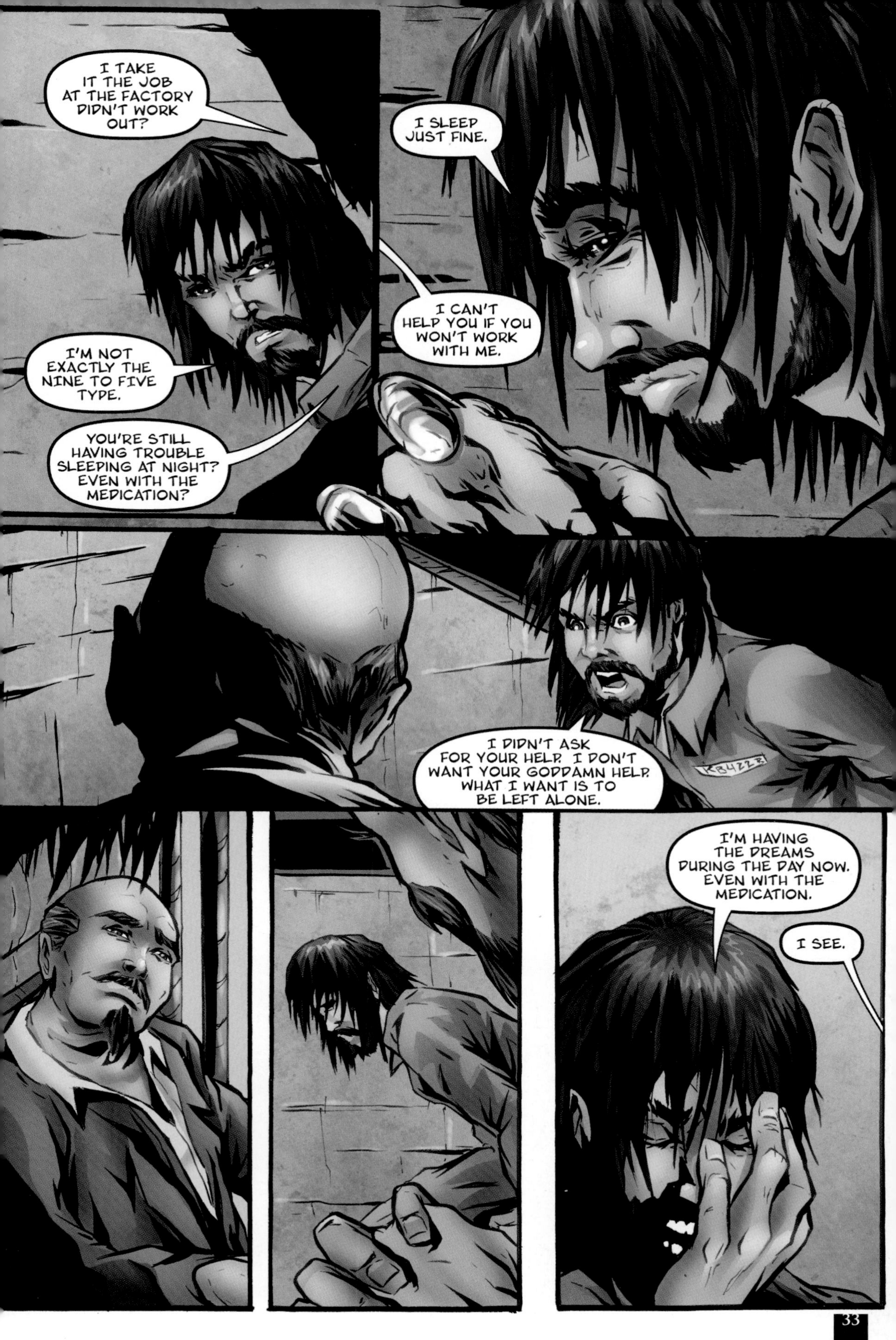
I TAKE IT THE JOB AT THE FACTORY DIDN'T WORK OUT?
I'M NOT EXACTLY THE NINE TO FIVE TYPE.
YOU'RE STILL HAVING TROUBLE SLEEPING AT NIGHT? EVEN WITH THE MEDICATION?
I SLEEP JUST FINE.
I CAN'T HELP YOU IF YOU WON'T WORK WITH ME.
I DIDN'T ASK FOR YOUR HELP. I DON'T WANT YOUR GODDAMN HELP. WHAT I WANT IS TO BE LEFT ALONE.
KB4228
I'M HAVING THE DREAMS DURING THE DAY NOW. EVEN WITH THE MEDICATION.
I SEE.

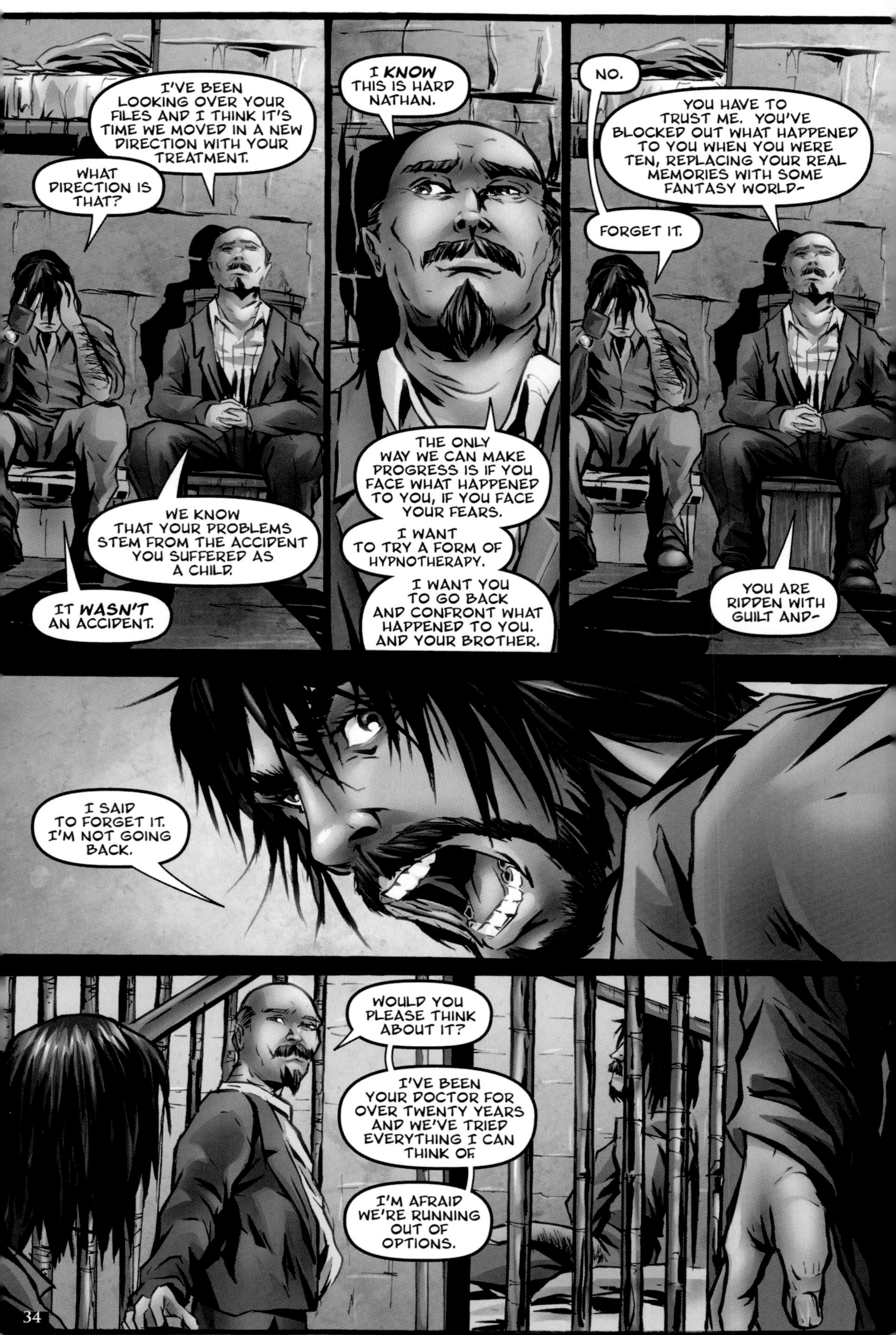
I'VE BEEN LOOKING OVER YOUR FILES AND I THINK IT'S TIME WE MOVED IN A NEW DIRECTION WITH YOUR TREATMENT.
WHAT DIRECTION IS THAT?
WE KNOW THAT YOUR PROBLEMS STEM FROM THE ACCIDENT YOU SUFFERED AS A CHILD.
IT WASN'T AN ACCIDENT.
I KNOW THIS IS HARD NATHAN.
THE ONLY WAY WE CAN MAKE PROGRESS IS IF YOU FACE WHAT HAPPENED TO YOU, IF YOU FACE YOUR FEARS.
I WANT TO TRY A FORM OF HYPNOTHERAPY.
I WANT YOU TO GO BACK AND CONFRONT WHAT HAPPENED TO YOU. AND YOUR BROTHER.
NO.
YOU HAVE TO TRUST ME. YOU'VE BLOCKED OUT WHAT HAPPENED TO YOU WHEN YOU WERE TEN, REPLACING YOUR REAL MEMORIES WITH SOME FANTASY WORLD-
FORGET IT.
YOU ARE RIDDEN WITH GUILT AND-
I SAID TO FORGET IT. I'M NOT GOING BACK.
WOULD YOU PLEASE THINK ABOUT IT?
I'VE BEEN YOUR DOCTOR FOR OVER TWENTY YEARS AND WE'VE TRIED EVERYTHING I CAN THINK OF.
I'M AFRAID WE'RE RUNNING OUT OF OPTIONS.

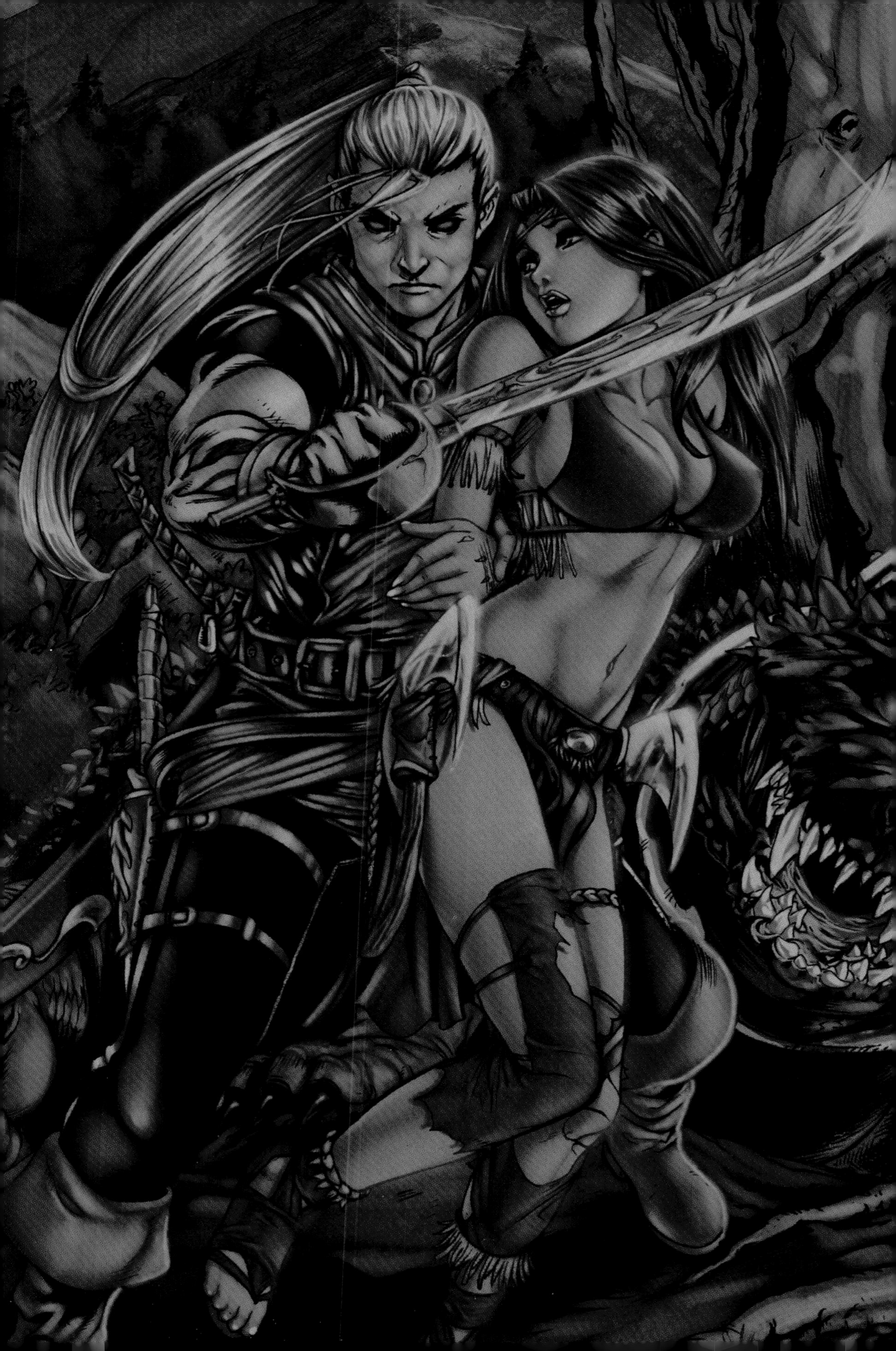

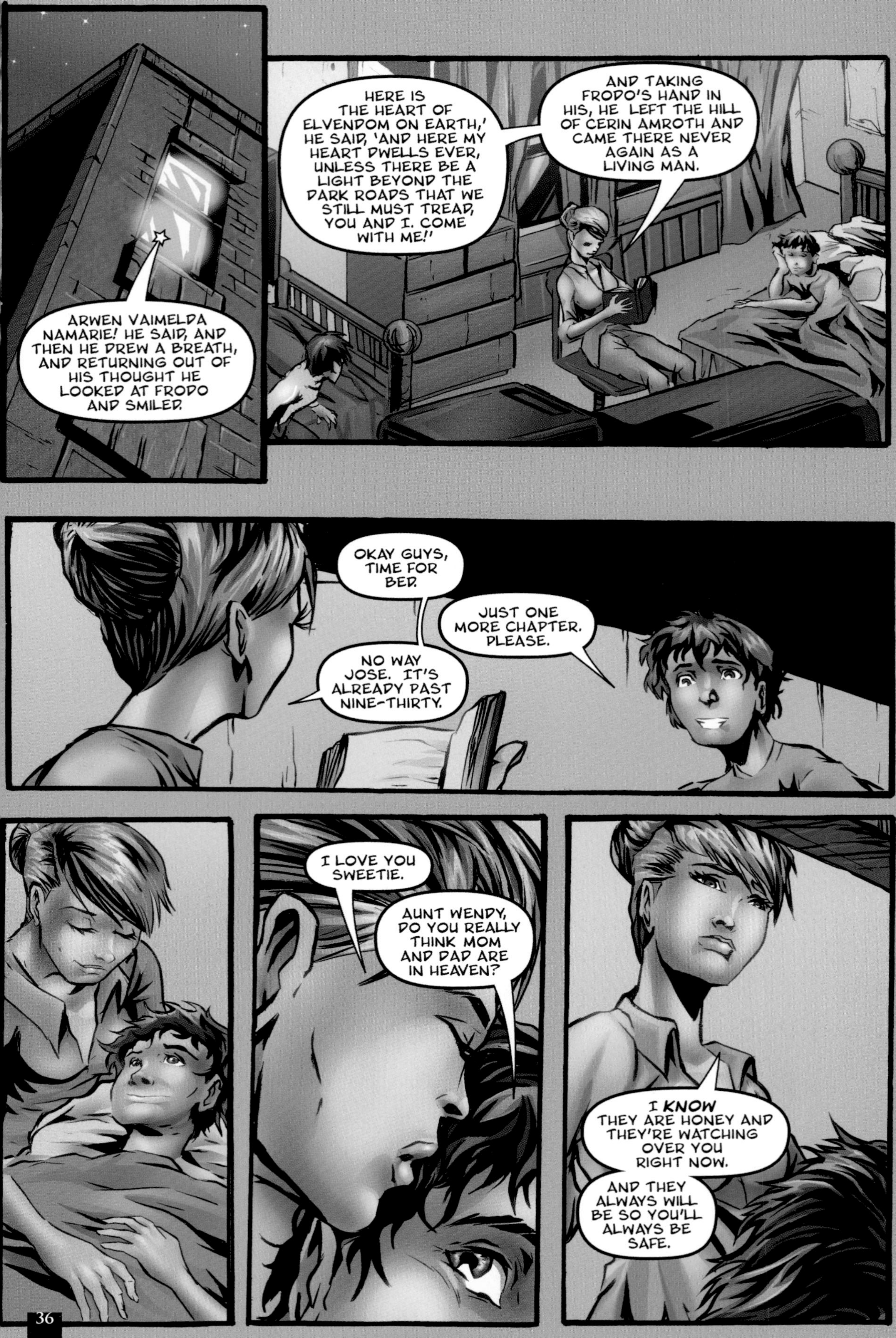
ARWEN VAIMELDA NAMARIE! HE SAID, AND THEN HE DREW A BREATH, AND RETURNING OUT OF HIS THOUGHT HE LOOKED AT FRODO AND SMILED.
HERE IS THE HEART OF ELVENDOM ON EARTH,' HE SAID, 'AND HERE MY HEART DWELLS EVER, UNLESS THERE BE A LIGHT BEYOND THE DARK ROADS THAT WE STILL MUST TREAD, YOU AND I. COME WITH ME!'
AND TAKING FRODO'S HAND IN HIS, HE LEFT THE HILL OF CERIN AMROTH AND CAME THERE NEVER AGAIN AS A LIVING MAN.
OKAY GUYS, TIME FOR BED.
JUST ONE MORE CHAPTER. PLEASE.
NO WAY JOSE. IT'S ALREADY PAST NINE-THIRTY.
I LOVE YOU SWEETIE.
AUNT WENDY, DO YOU REALLY THINK MOM AND DAD ARE IN HEAVEN?
I KNOW THEY ARE HONEY AND THEY'RE WATCHING OVER YOU RIGHT NOW.
AND THEY ALWAYS WILL BE SO YOU'LL ALWAYS BE SAFE.

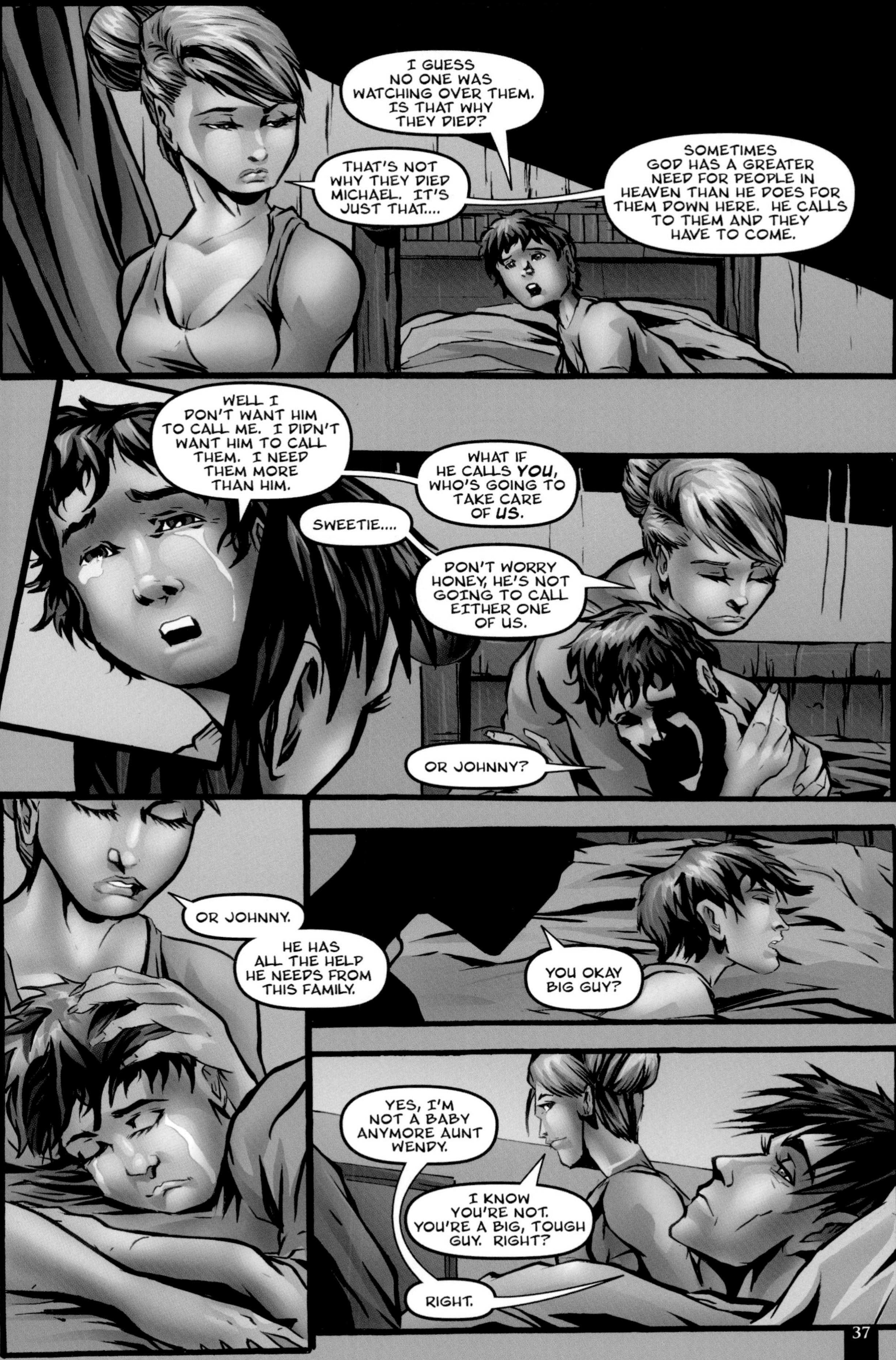
I GUESS NO ONE WAS WATCHING OVER THEM. IS THAT WHY THEY DIED?
THAT'S NOT WHY THEY DIED MICHAEL. IT'S JUST THAT....
SOMETIMES GOD HAS A GREATER NEED FOR PEOPLE IN HEAVEN THAN HE DOES FOR THEM DOWN HERE. HE CALLS TO THEM AND THEY HAVE TO COME.
WELL I DON'T WANT HIM TO CALL ME. I DIDN'T WANT HIM TO CALL THEM. I NEED THEM MORE THAN HIM.
WHAT IF HE CALLS YOU, WHO'S GOING TO TAKE CARE OF US.
SWEETIE....
DON'T WORRY HONEY, HE'S NOT GOING TO CALL EITHER ONE OF US.
OR JOHNNY?
OR JOHNNY.
HE HAS ALL THE HELP HE NEEDS FROM THIS FAMILY.
YOU OKAY BIG GUY?
YES, I'M NOT A BABY ANYMORE AUNT WENDY.
I KNOW YOU'RE NOT. YOU'RE A BIG, TOUGH GUY. RIGHT?
RIGHT.

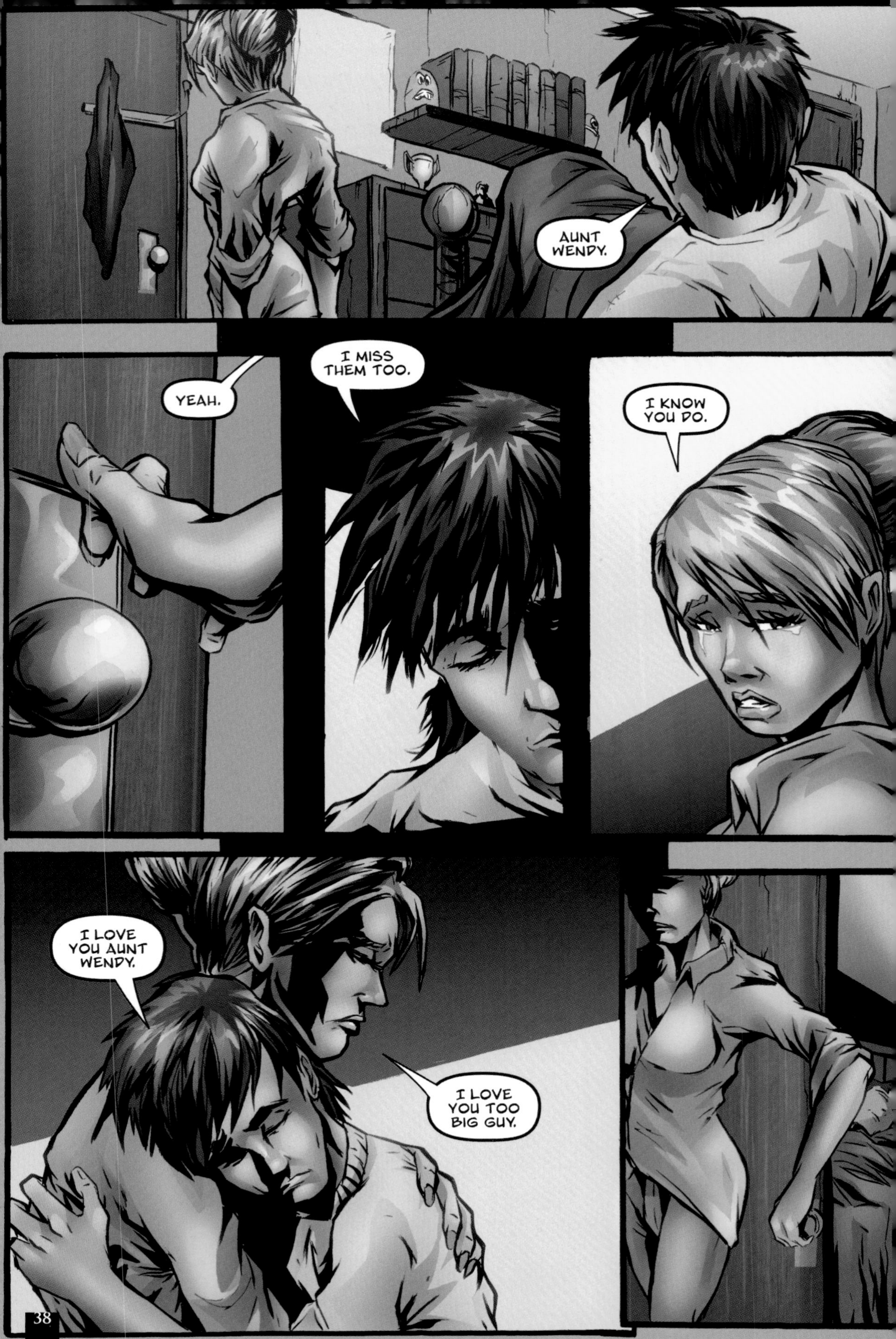
AUNT WENDY.
YEAH.
I MISS THEM TOO.
I KNOW YOU DO.
I LOVE YOU AUNT WENDY.
I LOVE YOU TOO BIG GUY.

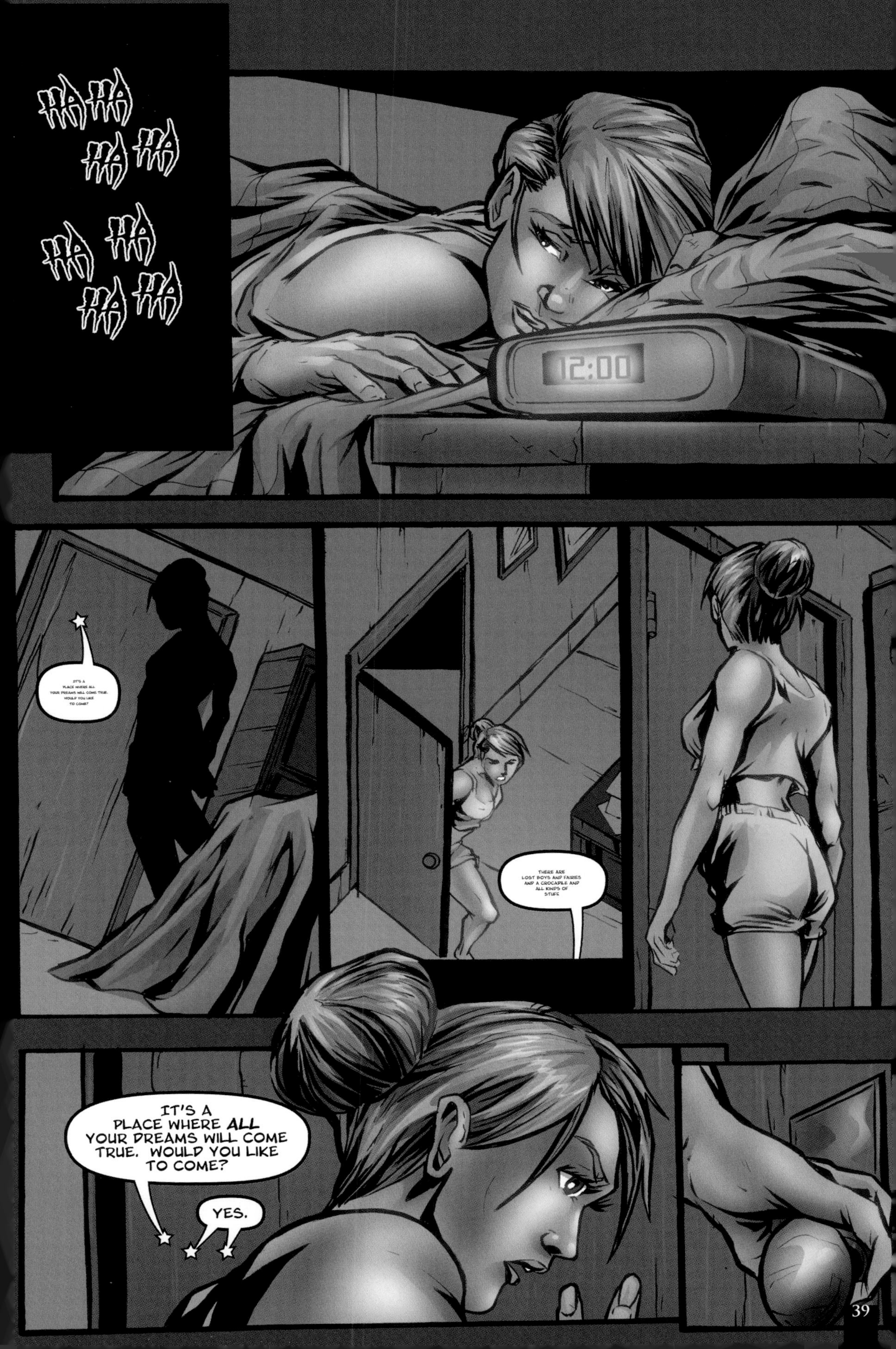
HA HA HA HA
HA HA HA HA
IT'S A PLACE WHERE ALL YOUR DREAMS WILL COME TRUE. WOULD YOU LIKE TO COME?
THERE ARE LOST BOYS AND FAIRIES AND A CROCADILE AND ALL KINDS OF STUFF
IT'S A PLACE WHERE ALL YOUR DREAMS WILL COME TRUE. WOULD YOU LIKE TO COME?
YES.

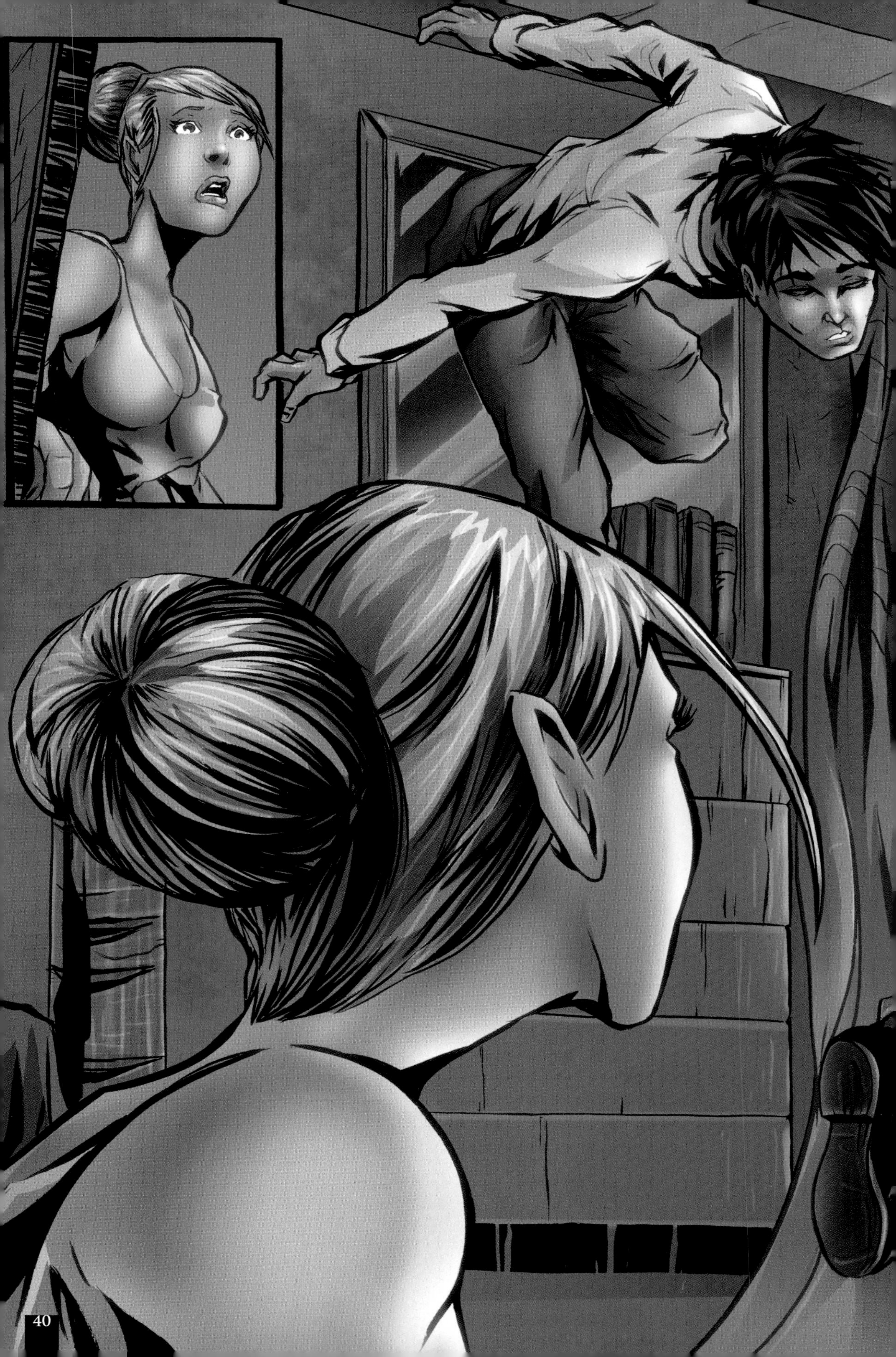

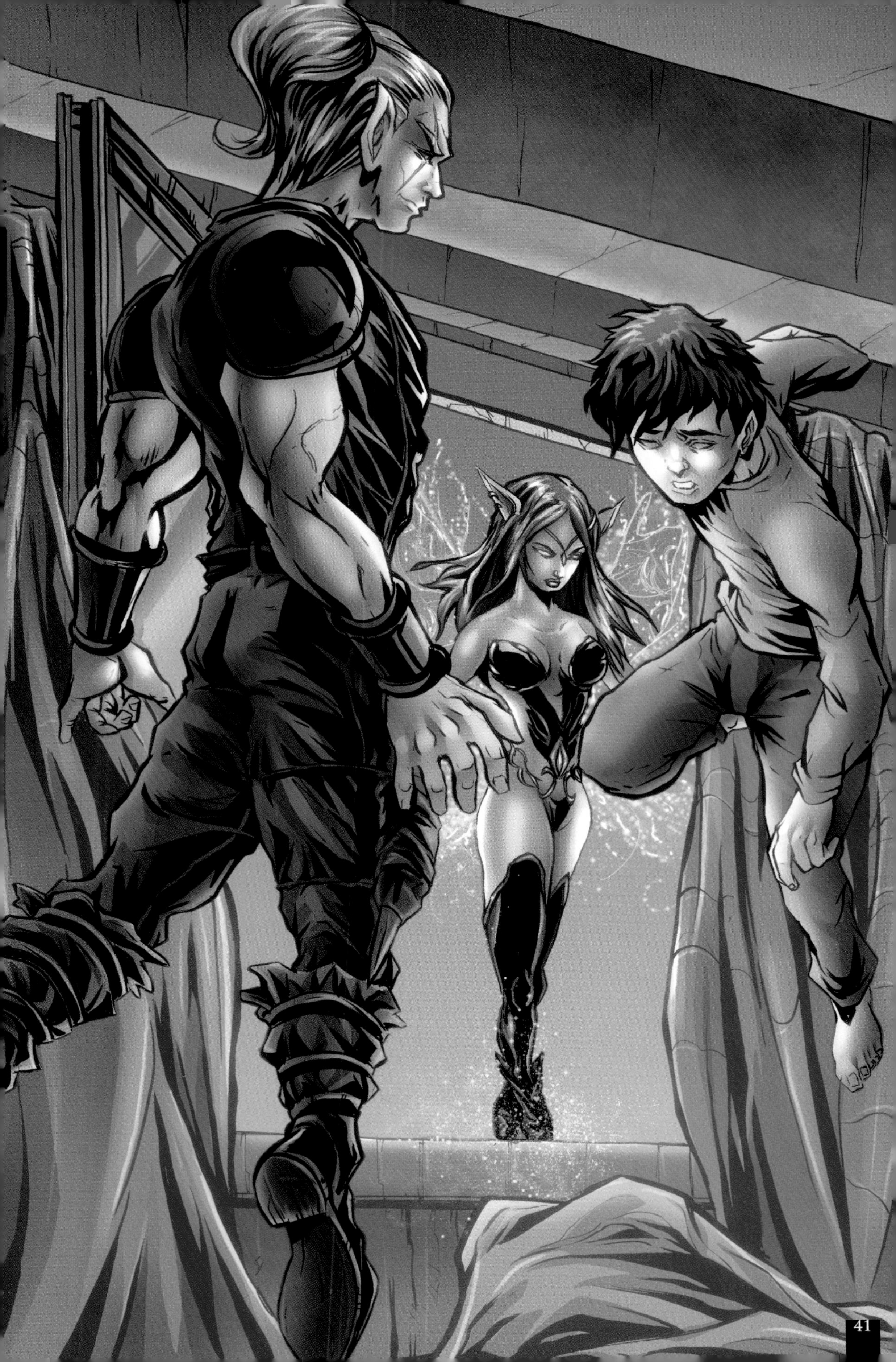

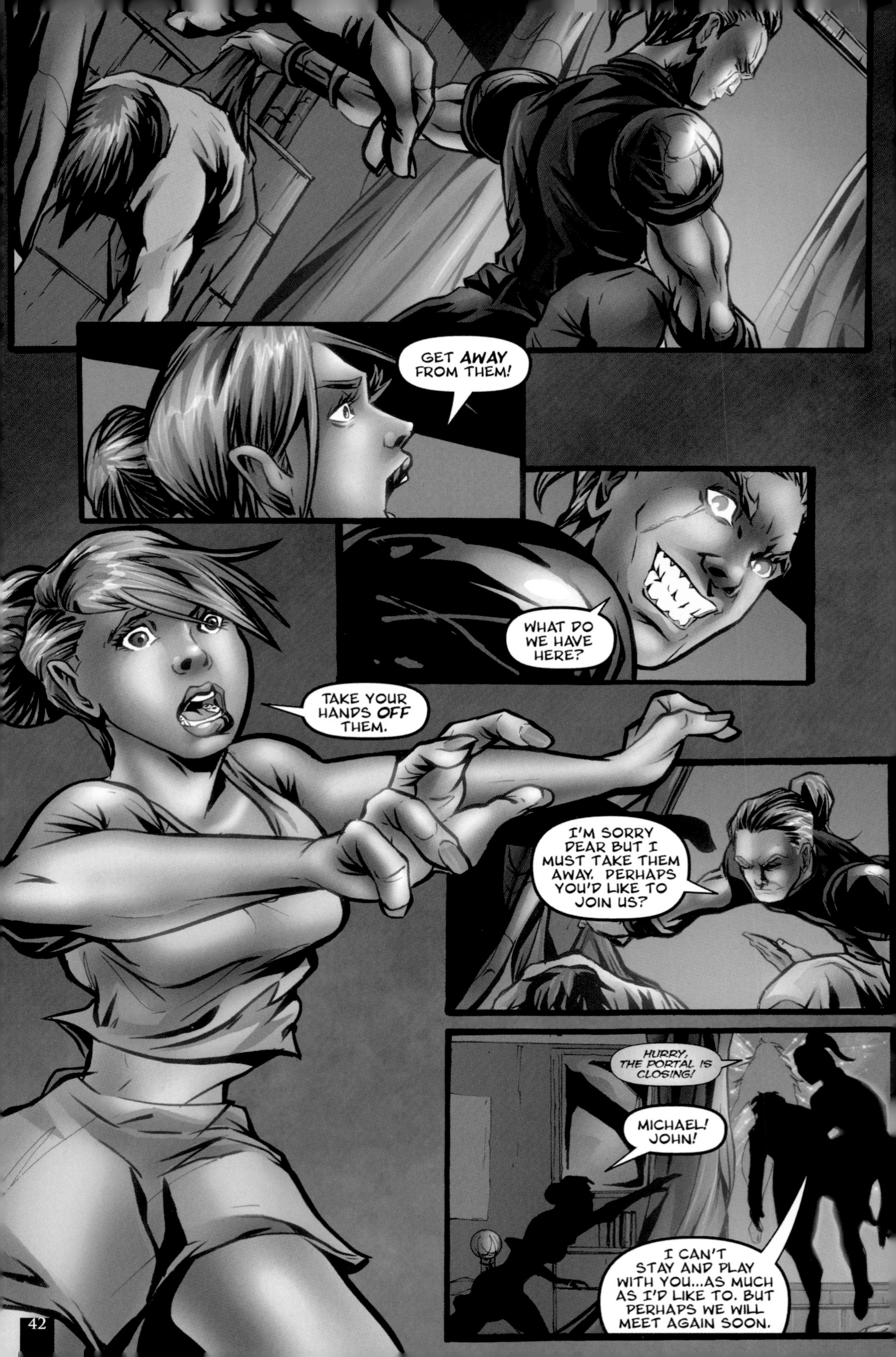
GET AWAY FROM THEM!
WHAT DO WE HAVE HERE?
TAKE YOUR HANDS OFF THEM.
I'M SORRY DEAR BUT I MUST TAKE THEM AWAY. PERHAPS YOU'D LIKE TO JOIN US?
HURRY, THE PORTAL IS CLOSING!
MICHAEL! JOHN!
I CAN'T STAY AND PLAY WITH YOU...AS MUCH AS I'D LIKE TO. BUT PERHAPS WE WILL MEET AGAIN SOON.

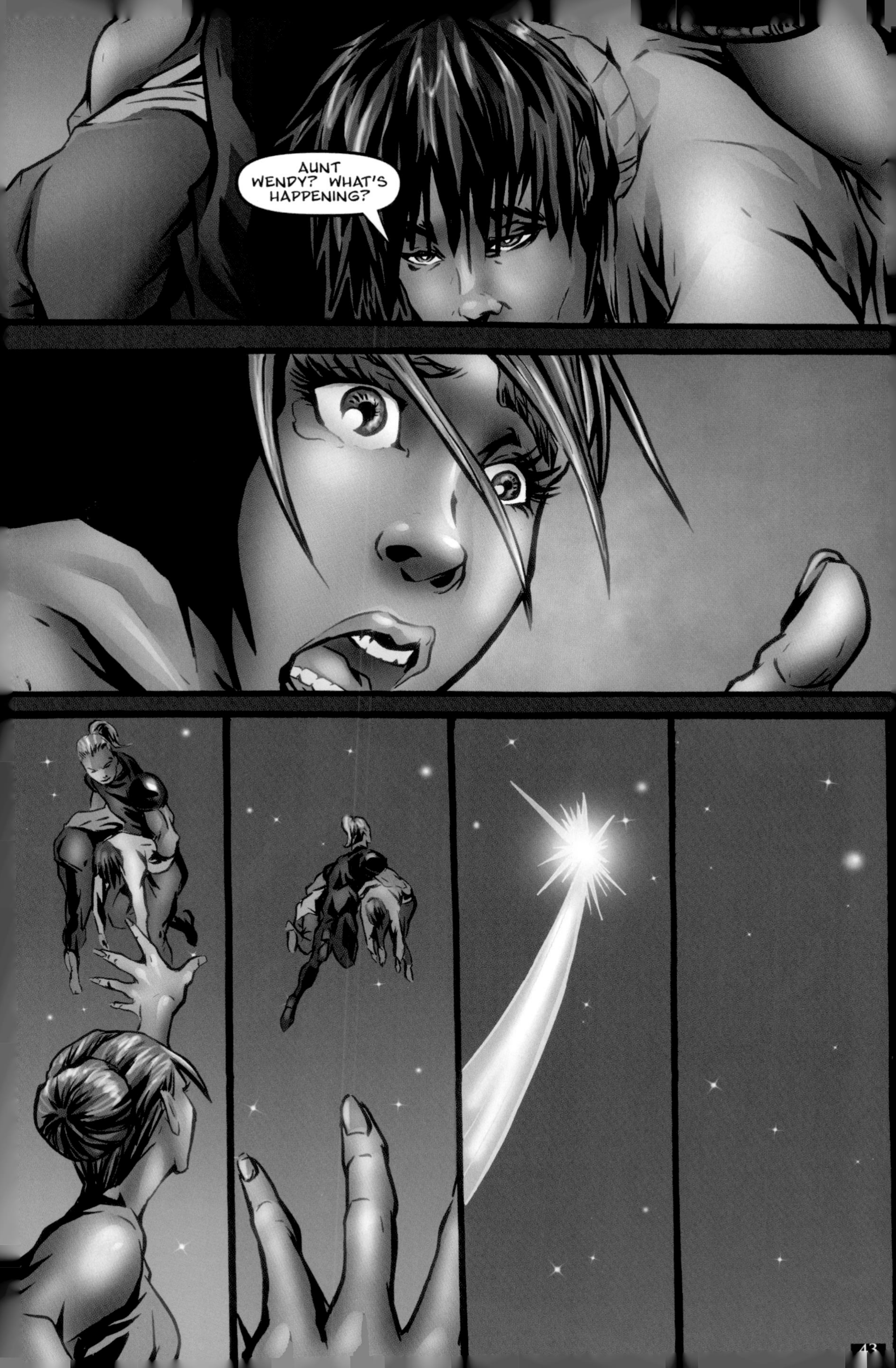
AUNT WENDY? WHAT'S HAPPENING?

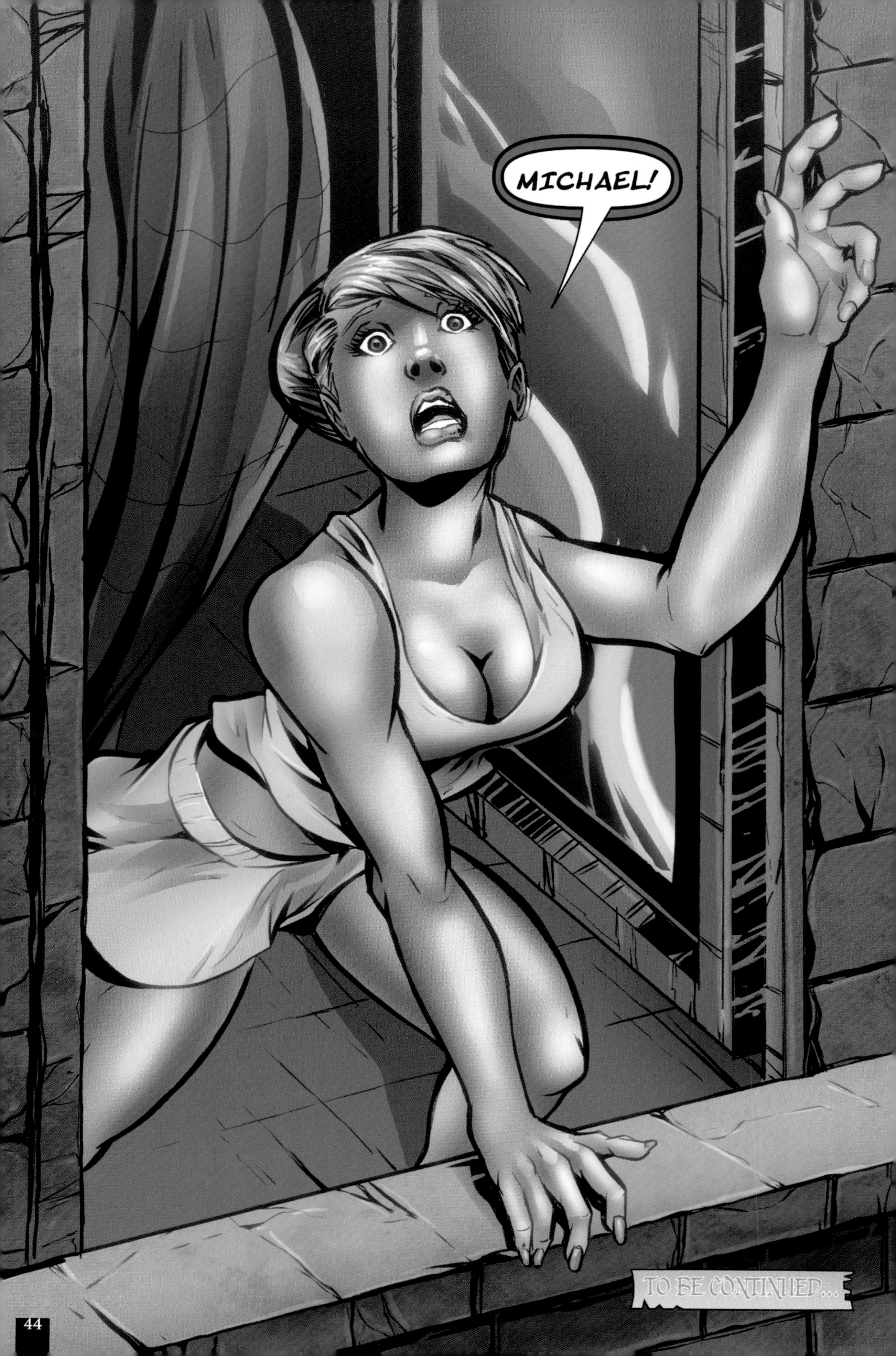
MICHAEL!
TO BE CONTINUED...

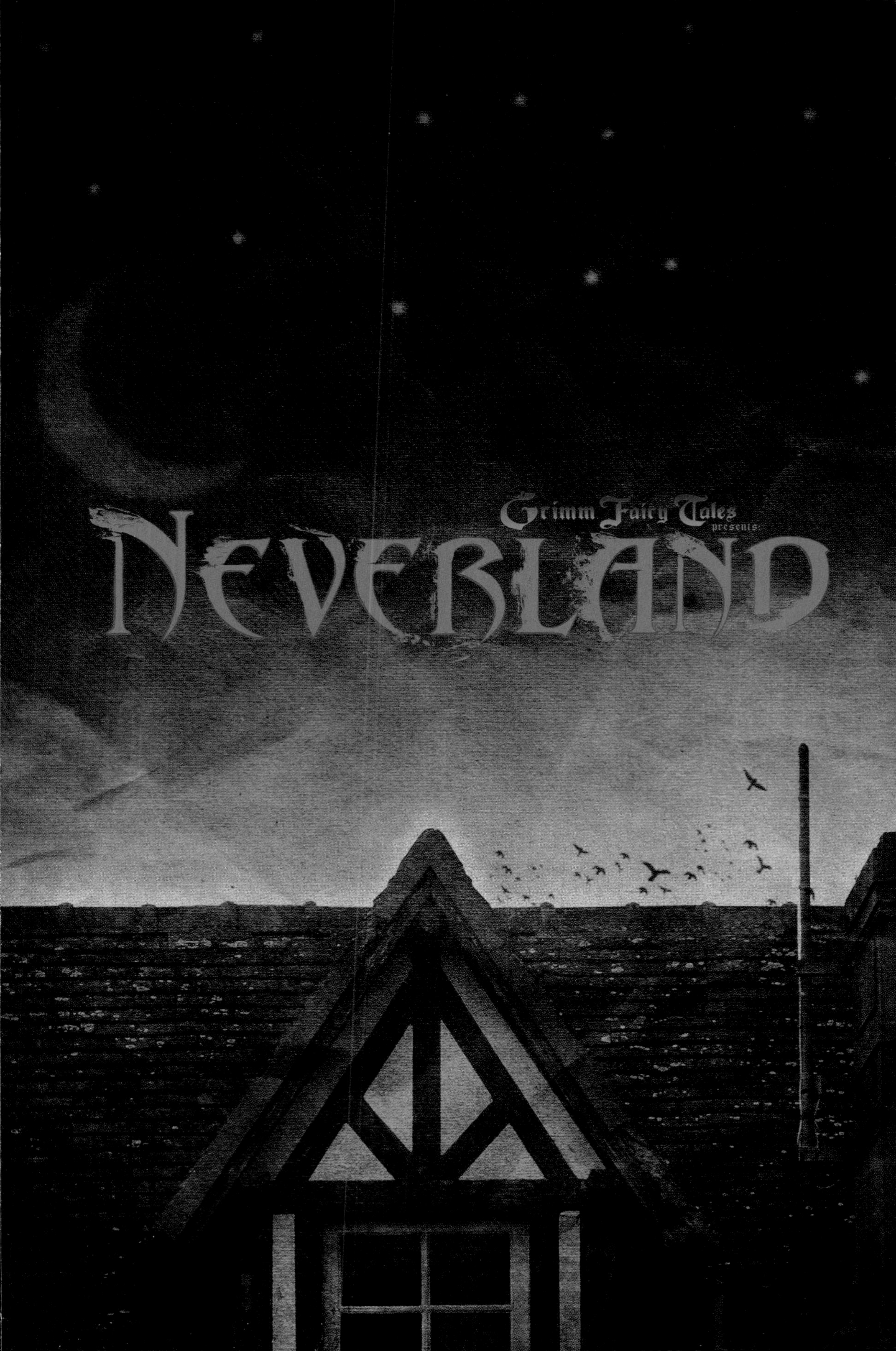
Grimm Fairy Tales
presents:
NEVERLAND

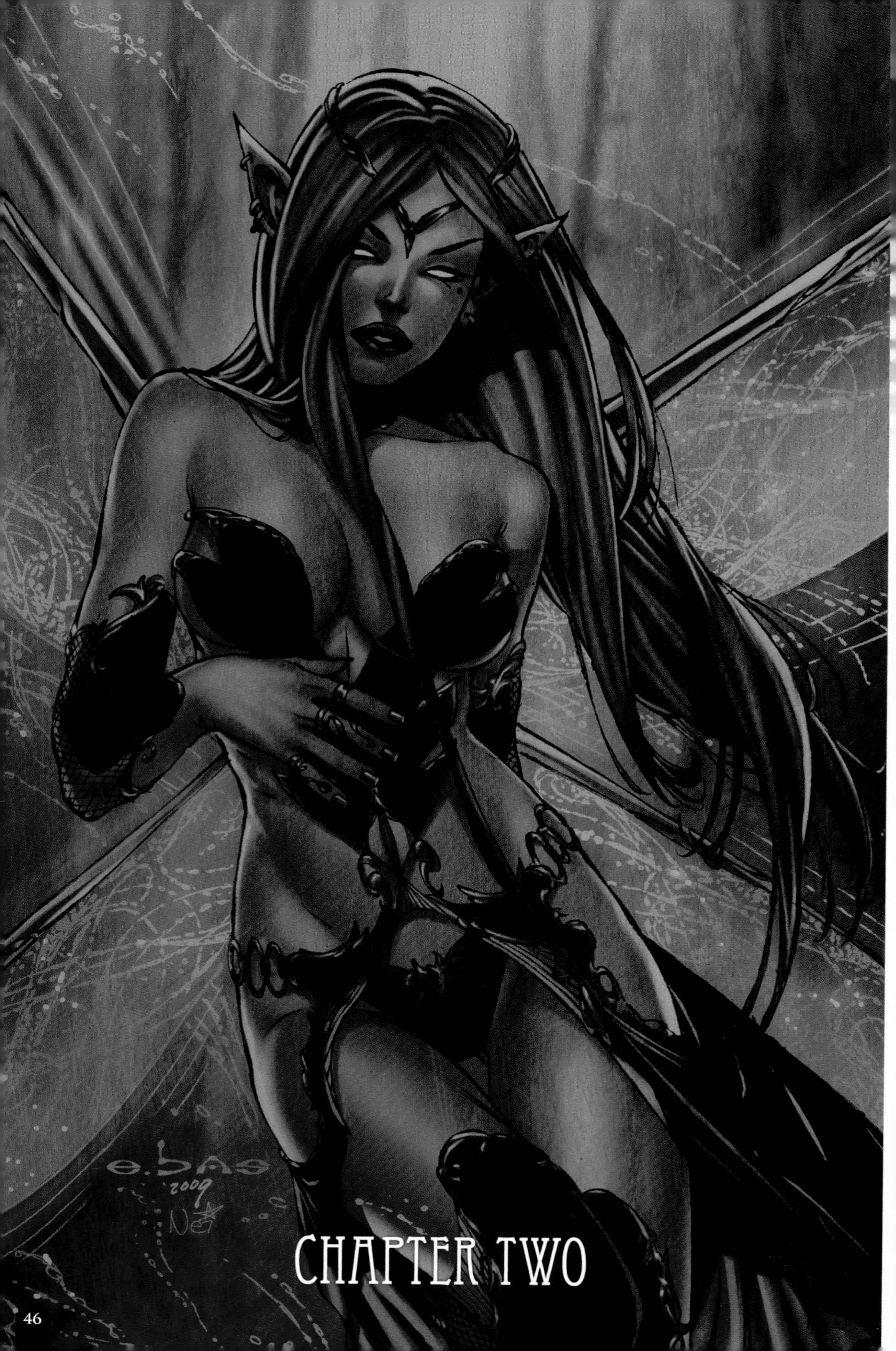

CHAPTER TWO

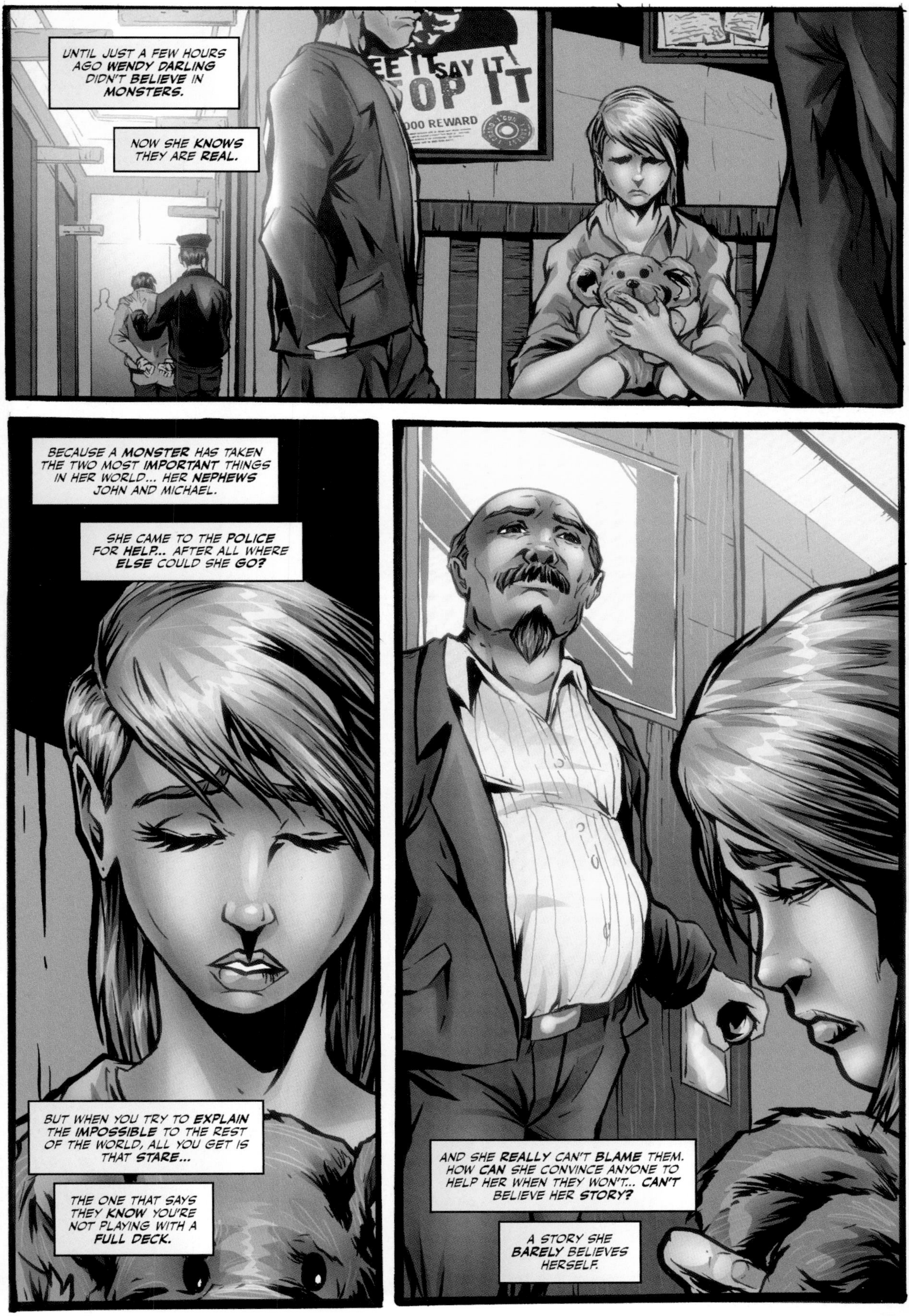
UNTIL JUST A FEW HOURS AGO WENDY DARLING DIDN'T BELIEVE IN MONSTERS.
NOW SHE KNOWS THEY ARE REAL.
SAY IT
000 REWARD
BECAUSE A MONSTER HAS TAKEN THE TWO MOST IMPORTANT THINGS IN HER WORLD... HER NEPHEWS JOHN AND MICHAEL.
SHE CAME TO THE POLICE FOR HELP... AFTER ALL WHERE ELSE COULD SHE GO?
BUT WHEN YOU TRY TO EXPLAIN THE IMPOSSIBLE TO THE REST OF THE WORLD, ALL YOU GET IS THAT STARE...
THE ONE THAT SAYS THEY KNOW YOU'RE NOT PLAYING WITH A FULL DECK.
AND SHE REALLY CAN'T BLAME THEM. HOW CAN SHE CONVINCE ANYONE TO HELP HER WHEN THEY WON'T... CAN'T BELIEVE HER STORY?
A STORY SHE BARELY BELIEVES HERSELF.

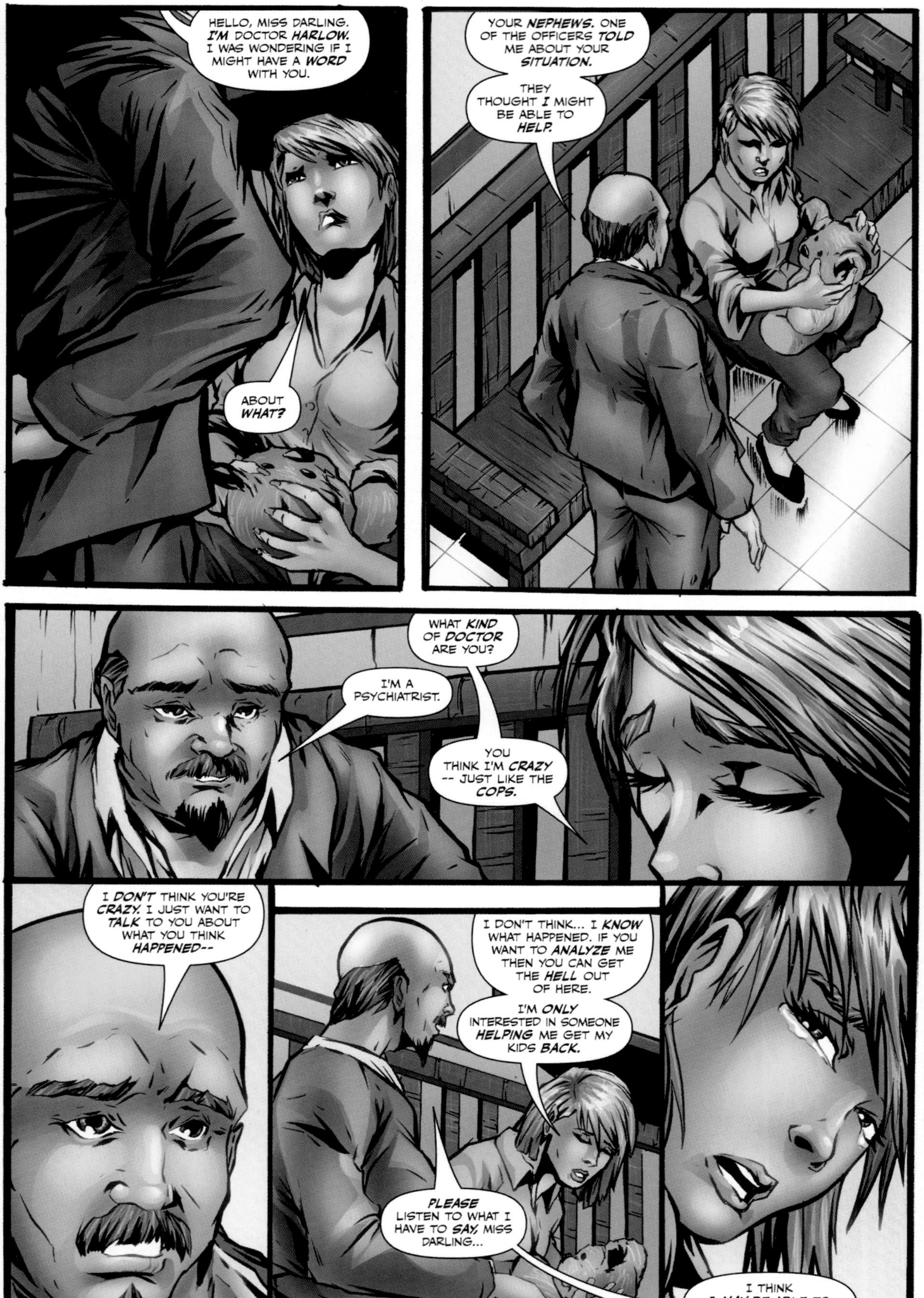
HELLO, MISS DARLING. I'M DOCTOR HARLOW. I WAS WONDERING IF I MIGHT HAVE A WORD WITH YOU.
ABOUT WHAT?
YOUR NEPHEWS. ONE OF THE OFFICERS TOLD ME ABOUT YOUR SITUATION.
THEY THOUGHT I MIGHT BE ABLE TO HELP.
WHAT KIND OF DOCTOR ARE YOU?
I'M A PSYCHIATRIST.
YOU THINK I'M CRAZY -- JUST LIKE THE COPS.
I DON'T THINK YOU'RE CRAZY. I JUST WANT TO TALK TO YOU ABOUT WHAT YOU THINK HAPPENED--
I DON'T THINK... I KNOW WHAT HAPPENED. IF YOU WANT TO ANALYZE ME THEN YOU CAN GET THE HELL OUT OF HERE.
I'M ONLY INTERESTED IN SOMEONE HELPING ME GET MY KIDS BACK.
PLEASE LISTEN TO WHAT I HAVE TO SAY, MISS DARLING...
I THINK I MAY BE ABLE TO HELP YOU FIND YOUR NEPHEWS.

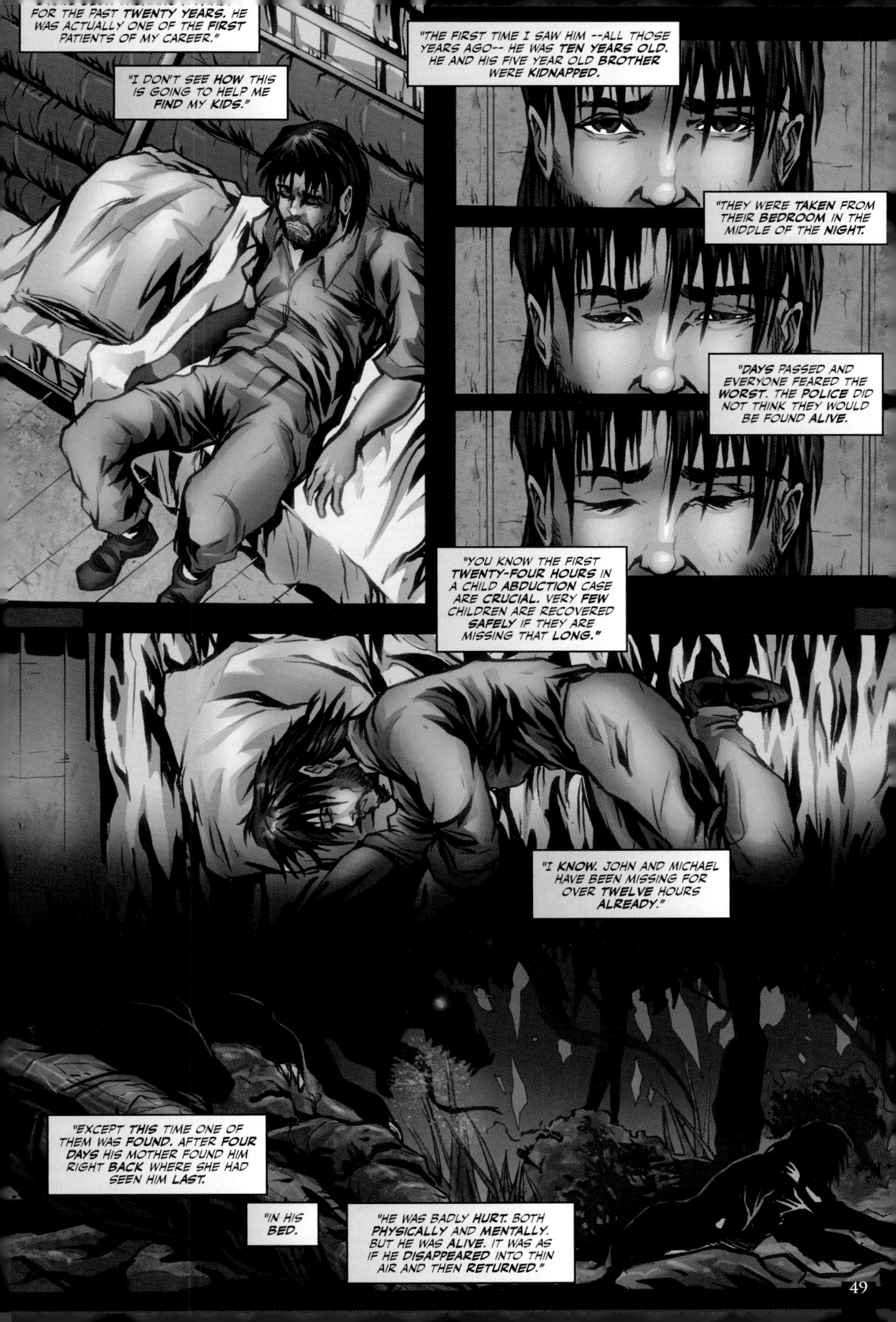
FOR THE PAST TWENTY YEARS. HE WAS ACTUALLY ONE OF THE FIRST PATIENTS OF MY CAREER."
"I DON'T SEE HOW THIS IS GOING TO HELP ME FIND MY KIDS."
"THE FIRST TIME I SAW HIM --ALL THOSE YEARS AGO-- HE WAS TEN YEARS OLD. HE AND HIS FIVE YEAR OLD BROTHER WERE KIDNAPPED.
"THEY WERE TAKEN FROM THEIR BEDROOM IN THE MIDDLE OF THE NIGHT.
"DAYS PASSED AND EVERYONE FEARED THE WORST. THE POLICE DID NOT THINK THEY WOULD BE FOUND ALIVE.
"YOU KNOW THE FIRST TWENTY-FOUR HOURS IN A CHILD ABDUCTION CASE ARE CRUCIAL. VERY FEW CHILDREN ARE RECOVERED SAFELY IF THEY ARE MISSING THAT LONG."
"I KNOW. JOHN AND MICHAEL HAVE BEEN MISSING FOR OVER TWELVE HOURS ALREADY."
"EXCEPT THIS TIME ONE OF THEM WAS FOUND. AFTER FOUR DAYS HIS MOTHER FOUND HIM RIGHT BACK WHERE SHE HAD SEEN HIM LAST.
"IN HIS BED.
"HE WAS BADLY HURT. BOTH PHYSICALLY AND MENTALLY. BUT HE WAS ALIVE. IT WAS AS IF HE DISAPPEARED INTO THIN AIR AND THEN RETURNED."

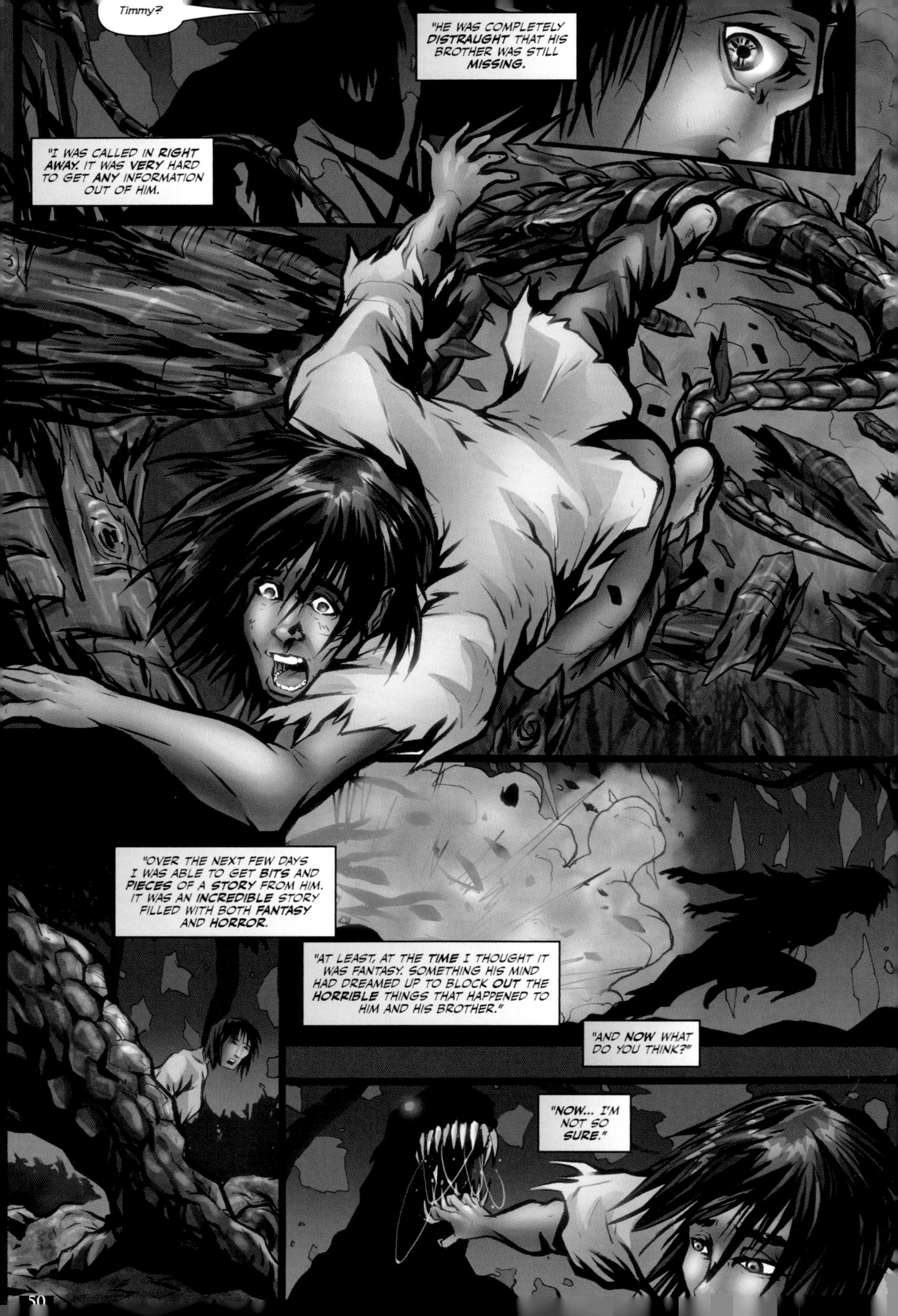

Timmy?
"HE WAS COMPLETELY DISTRAUGHT THAT HIS BROTHER WAS STILL MISSING.
"I WAS CALLED IN RIGHT AWAY. IT WAS VERY HARD TO GET ANY INFORMATION OUT OF HIM.
"OVER THE NEXT FEW DAYS I WAS ABLE TO GET BITS AND PIECES OF A STORY FROM HIM. IT WAS AN INCREDIBLE STORY FILLED WITH BOTH FANTASY AND HORROR.
"AT LEAST, AT THE TIME I THOUGHT IT WAS FANTASY. SOMETHING HIS MIND HAD DREAMED UP TO BLOCK OUT THE HORRIBLE THINGS THAT HAPPENED TO HIM AND HIS BROTHER."
"AND NOW WHAT DO YOU THINK?"
"NOW... I'M NOT SO SURE."

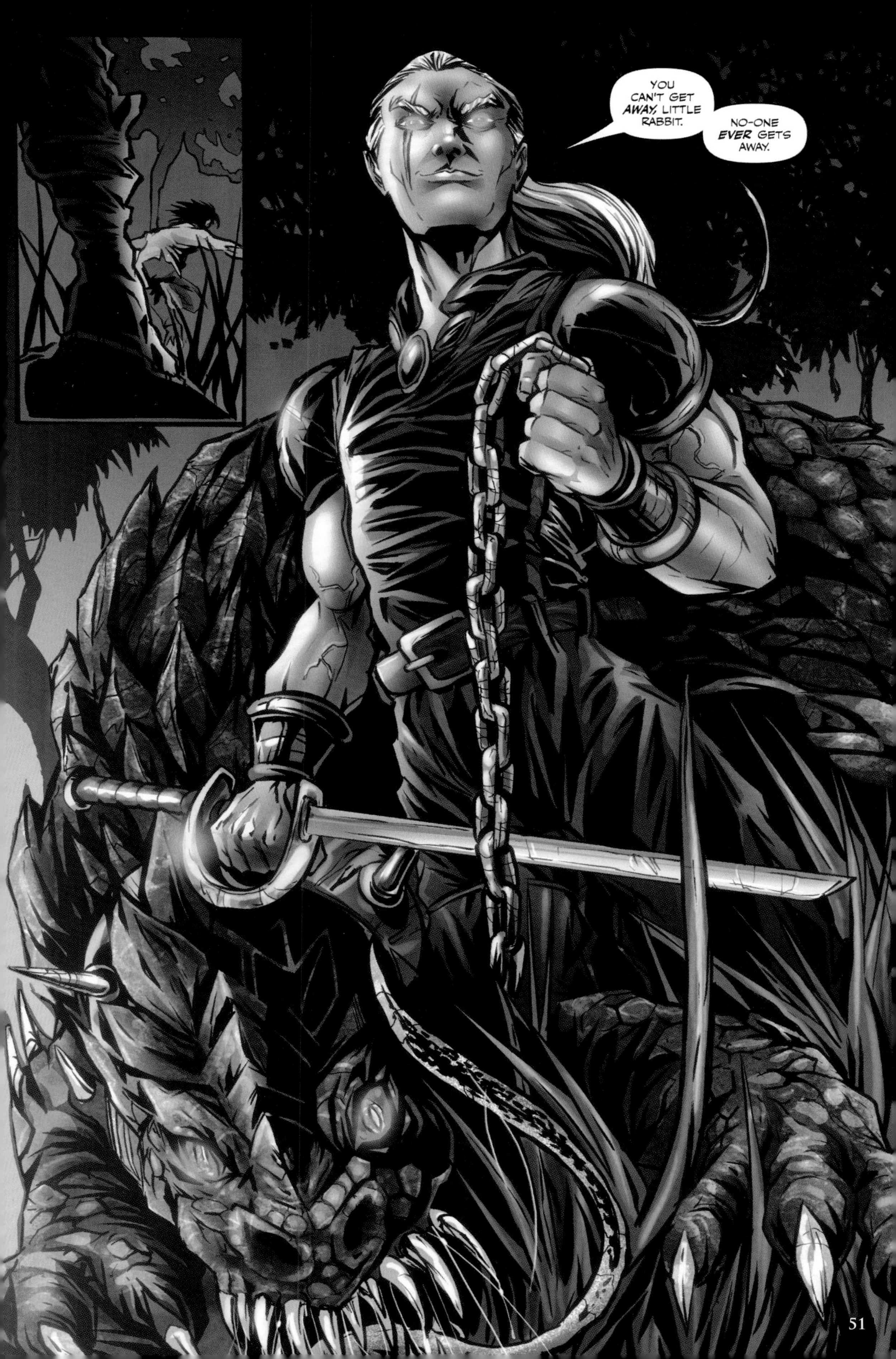
YOU CAN'T GET AWAY, LITTLE RABBIT.
NO-ONE EVER GETS AWAY.

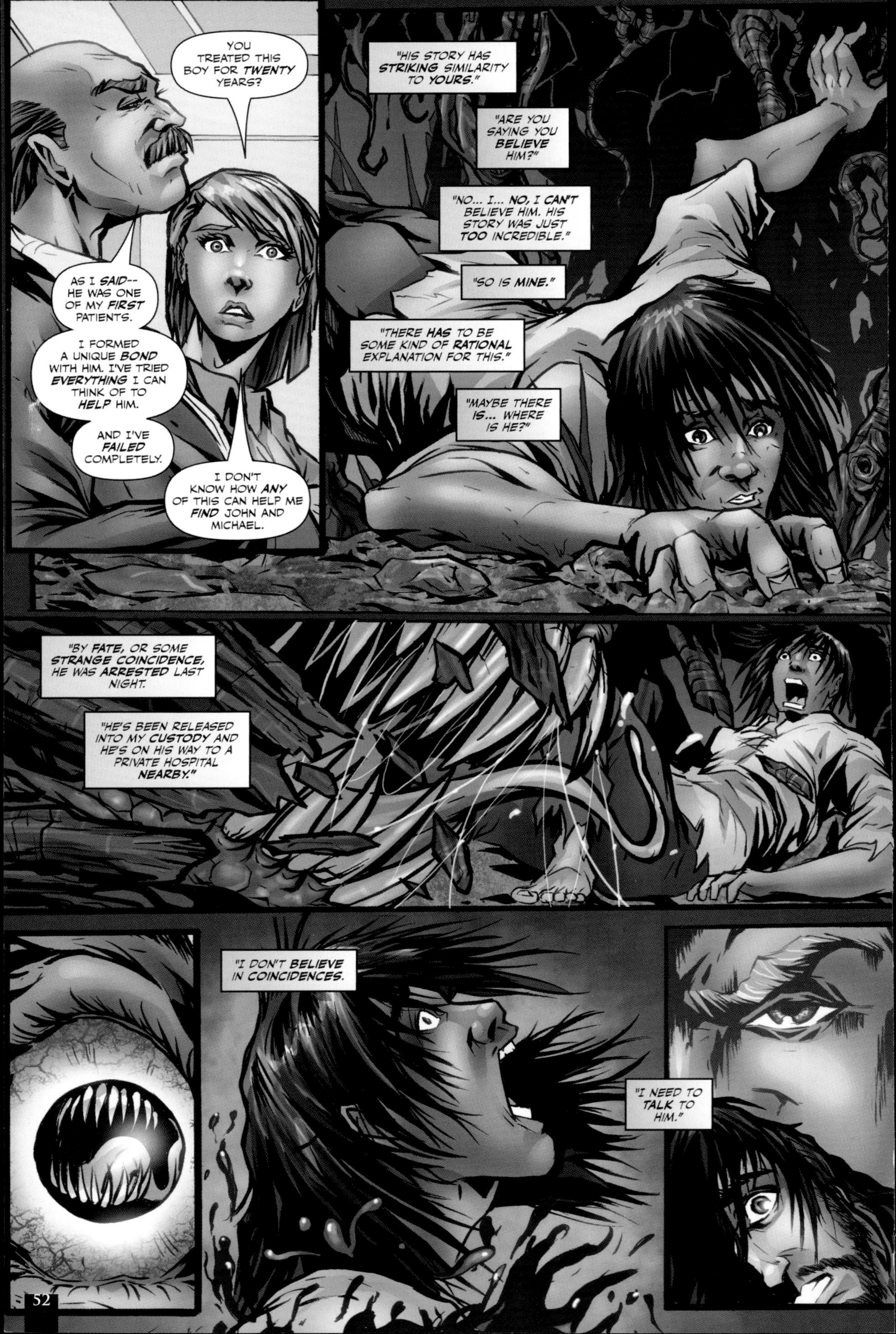

YOU TREATED THIS BOY FOR *TWENTY* YEARS?
AS I *SAID*-- HE WAS ONE OF MY *FIRST* PATIENTS.
I FORMED A UNIQUE *BOND* WITH HIM. I'VE TRIED *EVERYTHING* I CAN THINK OF TO *HELP* HIM.
AND I'VE *FAILED* COMPLETELY.
I DON'T KNOW HOW *ANY* OF THIS CAN HELP ME *FIND* JOHN AND MICHAEL.
"HIS STORY HAS *STRIKING* SIMILARITY TO *YOURS*."
"ARE YOU SAYING YOU *BELIEVE* HIM?"
"NO... I... *NO*, I *CAN'T* BELIEVE HIM. HIS STORY WAS JUST *TOO* INCREDIBLE."
"SO IS *MINE*."
"THERE *HAS* TO BE SOME KIND OF *RATIONAL* EXPLANATION FOR THIS."
"MAYBE THERE *IS*... WHERE IS HE?"
"BY *FATE*, OR SOME *STRANGE COINCIDENCE*, HE WAS *ARRESTED* LAST NIGHT.
"HE'S BEEN RELEASED INTO MY *CUSTODY* AND HE'S ON HIS WAY TO A PRIVATE HOSPITAL *NEARBY*."
"I DON'T *BELIEVE* IN *COINCIDENCES*.
"I NEED TO *TALK* TO HIM."

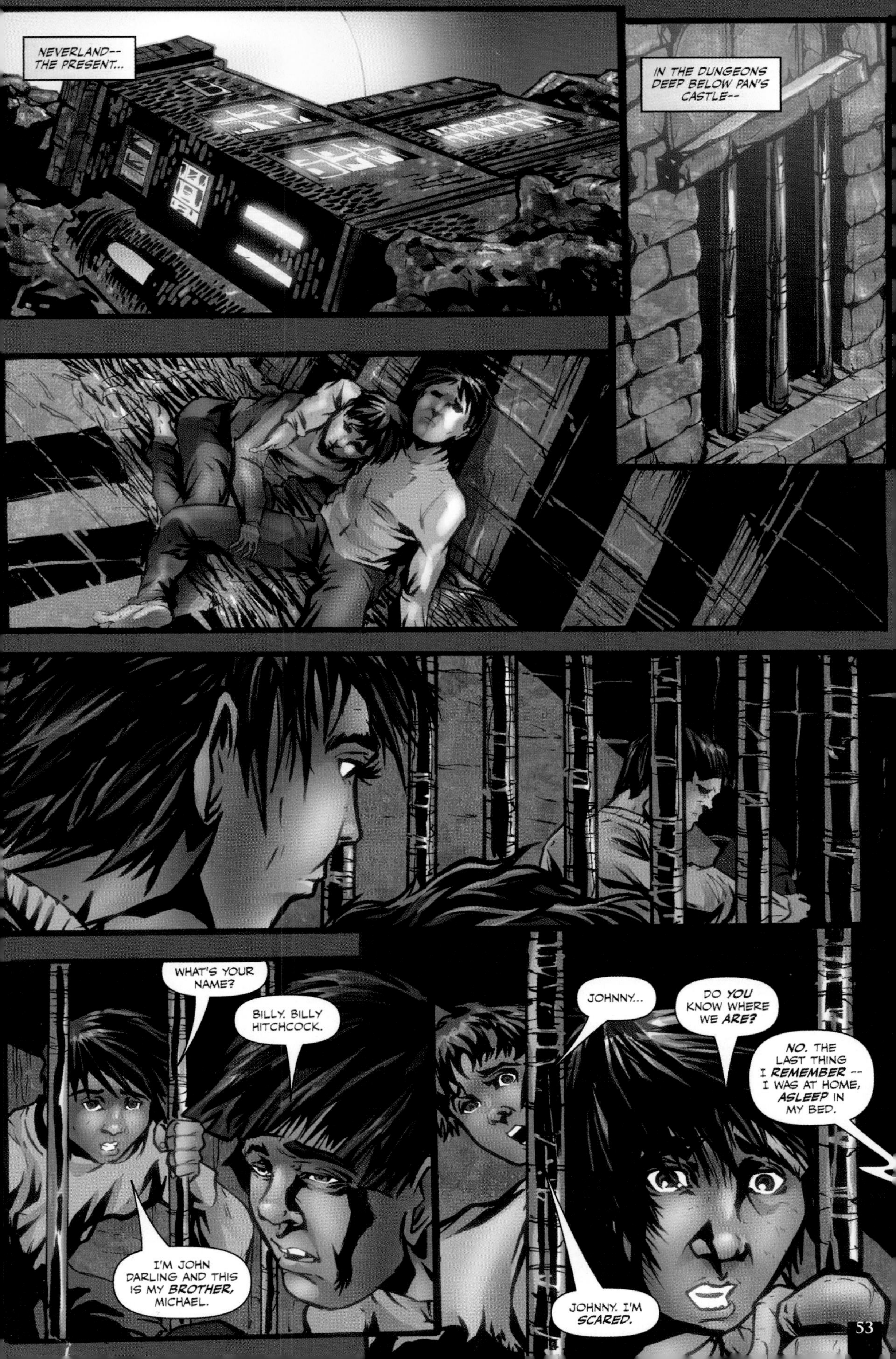
NEVERLAND-- THE PRESENT...
IN THE DUNGEONS DEEP BELOW PAN'S CASTLE--
WHAT'S YOUR NAME?
BILLY. BILLY HITCHCOCK.
I'M JOHN DARLING AND THIS IS MY BROTHER, MICHAEL.
JOHNNY...
DO YOU KNOW WHERE WE ARE?
NO. THE LAST THING I REMEMBER -- I WAS AT HOME, ASLEEP IN MY BED.
JOHNNY. I'M SCARED.

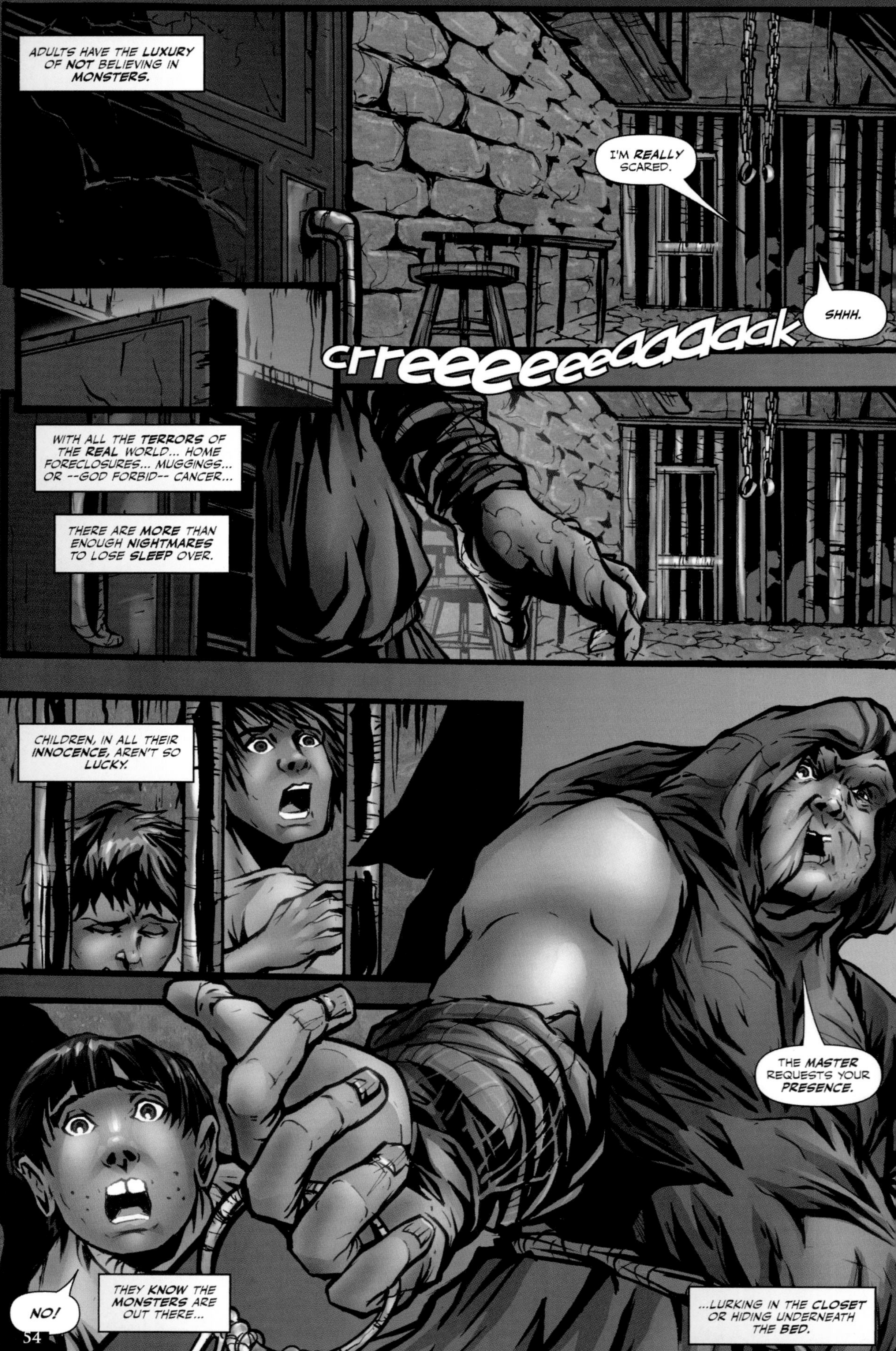
ADULTS HAVE THE LUXURY OF NOT BELIEVING IN MONSTERS.
I'M REALLY SCARED.
SHHH.
CRREEEEEEEAAAAAK
WITH ALL THE TERRORS OF THE REAL WORLD... HOME FORECLOSURES... MUGGINGS... OR --GOD FORBID-- CANCER...
THERE ARE MORE THAN ENOUGH NIGHTMARES TO LOSE SLEEP OVER.
CHILDREN, IN ALL THEIR INNOCENCE, AREN'T SO LUCKY.
THE MASTER REQUESTS YOUR PRESENCE.
NO!
THEY KNOW THE MONSTERS ARE OUT THERE...
...LURKING IN THE CLOSET OR HIDING UNDERNEATH THE BED.

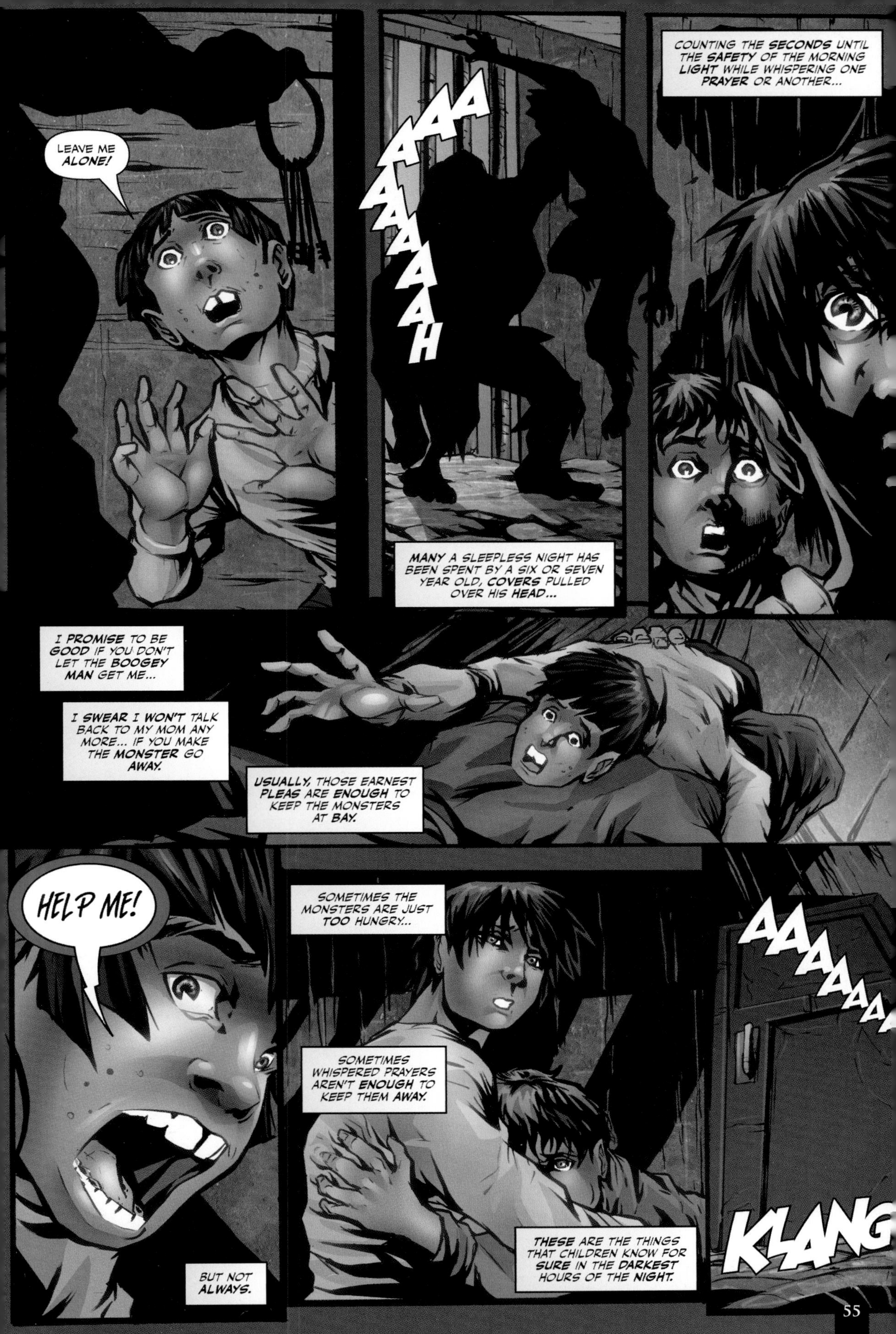
LEAVE ME ALONE!
AAAAAAAAAH
MANY A SLEEPLESS NIGHT HAS BEEN SPENT BY A SIX OR SEVEN YEAR OLD, COVERS PULLED OVER HIS HEAD...
COUNTING THE SECONDS UNTIL THE SAFETY OF THE MORNING LIGHT WHILE WHISPERING ONE PRAYER OR ANOTHER...
I PROMISE TO BE GOOD IF YOU DON'T LET THE BOOGEY MAN GET ME...
I SWEAR I WON'T TALK BACK TO MY MOM ANY MORE... IF YOU MAKE THE MONSTER GO AWAY.
USUALLY, THOSE EARNEST PLEAS ARE ENOUGH TO KEEP THE MONSTERS AT BAY.
HELP ME!
BUT NOT ALWAYS.
SOMETIMES THE MONSTERS ARE JUST TOO HUNGRY...
SOMETIMES WHISPERED PRAYERS AREN'T ENOUGH TO KEEP THEM AWAY.
THESE ARE THE THINGS THAT CHILDREN KNOW FOR SURE IN THE DARKEST HOURS OF THE NIGHT.
AAAAAAA
KLANG

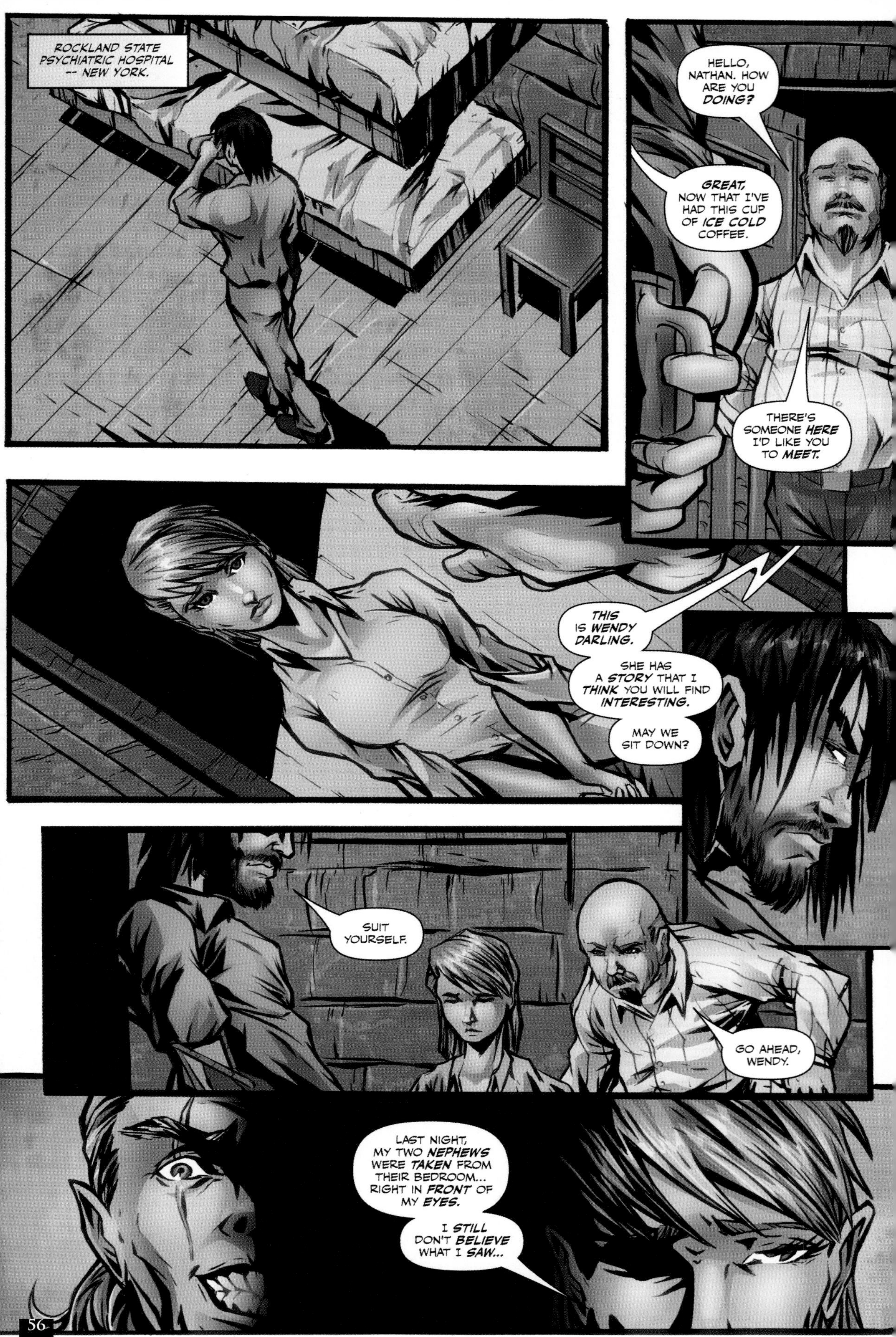
ROCKLAND STATE PSYCHIATRIC HOSPITAL -- NEW YORK.
HELLO, NATHAN. HOW ARE YOU DOING?
GREAT, NOW THAT I'VE HAD THIS CUP OF ICE COLD COFFEE.
THERE'S SOMEONE HERE I'D LIKE YOU TO MEET.
THIS IS WENDY DARLING.
SHE HAS A STORY THAT I THINK YOU WILL FIND INTERESTING.
MAY WE SIT DOWN?
SUIT YOURSELF.
GO AHEAD, WENDY.
LAST NIGHT, MY TWO NEPHEWS WERE TAKEN FROM THEIR BEDROOM... RIGHT IN FRONT OF MY EYES.
I STILL DON'T BELIEVE WHAT I SAW...

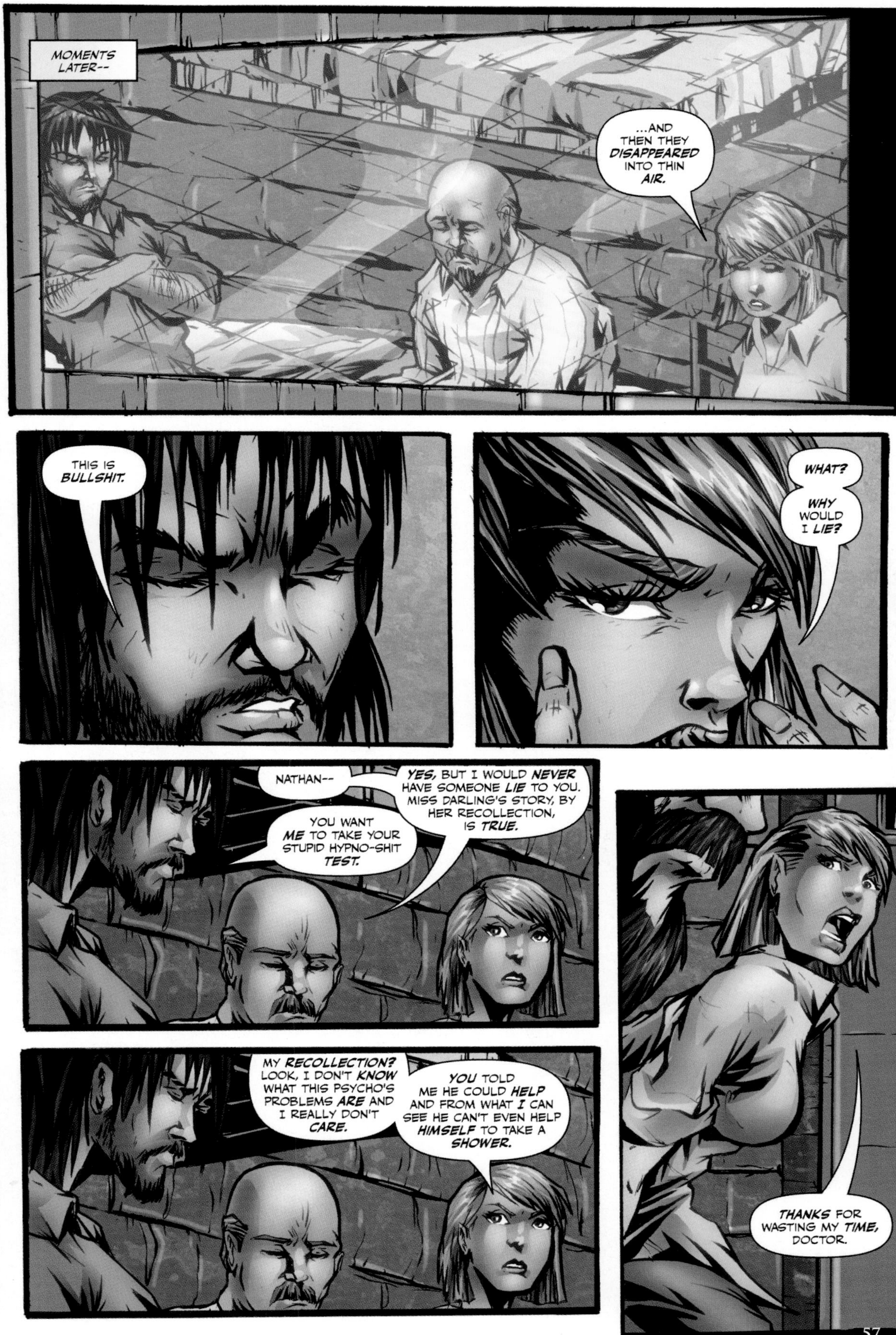
MOMENTS LATER--
...AND THEN THEY DISAPPEARED INTO THIN AIR.
THIS IS BULLSHIT.
WHAT?
WHY WOULD I LIE?
NATHAN--
YOU WANT ME TO TAKE YOUR STUPID HYPNO-SHIT TEST.
YES, BUT I WOULD NEVER HAVE SOMEONE LIE TO YOU. MISS DARLING'S STORY, BY HER RECOLLECTION, IS TRUE.
MY RECOLLECTION? LOOK, I DON'T KNOW WHAT THIS PSYCHO'S PROBLEMS ARE AND I REALLY DON'T CARE.
YOU TOLD ME HE COULD HELP AND FROM WHAT I CAN SEE HE CAN'T EVEN HELP HIMSELF TO TAKE A SHOWER.
THANKS FOR WASTING MY TIME, DOCTOR.

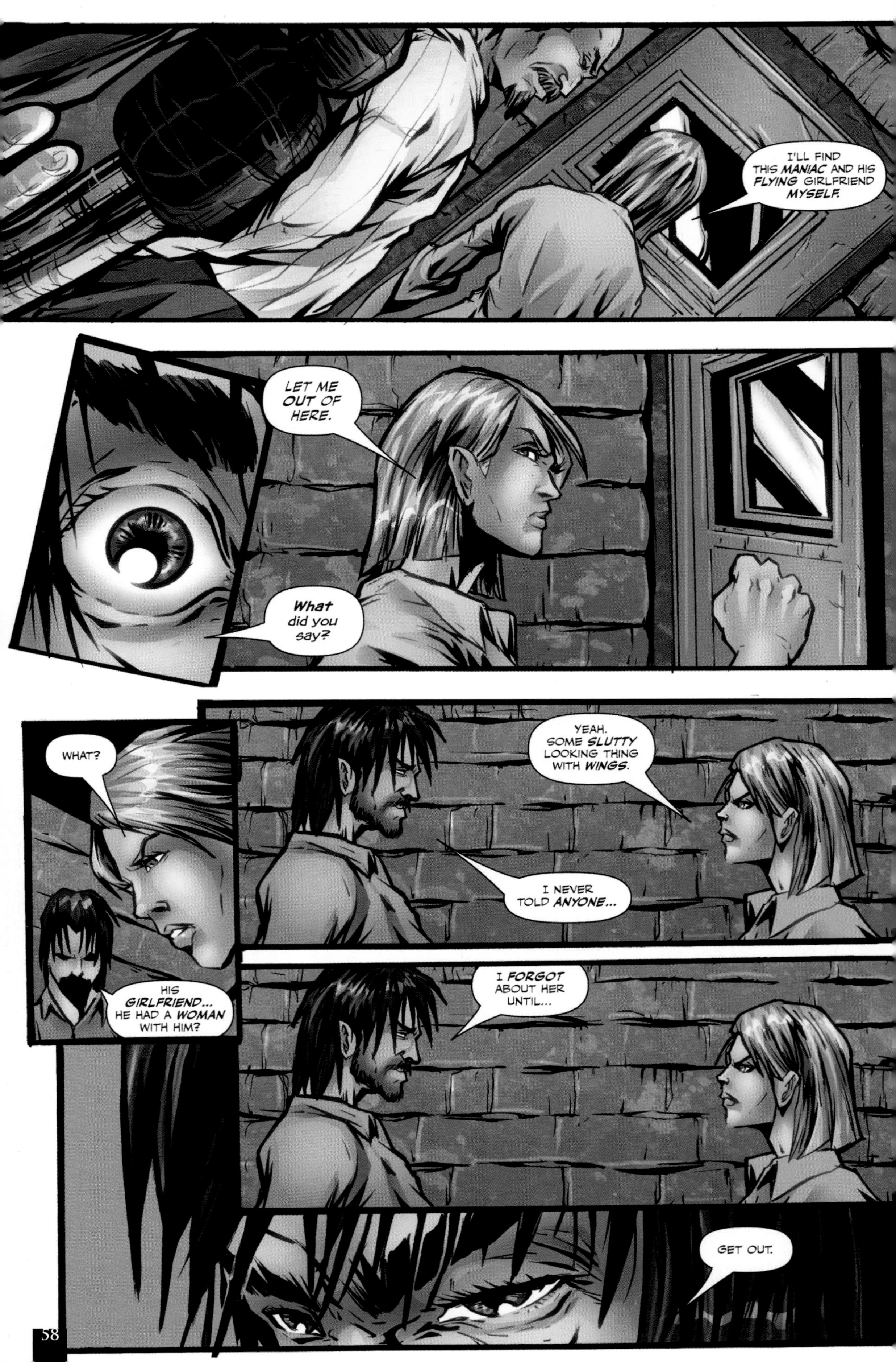
I'LL FIND THIS MANIAC AND HIS FLYING GIRLFRIEND MYSELF.
LET ME OUT OF HERE.
What did you say?
WHAT?
YEAH. SOME SLUTTY LOOKING THING WITH WINGS.
I NEVER TOLD ANYONE...
HIS GIRLFRIEND... HE HAD A WOMAN WITH HIM?
I FORGOT ABOUT HER UNTIL...
GET OUT.

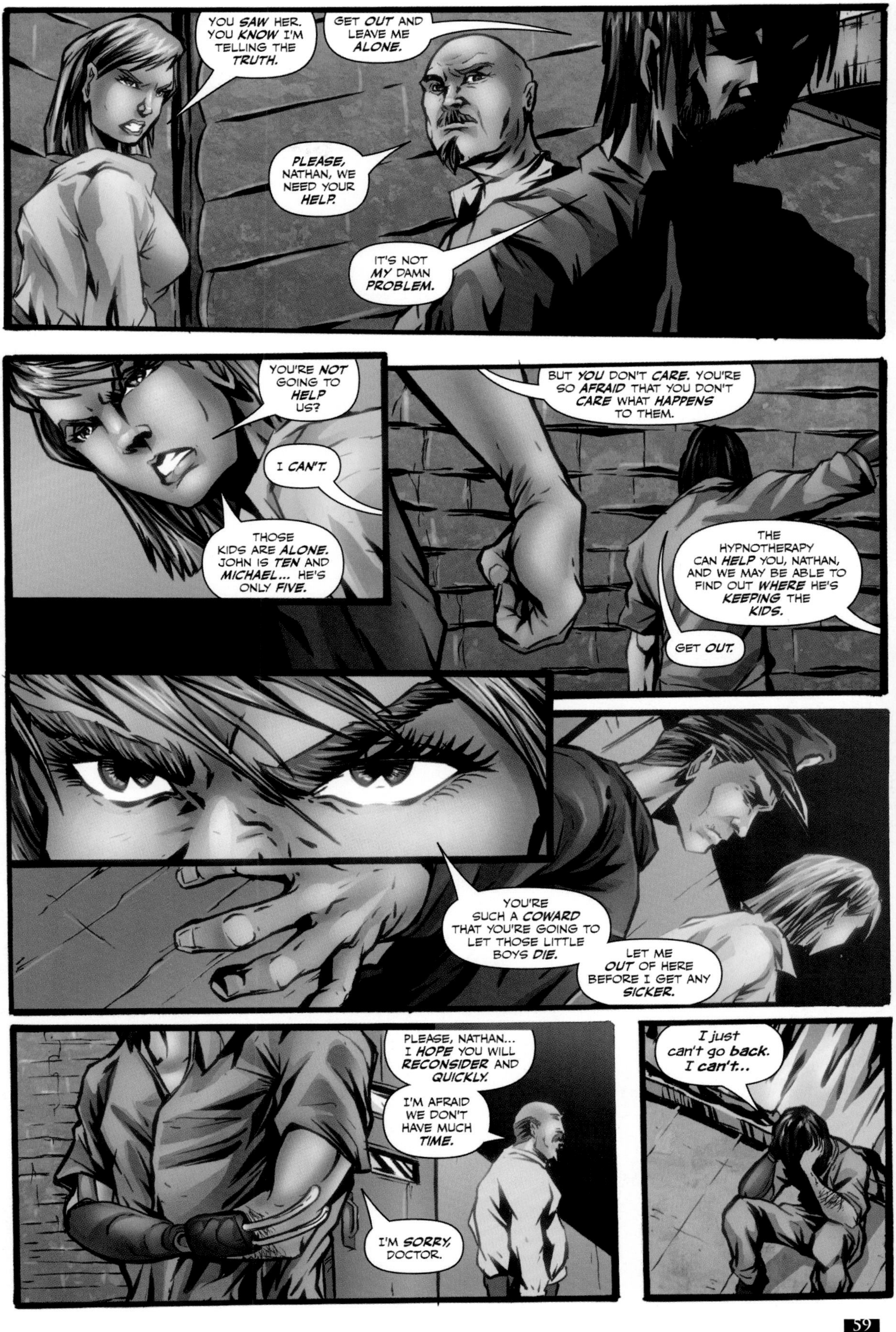

YOU SAW HER. YOU KNOW I'M TELLING THE TRUTH.
GET OUT AND LEAVE ME ALONE.
PLEASE, NATHAN, WE NEED YOUR HELP.
IT'S NOT MY DAMN PROBLEM.
YOU'RE NOT GOING TO HELP US?
I CAN'T.
THOSE KIDS ARE ALONE. JOHN IS TEN AND MICHAEL... HE'S ONLY FIVE.
BUT YOU DON'T CARE. YOU'RE SO AFRAID THAT YOU DON'T CARE WHAT HAPPENS TO THEM.
THE HYPNOTHERAPY CAN HELP YOU, NATHAN, AND WE MAY BE ABLE TO FIND OUT WHERE HE'S KEEPING THE KIDS.
GET OUT.
YOU'RE SUCH A COWARD THAT YOU'RE GOING TO LET THOSE LITTLE BOYS DIE.
LET ME OUT OF HERE BEFORE I GET ANY SICKER.
PLEASE, NATHAN... I HOPE YOU WILL RECONSIDER AND QUICKLY.
I'M AFRAID WE DON'T HAVE MUCH TIME.
I'M SORRY, DOCTOR.
I just can't go back. I can't...

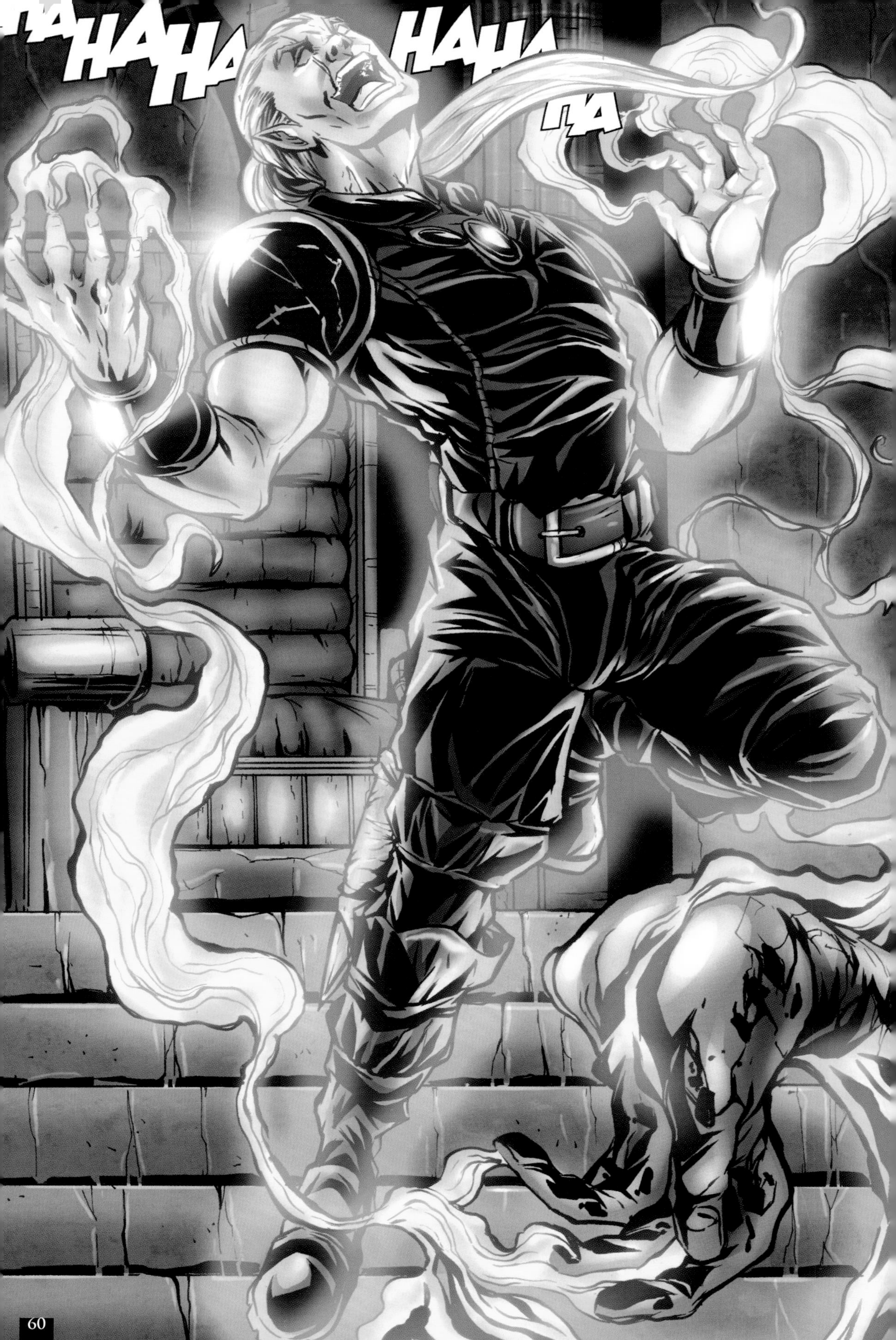
HA HA HA
HAHA
HA

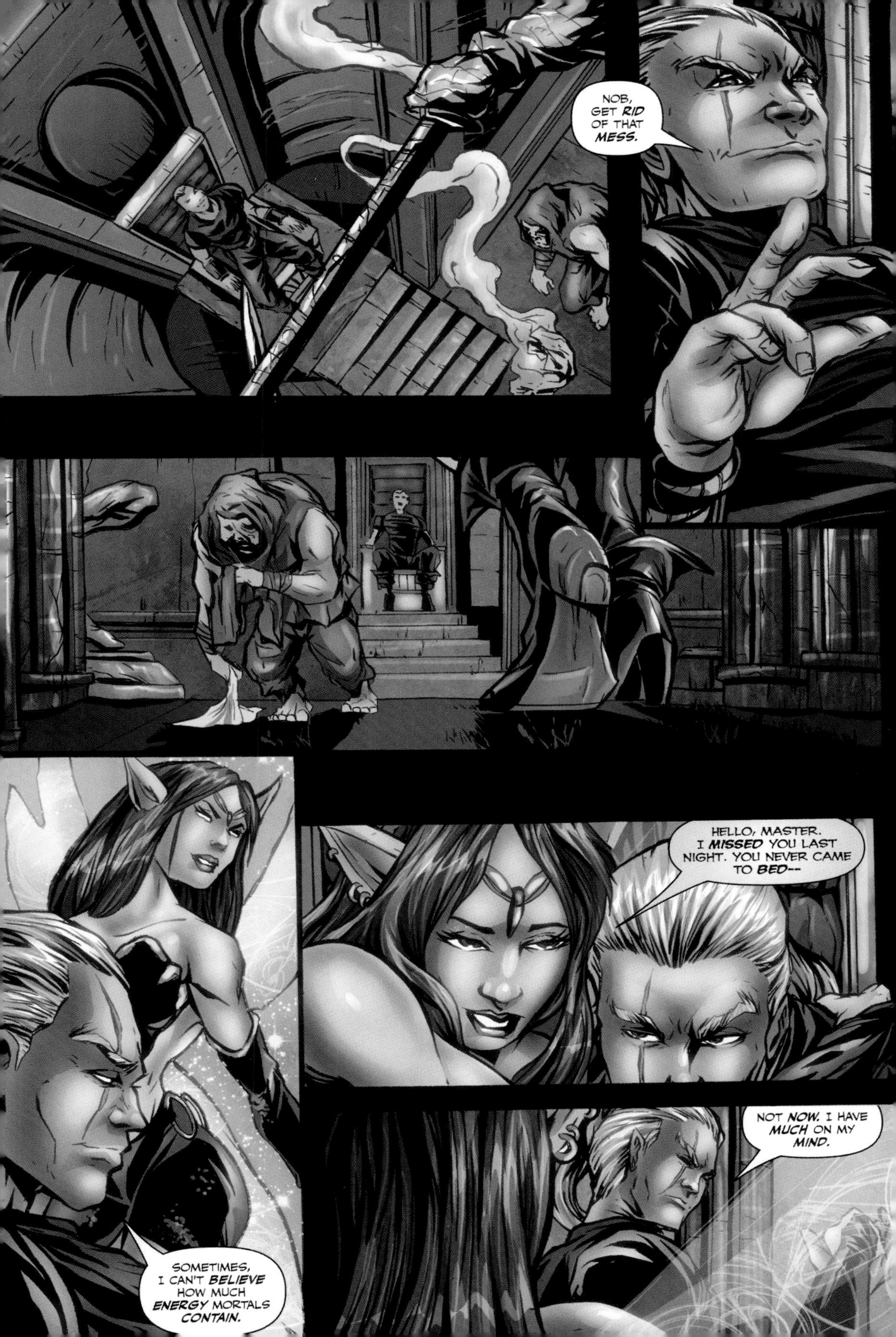
NOB, GET RID OF THAT MESS.
HELLO, MASTER. I MISSED YOU LAST NIGHT. YOU NEVER CAME TO BED--
NOT NOW. I HAVE MUCH ON MY MIND.
SOMETIMES, I CAN'T BELIEVE HOW MUCH ENERGY MORTALS CONTAIN.

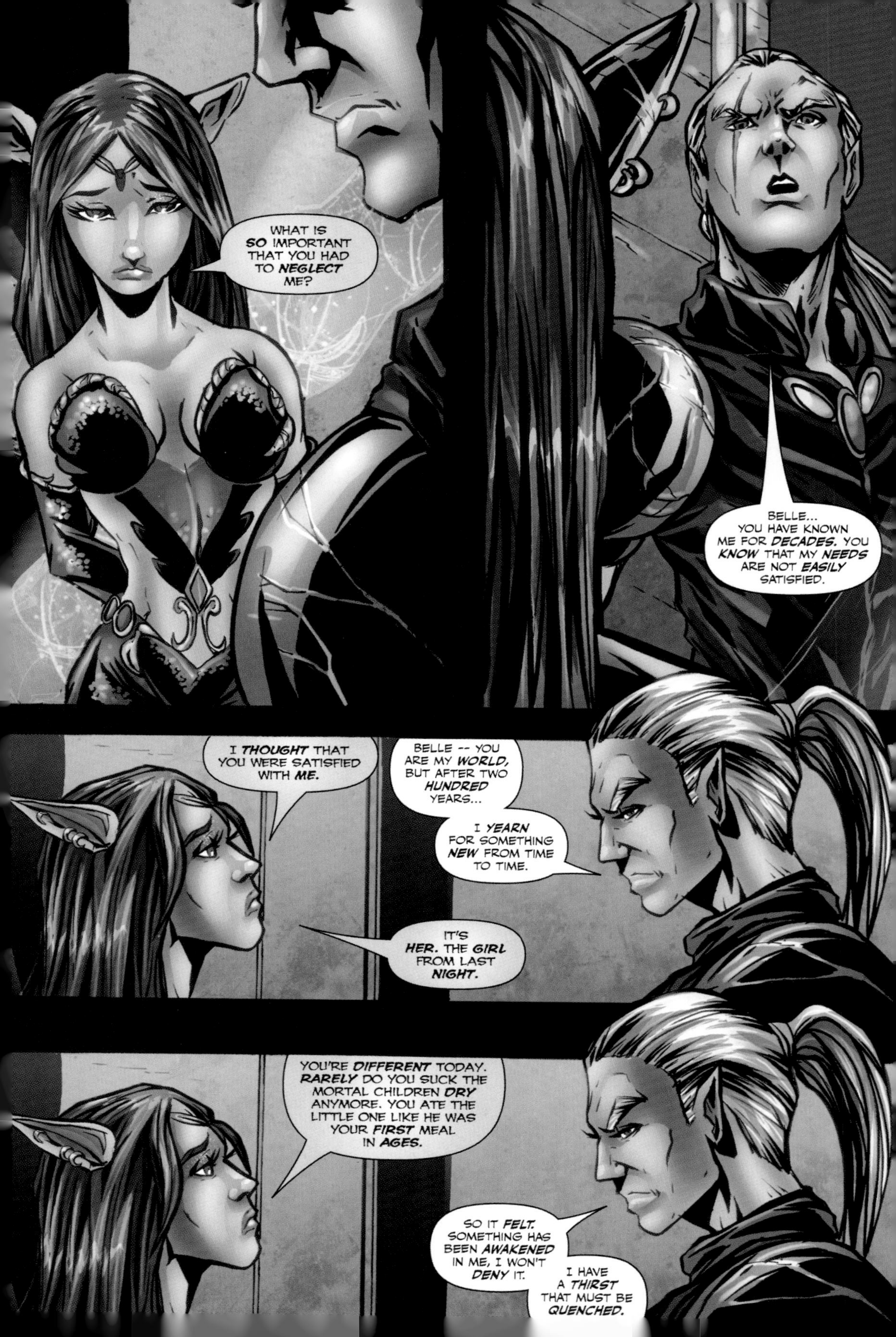
WHAT IS SO IMPORTANT THAT YOU HAD TO NEGLECT ME?
BELLE... YOU HAVE KNOWN ME FOR DECADES. YOU KNOW THAT MY NEEDS ARE NOT EASILY SATISFIED.
I THOUGHT THAT YOU WERE SATISFIED WITH ME.
BELLE -- YOU ARE MY WORLD, BUT AFTER TWO HUNDRED YEARS...
I YEARN FOR SOMETHING NEW FROM TIME TO TIME.
IT'S HER. THE GIRL FROM LAST NIGHT.
YOU'RE DIFFERENT TODAY. RARELY DO YOU SUCK THE MORTAL CHILDREN DRY ANYMORE. YOU ATE THE LITTLE ONE LIKE HE WAS YOUR FIRST MEAL IN AGES.
SO IT FELT. SOMETHING HAS BEEN AWAKENED IN ME, I WON'T DENY IT.
I HAVE A THIRST THAT MUST BE QUENCHED.

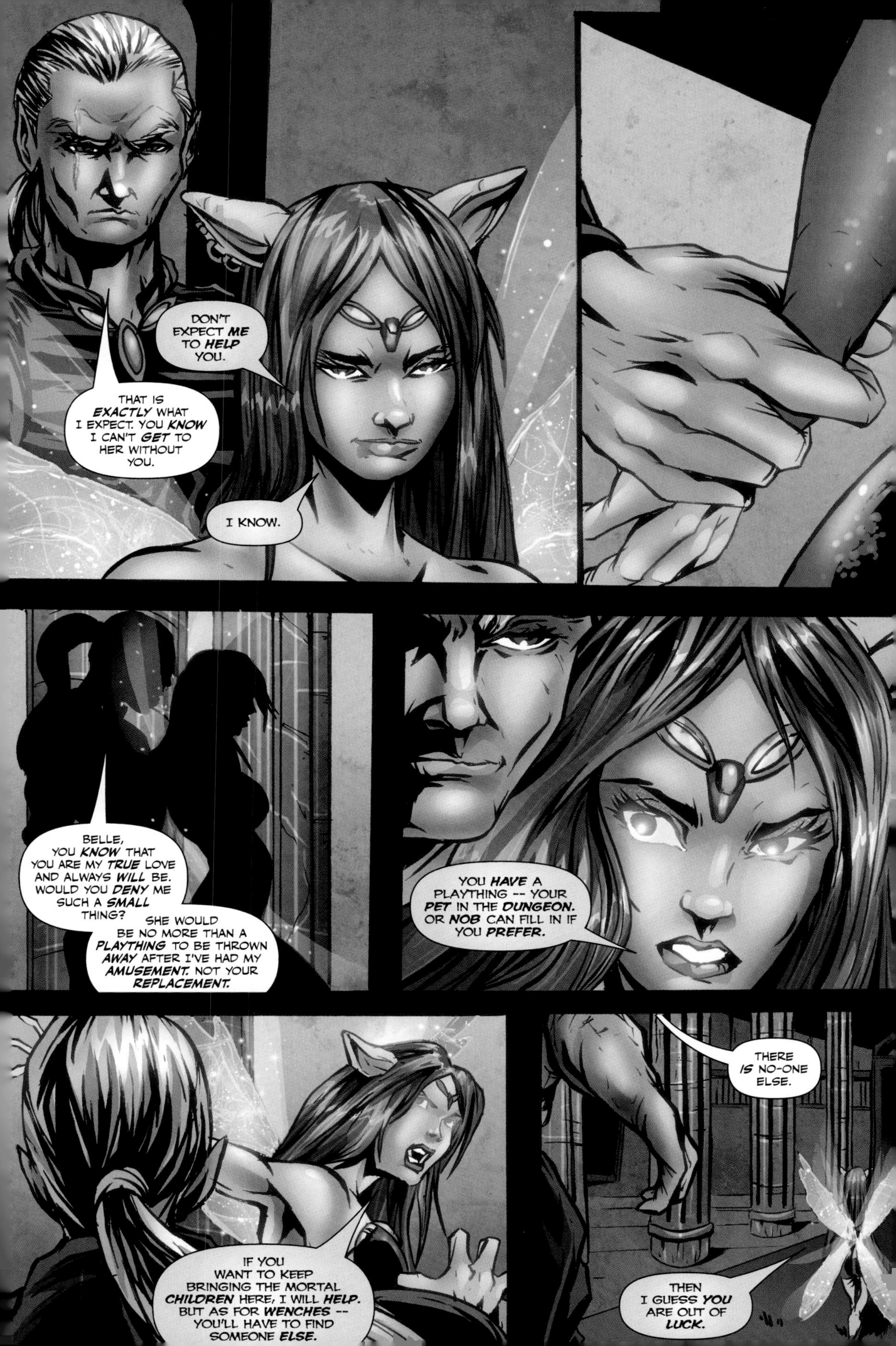
DON'T EXPECT ME TO HELP YOU.
THAT IS EXACTLY WHAT I EXPECT. YOU KNOW I CAN'T GET TO HER WITHOUT YOU.
I KNOW.
BELLE, YOU KNOW THAT YOU ARE MY TRUE LOVE AND ALWAYS WILL BE. WOULD YOU DENY ME SUCH A SMALL THING?
SHE WOULD BE NO MORE THAN A PLAYTHING TO BE THROWN AWAY AFTER I'VE HAD MY AMUSEMENT. NOT YOUR REPLACEMENT.
YOU HAVE A PLAYTHING -- YOUR PET IN THE DUNGEON. OR NOB CAN FILL IN IF YOU PREFER.
IF YOU WANT TO KEEP BRINGING THE MORTAL CHILDREN HERE, I WILL HELP. BUT AS FOR WENCHES -- YOU'LL HAVE TO FIND SOMEONE ELSE.
THERE IS NO-ONE ELSE.
THEN I GUESS YOU ARE OUT OF LUCK.

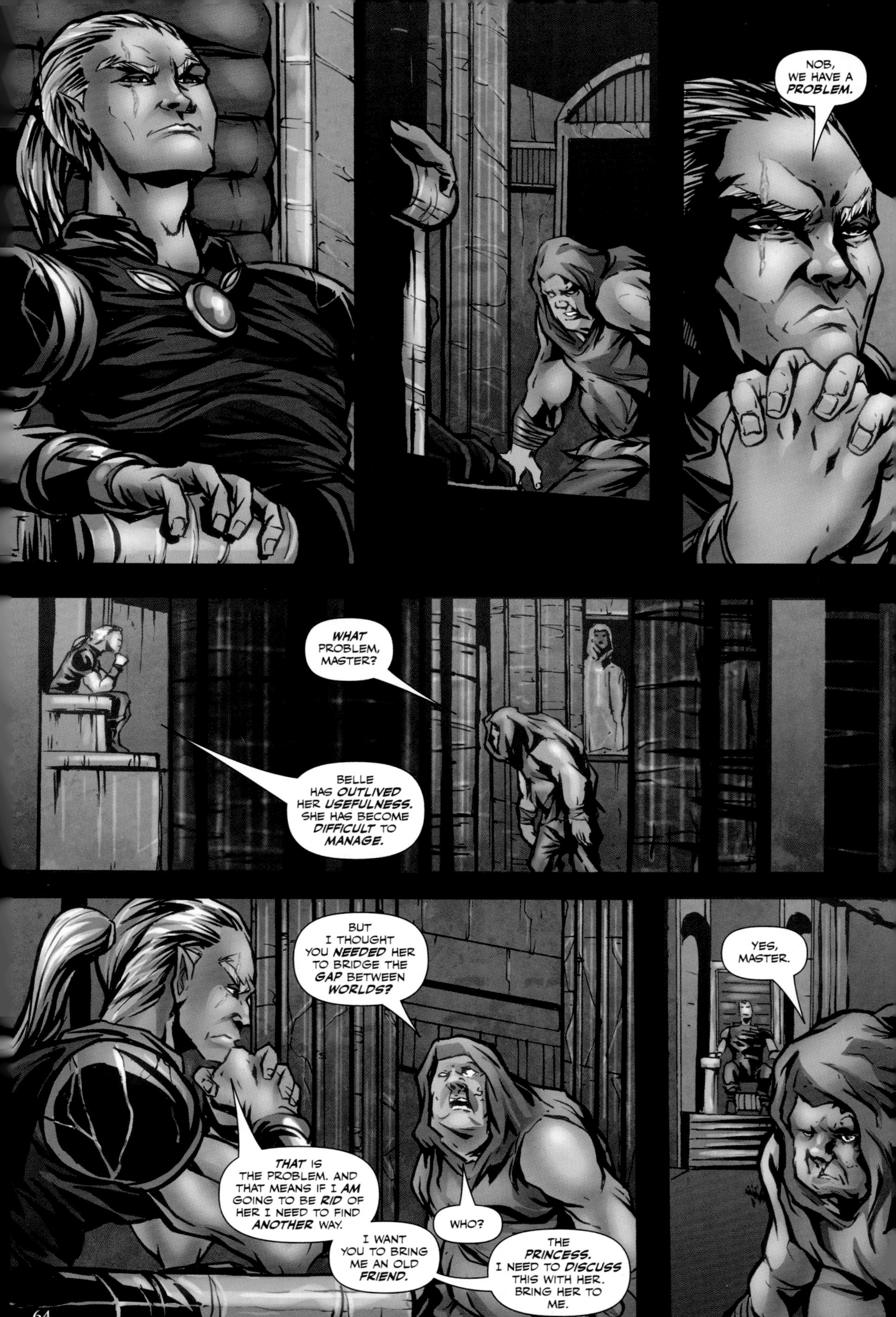
NOB, WE HAVE A PROBLEM.
WHAT PROBLEM, MASTER?
BELLE HAS OUTLIVED HER USEFULNESS. SHE HAS BECOME DIFFICULT TO MANAGE.
BUT I THOUGHT YOU NEEDED HER TO BRIDGE THE GAP BETWEEN WORLDS?
THAT IS THE PROBLEM. AND THAT MEANS IF I AM GOING TO BE RID OF HER I NEED TO FIND ANOTHER WAY.
I WANT YOU TO BRING ME AN OLD FRIEND.
WHO?
THE PRINCESS. I NEED TO DISCUSS THIS WITH HER. BRING HER TO ME.
YES, MASTER.

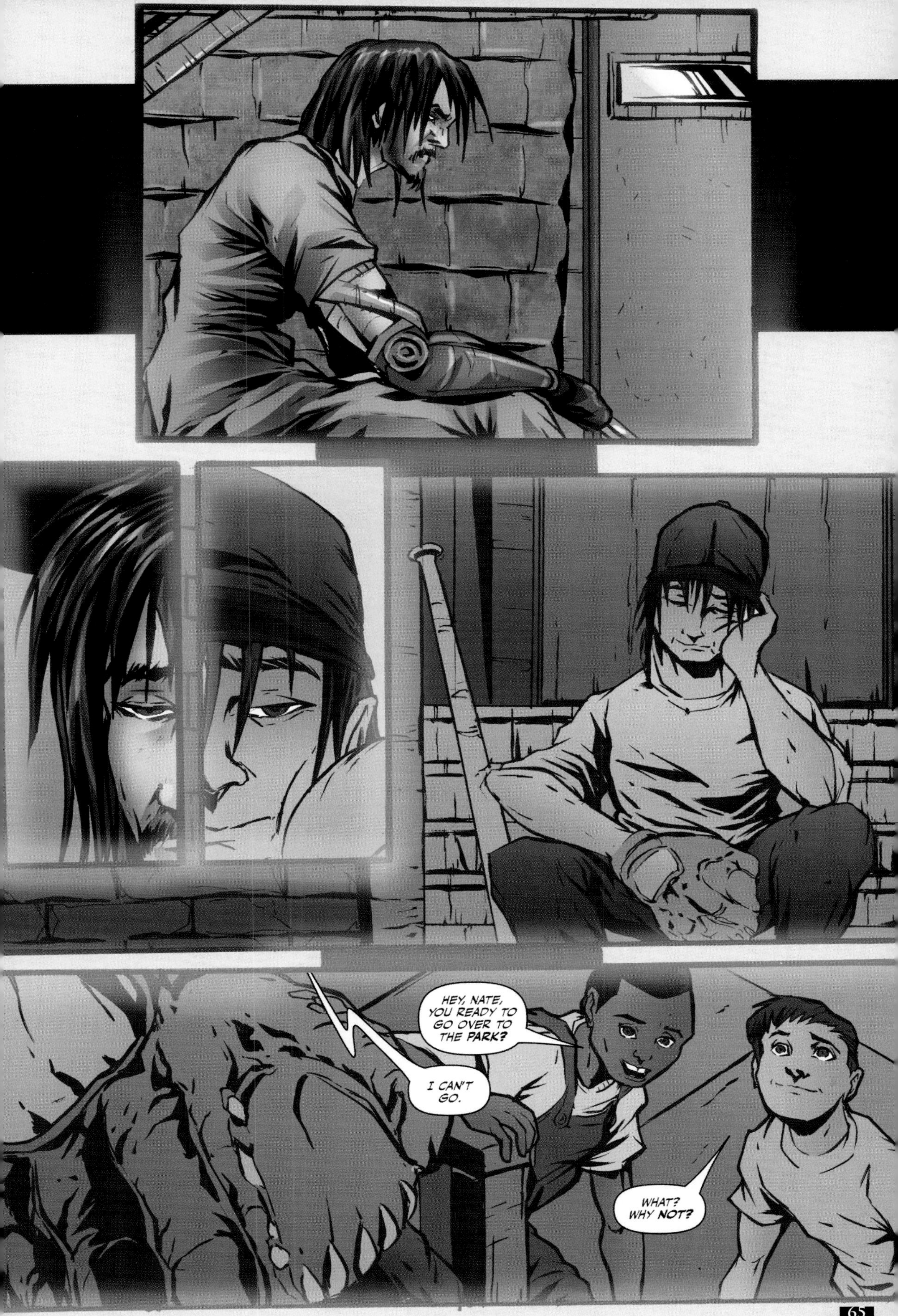

HEY, NATE, YOU READY TO GO OVER TO THE PARK?
I CAN'T GO.
WHAT? WHY NOT?

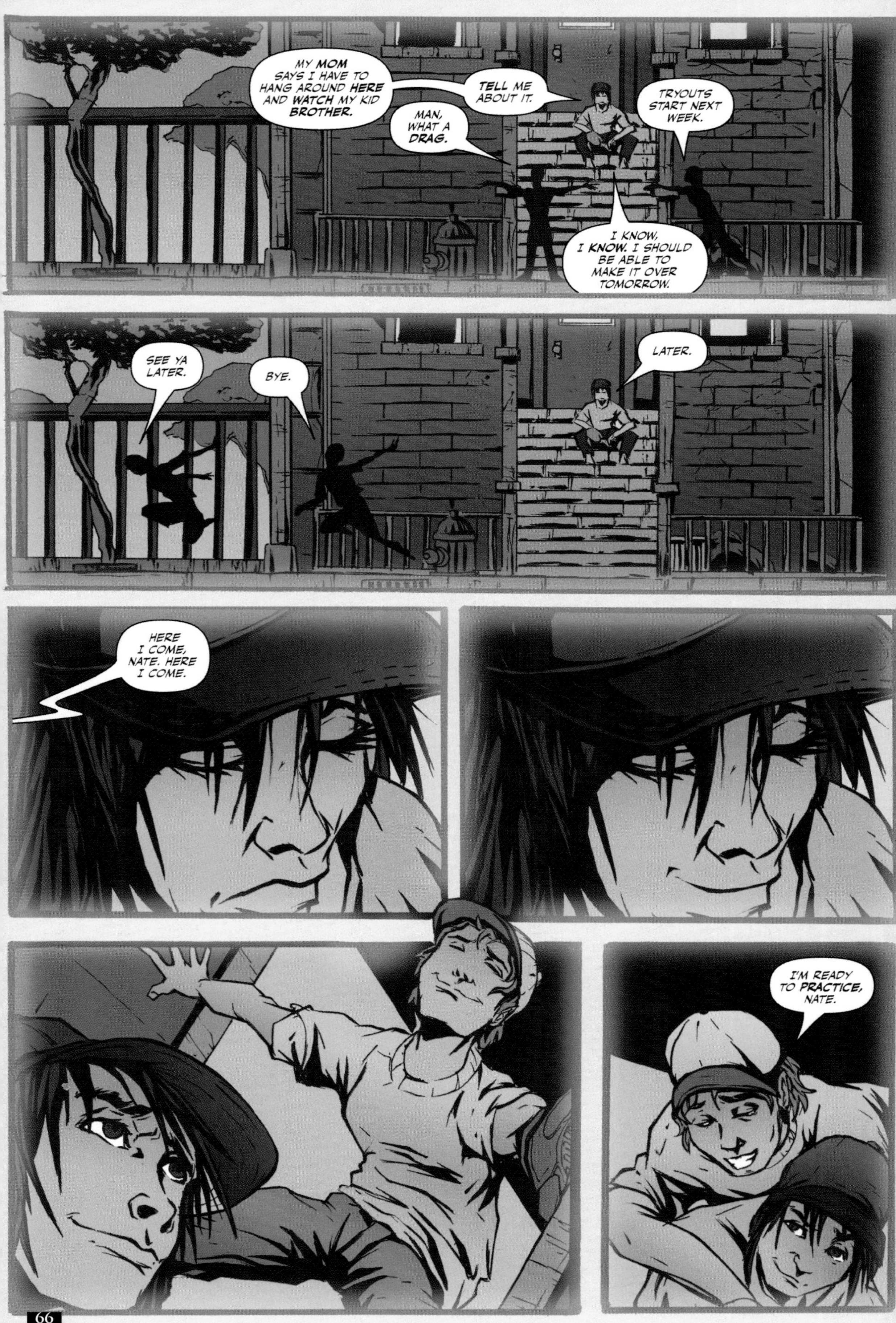
MY MOM SAYS I HAVE TO HANG AROUND HERE AND WATCH MY KID BROTHER.
TELL ME ABOUT IT.
MAN, WHAT A DRAG.
TRYOUTS START NEXT WEEK.
I KNOW, I KNOW. I SHOULD BE ABLE TO MAKE IT OVER TOMORROW.
SEE YA LATER.
BYE.
LATER.
HERE I COME, NATE. HERE I COME.
I'M READY TO PRACTICE, NATE.

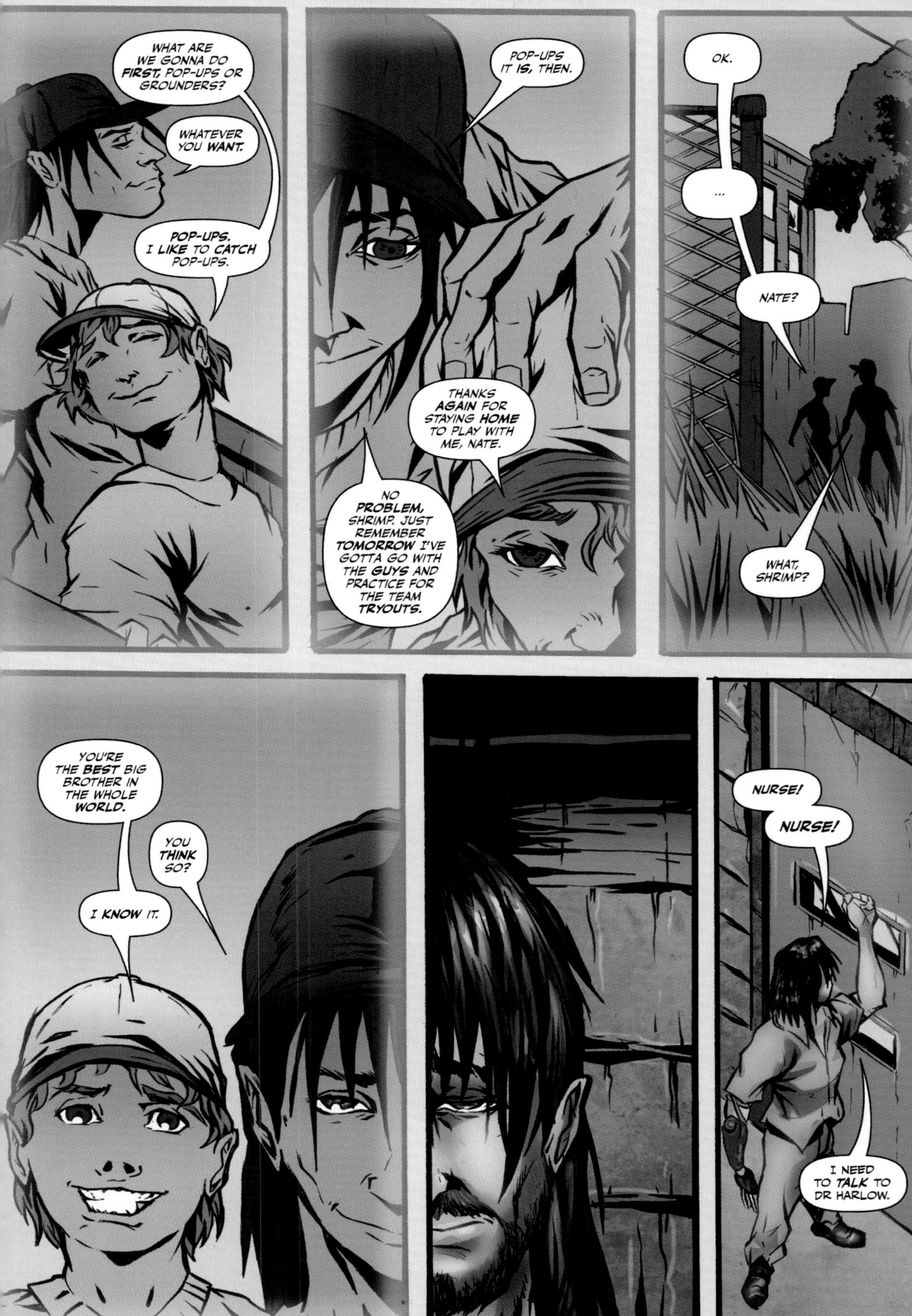
WHAT ARE WE GONNA DO FIRST, POP-UPS OR GROUNDERS?
WHATEVER YOU WANT.
POP-UPS. I LIKE TO CATCH POP-UPS.
POP-UPS IT IS, THEN.
THANKS AGAIN FOR STAYING HOME TO PLAY WITH ME, NATE.
NO PROBLEM, SHRIMP. JUST REMEMBER TOMORROW I'VE GOTTA GO WITH THE GUYS AND PRACTICE FOR THE TEAM TRYOUTS.
OK.
...
NATE?
WHAT, SHRIMP?
YOU'RE THE BEST BIG BROTHER IN THE WHOLE WORLD.
YOU THINK SO?
I KNOW IT.
NURSE!
NURSE!
I NEED TO TALK TO DR HARLOW.

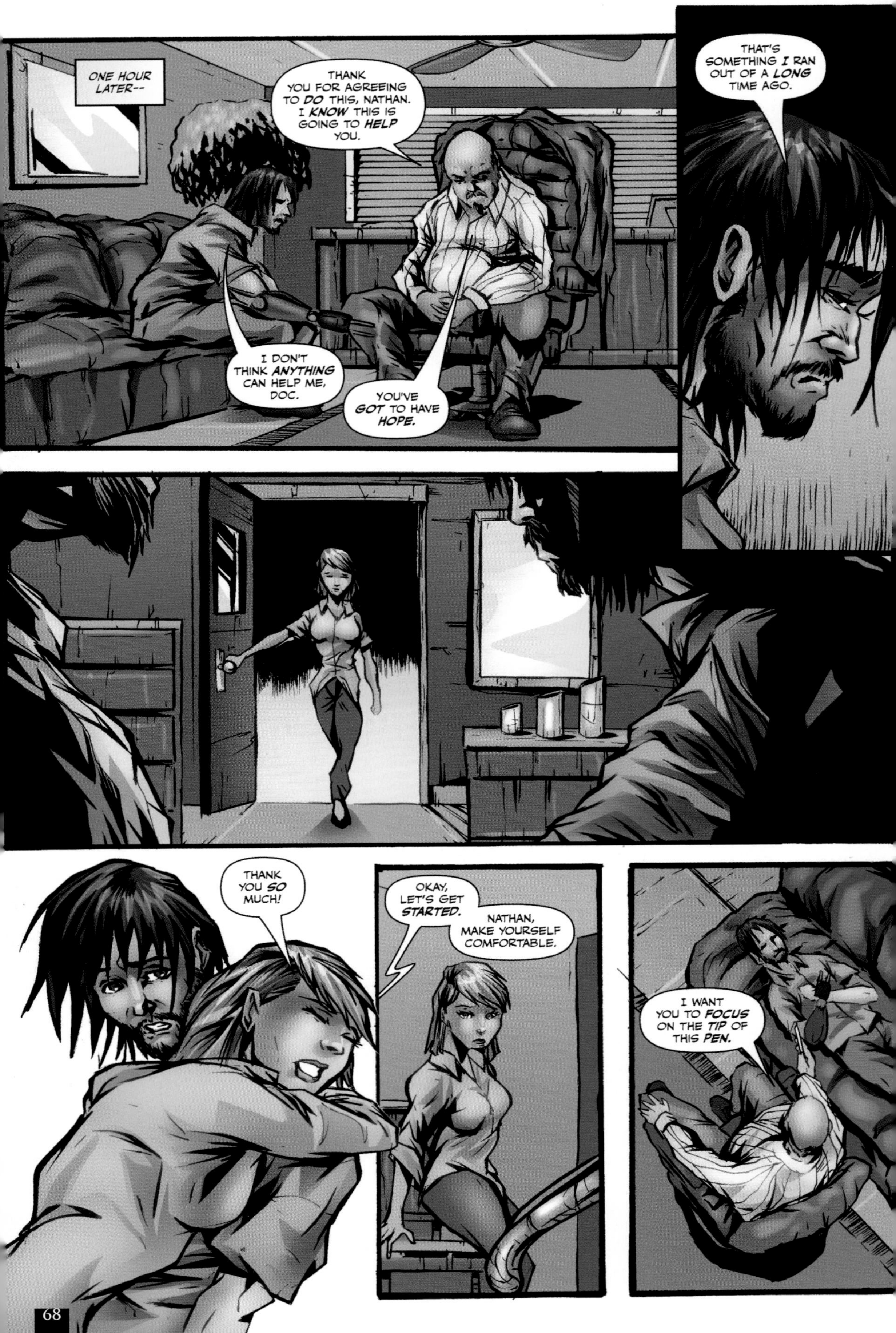
ONE HOUR LATER--
THANK YOU FOR AGREEING TO DO THIS, NATHAN. I KNOW THIS IS GOING TO HELP YOU.
I DON'T THINK ANYTHING CAN HELP ME, DOC.
YOU'VE GOT TO HAVE HOPE.
THAT'S SOMETHING I RAN OUT OF A LONG TIME AGO.
THANK YOU SO MUCH!
OKAY, LET'S GET STARTED.
NATHAN, MAKE YOURSELF COMFORTABLE.
I WANT YOU TO FOCUS ON THE TIP OF THIS PEN.

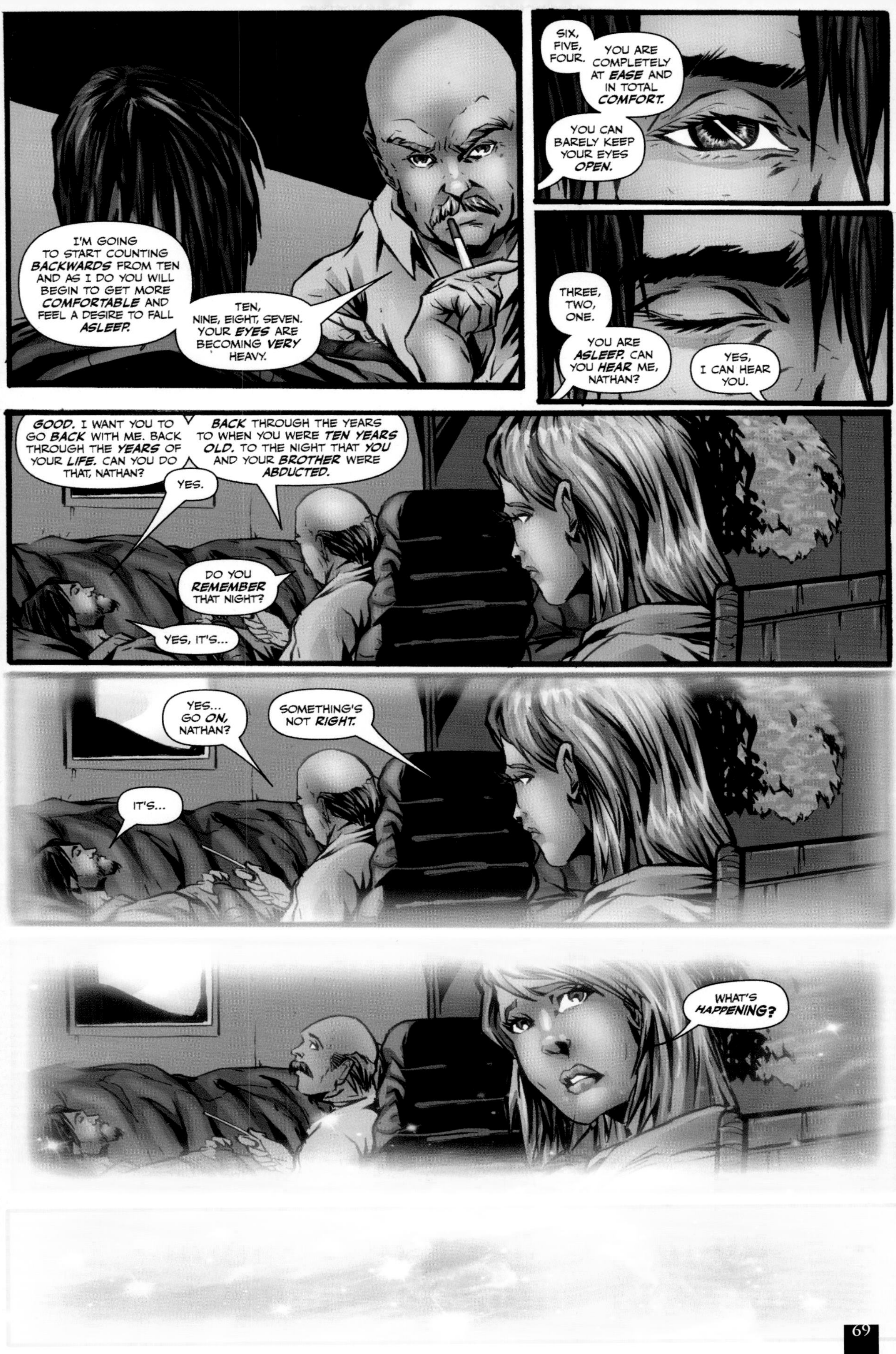
I'M GOING TO START COUNTING BACKWARDS FROM TEN AND AS I DO YOU WILL BEGIN TO GET MORE COMFORTABLE AND FEEL A DESIRE TO FALL ASLEEP.
TEN, NINE, EIGHT, SEVEN. YOUR EYES ARE BECOMING VERY HEAVY.
SIX, FIVE, FOUR.
YOU ARE COMPLETELY AT EASE AND IN TOTAL COMFORT.
YOU CAN BARELY KEEP YOUR EYES OPEN.
THREE, TWO, ONE.
YOU ARE ASLEEP. CAN YOU HEAR ME, NATHAN?
YES, I CAN HEAR YOU.
GOOD. I WANT YOU TO GO BACK WITH ME. BACK THROUGH THE YEARS OF YOUR LIFE. CAN YOU DO THAT, NATHAN?
YES.
BACK THROUGH THE YEARS TO WHEN YOU WERE TEN YEARS OLD. TO THE NIGHT THAT YOU AND YOUR BROTHER WERE ABDUCTED.
DO YOU REMEMBER THAT NIGHT?
YES, IT'S...
YES... GO ON, NATHAN?
SOMETHING'S NOT RIGHT.
IT'S...
WHAT'S HAPPENING?

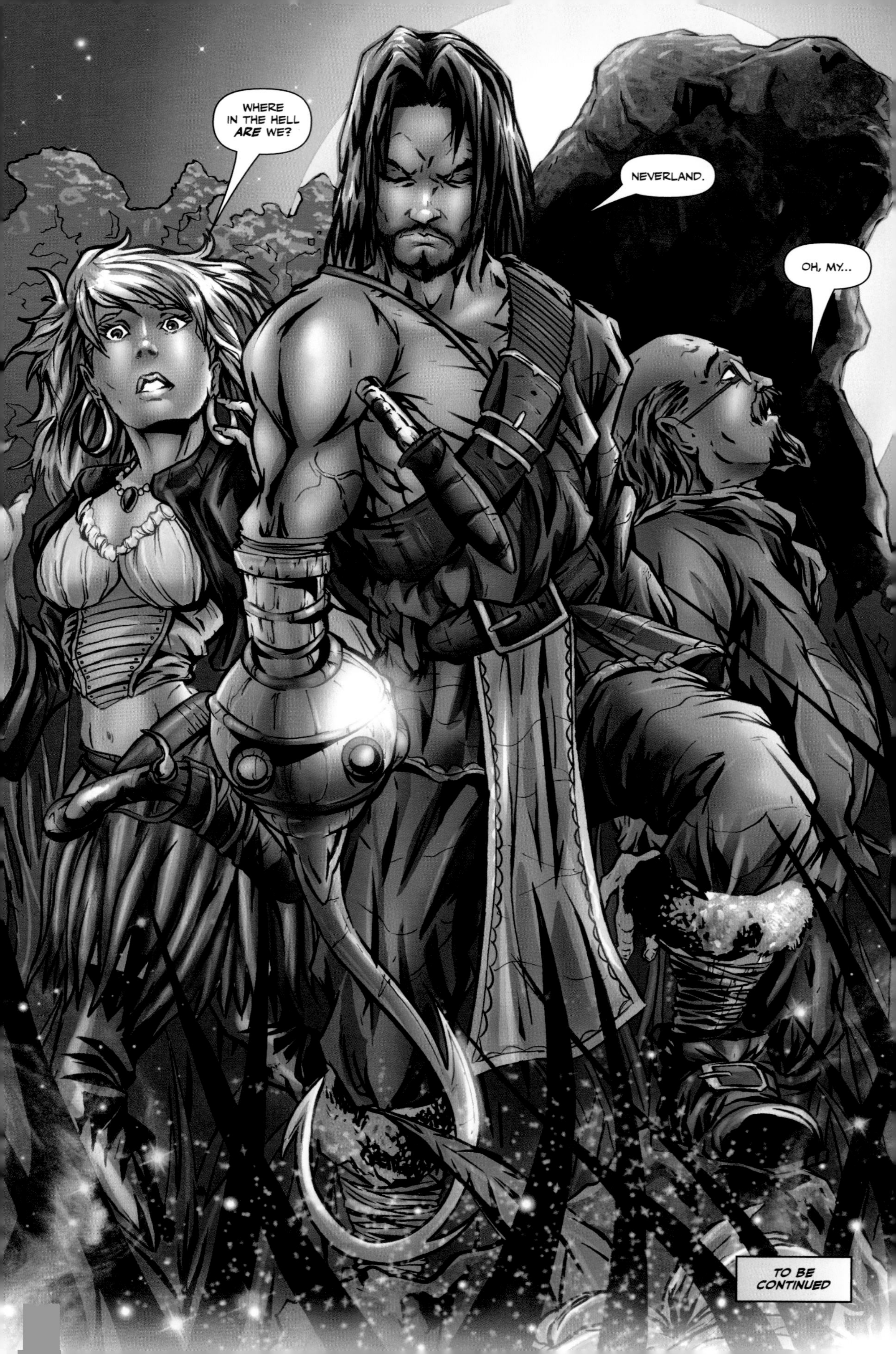
WHERE IN THE HELL *ARE* WE?
NEVERLAND.
OH, MY...
TO BE CONTINUED

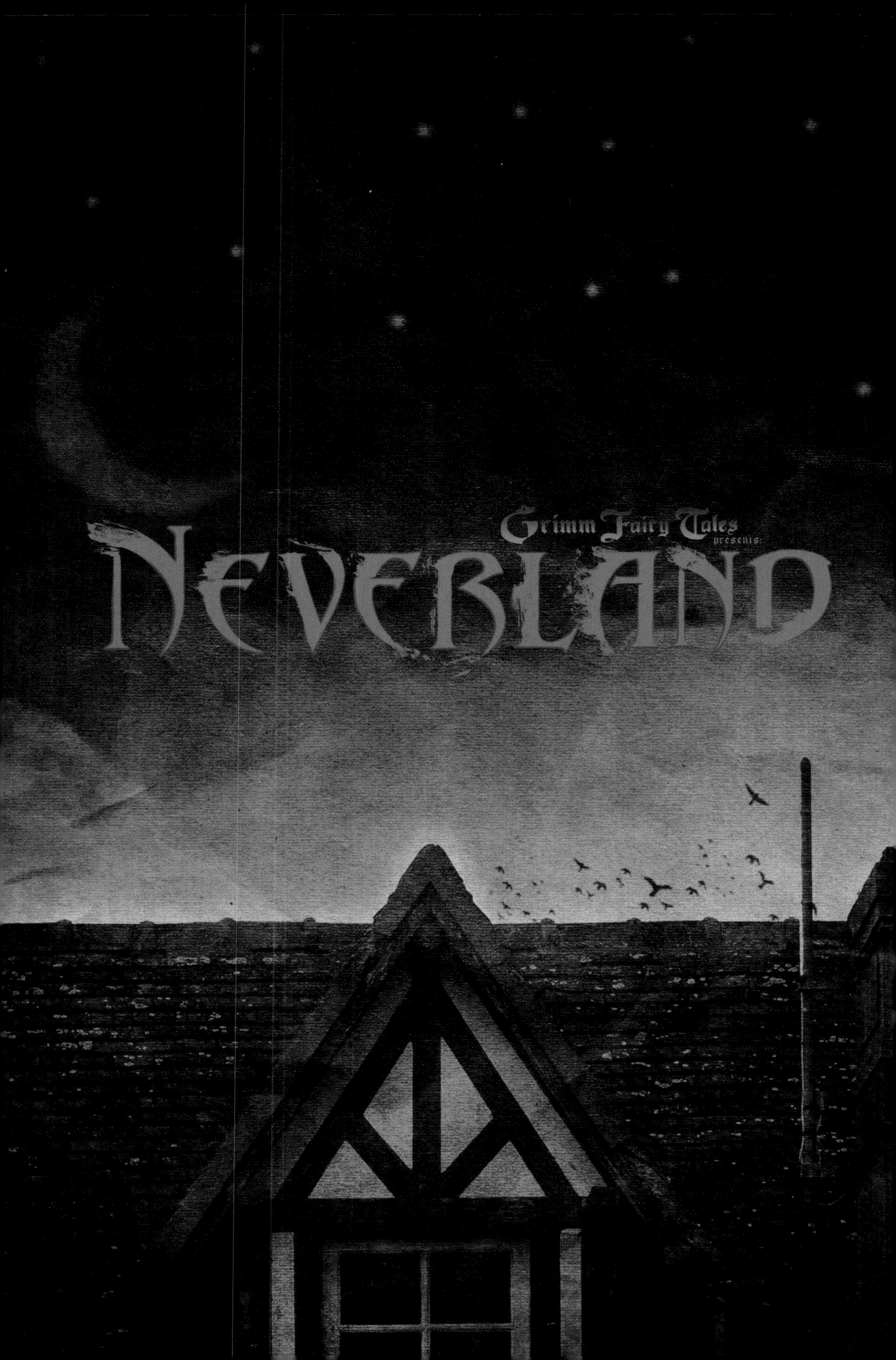
Grimm Fairy Tales
presents:
NEVERLAND

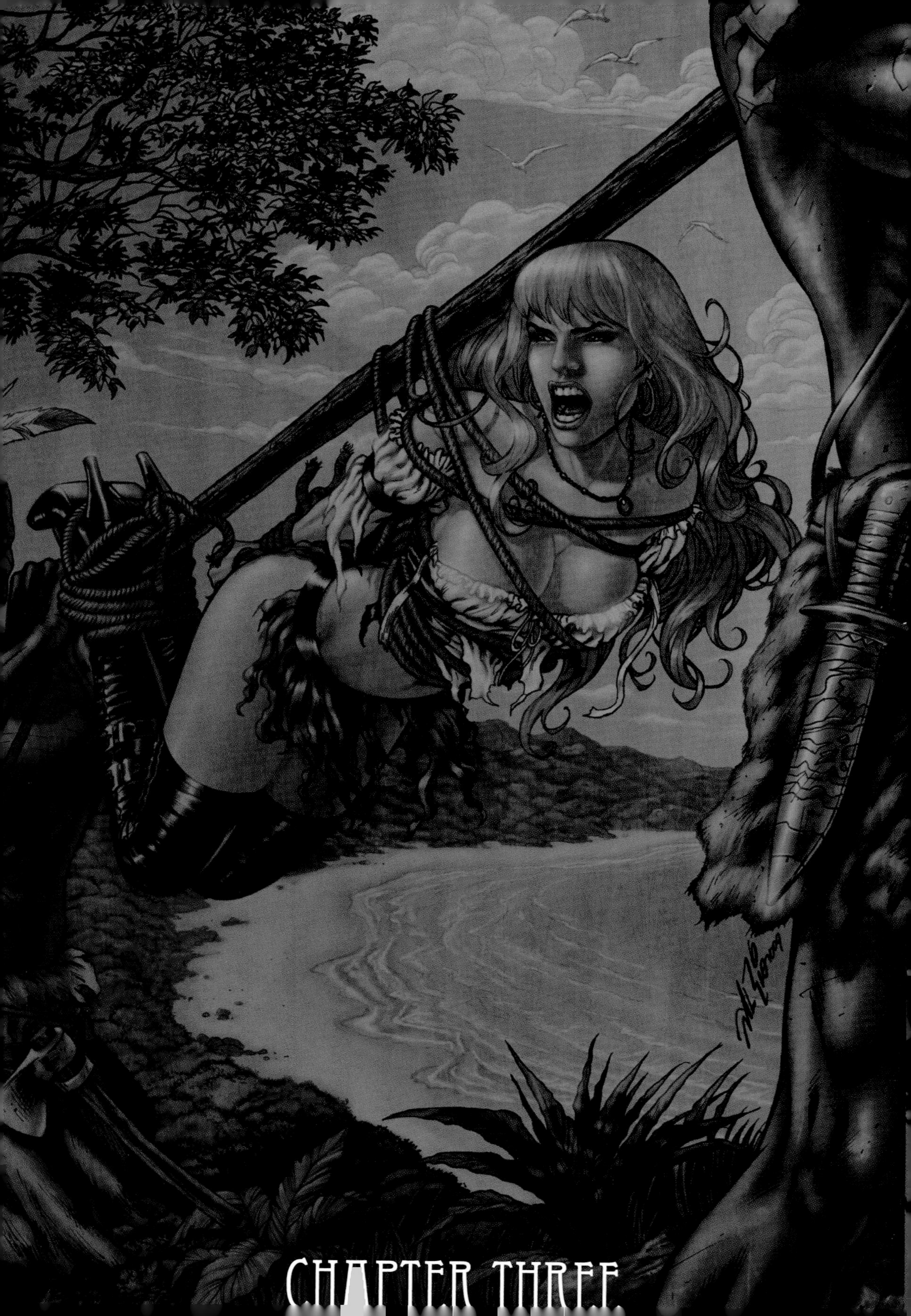

CHAPTER THREE

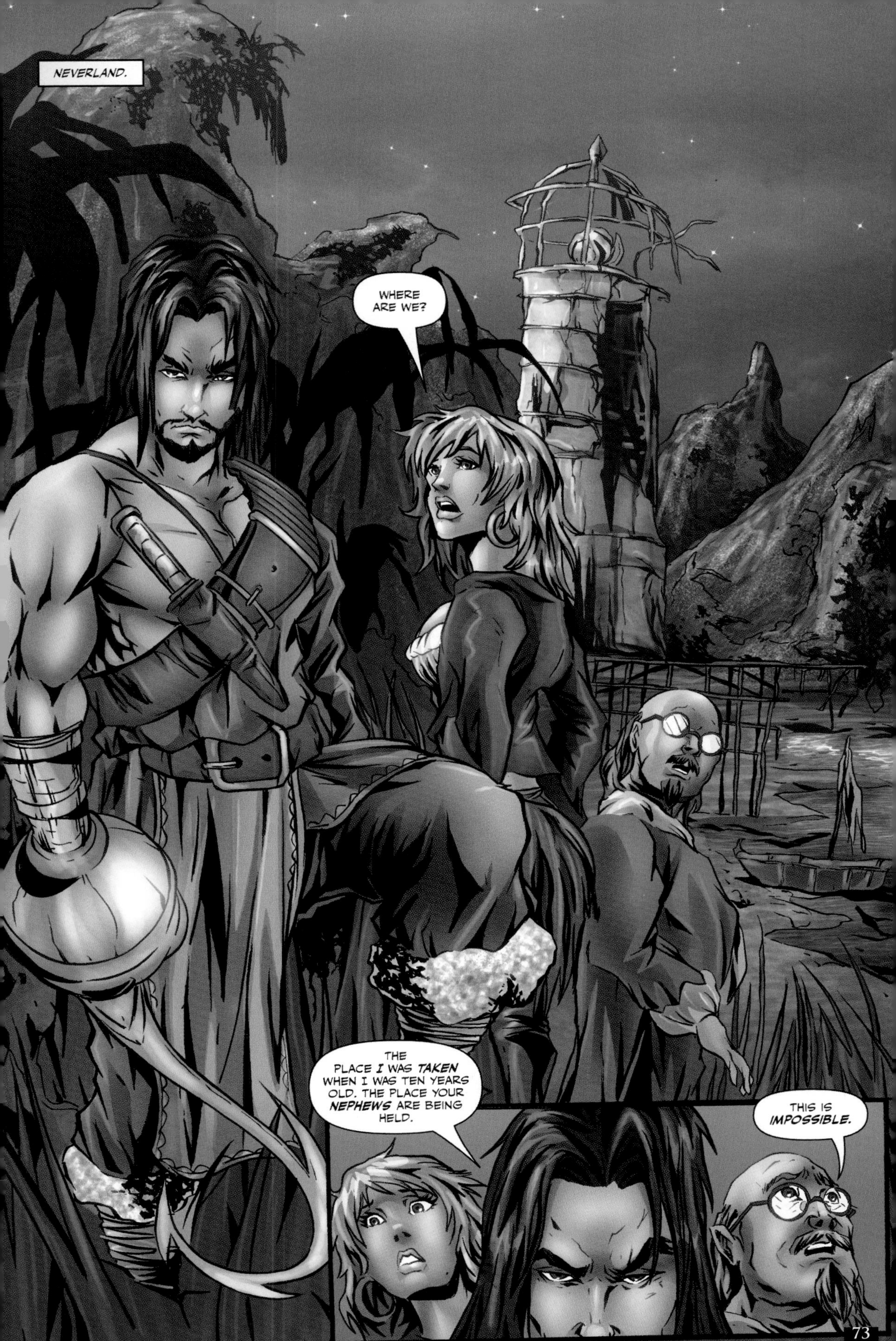
NEVERLAND.
WHERE ARE WE?
THE PLACE *I* WAS *TAKEN* WHEN I WAS TEN YEARS OLD. THE PLACE YOUR *NEPHEWS* ARE BEING HELD.
THIS IS *IMPOSSIBLE.*

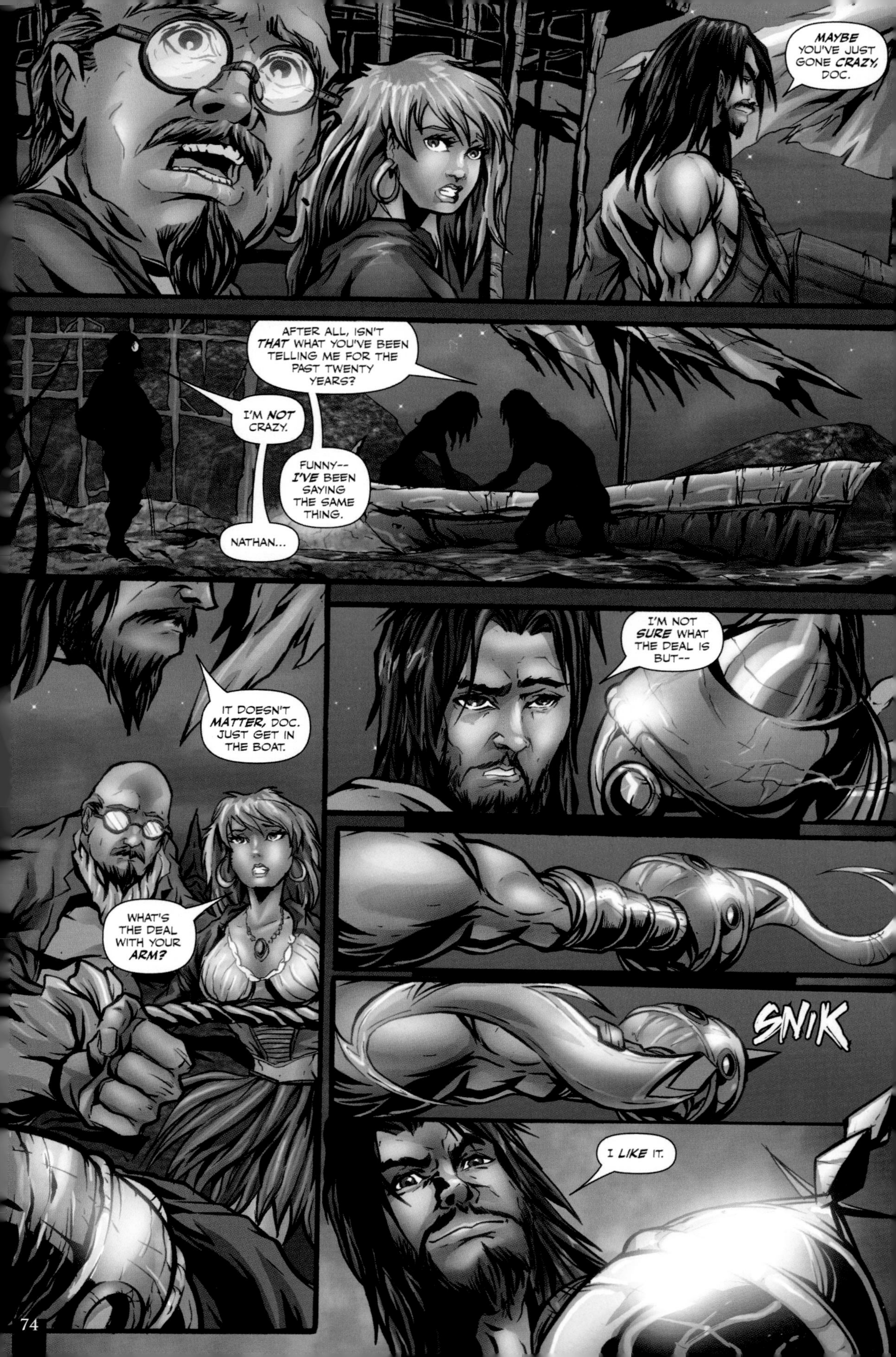
MAYBE YOU'VE JUST GONE CRAZY, DOC.
AFTER ALL, ISN'T THAT WHAT YOU'VE BEEN TELLING ME FOR THE PAST TWENTY YEARS?
I'M NOT CRAZY.
FUNNY-- I'VE BEEN SAYING THE SAME THING.
NATHAN...
IT DOESN'T MATTER, DOC. JUST GET IN THE BOAT.
WHAT'S THE DEAL WITH YOUR ARM?
I'M NOT SURE WHAT THE DEAL IS BUT--
SNIK
I LIKE IT.

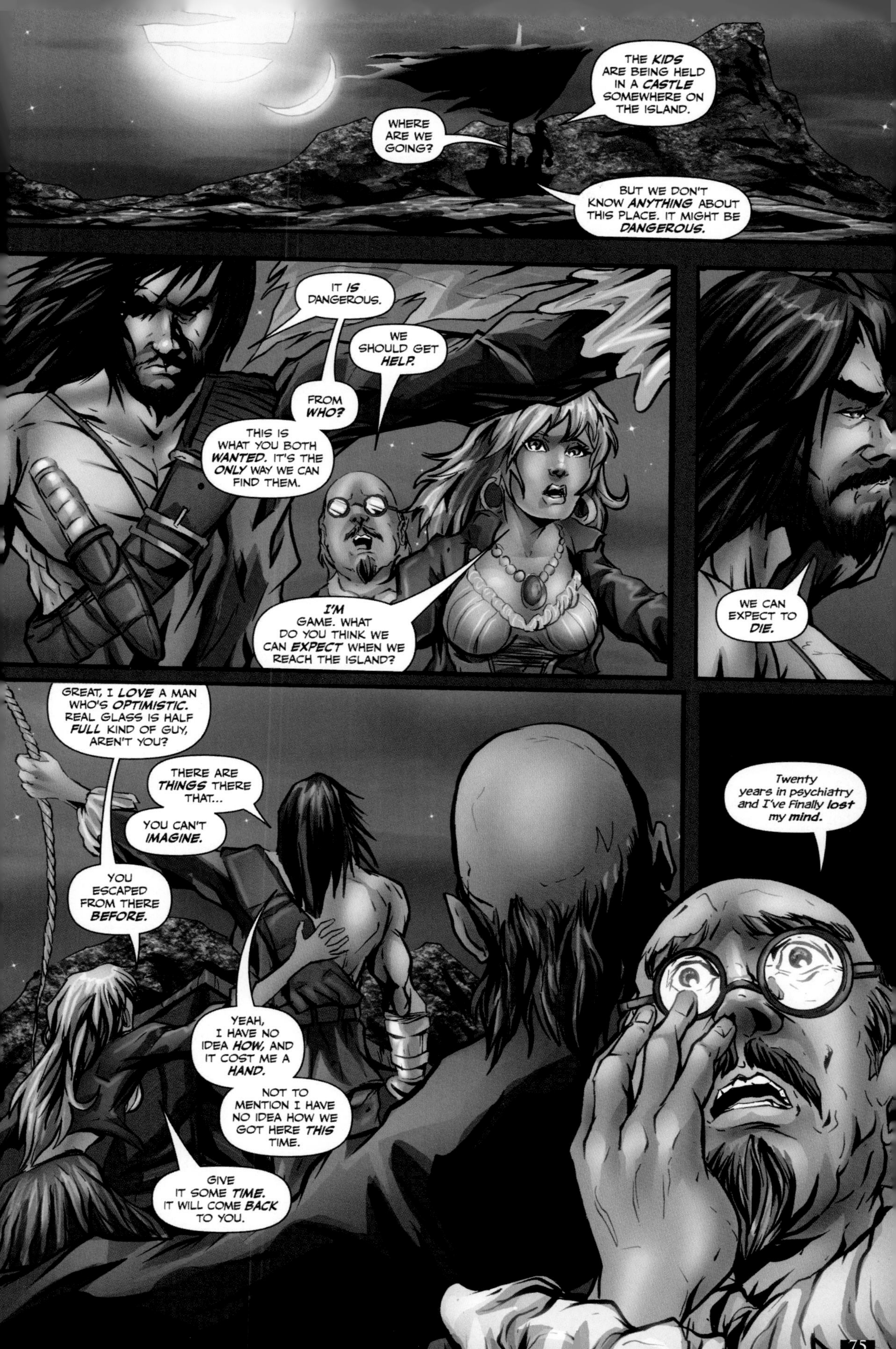

THE KIDS ARE BEING HELD IN A CASTLE SOMEWHERE ON THE ISLAND.
WHERE ARE WE GOING?
BUT WE DON'T KNOW ANYTHING ABOUT THIS PLACE. IT MIGHT BE DANGEROUS.
IT IS DANGEROUS.
WE SHOULD GET HELP.
FROM WHO?
THIS IS WHAT YOU BOTH WANTED. IT'S THE ONLY WAY WE CAN FIND THEM.
I'M GAME. WHAT DO YOU THINK WE CAN EXPECT WHEN WE REACH THE ISLAND?
WE CAN EXPECT TO DIE.
GREAT, I LOVE A MAN WHO'S OPTIMISTIC. REAL GLASS IS HALF FULL KIND OF GUY, AREN'T YOU?
THERE ARE THINGS THERE THAT...
YOU CAN'T IMAGINE.
YOU ESCAPED FROM THERE BEFORE.
YEAH, I HAVE NO IDEA HOW, AND IT COST ME A HAND.
NOT TO MENTION I HAVE NO IDEA HOW WE GOT HERE THIS TIME.
GIVE IT SOME TIME. IT WILL COME BACK TO YOU.
Twenty years in psychiatry and I've finally lost my mind.

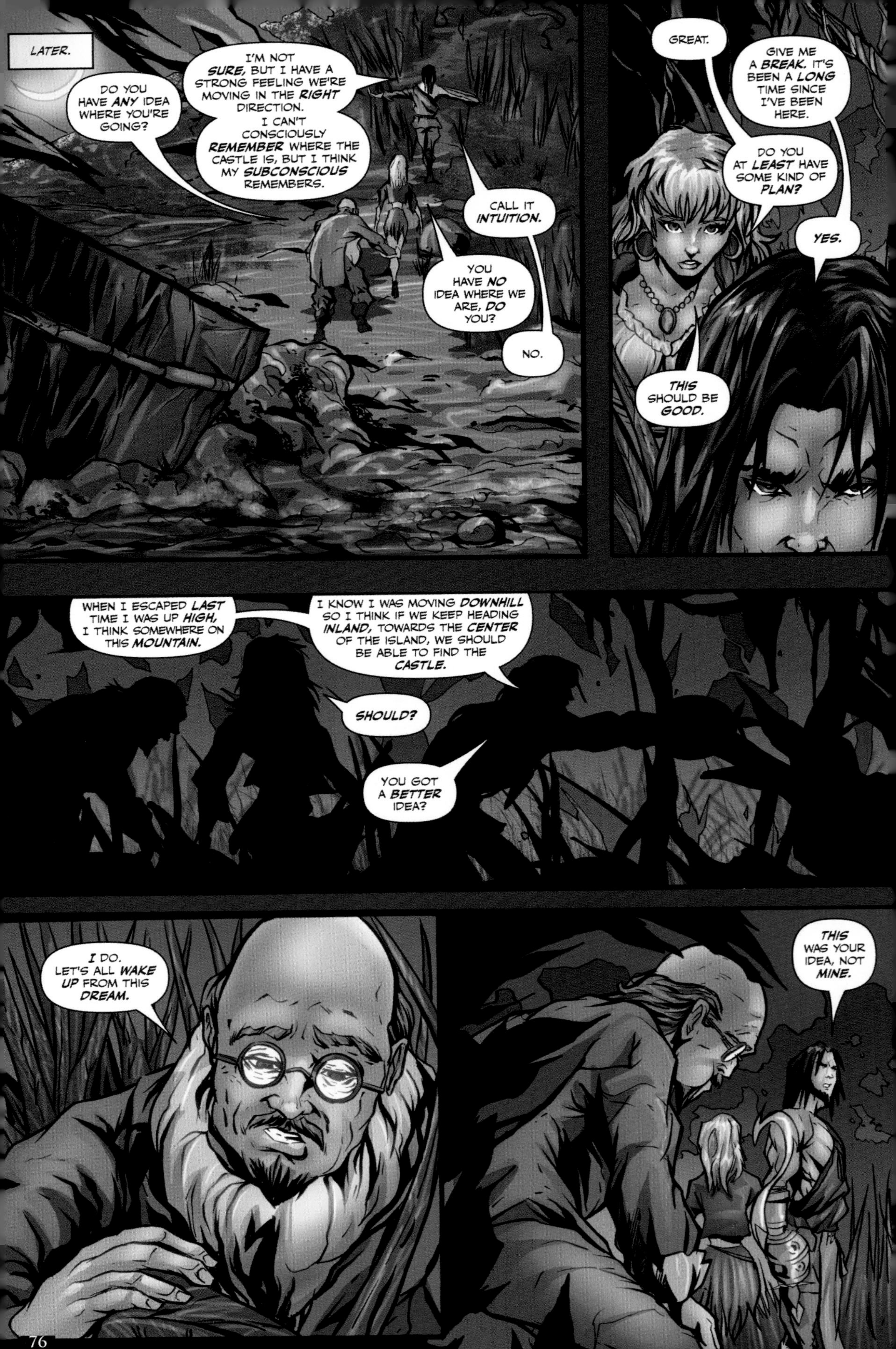
LATER.
DO YOU HAVE ANY IDEA WHERE YOU'RE GOING?
I'M NOT SURE, BUT I HAVE A STRONG FEELING WE'RE MOVING IN THE RIGHT DIRECTION.
I CAN'T CONSCIOUSLY REMEMBER WHERE THE CASTLE IS, BUT I THINK MY SUBCONSCIOUS REMEMBERS.
CALL IT INTUITION.
YOU HAVE NO IDEA WHERE WE ARE, DO YOU?
NO.
GREAT.
GIVE ME A BREAK. IT'S BEEN A LONG TIME SINCE I'VE BEEN HERE.
DO YOU AT LEAST HAVE SOME KIND OF PLAN?
YES.
THIS SHOULD BE GOOD.
WHEN I ESCAPED LAST TIME I WAS UP HIGH, I THINK SOMEWHERE ON THIS MOUNTAIN.
I KNOW I WAS MOVING DOWNHILL SO I THINK IF WE KEEP HEADING INLAND, TOWARDS THE CENTER OF THE ISLAND, WE SHOULD BE ABLE TO FIND THE CASTLE.
SHOULD?
YOU GOT A BETTER IDEA?
I DO. LET'S ALL WAKE UP FROM THIS DREAM.
THIS WAS YOUR IDEA, NOT MINE.

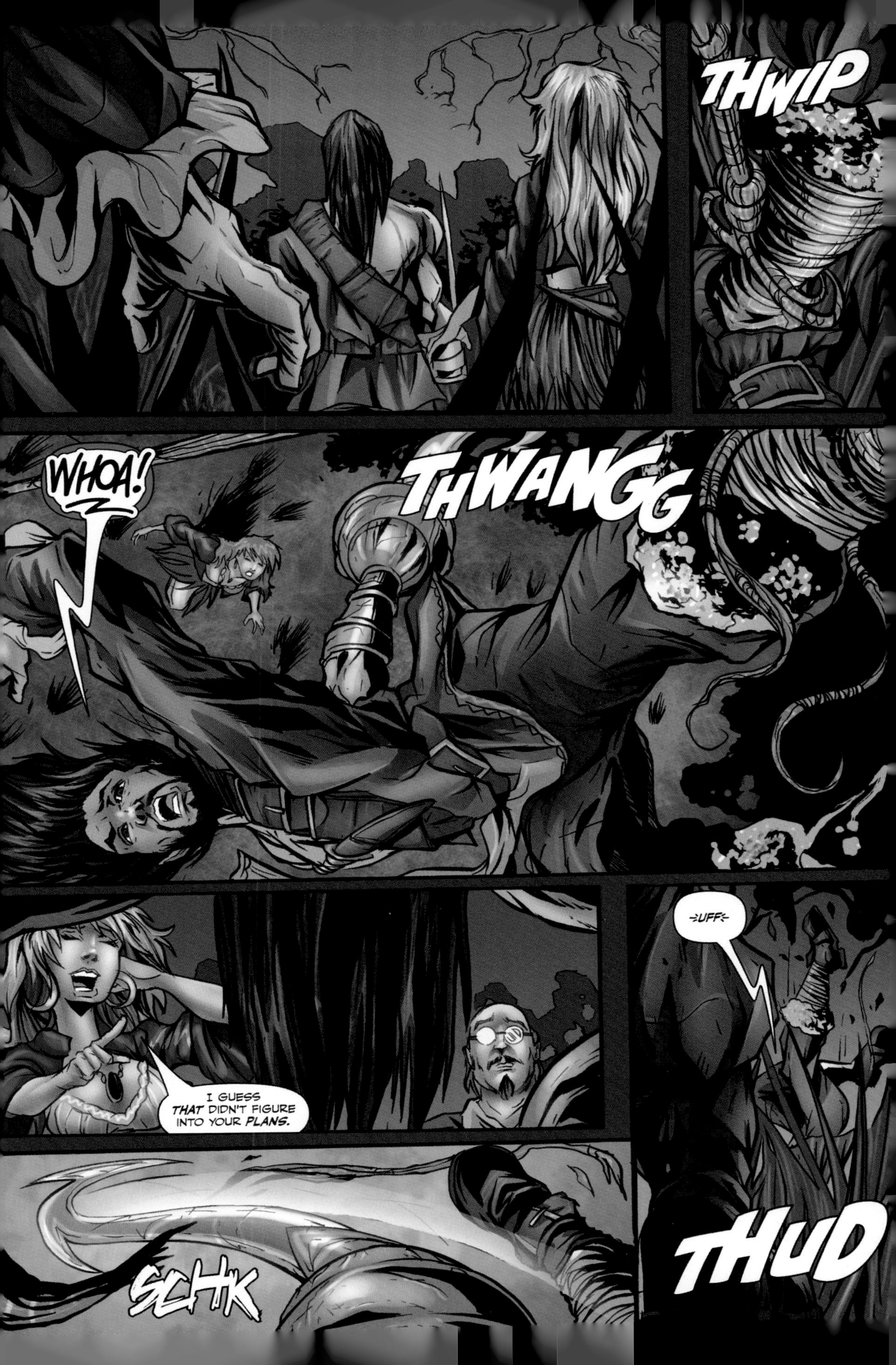
THWIP
WHOA!
THWANGG
I GUESS *THAT* DIDN'T FIGURE INTO YOUR *PLANS*.
UFF
SCHK
THUD

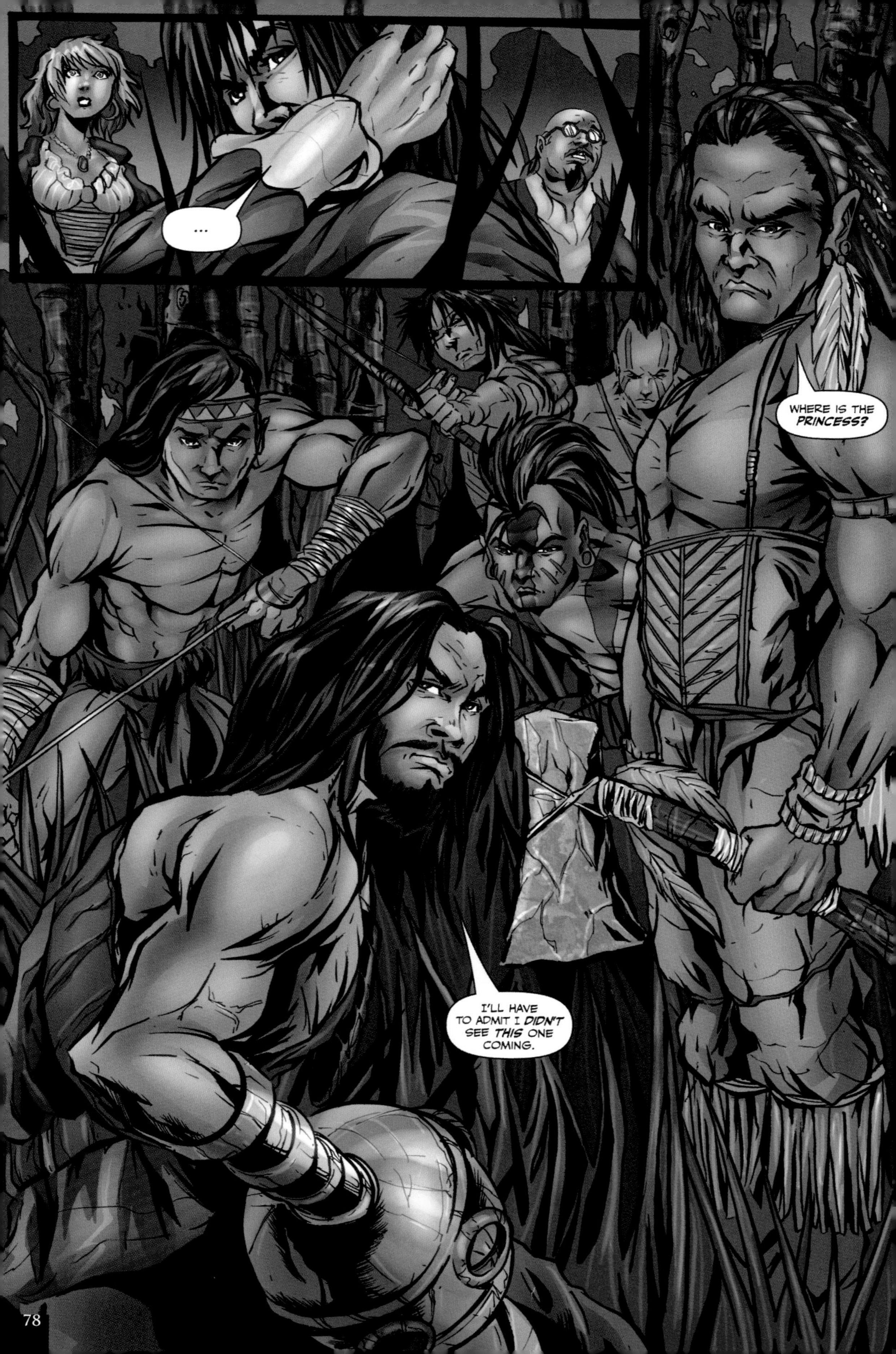
...
WHERE IS THE PRINCESS?
I'LL HAVE TO ADMIT I DIDN'T SEE THIS ONE COMING.

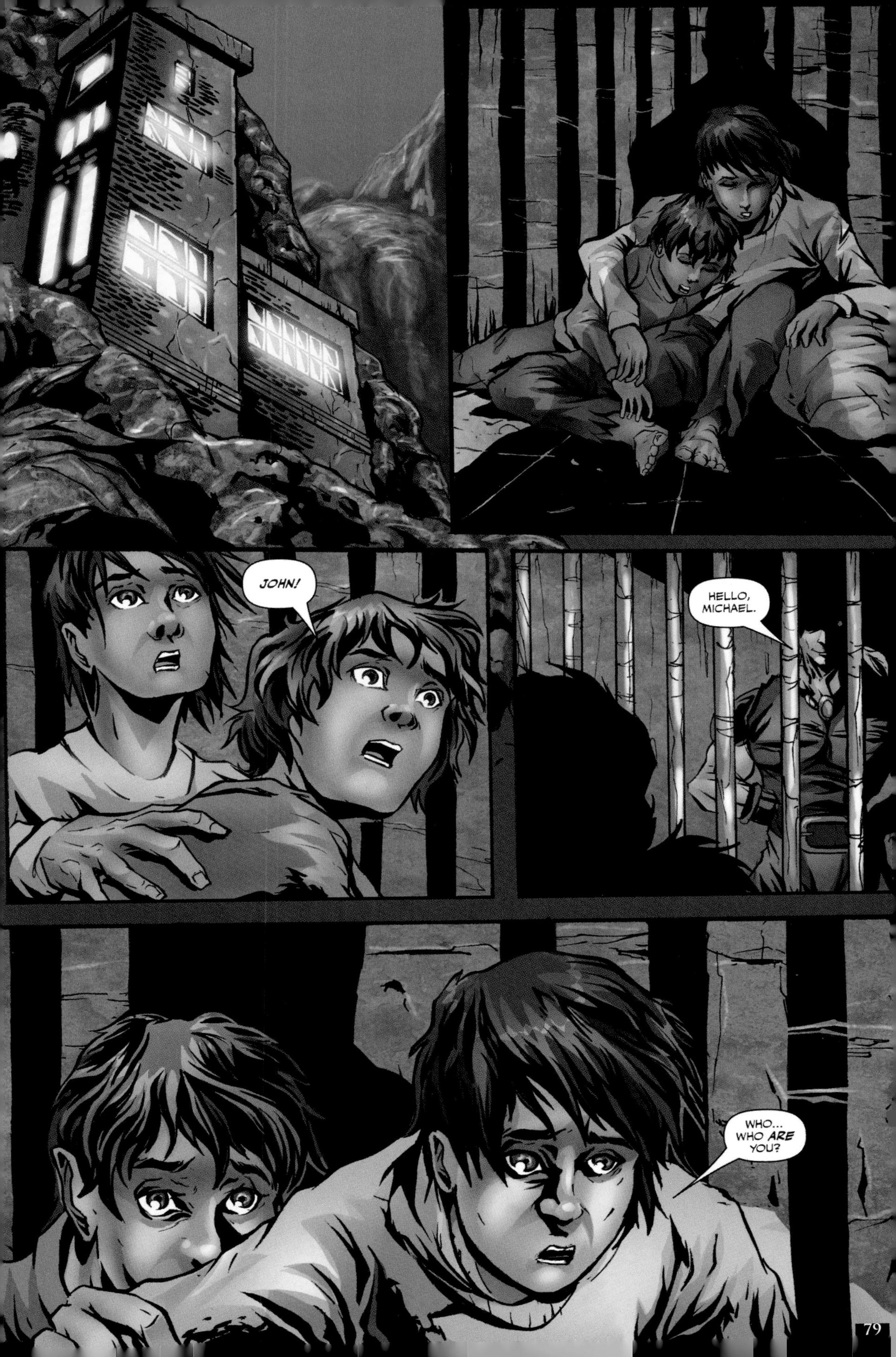
JOHN!
HELLO, MICHAEL.
WHO... WHO *ARE* YOU?

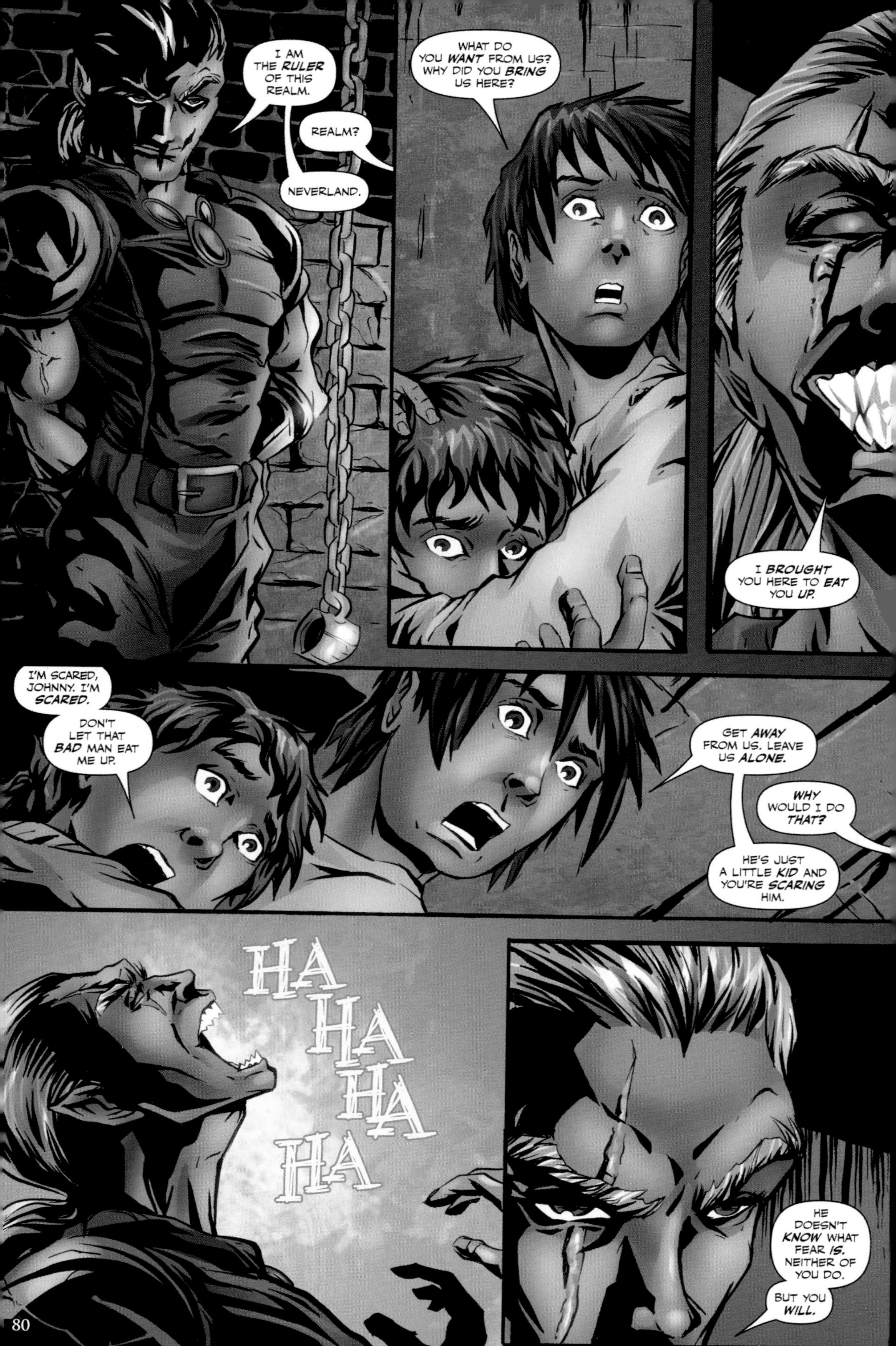
I AM THE RULER OF THIS REALM.
REALM?
NEVERLAND.
WHAT DO YOU WANT FROM US? WHY DID YOU BRING US HERE?
I BROUGHT YOU HERE TO EAT YOU UP.
I'M SCARED, JOHNNY. I'M SCARED.
DON'T LET THAT BAD MAN EAT ME UP.
GET AWAY FROM US. LEAVE US ALONE.
HE'S JUST A LITTLE KID AND YOU'RE SCARING HIM.
WHY WOULD I DO THAT?
HA HA HA HA
HE DOESN'T KNOW WHAT FEAR IS. NEITHER OF YOU DO.
BUT YOU WILL.

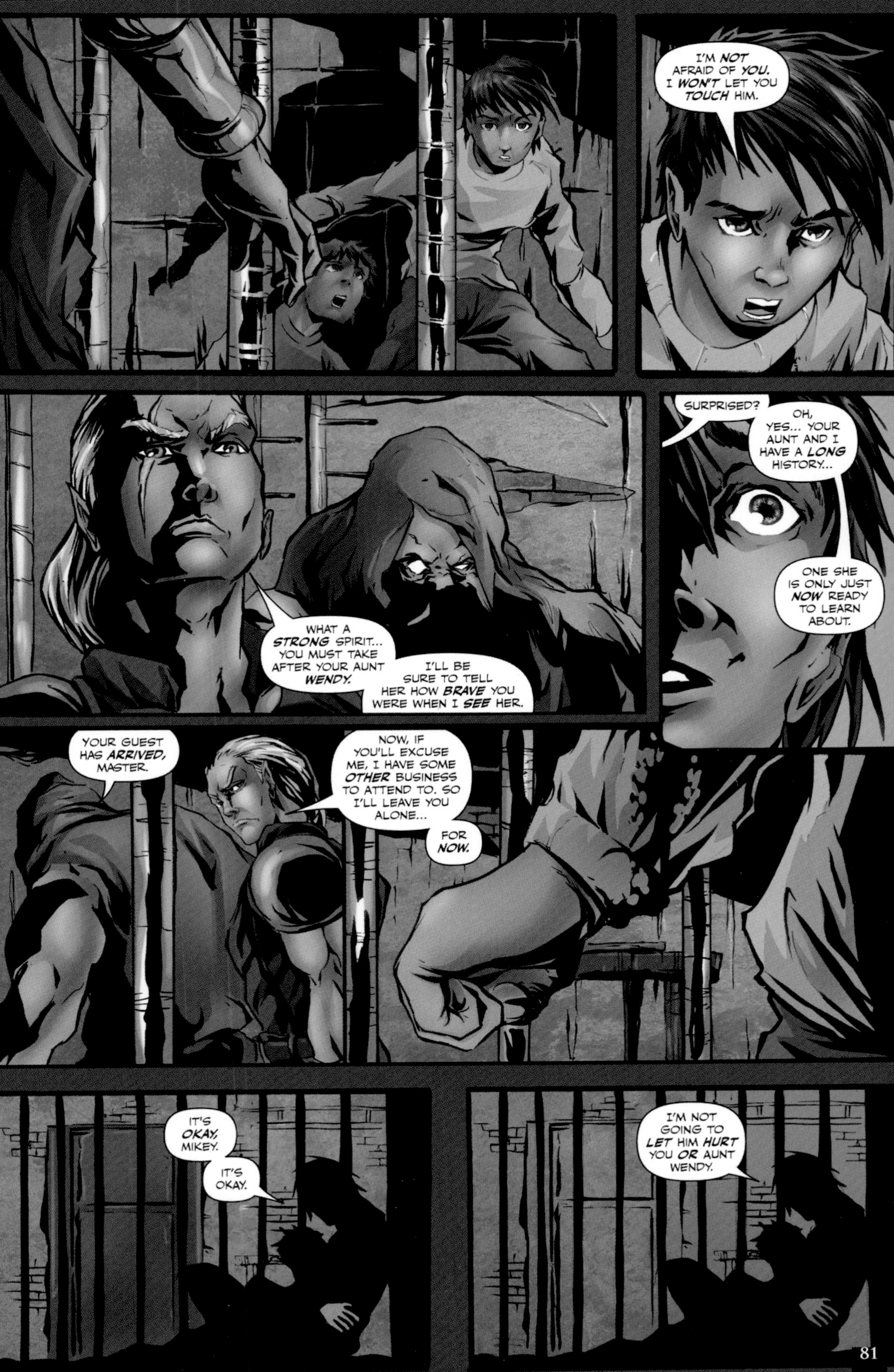
I'M NOT AFRAID OF YOU. I WON'T LET YOU TOUCH HIM.
WHAT A STRONG SPIRIT... YOU MUST TAKE AFTER YOUR AUNT WENDY.
I'LL BE SURE TO TELL HER HOW BRAVE YOU WERE WHEN I SEE HER.
SURPRISED?
OH, YES... YOUR AUNT AND I HAVE A LONG HISTORY...
ONE SHE IS ONLY JUST NOW READY TO LEARN ABOUT.
YOUR GUEST HAS ARRIVED, MASTER.
NOW, IF YOU'LL EXCUSE ME, I HAVE SOME OTHER BUSINESS TO ATTEND TO. SO I'LL LEAVE YOU ALONE...
FOR NOW.
IT'S OKAY, MIKEY.
IT'S OKAY.
I'M NOT GOING TO LET HIM HURT YOU OR AUNT WENDY.

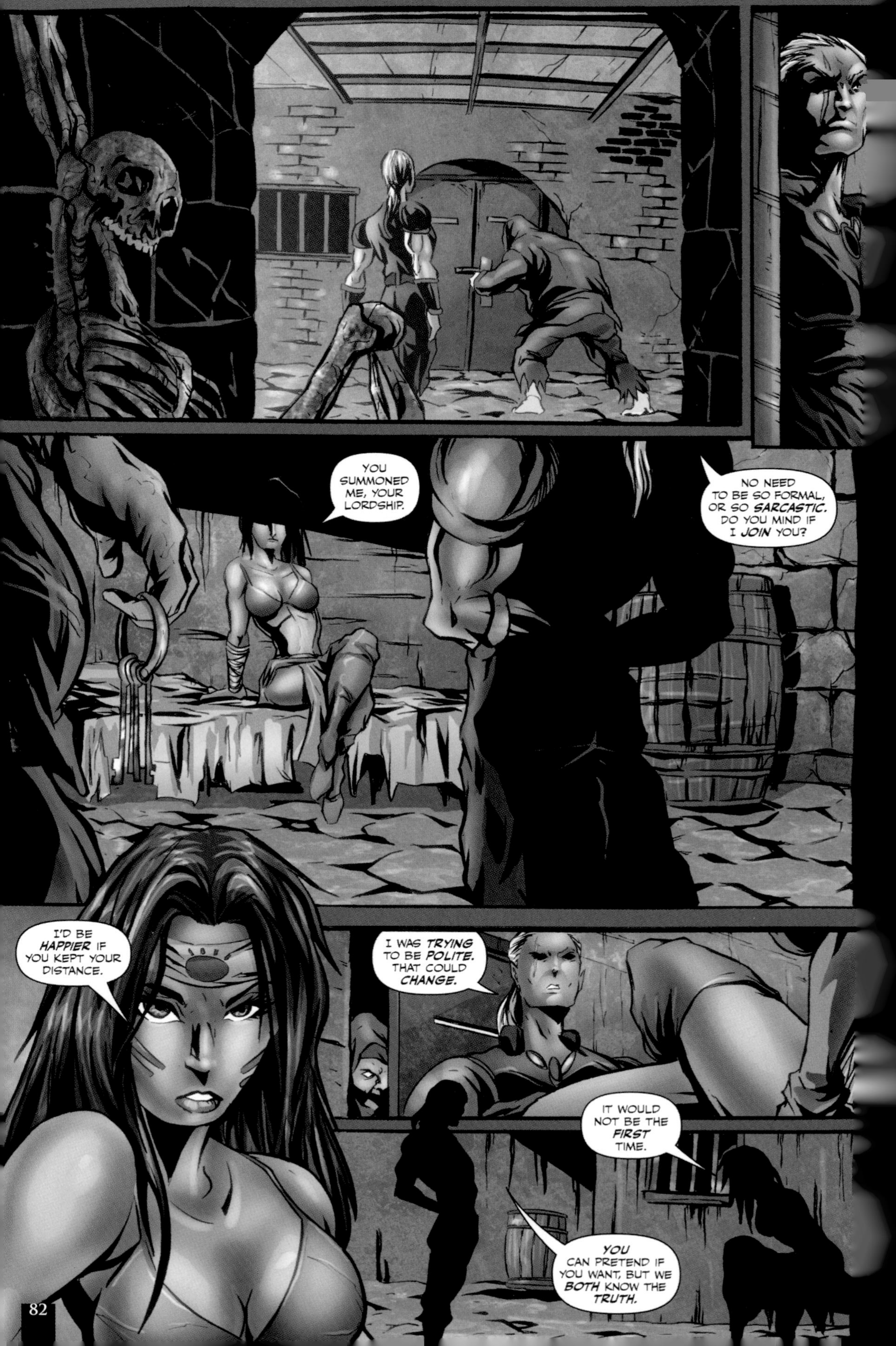
YOU SUMMONED ME, YOUR LORDSHIP.
NO NEED TO BE SO FORMAL, OR SO SARCASTIC. DO YOU MIND IF I JOIN YOU?
I'D BE HAPPIER IF YOU KEPT YOUR DISTANCE.
I WAS TRYING TO BE POLITE. THAT COULD CHANGE.
IT WOULD NOT BE THE FIRST TIME.
YOU CAN PRETEND IF YOU WANT, BUT WE BOTH KNOW THE TRUTH.

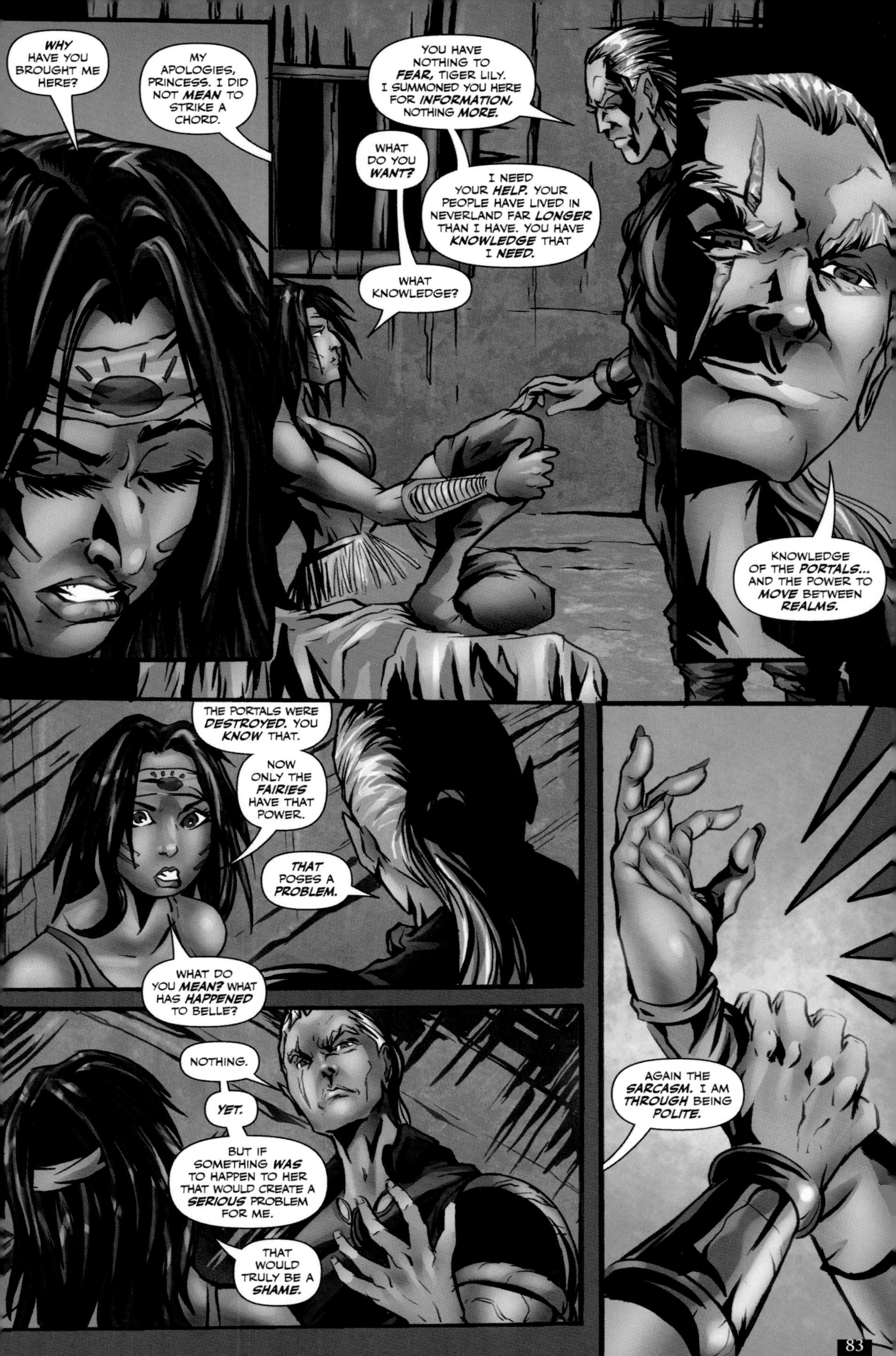
WHY HAVE YOU BROUGHT ME HERE?
MY APOLOGIES, PRINCESS. I DID NOT MEAN TO STRIKE A CHORD.
YOU HAVE NOTHING TO FEAR, TIGER LILY. I SUMMONED YOU HERE FOR INFORMATION, NOTHING MORE.
WHAT DO YOU WANT?
I NEED YOUR HELP. YOUR PEOPLE HAVE LIVED IN NEVERLAND FAR LONGER THAN I HAVE. YOU HAVE KNOWLEDGE THAT I NEED.
WHAT KNOWLEDGE?
KNOWLEDGE OF THE PORTALS... AND THE POWER TO MOVE BETWEEN REALMS.
THE PORTALS WERE DESTROYED. YOU KNOW THAT.
NOW ONLY THE FAIRIES HAVE THAT POWER.
THAT POSES A PROBLEM.
WHAT DO YOU MEAN? WHAT HAS HAPPENED TO BELLE?
NOTHING.
YET.
BUT IF SOMETHING WAS TO HAPPEN TO HER THAT WOULD CREATE A SERIOUS PROBLEM FOR ME.
THAT WOULD TRULY BE A SHAME.
AGAIN THE SARCASM. I AM THROUGH BEING POLITE.

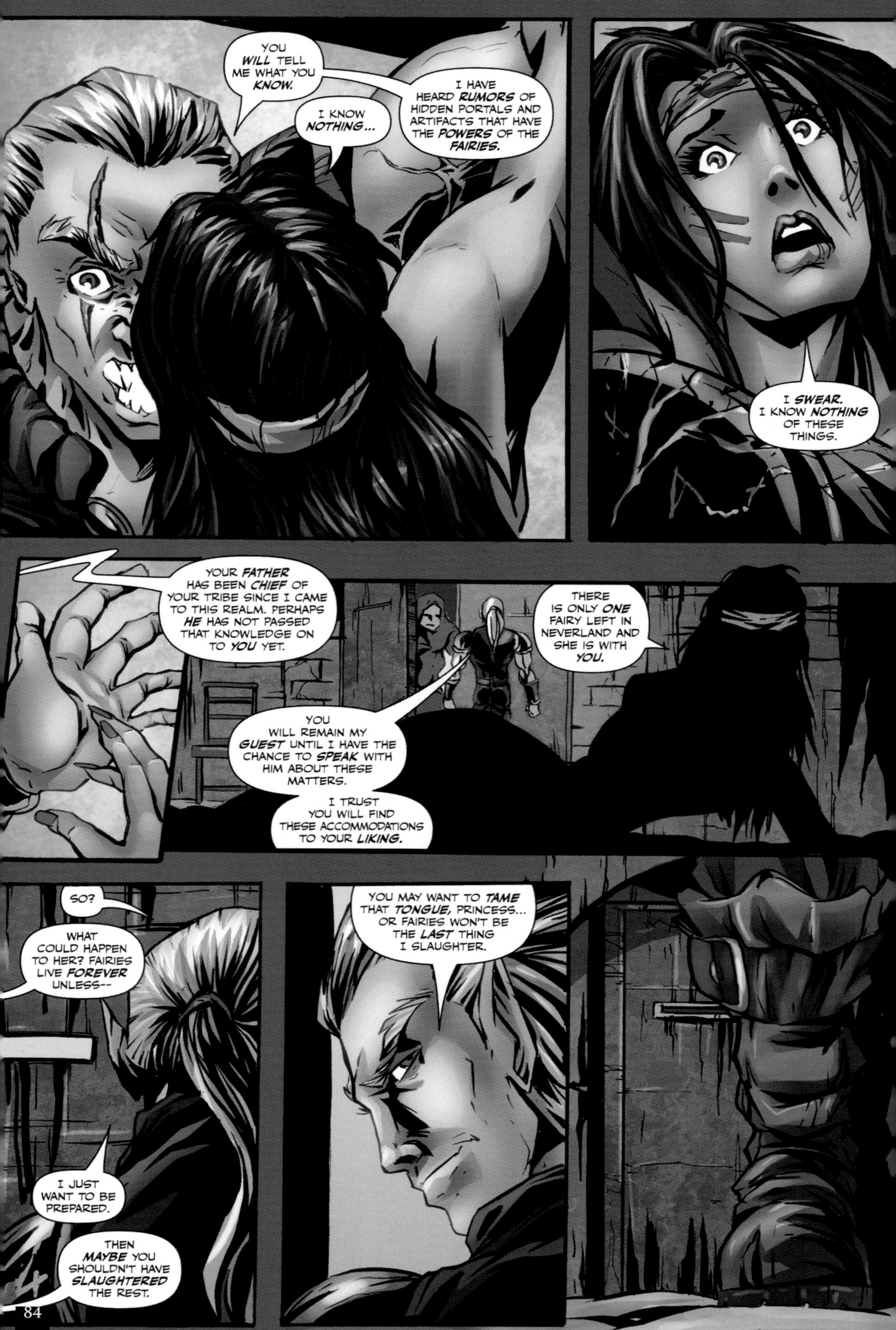
YOU WILL TELL ME WHAT YOU KNOW.
I KNOW NOTHING...
I HAVE HEARD RUMORS OF HIDDEN PORTALS AND ARTIFACTS THAT HAVE THE POWERS OF THE FAIRIES.
I SWEAR. I KNOW NOTHING OF THESE THINGS.
YOUR FATHER HAS BEEN CHIEF OF YOUR TRIBE SINCE I CAME TO THIS REALM. PERHAPS HE HAS NOT PASSED THAT KNOWLEDGE ON TO YOU YET.
YOU WILL REMAIN MY GUEST UNTIL I HAVE THE CHANCE TO SPEAK WITH HIM ABOUT THESE MATTERS.
I TRUST YOU WILL FIND THESE ACCOMMODATIONS TO YOUR LIKING.
THERE IS ONLY ONE FAIRY LEFT IN NEVERLAND AND SHE IS WITH YOU.
SO?
WHAT COULD HAPPEN TO HER? FAIRIES LIVE FOREVER UNLESS--
I JUST WANT TO BE PREPARED.
THEN MAYBE YOU SHOULDN'T HAVE SLAUGHTERED THE REST.
YOU MAY WANT TO TAME THAT TONGUE, PRINCESS... OR FAIRIES WON'T BE THE LAST THING I SLAUGHTER.

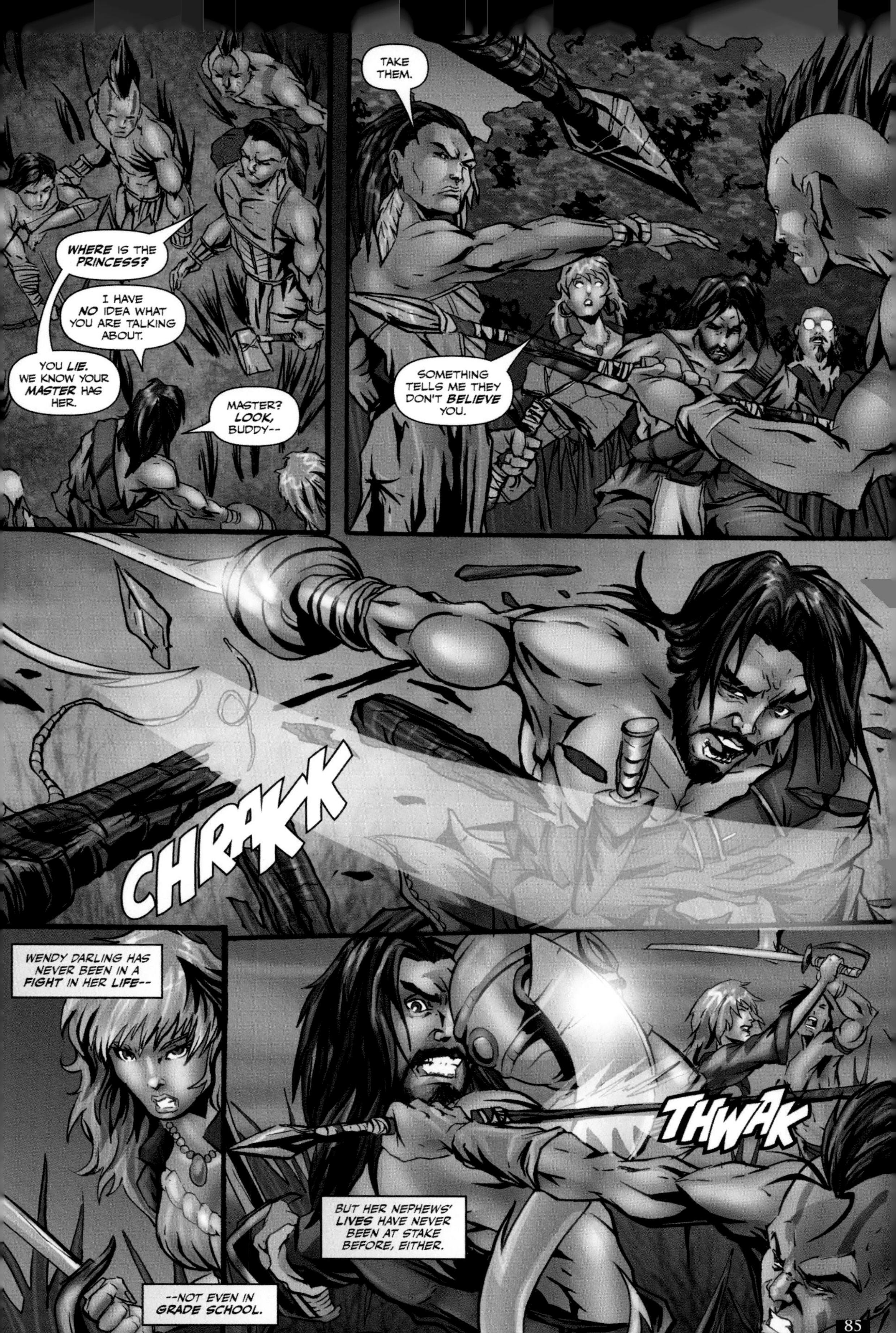
WHERE IS THE PRINCESS?
I HAVE NO IDEA WHAT YOU ARE TALKING ABOUT.
YOU LIE. WE KNOW YOUR MASTER HAS HER.
MASTER? LOOK, BUDDY--
TAKE THEM.
SOMETHING TELLS ME THEY DON'T BELIEVE YOU.
CHRAKK
WENDY DARLING HAS NEVER BEEN IN A FIGHT IN HER LIFE--
THWAK
BUT HER NEPHEWS' LIVES HAVE NEVER BEEN AT STAKE BEFORE, EITHER.
--NOT EVEN IN GRADE SCHOOL.

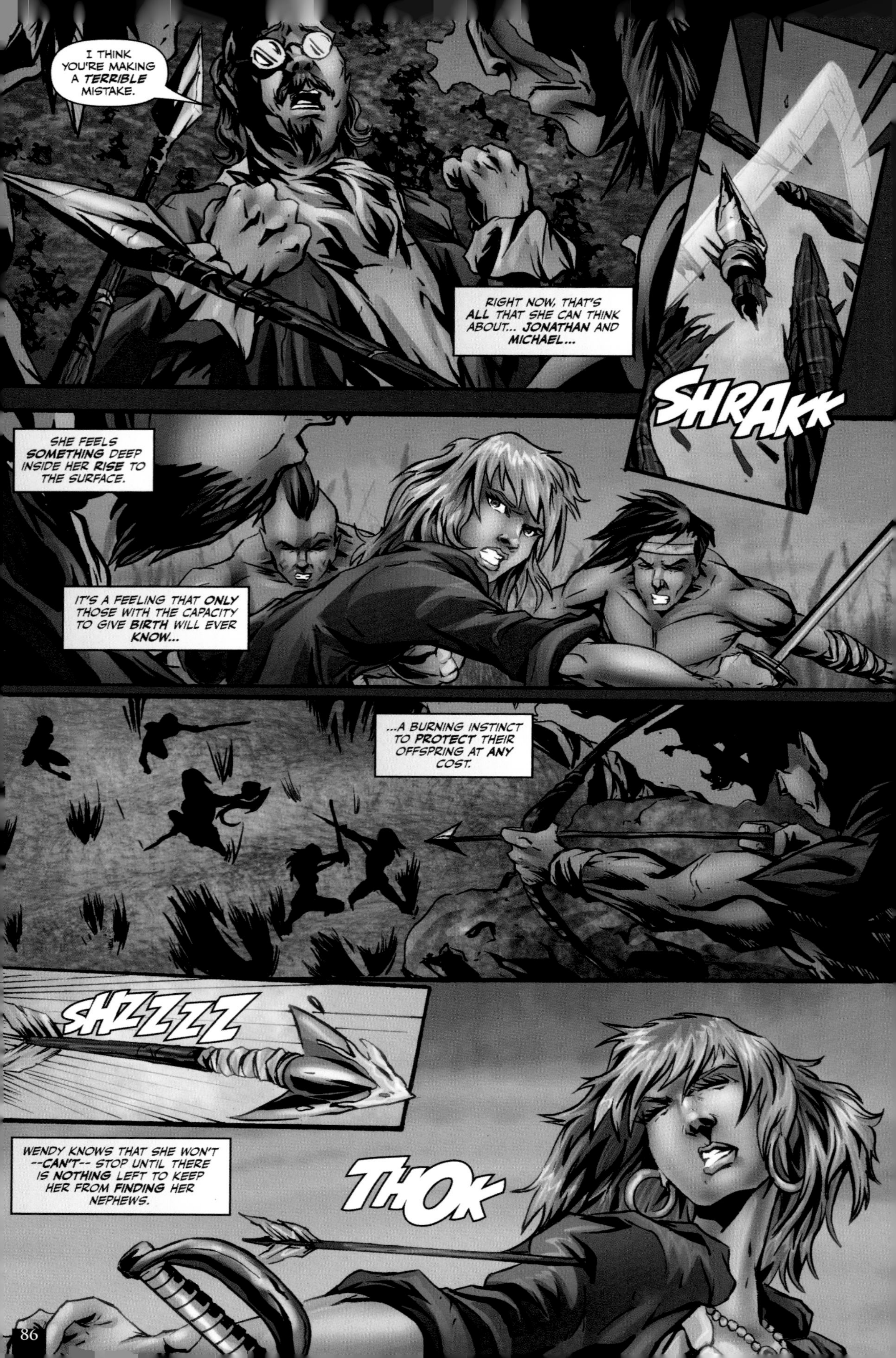

I THINK YOU'RE MAKING A TERRIBLE MISTAKE.
RIGHT NOW, THAT'S ALL THAT SHE CAN THINK ABOUT... JONATHAN AND MICHAEL...
SHRAKK
SHE FEELS SOMETHING DEEP INSIDE HER RISE TO THE SURFACE.
IT'S A FEELING THAT ONLY THOSE WITH THE CAPACITY TO GIVE BIRTH WILL EVER KNOW...
...A BURNING INSTINCT TO PROTECT THEIR OFFSPRING AT ANY COST.
SHZZZZ
WENDY KNOWS THAT SHE WON'T --CAN'T-- STOP UNTIL THERE IS NOTHING LEFT TO KEEP HER FROM FINDING HER NEPHEWS.
THOK

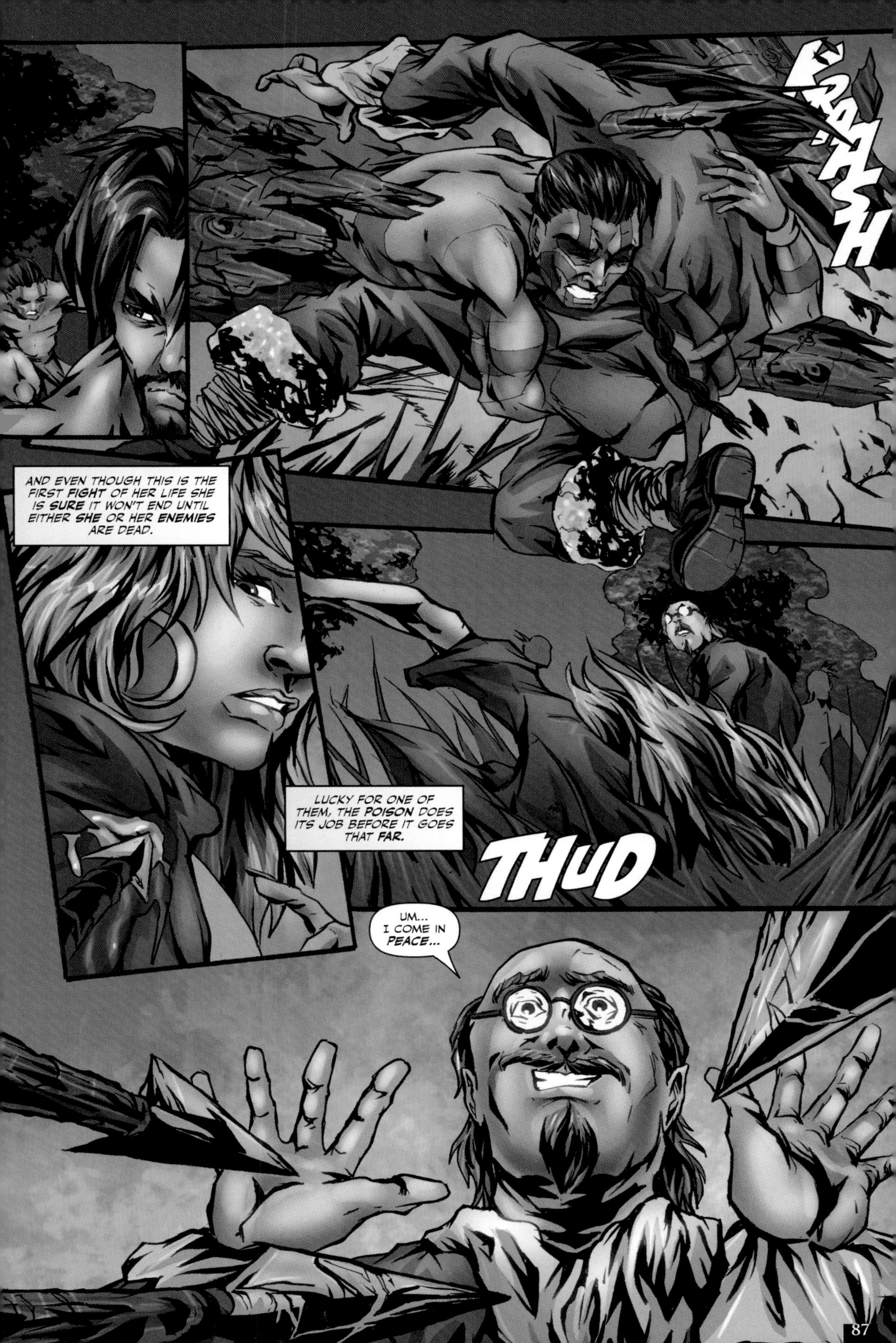
KRAASH
AND EVEN THOUGH THIS IS THE FIRST FIGHT OF HER LIFE SHE IS SURE IT WON'T END UNTIL EITHER SHE OR HER ENEMIES ARE DEAD.
LUCKY FOR ONE OF THEM, THE POISON DOES ITS JOB BEFORE IT GOES THAT FAR.
THUD
UM... I COME IN PEACE...

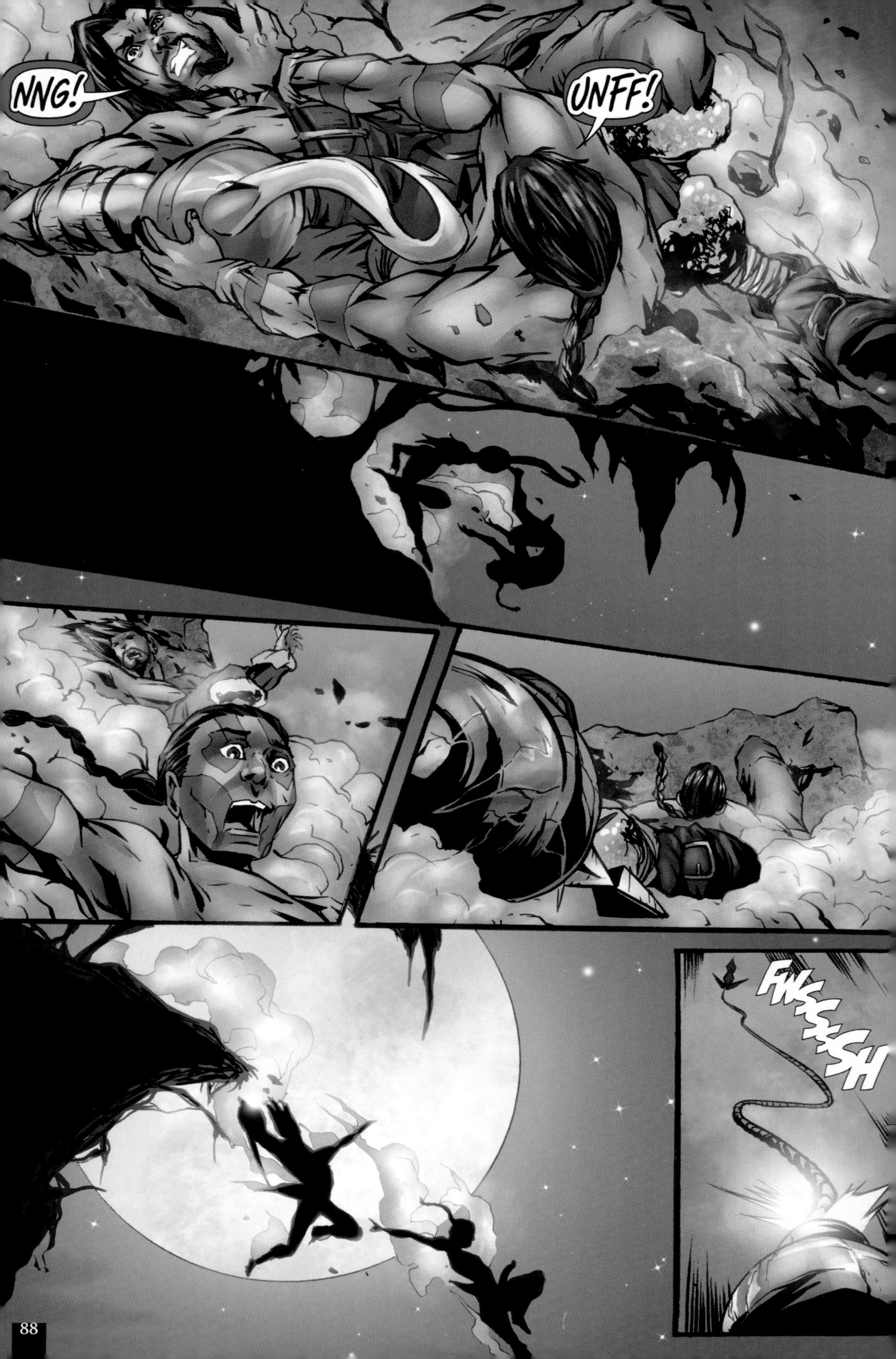
NNG!
UNFF!
FWSSSH

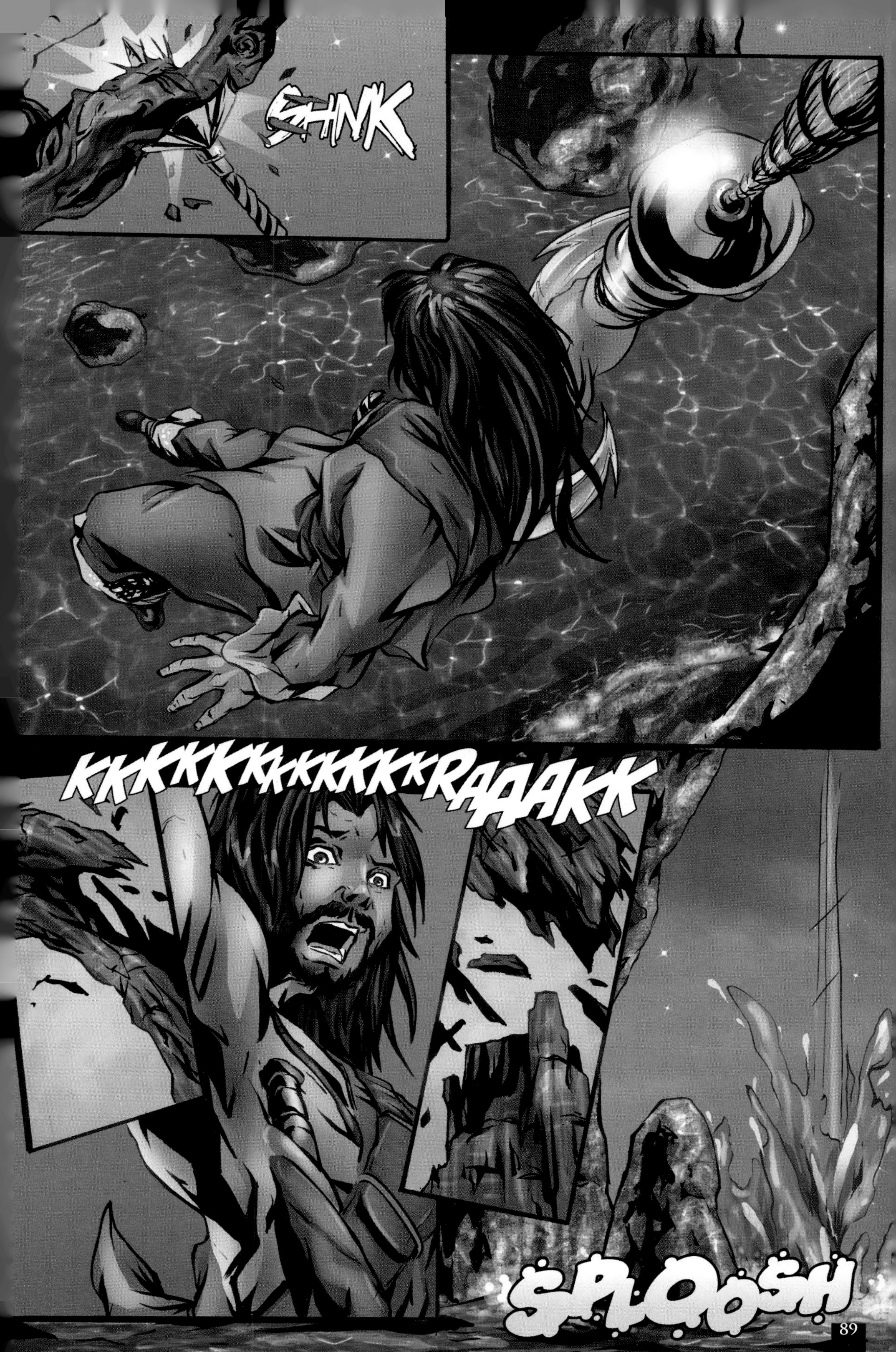
SHNK
KKKKKKKKKKKKRAAAKK
SPLOOSH

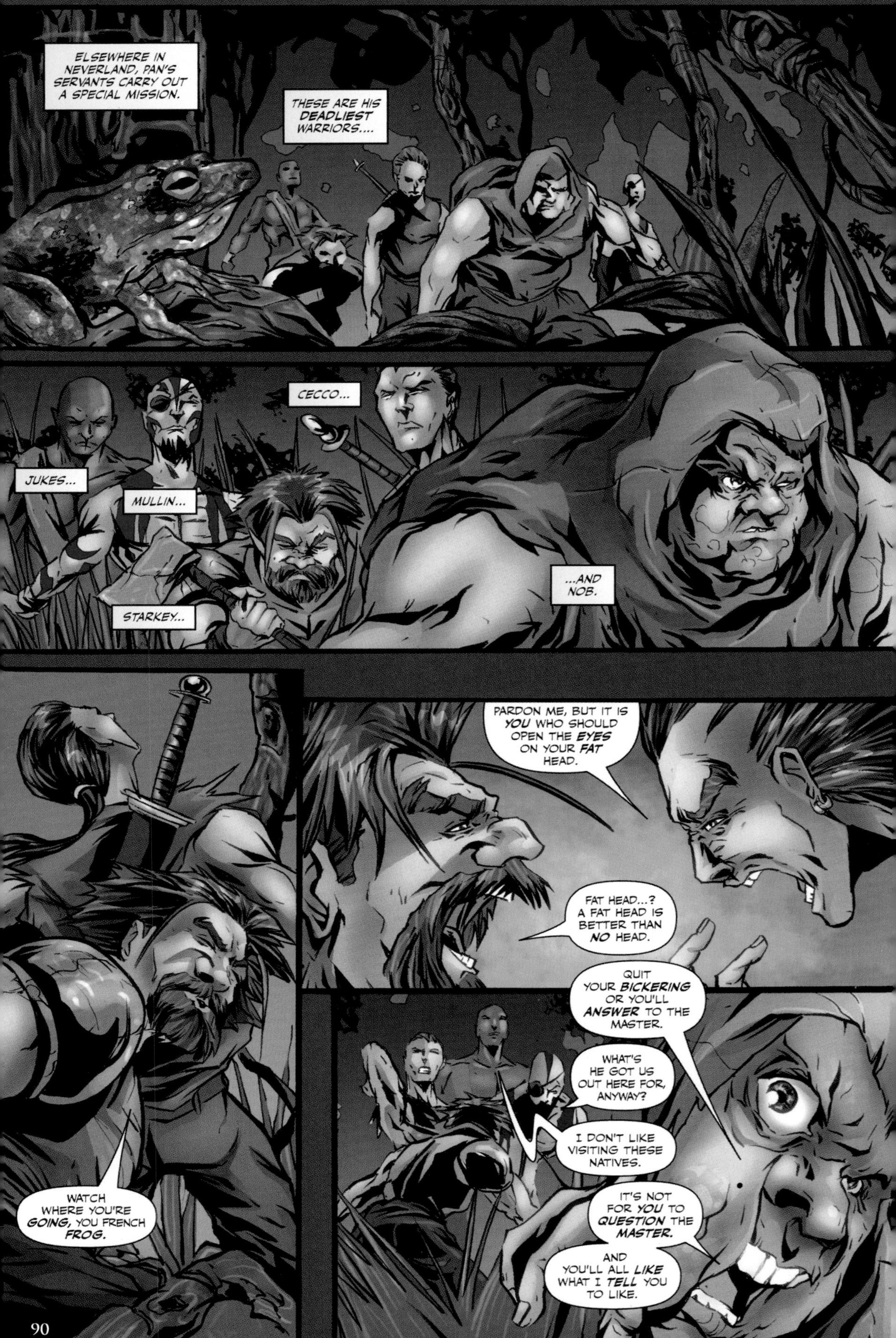
ELSEWHERE IN NEVERLAND, PAN'S SERVANTS CARRY OUT A SPECIAL MISSION.
THESE ARE HIS DEADLIEST WARRIORS....
JUKES...
MULLIN...
STARKEY...
CECCO...
...AND NOB.
WATCH WHERE YOU'RE GOING, YOU FRENCH FROG.
PARDON ME, BUT IT IS YOU WHO SHOULD OPEN THE EYES ON YOUR FAT HEAD.
FAT HEAD...? A FAT HEAD IS BETTER THAN NO HEAD.
QUIT YOUR BICKERING OR YOU'LL ANSWER TO THE MASTER.
WHAT'S HE GOT US OUT HERE FOR, ANYWAY?
I DON'T LIKE VISITING THESE NATIVES.
IT'S NOT FOR YOU TO QUESTION THE MASTER.
AND YOU'LL ALL LIKE WHAT I TELL YOU TO LIKE.

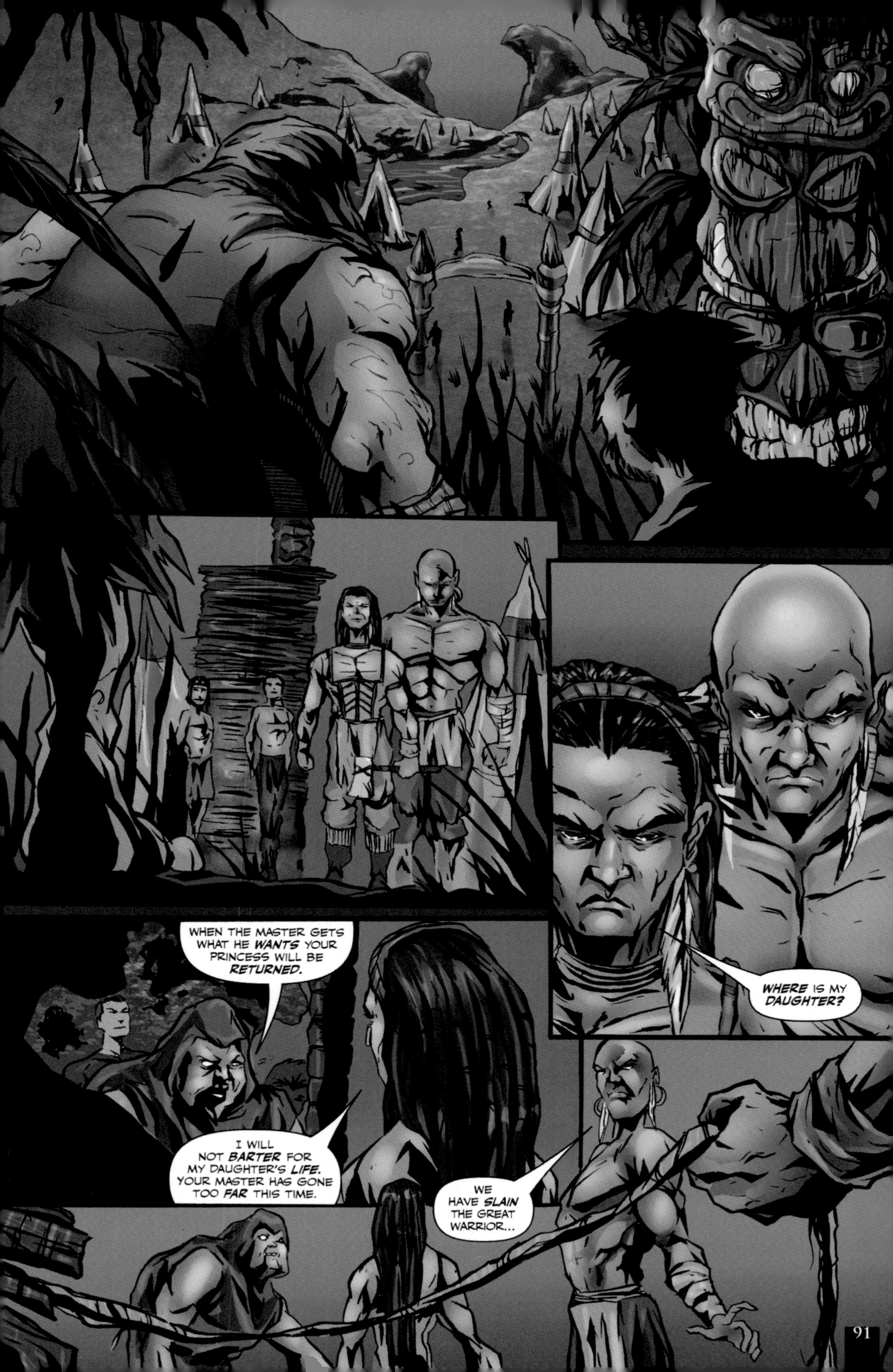
WHERE IS MY DAUGHTER?
WHEN THE MASTER GETS WHAT HE WANTS YOUR PRINCESS WILL BE RETURNED.
I WILL NOT BARTER FOR MY DAUGHTER'S LIFE. YOUR MASTER HAS GONE TOO FAR THIS TIME.
WE HAVE SLAIN THE GREAT WARRIOR...

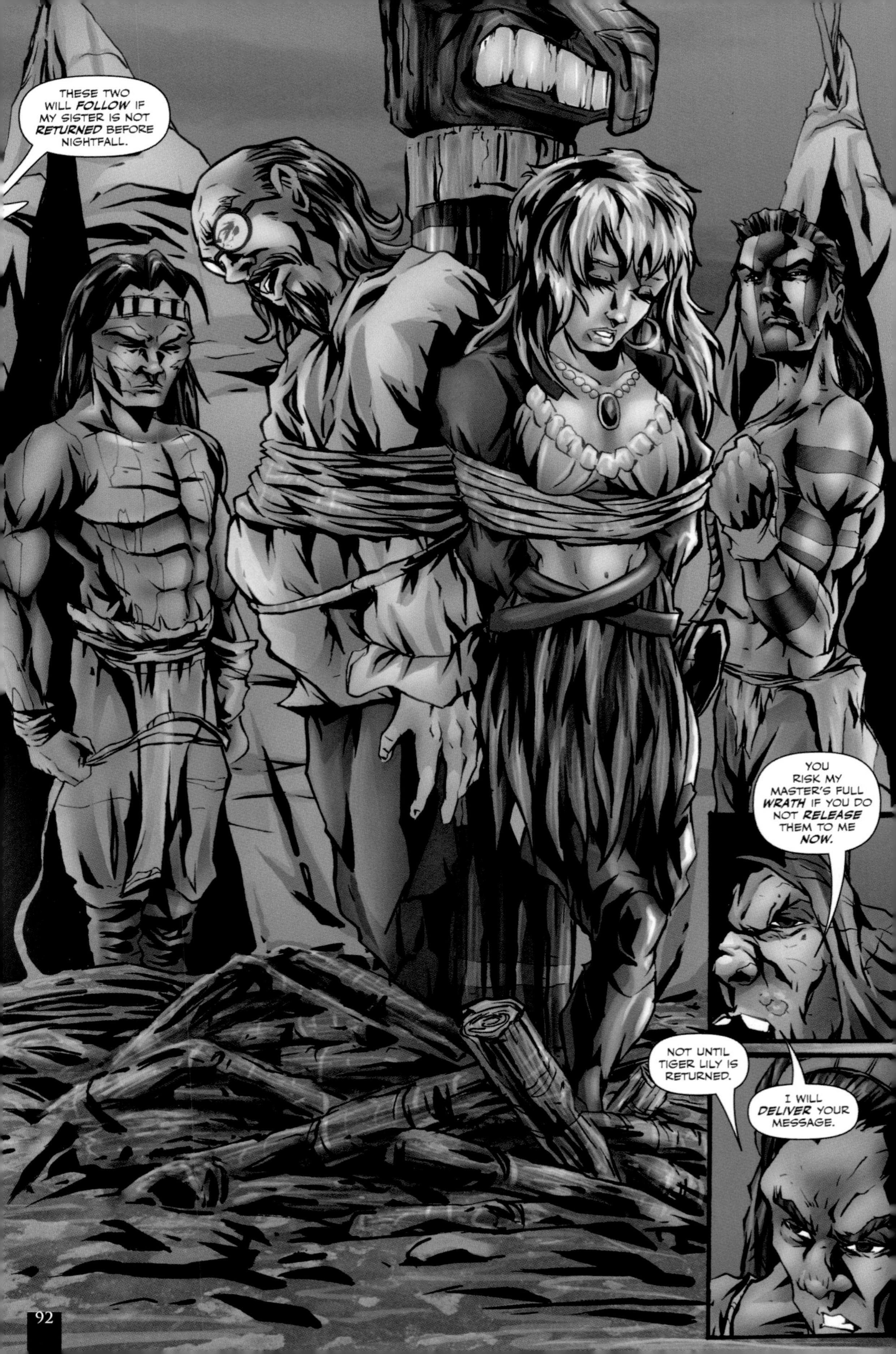
THESE TWO WILL FOLLOW IF MY SISTER IS NOT RETURNED BEFORE NIGHTFALL.
YOU RISK MY MASTER'S FULL WRATH IF YOU DO NOT RELEASE THEM TO ME NOW.
NOT UNTIL TIGER LILY IS RETURNED.
I WILL DELIVER YOUR MESSAGE.

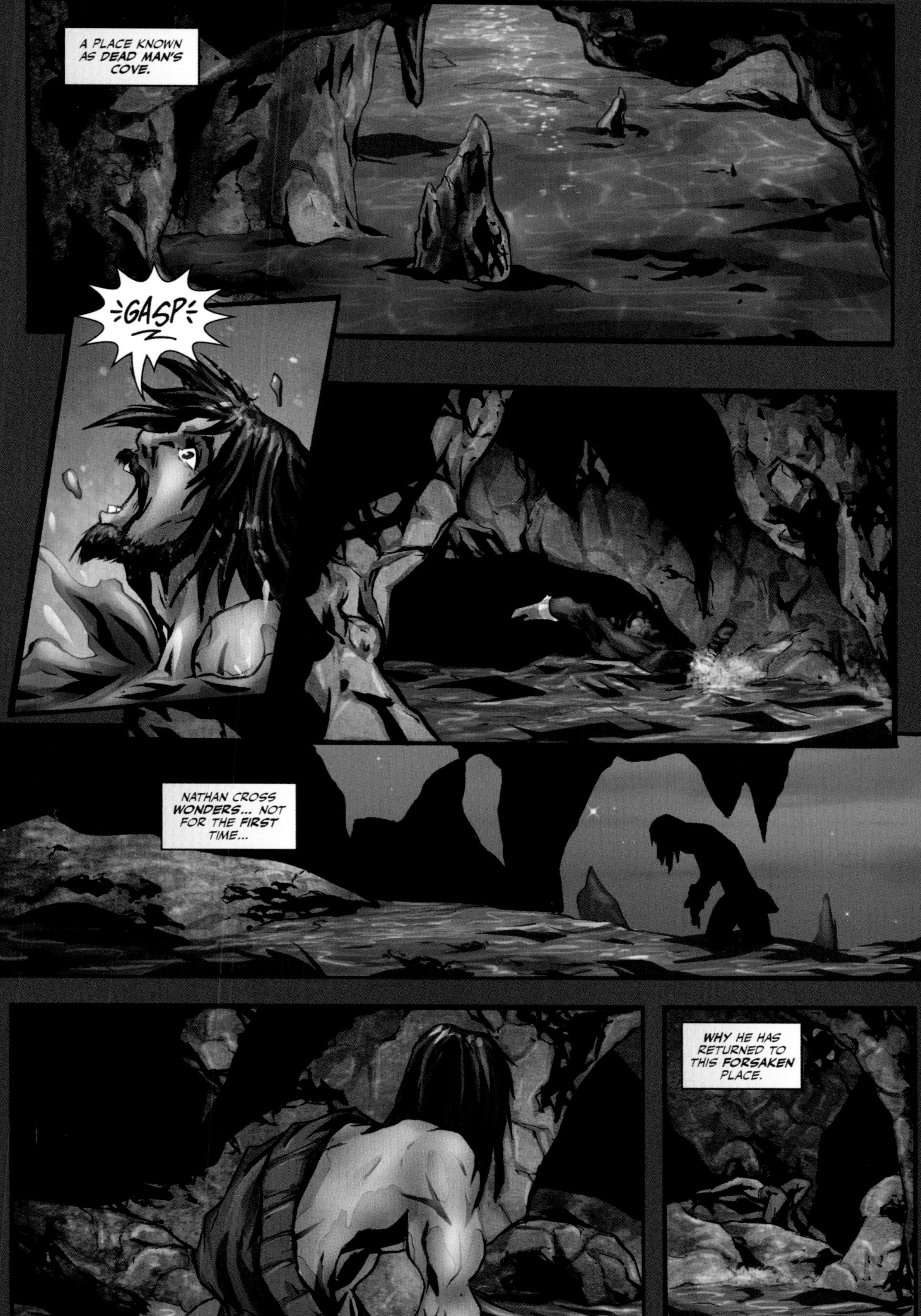
A PLACE KNOWN AS DEAD MAN'S COVE.
GASP
NATHAN CROSS WONDERS... NOT FOR THE FIRST TIME...
WHY HE HAS RETURNED TO THIS FORSAKEN PLACE.

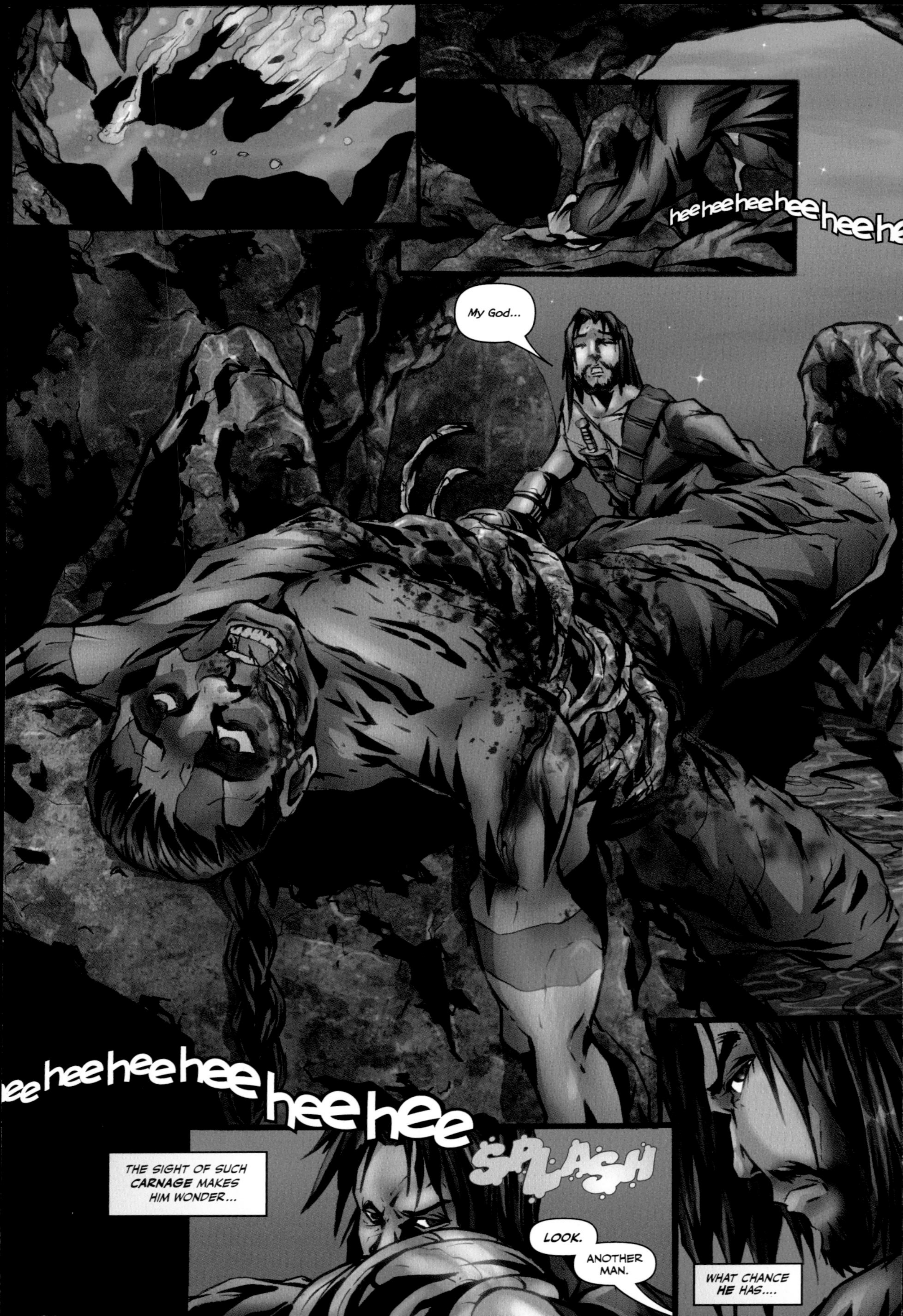
heeheeheeheeheehe
My God...
eeheeheeheeheehee
SPLASH
THE SIGHT OF SUCH CARNAGE MAKES HIM WONDER...
LOOK.
ANOTHER MAN.
WHAT CHANCE HE HAS....

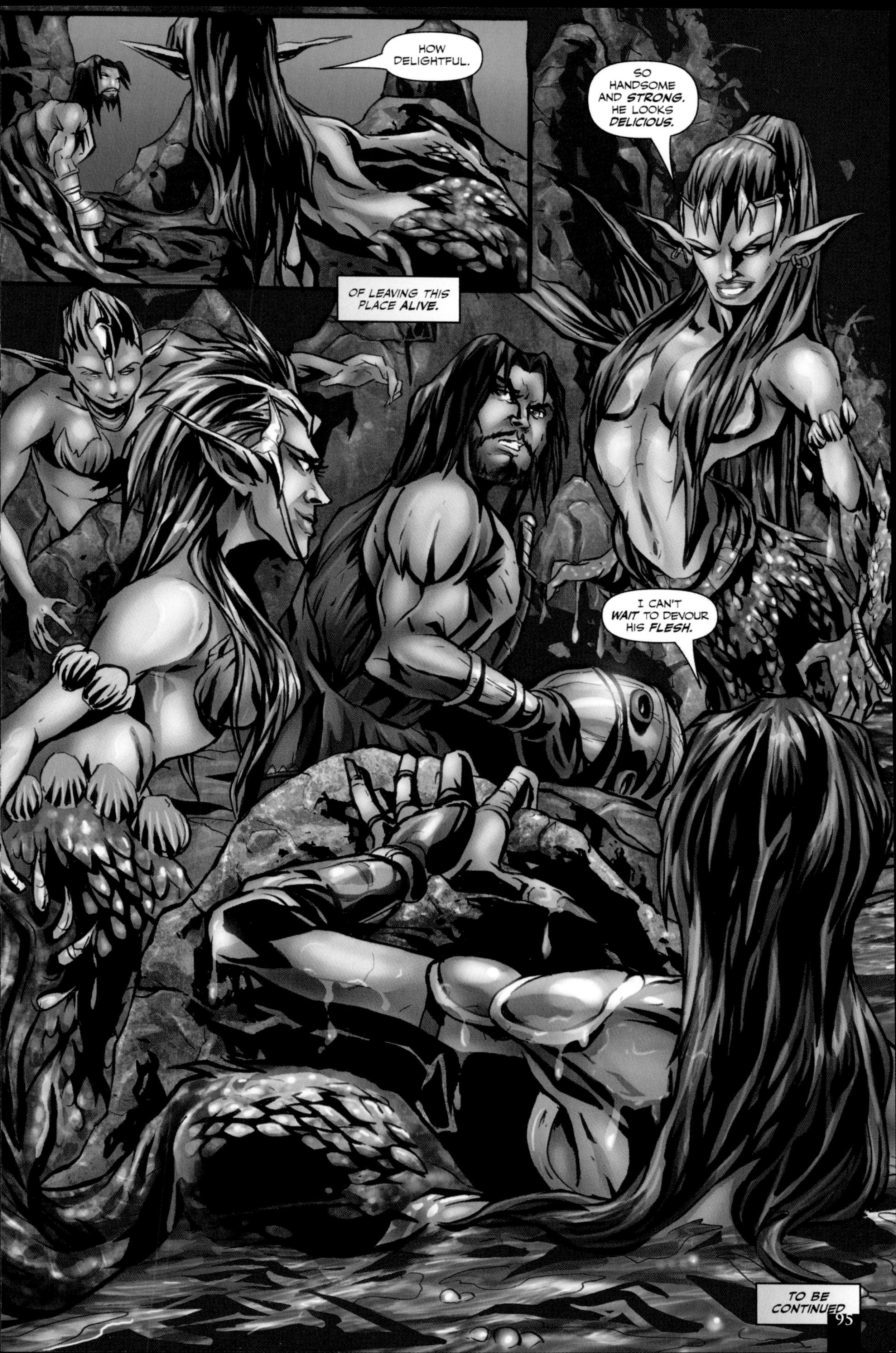
HOW DELIGHTFUL.
SO HANDSOME AND STRONG. HE LOOKS DELICIOUS.
OF LEAVING THIS PLACE ALIVE.
I CAN'T WAIT TO DEVOUR HIS FLESH.
TO BE CONTINUED

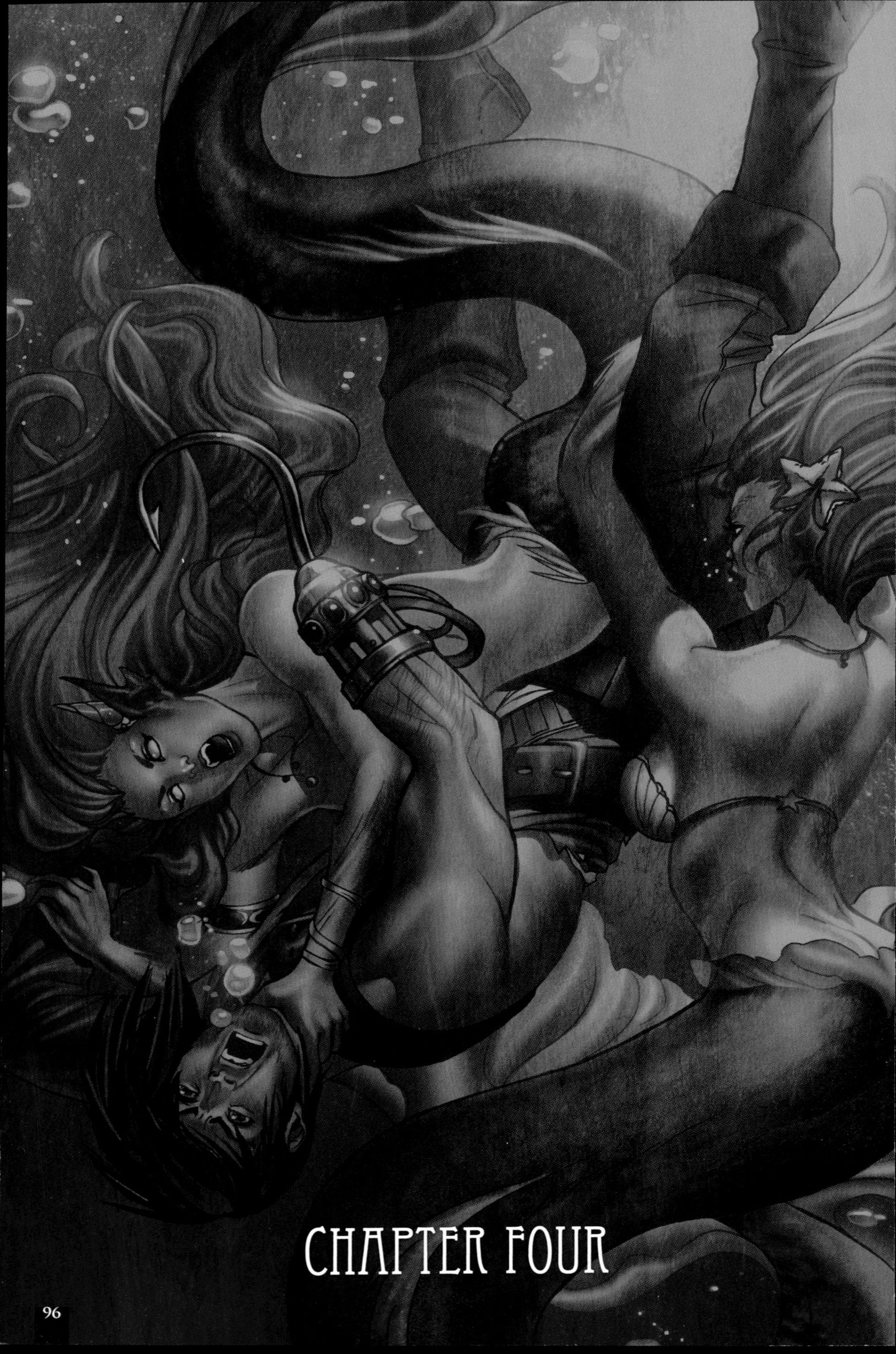

CHAPTER FOUR

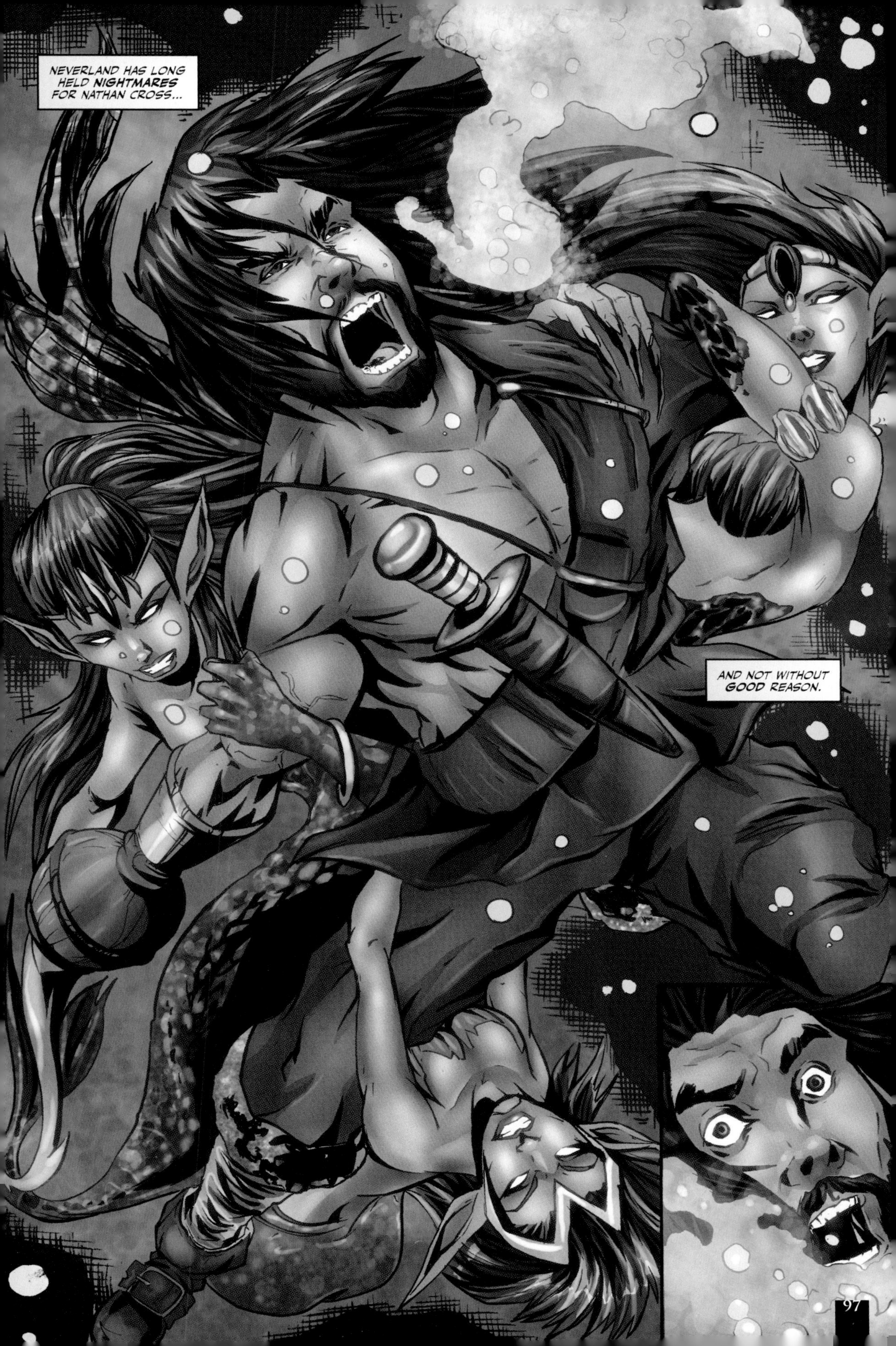
NEVERLAND HAS LONG HELD NIGHTMARES FOR NATHAN CROSS...
AND NOT WITHOUT GOOD REASON.

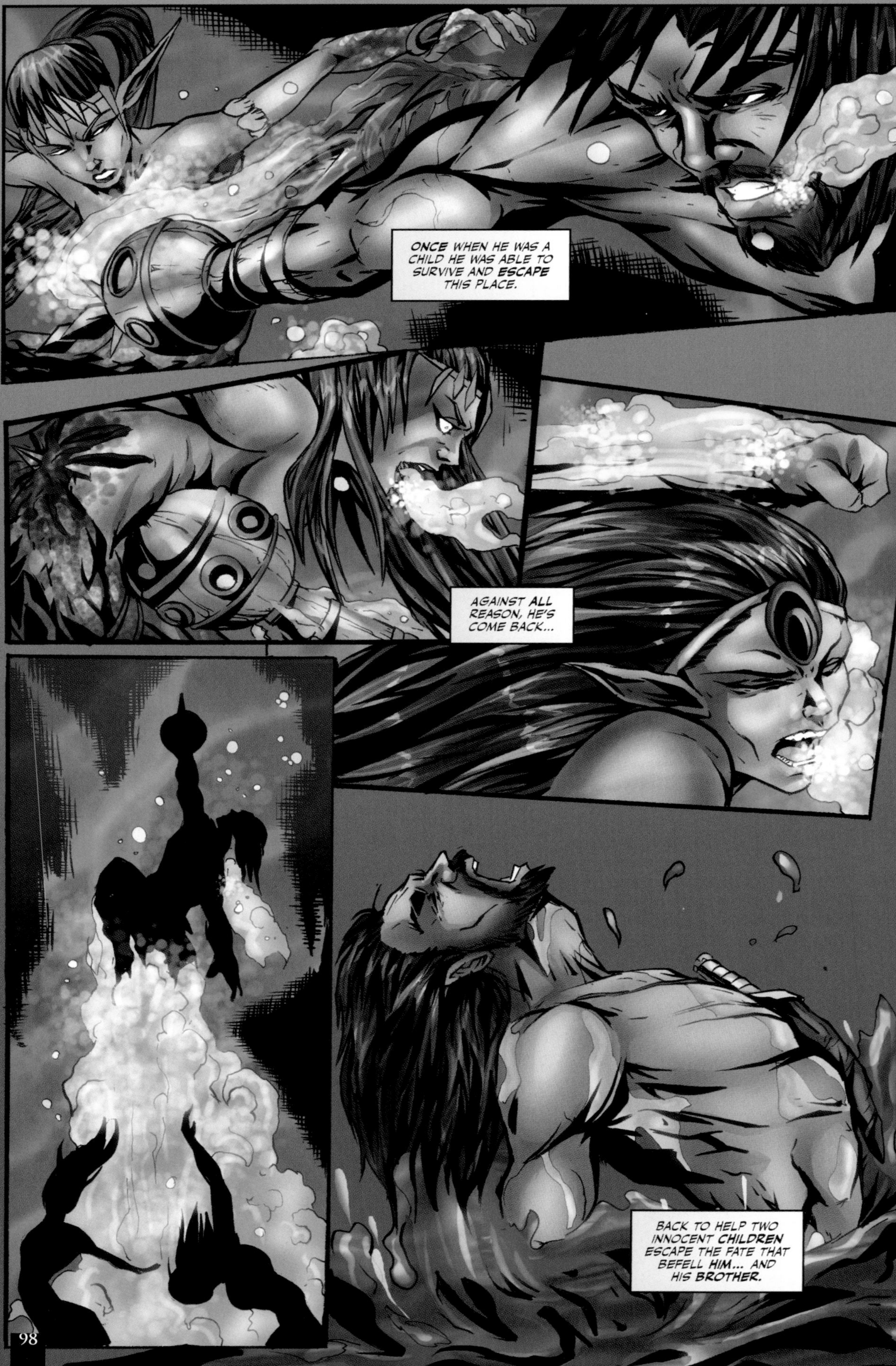
ONCE WHEN HE WAS A CHILD HE WAS ABLE TO SURVIVE AND ESCAPE THIS PLACE.
AGAINST ALL REASON, HE'S COME BACK...
BACK TO HELP TWO INNOCENT CHILDREN ESCAPE THE FATE THAT BEFELL HIM... AND HIS BROTHER.

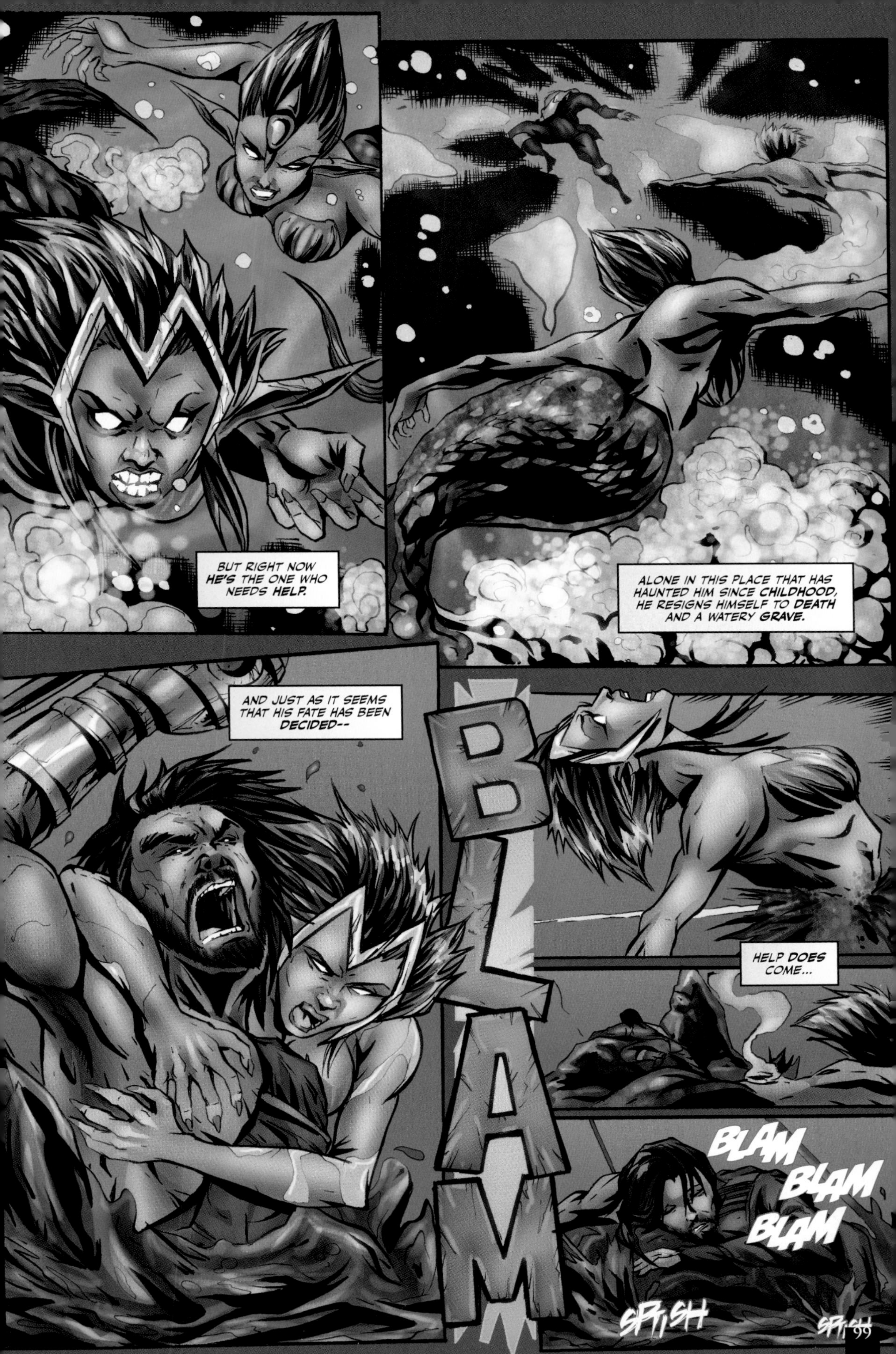
BUT RIGHT NOW HE'S THE ONE WHO NEEDS HELP.
ALONE IN THIS PLACE THAT HAS HAUNTED HIM SINCE CHILDHOOD, HE RESIGNS HIMSELF TO DEATH AND A WATERY GRAVE.
AND JUST AS IT SEEMS THAT HIS FATE HAS BEEN DECIDED--
BLAM
HELP DOES COME...
BLAM
BLAM
BLAM
SPLISH
SPLISH

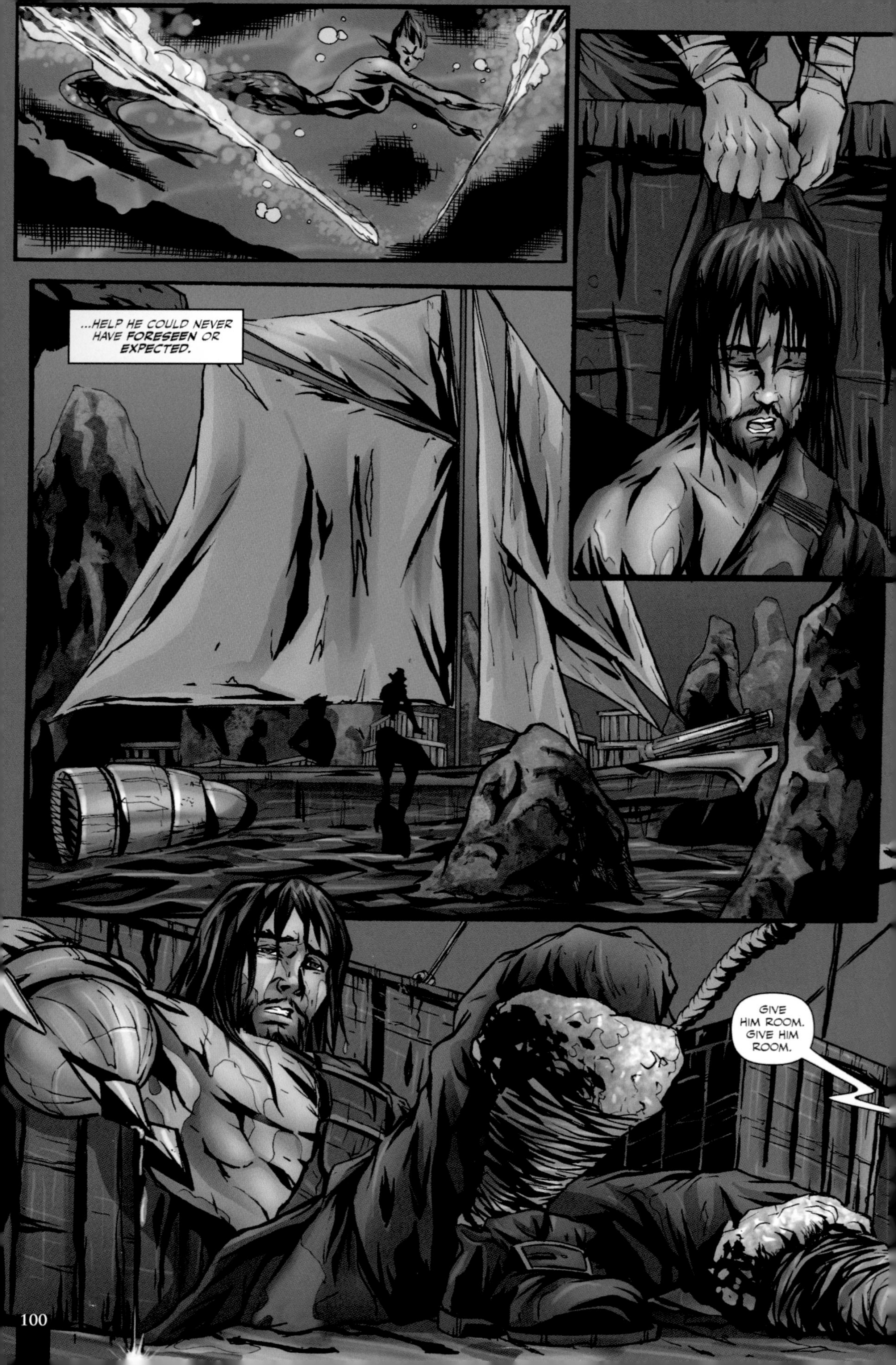
...HELP HE COULD NEVER HAVE FORESEEN OR EXPECTED.
GIVE HIM ROOM. GIVE HIM ROOM.

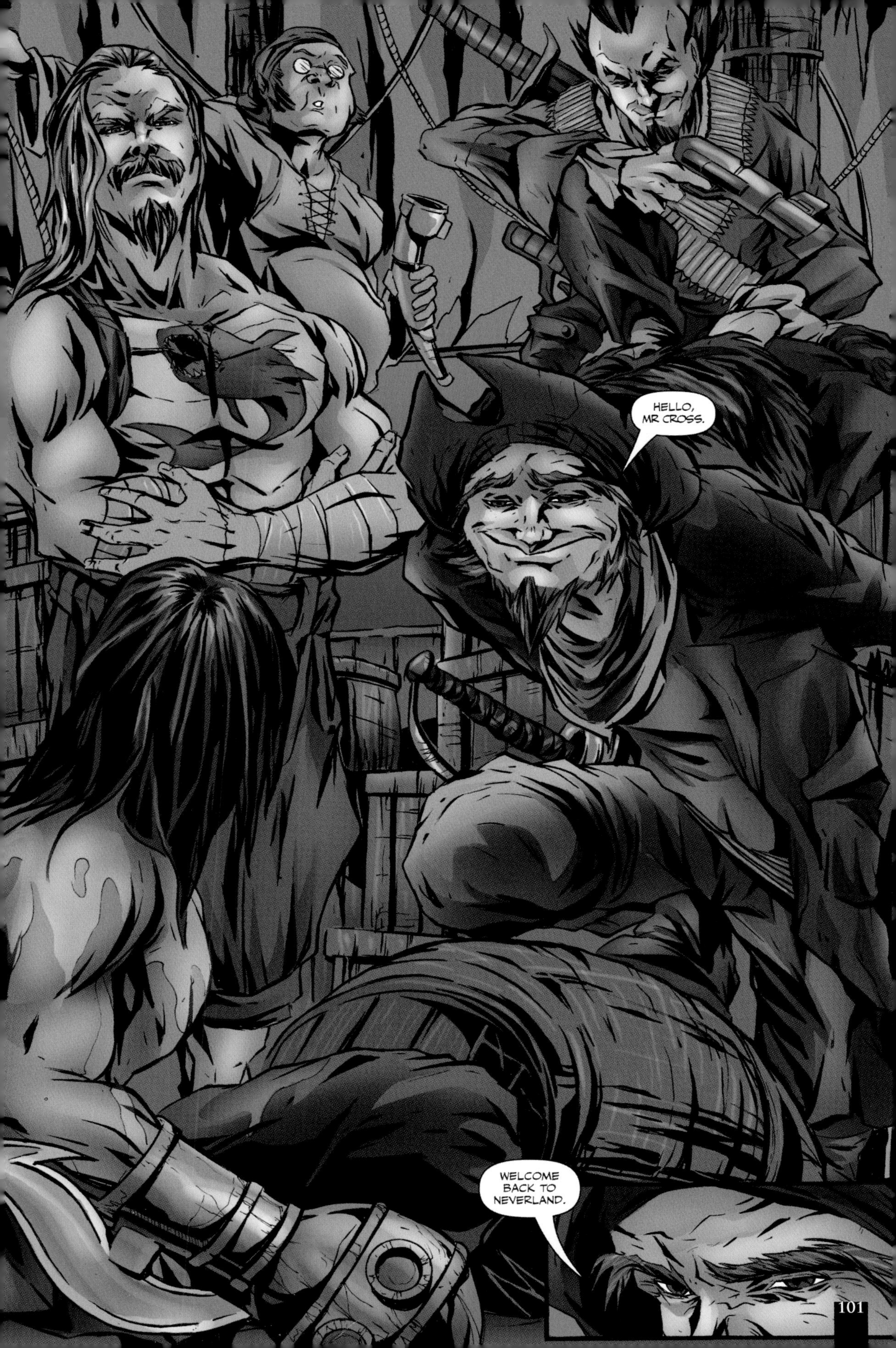
HELLO, MR CROSS.
WELCOME BACK TO NEVERLAND.

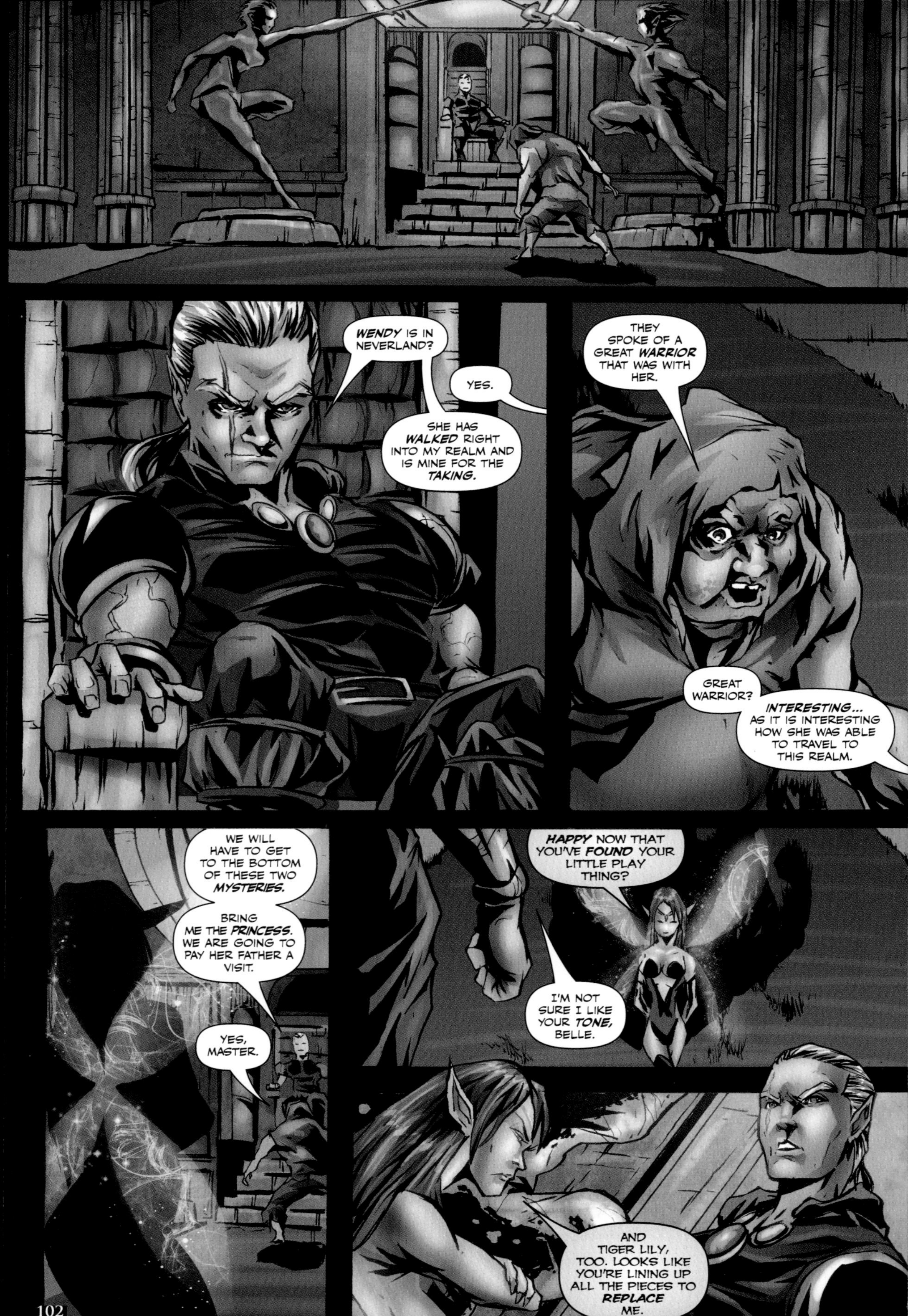
WENDY IS IN NEVERLAND?
YES.
SHE HAS WALKED RIGHT INTO MY REALM AND IS MINE FOR THE TAKING.
THEY SPOKE OF A GREAT WARRIOR THAT WAS WITH HER.
GREAT WARRIOR?
INTERESTING... AS IT IS INTERESTING HOW SHE WAS ABLE TO TRAVEL TO THIS REALM.
WE WILL HAVE TO GET TO THE BOTTOM OF THESE TWO MYSTERIES.
BRING ME THE PRINCESS. WE ARE GOING TO PAY HER FATHER A VISIT.
YES, MASTER.
HAPPY NOW THAT YOU'VE FOUND YOUR LITTLE PLAY THING?
I'M NOT SURE I LIKE YOUR TONE, BELLE.
AND TIGER LILY, TOO. LOOKS LIKE YOU'RE LINING UP ALL THE PIECES TO REPLACE ME.

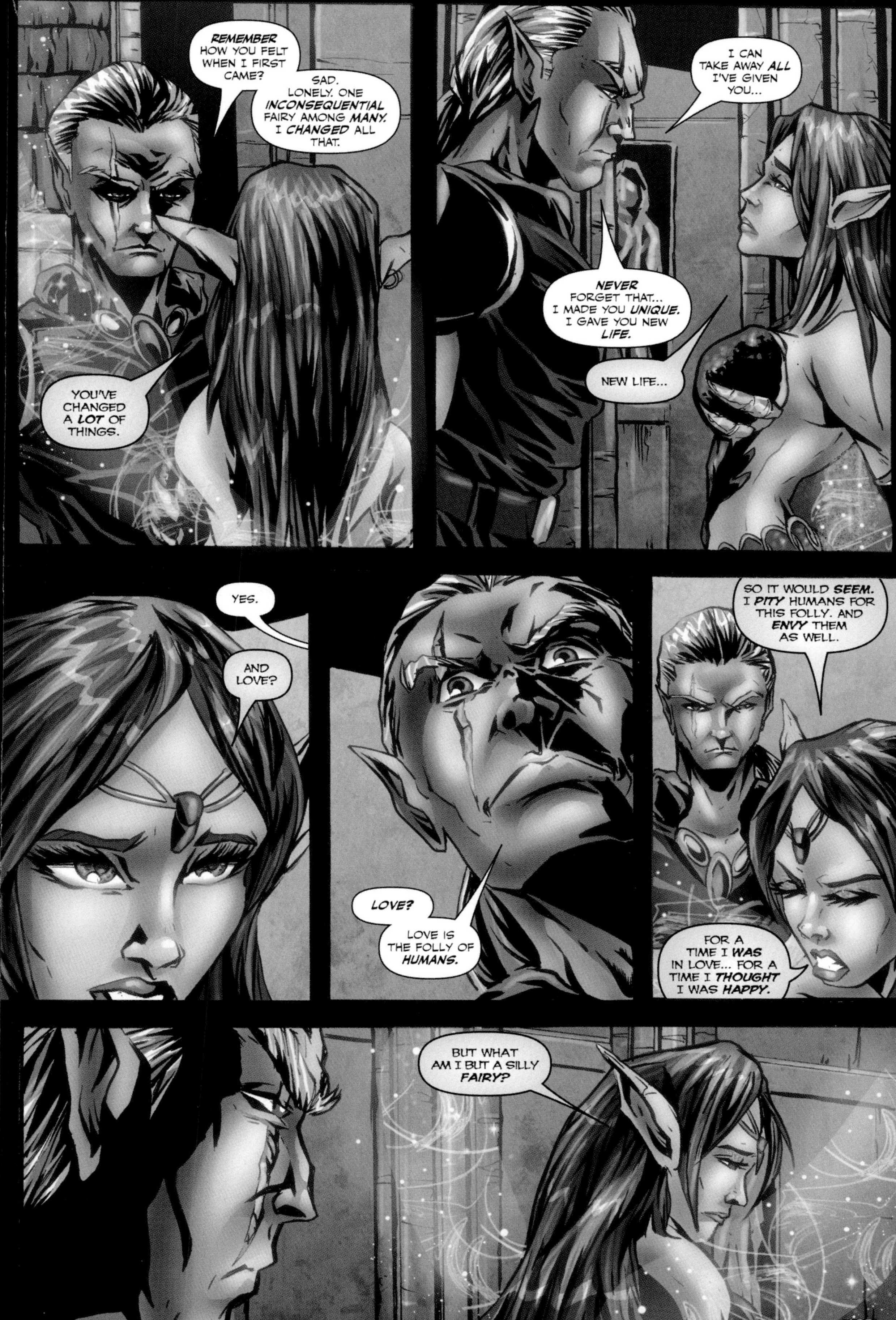
REMEMBER HOW YOU FELT WHEN I FIRST CAME?
SAD. LONELY. ONE INCONSEQUENTIAL FAIRY AMONG MANY. I CHANGED ALL THAT.
YOU'VE CHANGED A LOT OF THINGS.
I CAN TAKE AWAY ALL I'VE GIVEN YOU...
NEVER FORGET THAT... I MADE YOU UNIQUE. I GAVE YOU NEW LIFE.
NEW LIFE...
YES.
AND LOVE?
LOVE?
LOVE IS THE FOLLY OF HUMANS.
SO IT WOULD SEEM. I PITY HUMANS FOR THIS FOLLY. AND ENVY THEM AS WELL.
FOR A TIME I WAS IN LOVE... FOR A TIME I THOUGHT I WAS HAPPY.
BUT WHAT AM I BUT A SILLY FAIRY?

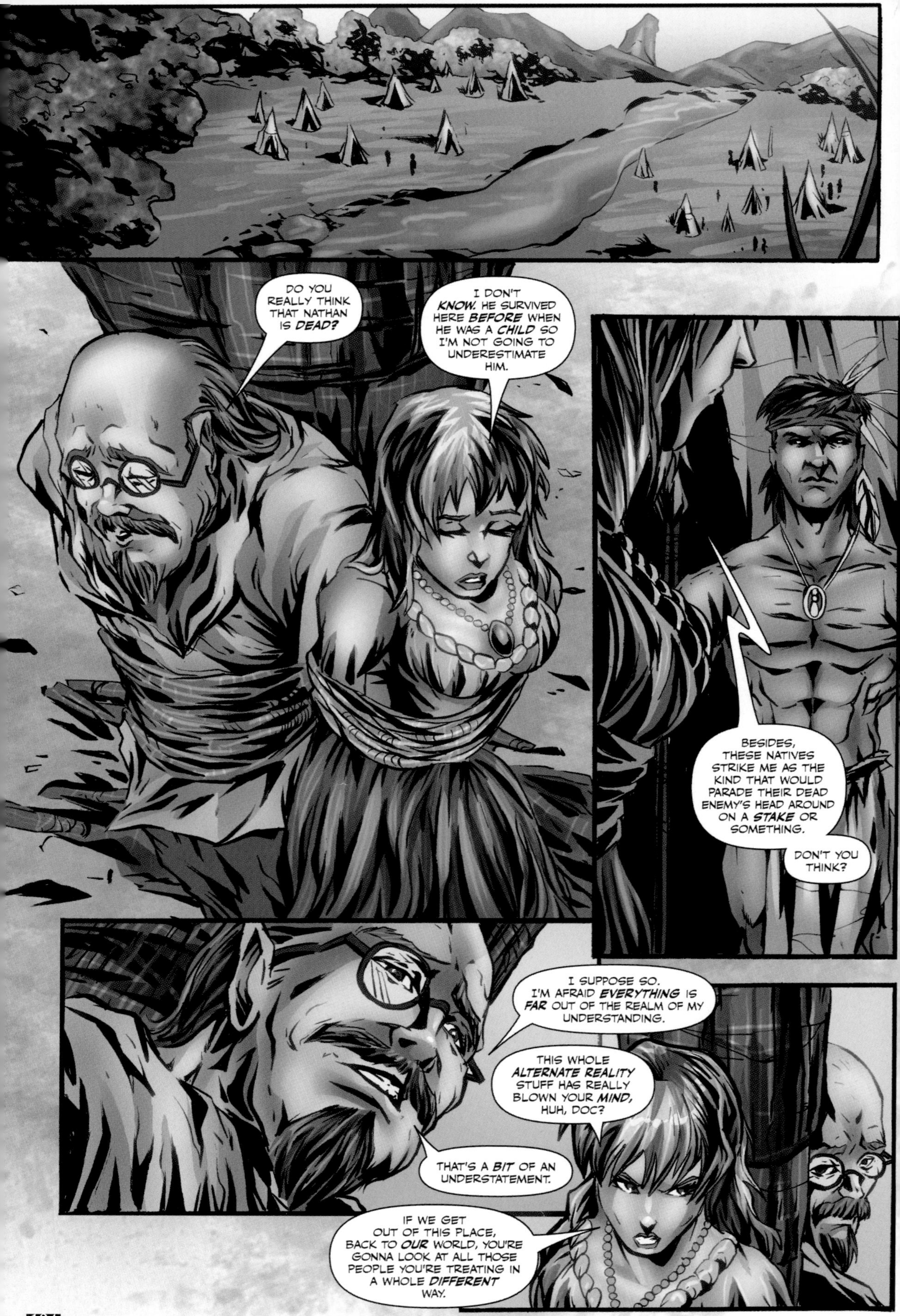
DO YOU REALLY THINK THAT NATHAN IS *DEAD?*
I DON'T *KNOW.* HE SURVIVED HERE *BEFORE* WHEN HE WAS A *CHILD* SO I'M NOT GOING TO UNDERESTIMATE HIM.
BESIDES, THESE NATIVES STRIKE ME AS THE KIND THAT WOULD PARADE THEIR DEAD ENEMY'S HEAD AROUND ON A *STAKE* OR SOMETHING.
DON'T YOU THINK?
I SUPPOSE SO. I'M AFRAID *EVERYTHING* IS *FAR* OUT OF THE REALM OF MY UNDERSTANDING.
THIS WHOLE *ALTERNATE REALITY* STUFF HAS REALLY BLOWN YOUR *MIND,* HUH, DOC?
THAT'S A *BIT* OF AN UNDERSTATEMENT.
IF WE GET OUT OF THIS PLACE, BACK TO *OUR* WORLD, YOU'RE GONNA LOOK AT ALL THOSE PEOPLE YOU'RE TREATING IN A WHOLE *DIFFERENT* WAY.

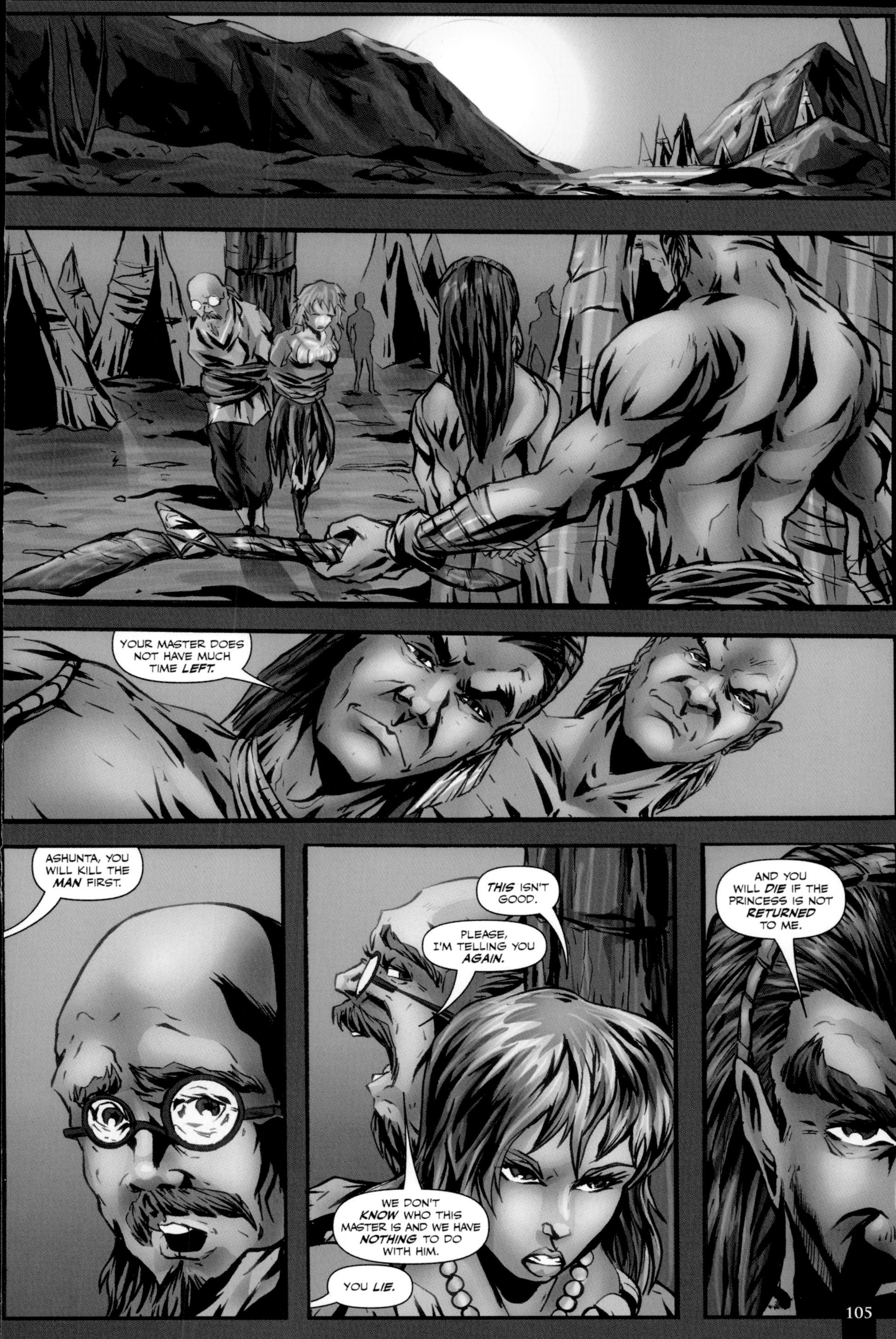

YOUR MASTER DOES NOT HAVE MUCH TIME *LEFT.*
ASHUNTA, YOU WILL KILL THE *MAN* FIRST.
THIS ISN'T GOOD.
PLEASE, I'M TELLING YOU *AGAIN.*
WE DON'T *KNOW* WHO THIS MASTER IS AND WE HAVE *NOTHING* TO DO WITH HIM.
YOU *LIE.*
AND YOU WILL *DIE* IF THE PRINCESS IS NOT *RETURNED* TO ME.

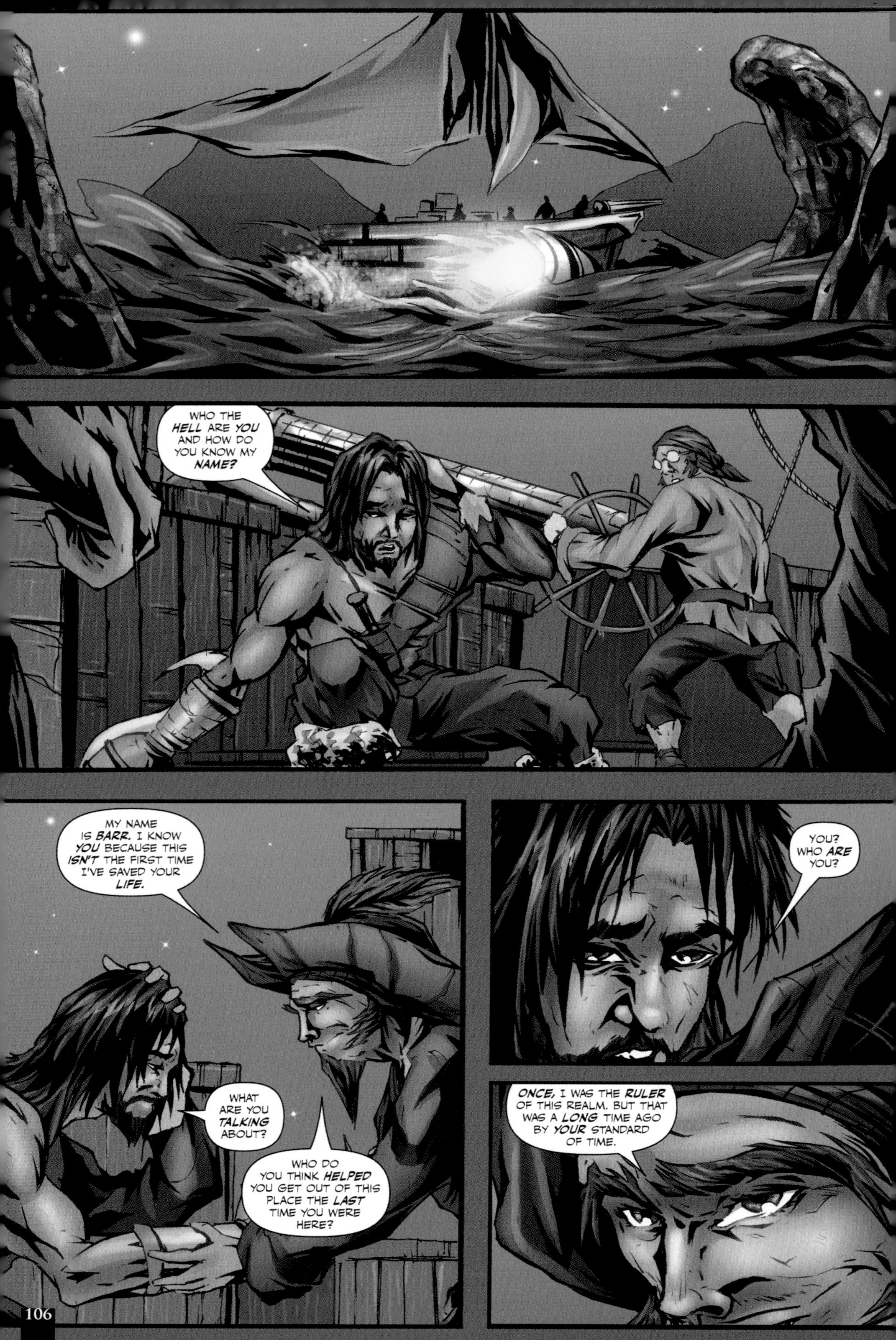

WHO THE HELL ARE YOU AND HOW DO YOU KNOW MY NAME?
MY NAME IS BARR. I KNOW YOU BECAUSE THIS ISN'T THE FIRST TIME I'VE SAVED YOUR LIFE.
WHAT ARE YOU TALKING ABOUT?
WHO DO YOU THINK HELPED YOU GET OUT OF THIS PLACE THE LAST TIME YOU WERE HERE?
YOU? WHO ARE YOU?
ONCE, I WAS THE RULER OF THIS REALM. BUT THAT WAS A LONG TIME AGO BY YOUR STANDARD OF TIME.

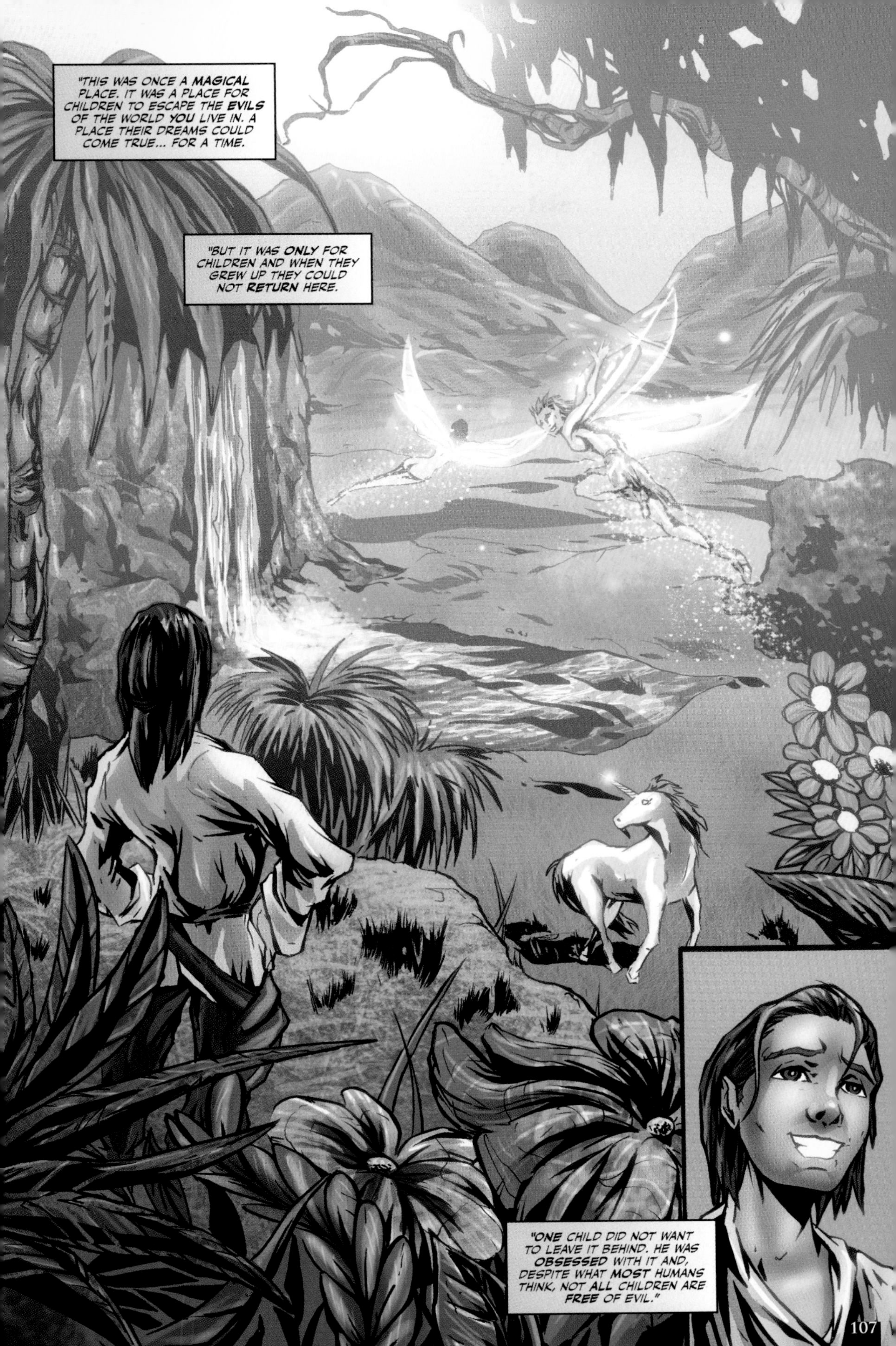
"THIS WAS ONCE A MAGICAL PLACE. IT WAS A PLACE FOR CHILDREN TO ESCAPE THE EVILS OF THE WORLD YOU LIVE IN. A PLACE THEIR DREAMS COULD COME TRUE... FOR A TIME.
"BUT IT WAS ONLY FOR CHILDREN AND WHEN THEY GREW UP THEY COULD NOT RETURN HERE.
"ONE CHILD DID NOT WANT TO LEAVE IT BEHIND. HE WAS OBSESSED WITH IT AND, DESPITE WHAT MOST HUMANS THINK, NOT ALL CHILDREN ARE FREE OF EVIL."

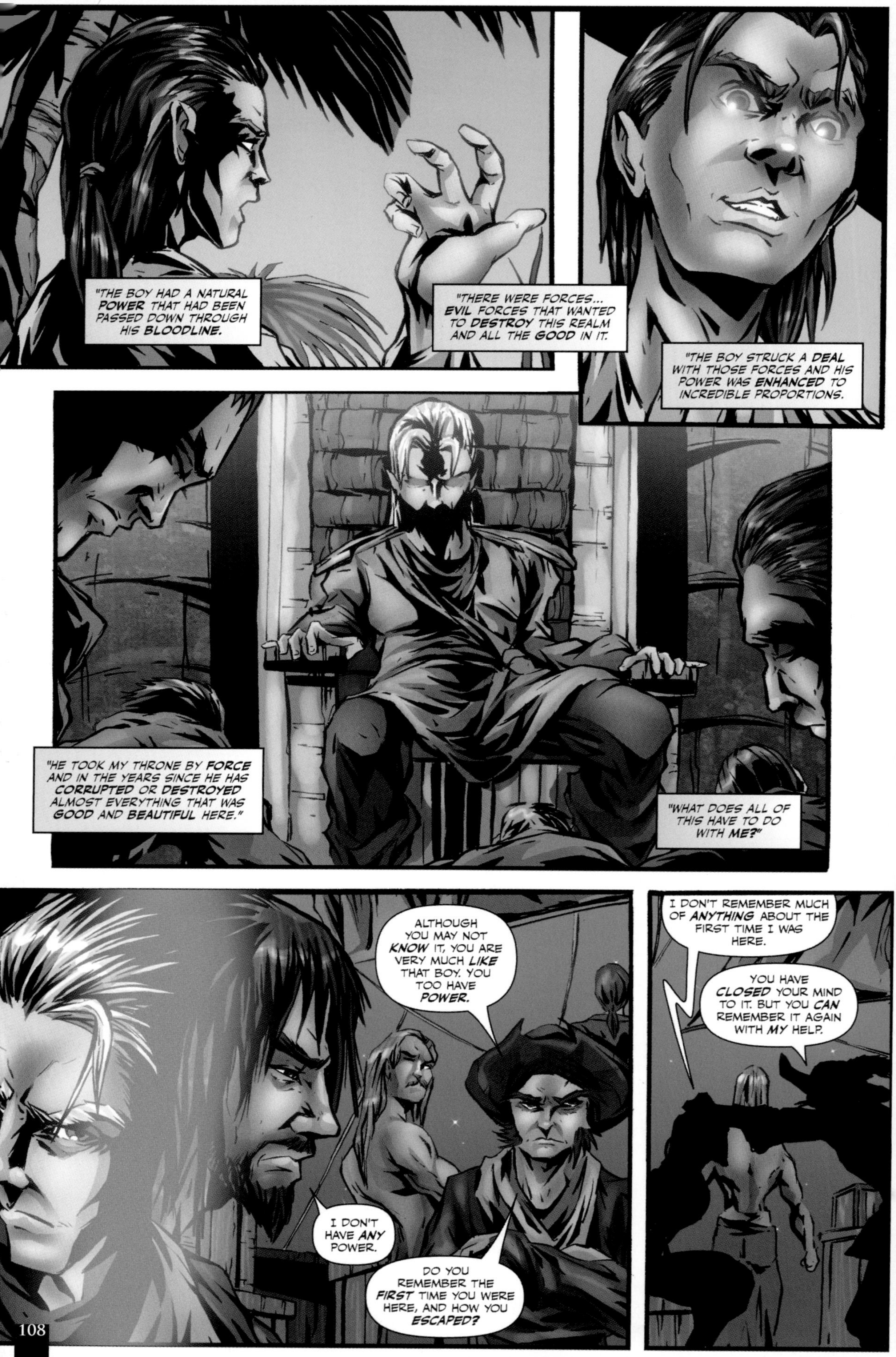
"THE BOY HAD A NATURAL POWER THAT HAD BEEN PASSED DOWN THROUGH HIS BLOODLINE.
"THERE WERE FORCES... EVIL FORCES THAT WANTED TO DESTROY THIS REALM AND ALL THE GOOD IN IT.
"THE BOY STRUCK A DEAL WITH THOSE FORCES AND HIS POWER WAS ENHANCED TO INCREDIBLE PROPORTIONS.
"HE TOOK MY THRONE BY FORCE AND IN THE YEARS SINCE HE HAS CORRUPTED OR DESTROYED ALMOST EVERYTHING THAT WAS GOOD AND BEAUTIFUL HERE."
"WHAT DOES ALL OF THIS HAVE TO DO WITH ME?"
ALTHOUGH YOU MAY NOT KNOW IT, YOU ARE VERY MUCH LIKE THAT BOY. YOU TOO HAVE POWER.
I DON'T HAVE ANY POWER.
DO YOU REMEMBER THE FIRST TIME YOU WERE HERE, AND HOW YOU ESCAPED?
I DON'T REMEMBER MUCH OF ANYTHING ABOUT THE FIRST TIME I WAS HERE.
YOU HAVE CLOSED YOUR MIND TO IT. BUT YOU CAN REMEMBER IT AGAIN WITH MY HELP.

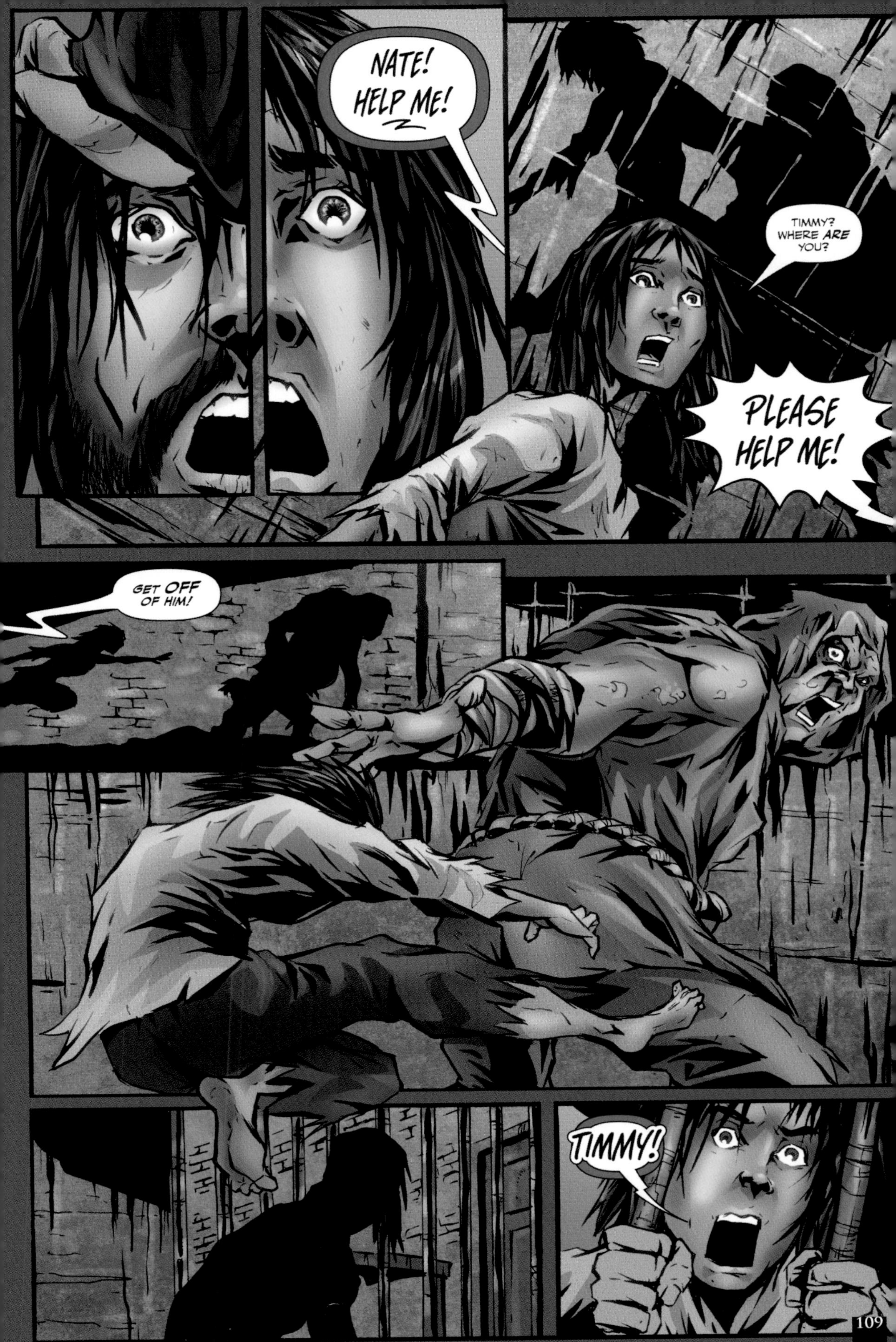
NATE! HELP ME!
TIMMY? WHERE ARE YOU?
PLEASE HELP ME!
GET OFF OF HIM!
TIMMY!

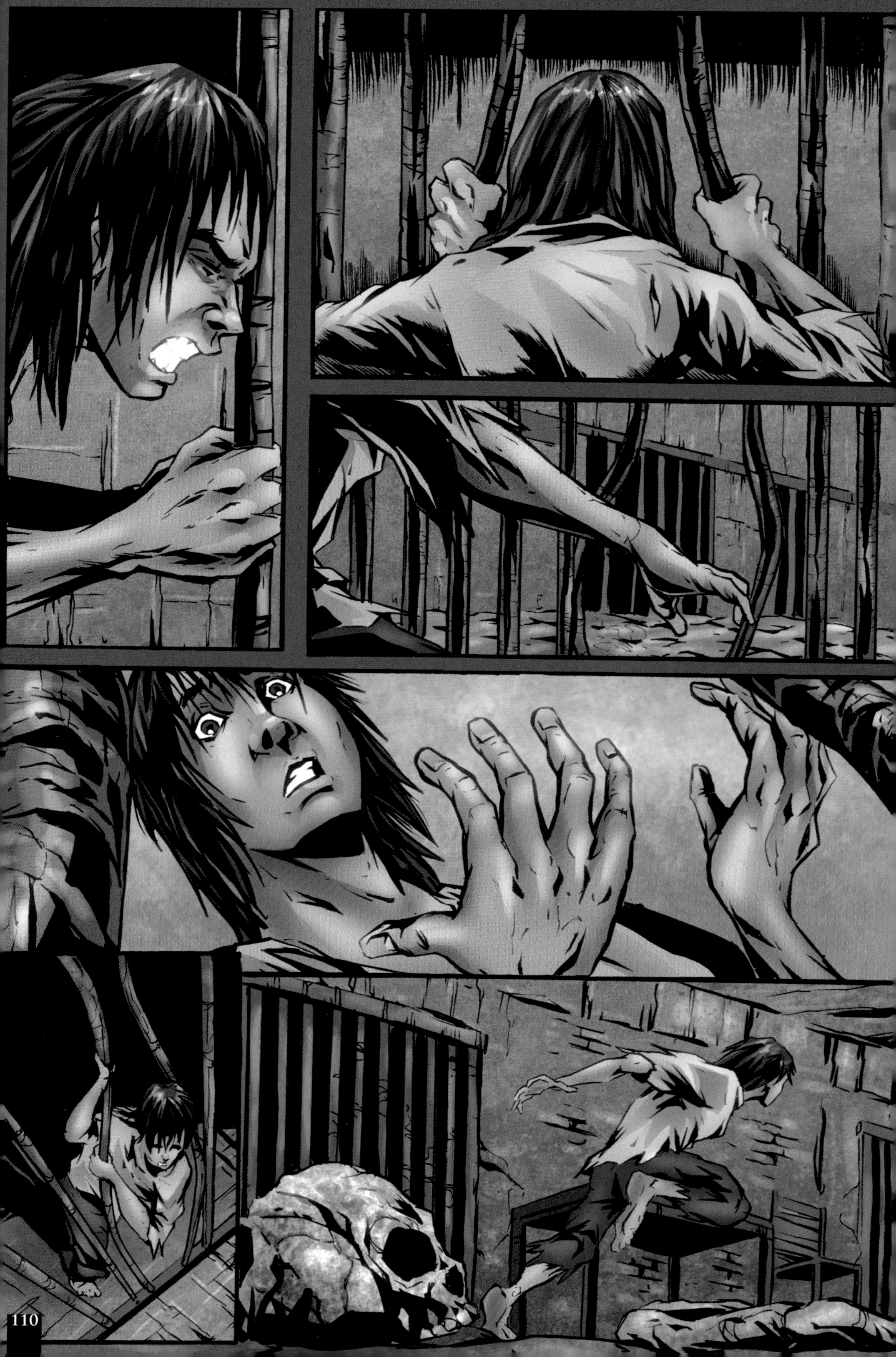

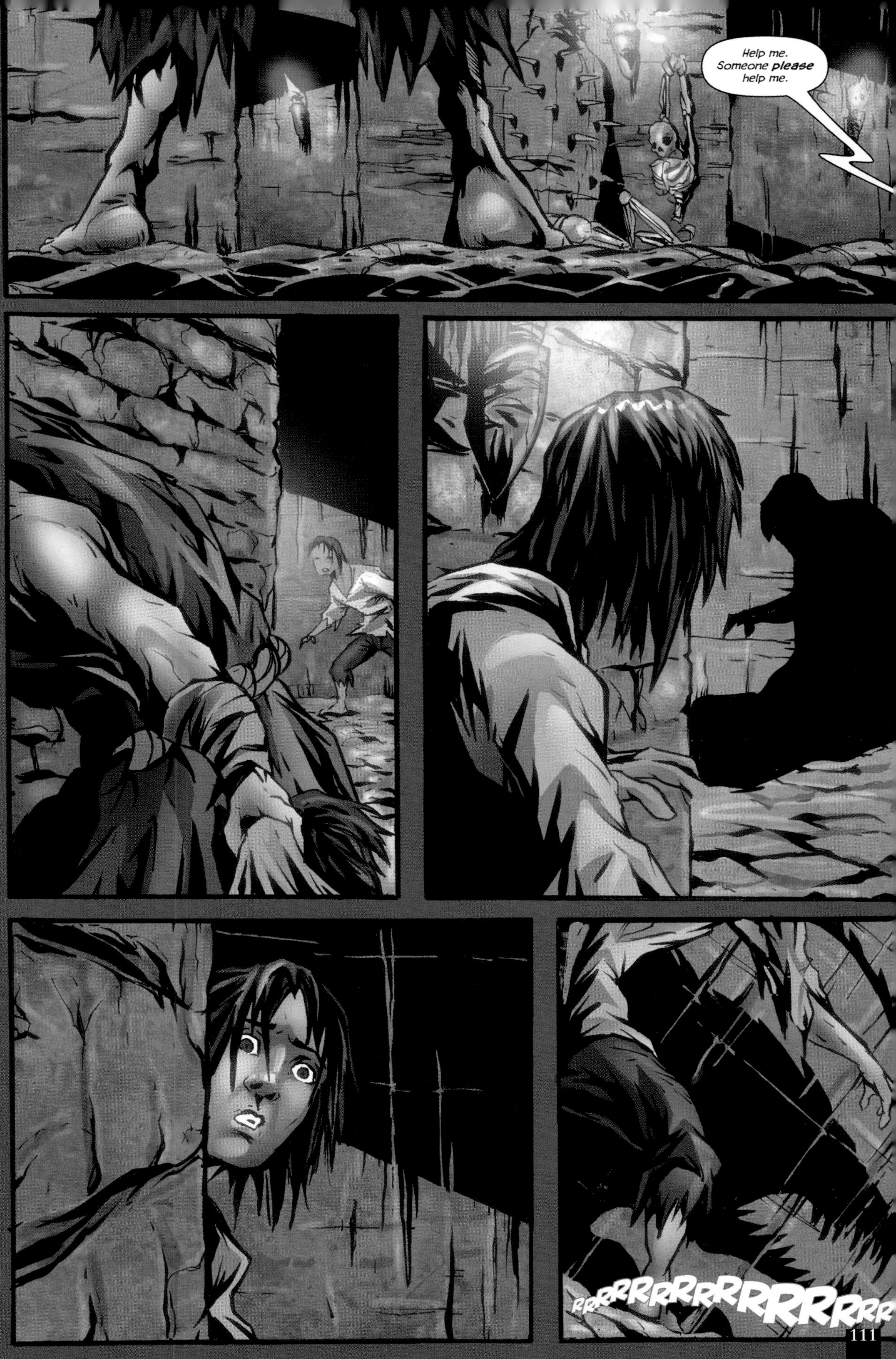

Help me. Someone **please** help me.
RRRRRRRRRRRRRRRRR

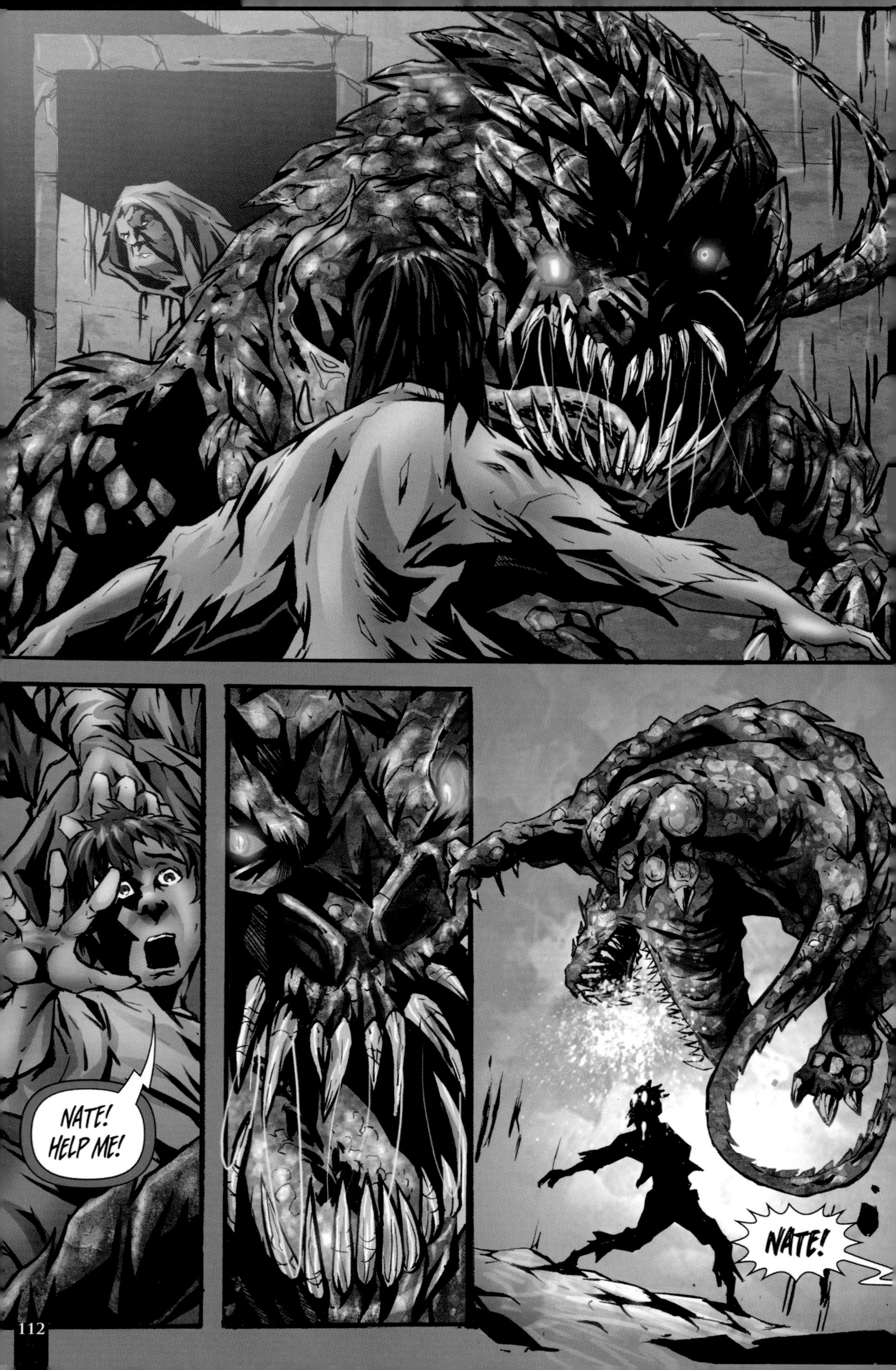
NATE!
HELP ME!
NATE!

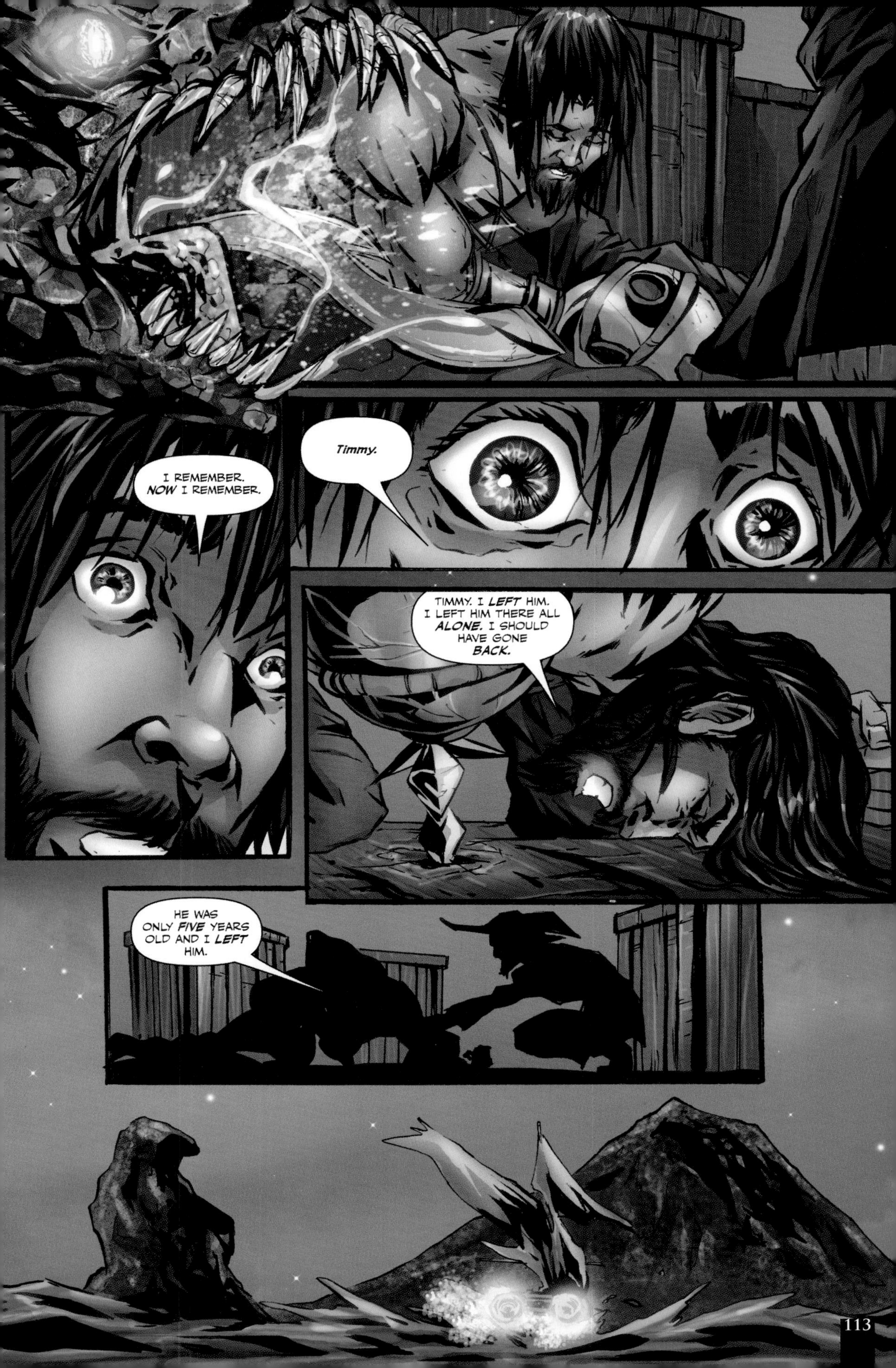
I REMEMBER. NOW I REMEMBER.
Timmy.
TIMMY. I LEFT HIM. I LEFT HIM THERE ALL ALONE. I SHOULD HAVE GONE BACK.
HE WAS ONLY FIVE YEARS OLD AND I LEFT HIM.

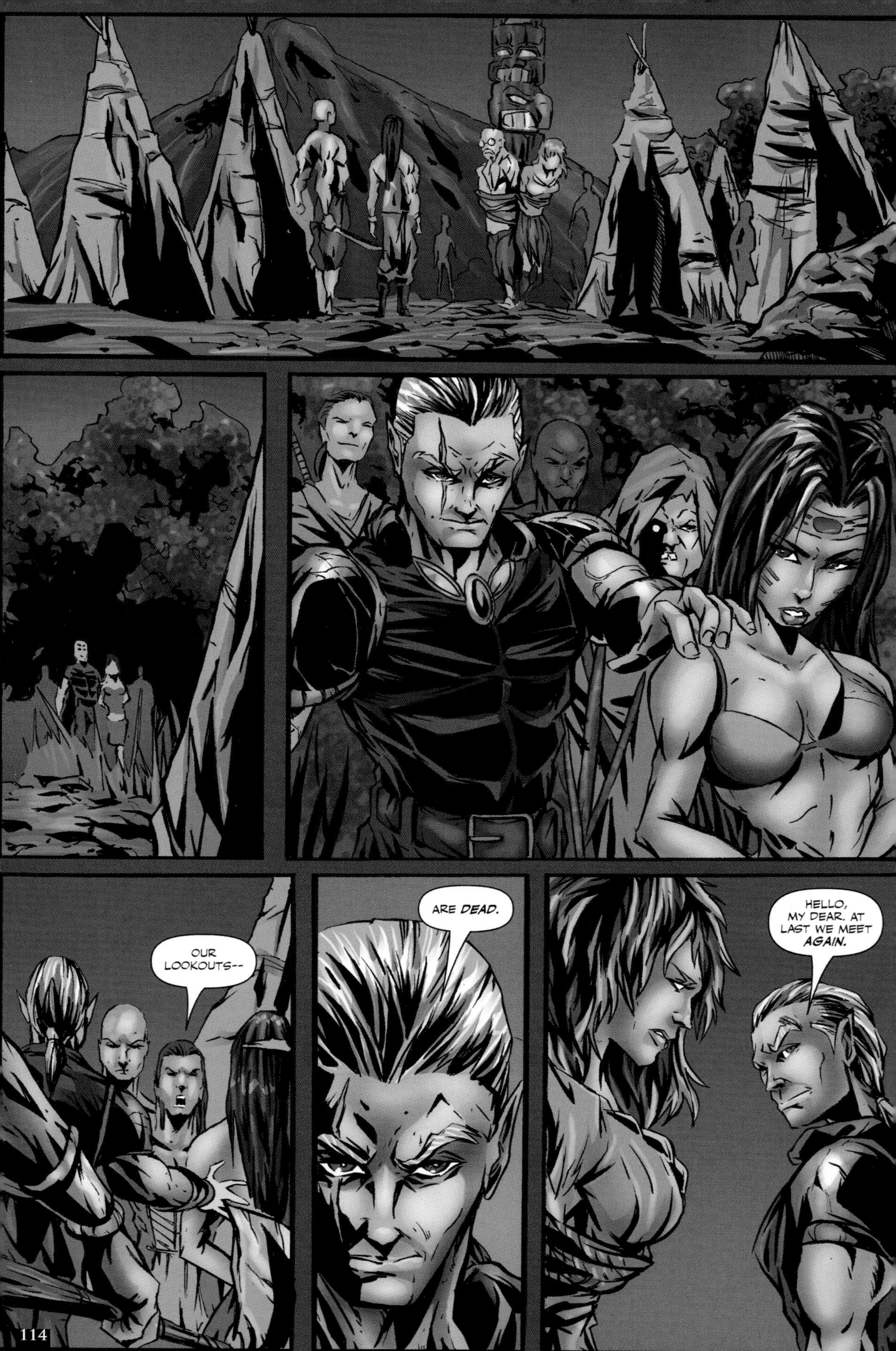
OUR LOOKOUTS--
ARE DEAD.
HELLO, MY DEAR. AT LAST WE MEET AGAIN.

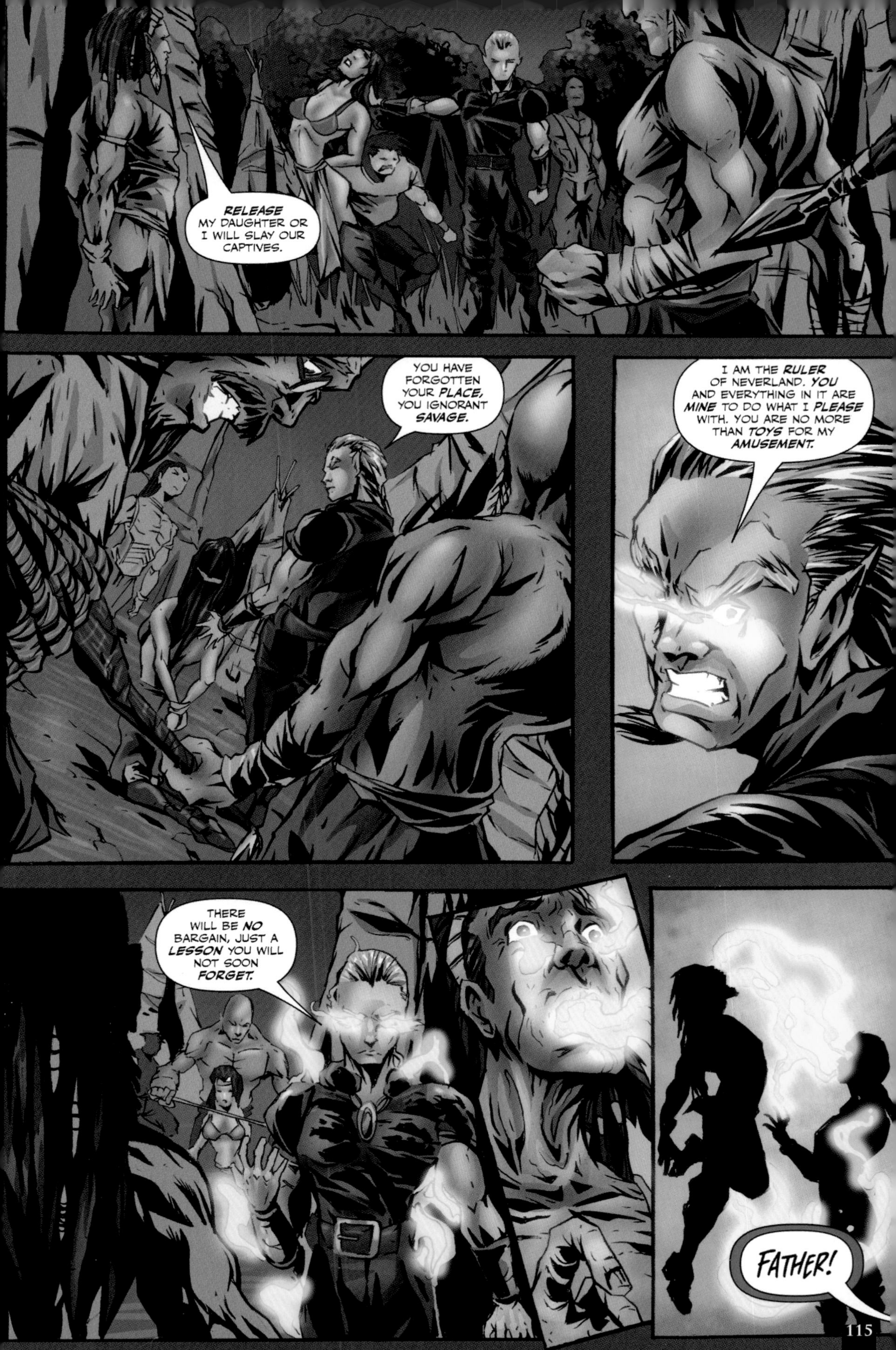
RELEASE MY DAUGHTER OR I WILL SLAY OUR CAPTIVES.
YOU HAVE FORGOTTEN YOUR PLACE, YOU IGNORANT SAVAGE.
I AM THE RULER OF NEVERLAND. YOU AND EVERYTHING IN IT ARE MINE TO DO WHAT I PLEASE WITH. YOU ARE NO MORE THAN TOYS FOR MY AMUSEMENT.
THERE WILL BE NO BARGAIN, JUST A LESSON YOU WILL NOT SOON FORGET.
FATHER!

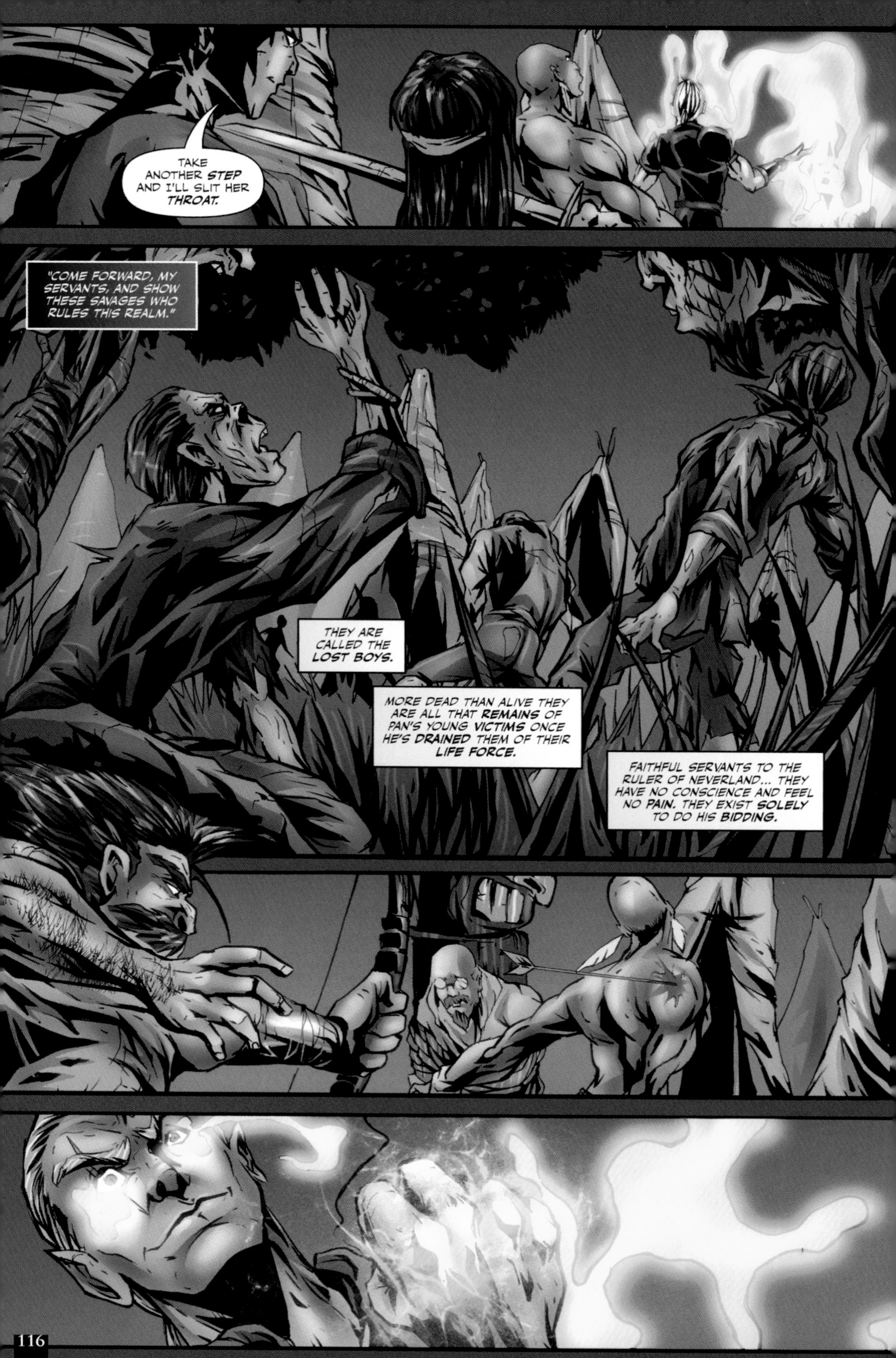
TAKE ANOTHER STEP AND I'LL SLIT HER THROAT.
"COME FORWARD, MY SERVANTS, AND SHOW THESE SAVAGES WHO RULES THIS REALM."
THEY ARE CALLED THE LOST BOYS.
MORE DEAD THAN ALIVE THEY ARE ALL THAT REMAINS OF PAN'S YOUNG VICTIMS ONCE HE'S DRAINED THEM OF THEIR LIFE FORCE.
FAITHFUL SERVANTS TO THE RULER OF NEVERLAND... THEY HAVE NO CONSCIENCE AND FEEL NO PAIN. THEY EXIST SOLELY TO DO HIS BIDDING.

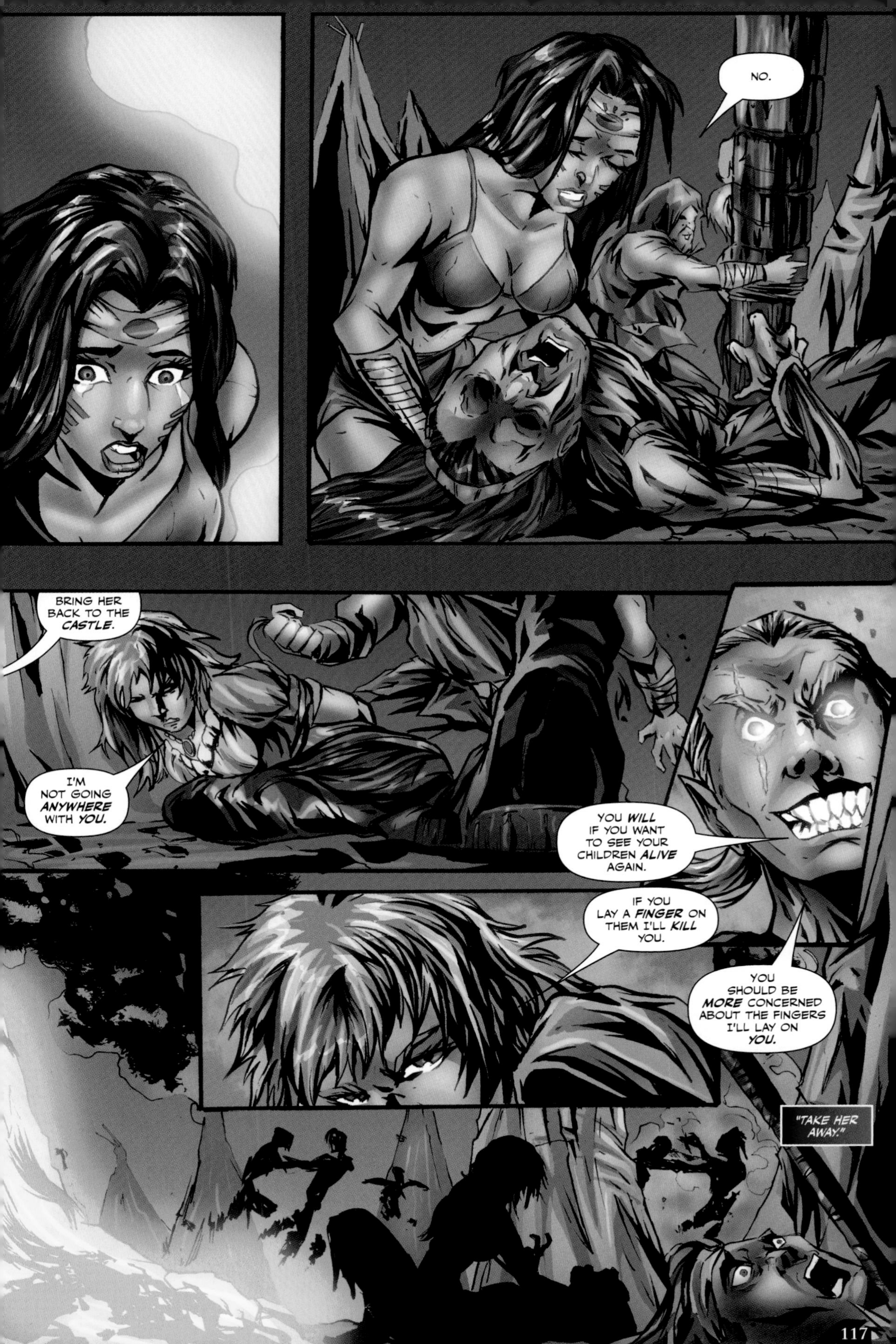
NO.
BRING HER BACK TO THE CASTLE.
I'M NOT GOING ANYWHERE WITH YOU.
YOU WILL IF YOU WANT TO SEE YOUR CHILDREN ALIVE AGAIN.
IF YOU LAY A FINGER ON THEM I'LL KILL YOU.
YOU SHOULD BE MORE CONCERNED ABOUT THE FINGERS I'LL LAY ON YOU.
"TAKE HER AWAY."

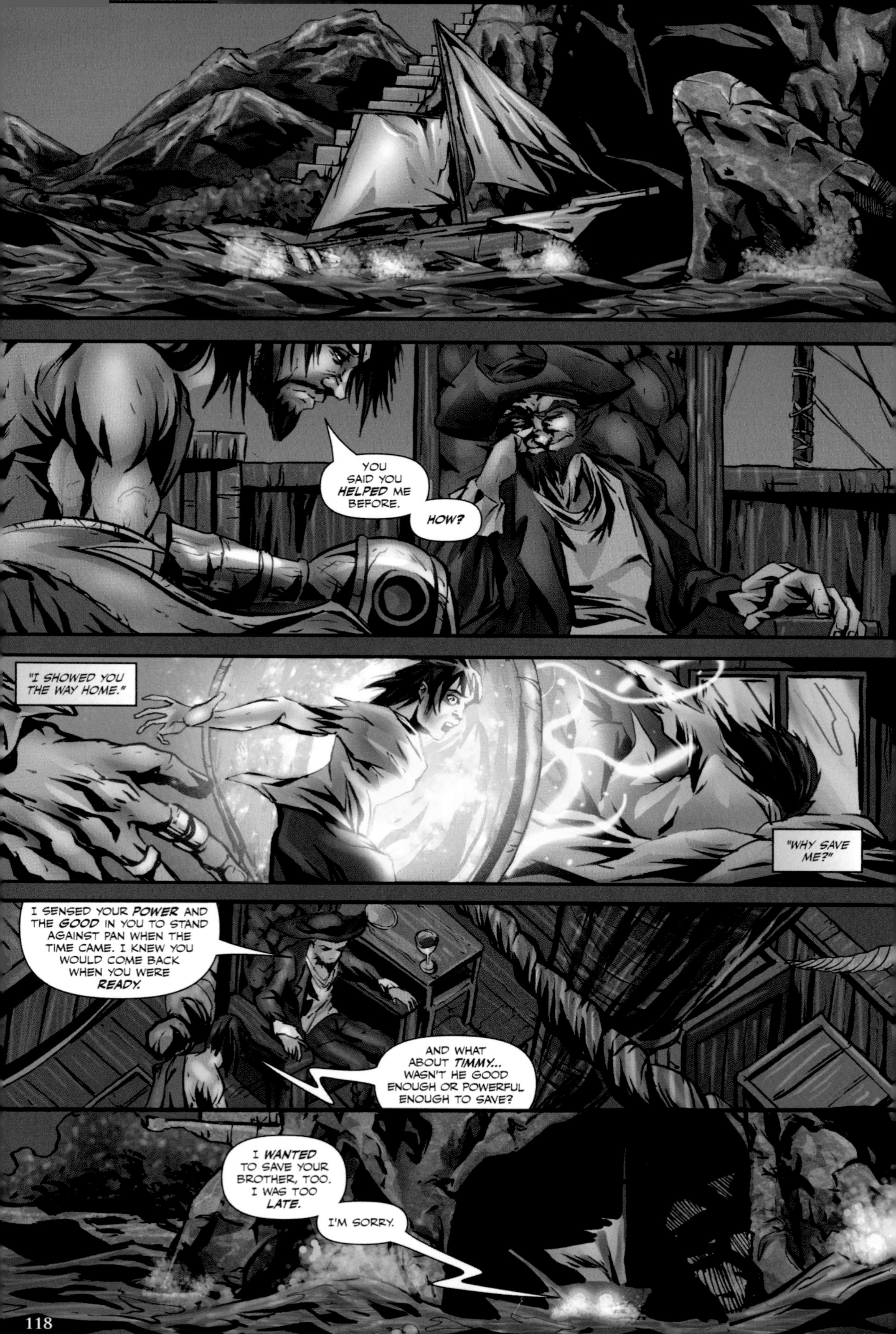
YOU SAID YOU HELPED ME BEFORE.
HOW?
"I SHOWED YOU THE WAY HOME."
"WHY SAVE ME?"
I SENSED YOUR POWER AND THE GOOD IN YOU TO STAND AGAINST PAN WHEN THE TIME CAME. I KNEW YOU WOULD COME BACK WHEN YOU WERE READY.
AND WHAT ABOUT TIMMY... WASN'T HE GOOD ENOUGH OR POWERFUL ENOUGH TO SAVE?
I WANTED TO SAVE YOUR BROTHER, TOO. I WAS TOO LATE.
I'M SORRY.

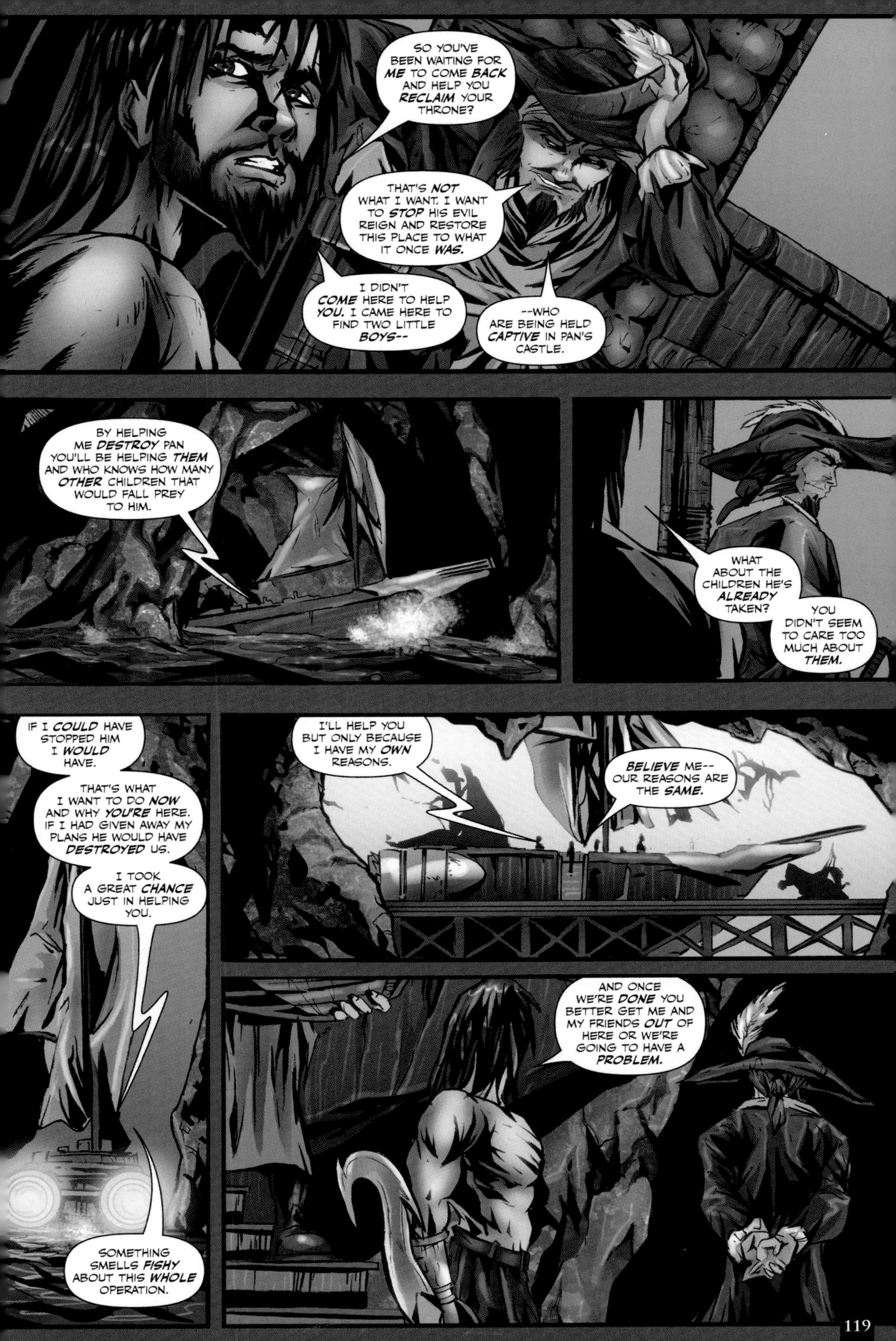
SO YOU'VE BEEN WAITING FOR ME TO COME BACK AND HELP YOU RECLAIM YOUR THRONE?
THAT'S NOT WHAT I WANT. I WANT TO STOP HIS EVIL REIGN AND RESTORE THIS PLACE TO WHAT IT ONCE WAS.
I DIDN'T COME HERE TO HELP YOU. I CAME HERE TO FIND TWO LITTLE BOYS--
--WHO ARE BEING HELD CAPTIVE IN PAN'S CASTLE.
BY HELPING ME DESTROY PAN YOU'LL BE HELPING THEM AND WHO KNOWS HOW MANY OTHER CHILDREN THAT WOULD FALL PREY TO HIM.
WHAT ABOUT THE CHILDREN HE'S ALREADY TAKEN?
YOU DIDN'T SEEM TO CARE TOO MUCH ABOUT THEM.
IF I COULD HAVE STOPPED HIM I WOULD HAVE.
THAT'S WHAT I WANT TO DO NOW AND WHY YOU'RE HERE. IF I HAD GIVEN AWAY MY PLANS HE WOULD HAVE DESTROYED US.
I TOOK A GREAT CHANCE JUST IN HELPING YOU.
SOMETHING SMELLS FISHY ABOUT THIS WHOLE OPERATION.
I'LL HELP YOU BUT ONLY BECAUSE I HAVE MY OWN REASONS.
BELIEVE ME-- OUR REASONS ARE THE SAME.
AND ONCE WE'RE DONE YOU BETTER GET ME AND MY FRIENDS OUT OF HERE OR WE'RE GOING TO HAVE A PROBLEM.

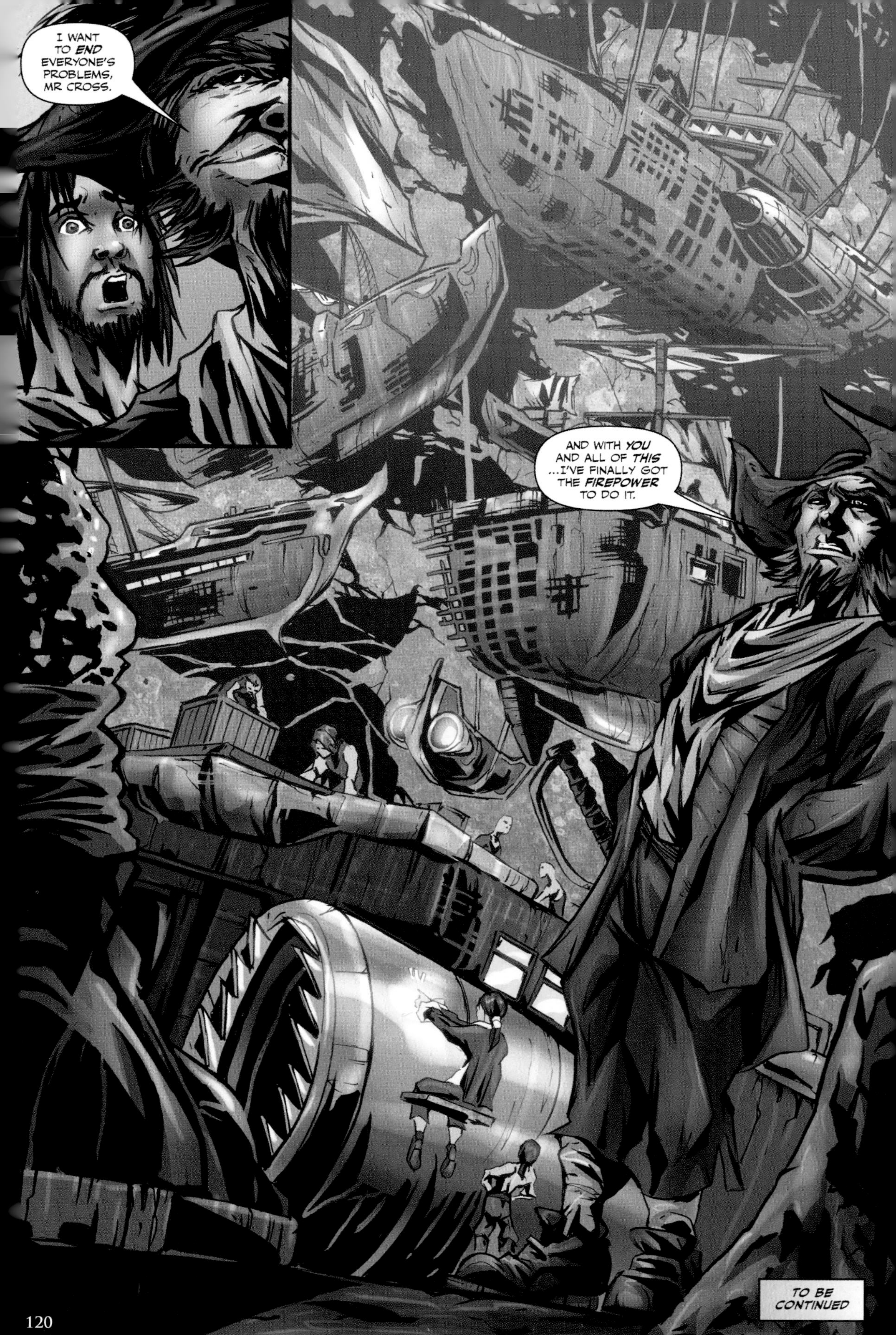
I WANT TO END EVERYONE'S PROBLEMS, MR CROSS.
AND WITH YOU AND ALL OF THIS ...I'VE FINALLY GOT THE FIREPOWER TO DO IT.
TO BE CONTINUED

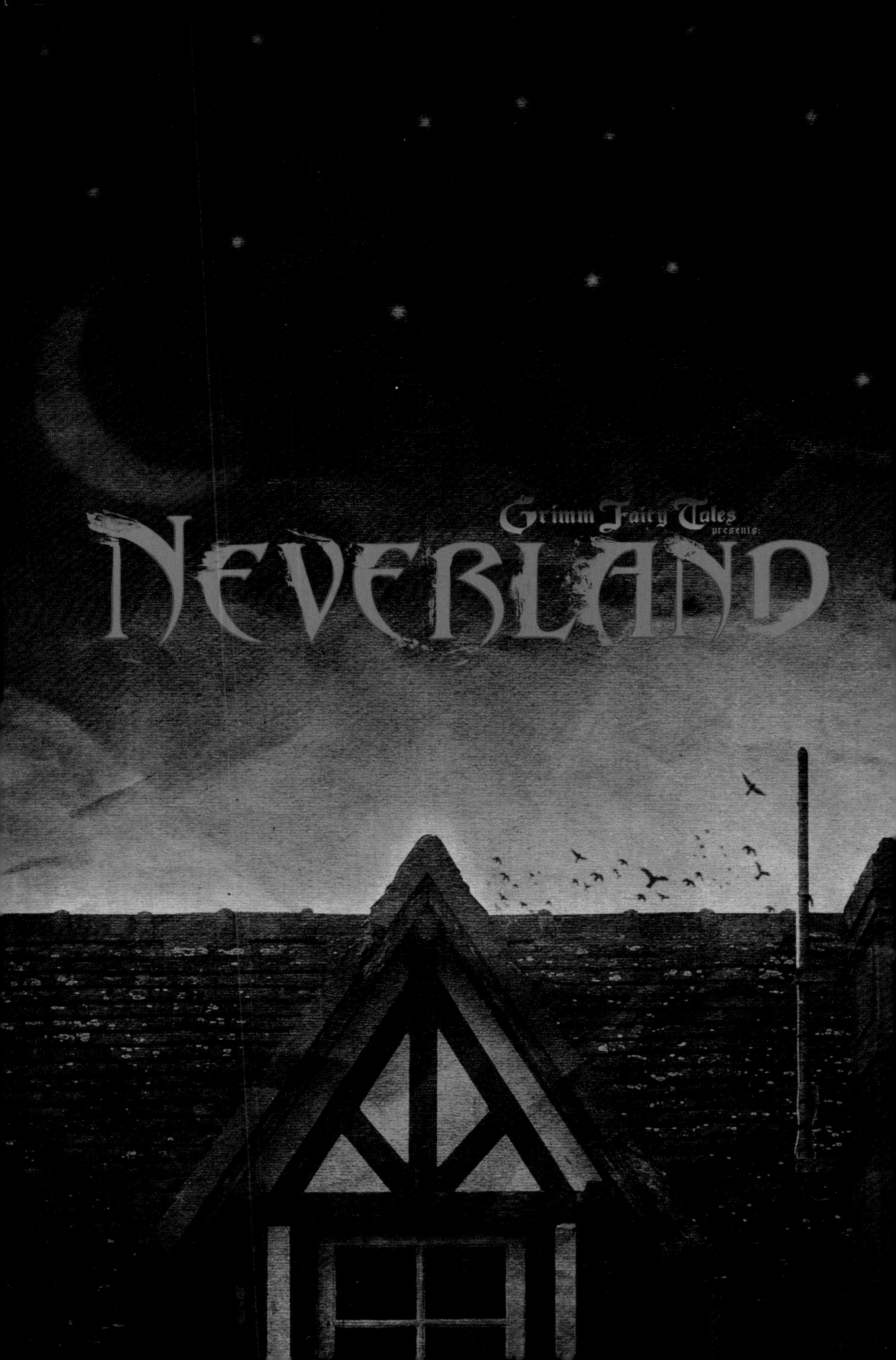
Grimm Fairy Tales presents:
NEVERLAND

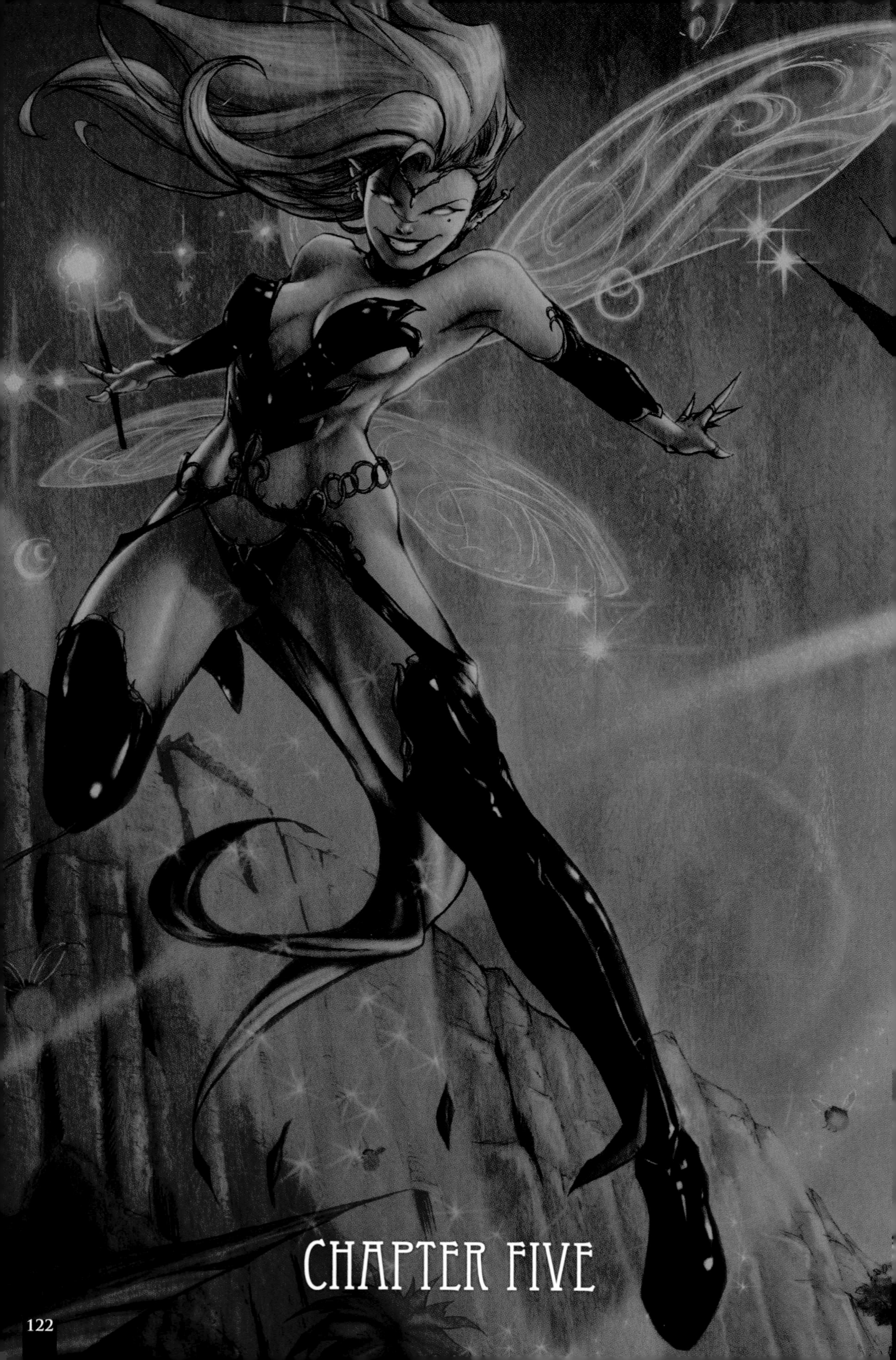

CHAPTER FIVE

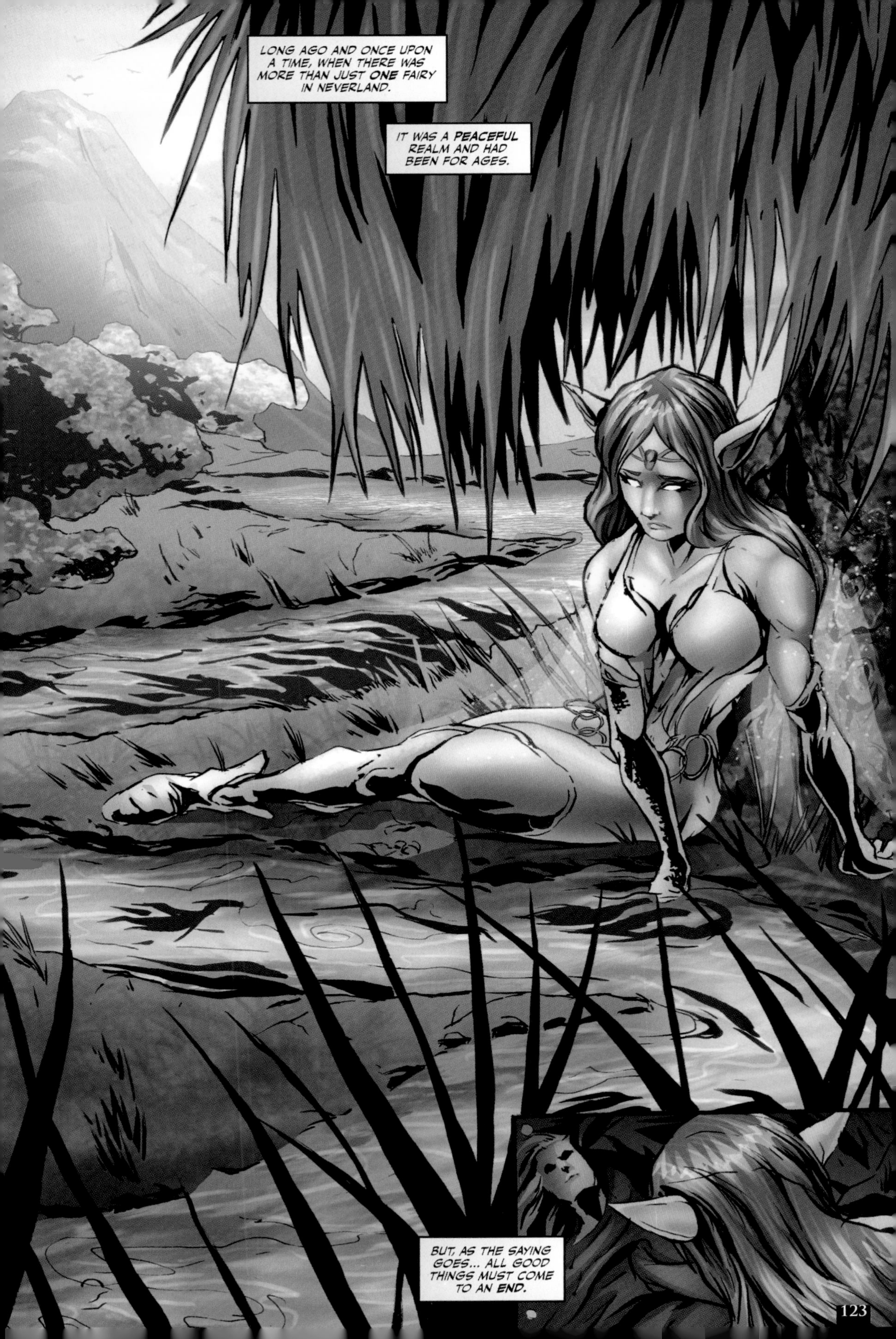
LONG AGO AND ONCE UPON A TIME, WHEN THERE WAS MORE THAN JUST ONE FAIRY IN NEVERLAND.
IT WAS A PEACEFUL REALM AND HAD BEEN FOR AGES.
BUT, AS THE SAYING GOES... ALL GOOD THINGS MUST COME TO AN END.

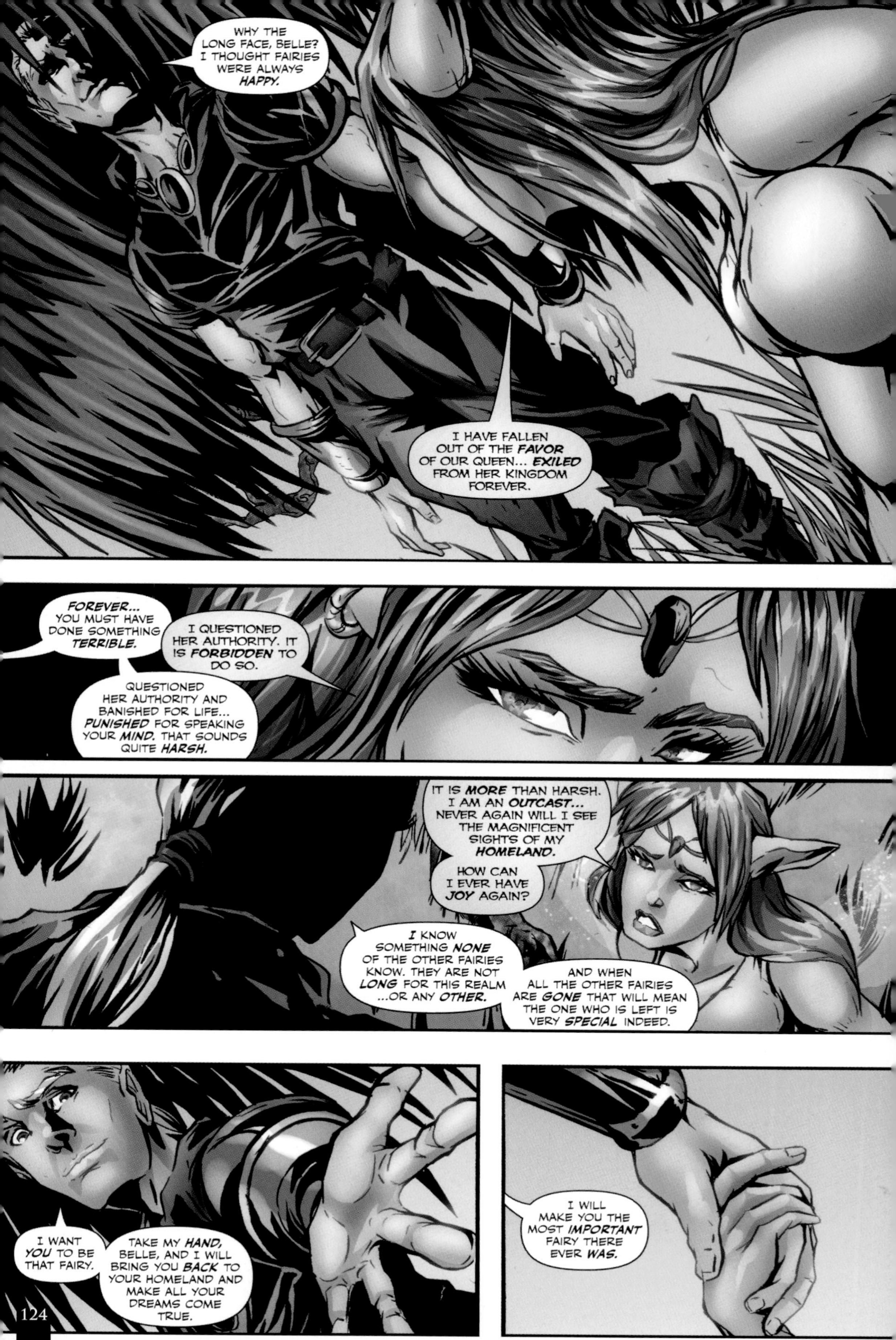
WHY THE LONG FACE, BELLE? I THOUGHT FAIRIES WERE ALWAYS *HAPPY.*
I HAVE FALLEN OUT OF THE *FAVOR* OF OUR QUEEN... *EXILED* FROM HER KINGDOM FOREVER.
FOREVER... YOU MUST HAVE DONE SOMETHING *TERRIBLE.*
I QUESTIONED HER AUTHORITY. IT IS *FORBIDDEN* TO DO SO.
QUESTIONED HER AUTHORITY AND BANISHED FOR LIFE... *PUNISHED* FOR SPEAKING YOUR *MIND.* THAT SOUNDS QUITE *HARSH.*
IT IS *MORE* THAN HARSH. I AM AN *OUTCAST...* NEVER AGAIN WILL I SEE THE MAGNIFICENT SIGHTS OF MY *HOMELAND.*
HOW CAN I EVER HAVE *JOY* AGAIN?
I KNOW SOMETHING *NONE* OF THE OTHER FAIRIES KNOW. THEY ARE NOT *LONG* FOR THIS REALM ...OR ANY *OTHER.*
AND WHEN ALL THE OTHER FAIRIES ARE *GONE* THAT WILL MEAN THE ONE WHO IS LEFT IS VERY *SPECIAL* INDEED.
I WANT *YOU* TO BE THAT FAIRY.
TAKE MY *HAND,* BELLE, AND I WILL BRING YOU *BACK* TO YOUR HOMELAND AND MAKE ALL YOUR DREAMS COME TRUE.
I WILL MAKE YOU THE MOST *IMPORTANT* FAIRY THERE EVER *WAS.*

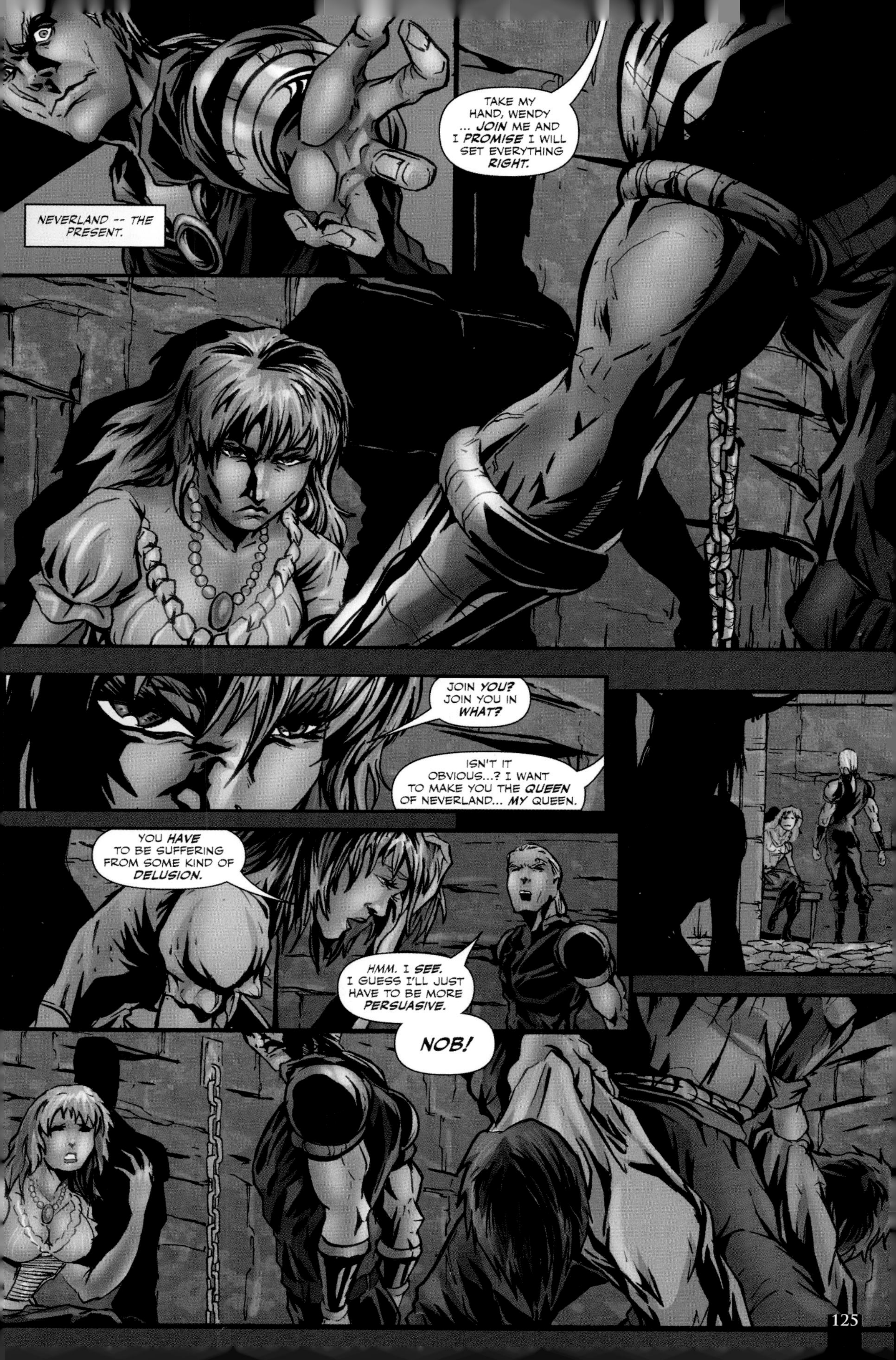

TAKE MY HAND, WENDY ... JOIN ME AND I PROMISE I WILL SET EVERYTHING RIGHT.
NEVERLAND -- THE PRESENT.
JOIN YOU? JOIN YOU IN WHAT?
ISN'T IT OBVIOUS...? I WANT TO MAKE YOU THE QUEEN OF NEVERLAND... MY QUEEN.
YOU HAVE TO BE SUFFERING FROM SOME KIND OF DELUSION.
HMM. I SEE. I GUESS I'LL JUST HAVE TO BE MORE PERSUASIVE.
NOB!

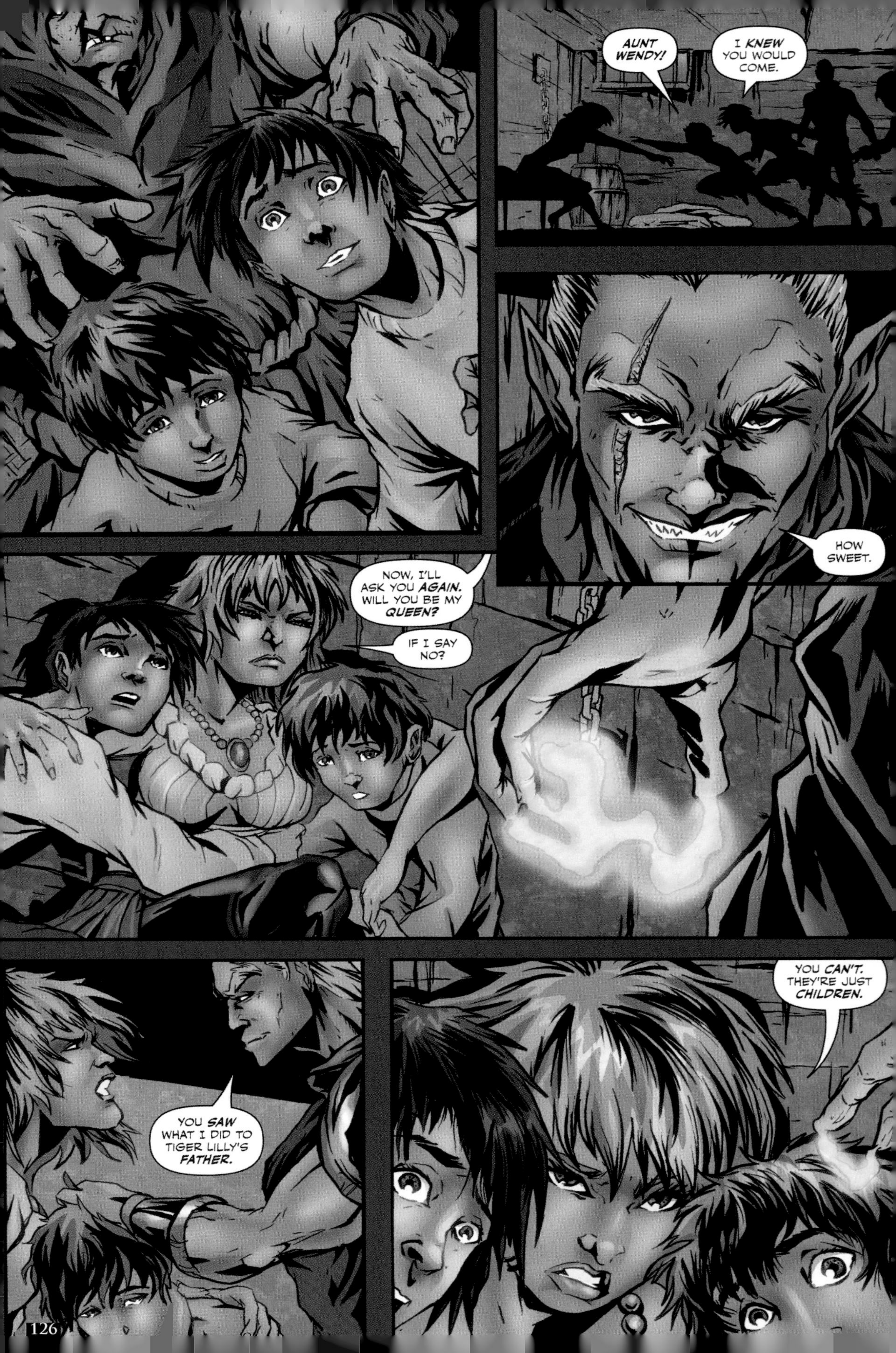
AUNT WENDY!
I KNEW YOU WOULD COME.
HOW SWEET.
NOW, I'LL ASK YOU AGAIN. WILL YOU BE MY QUEEN?
IF I SAY NO?
YOU SAW WHAT I DID TO TIGER LILLY'S FATHER.
YOU CAN'T. THEY'RE JUST CHILDREN.

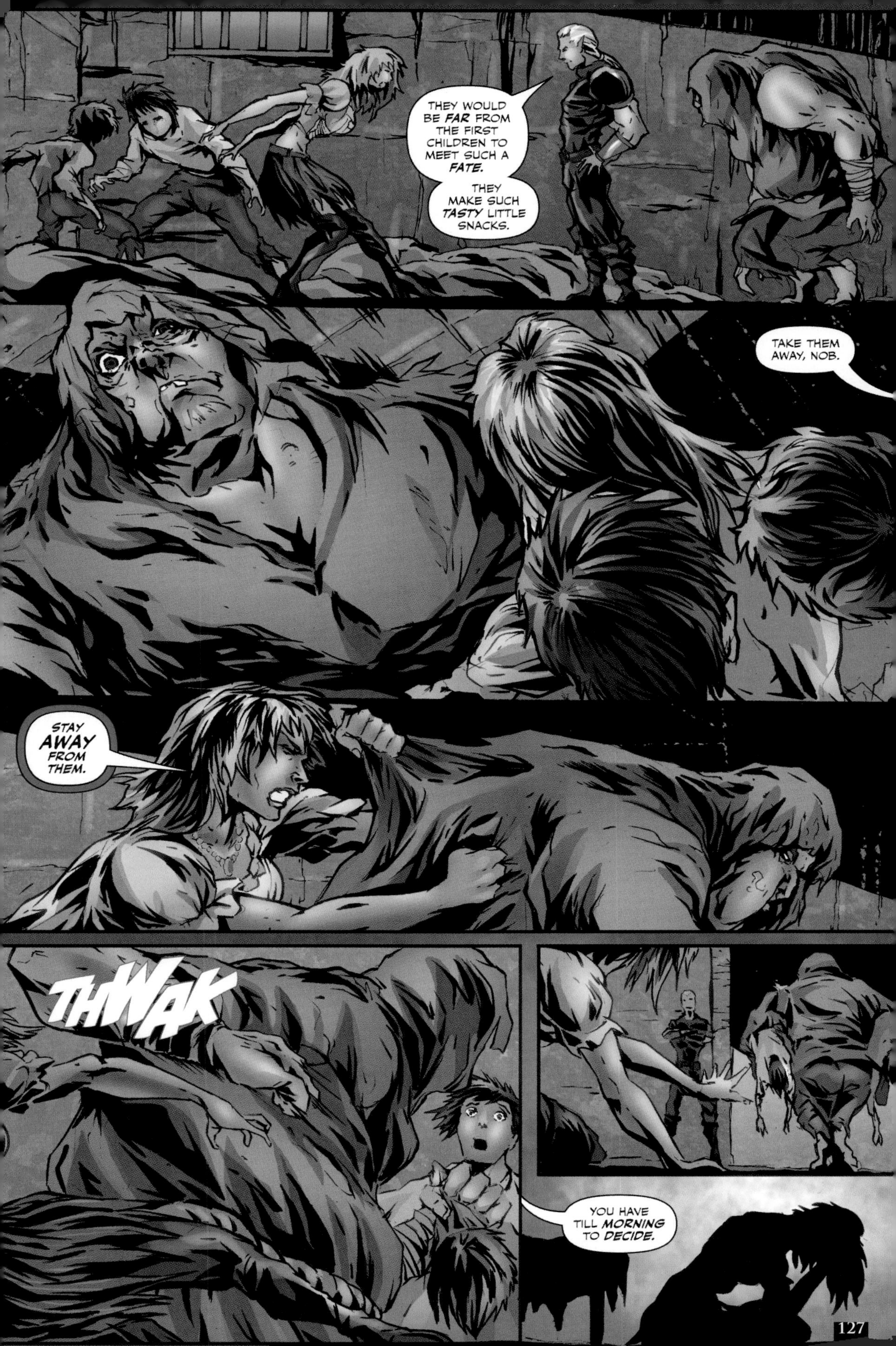
THEY WOULD BE FAR FROM THE FIRST CHILDREN TO MEET SUCH A FATE.
THEY MAKE SUCH TASTY LITTLE SNACKS.
TAKE THEM AWAY, NOB.
STAY AWAY FROM THEM.
THWAK
YOU HAVE TILL MORNING TO DECIDE.

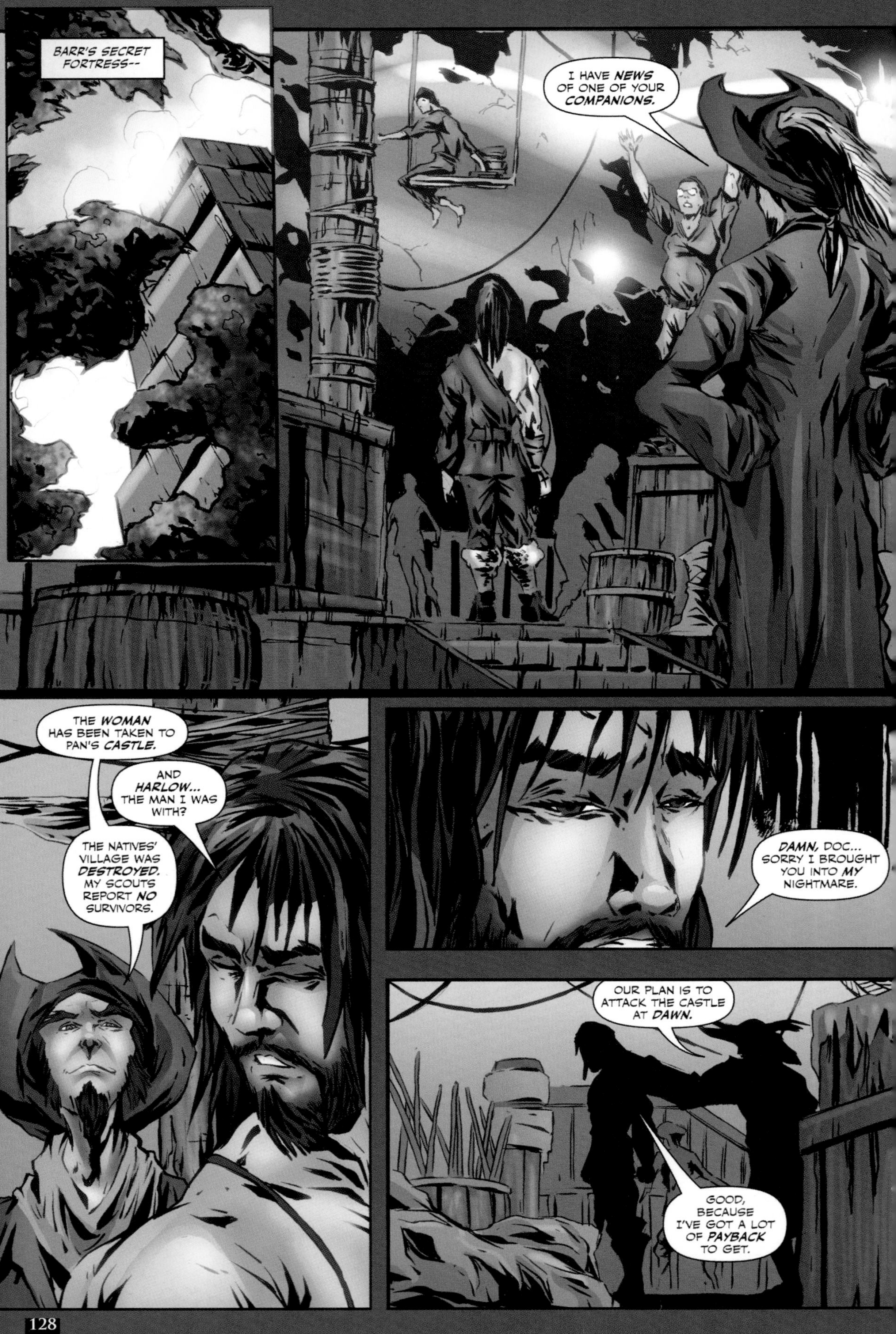
BARR'S SECRET FORTRESS--
I HAVE NEWS OF ONE OF YOUR COMPANIONS.
THE WOMAN HAS BEEN TAKEN TO PAN'S CASTLE.
AND HARLOW... THE MAN I WAS WITH?
THE NATIVES' VILLAGE WAS DESTROYED. MY SCOUTS REPORT NO SURVIVORS.
DAMN, DOC... SORRY I BROUGHT YOU INTO MY NIGHTMARE.
OUR PLAN IS TO ATTACK THE CASTLE AT DAWN.
GOOD, BECAUSE I'VE GOT A LOT OF PAYBACK TO GET.

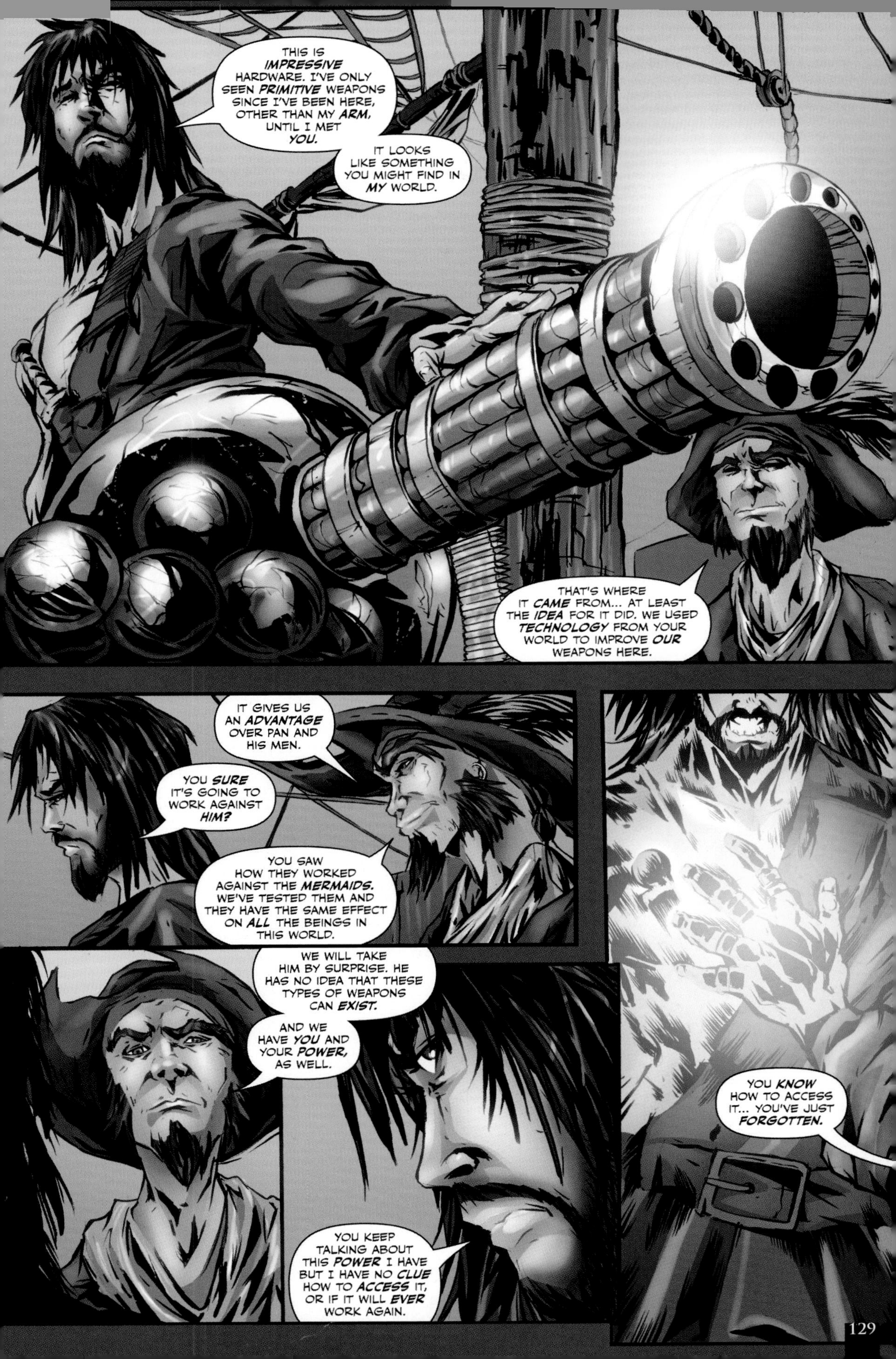

THIS IS IMPRESSIVE HARDWARE. I'VE ONLY SEEN PRIMITIVE WEAPONS SINCE I'VE BEEN HERE, OTHER THAN MY ARM, UNTIL I MET YOU.
IT LOOKS LIKE SOMETHING YOU MIGHT FIND IN MY WORLD.
THAT'S WHERE IT CAME FROM... AT LEAST THE IDEA FOR IT DID. WE USED TECHNOLOGY FROM YOUR WORLD TO IMPROVE OUR WEAPONS HERE.
IT GIVES US AN ADVANTAGE OVER PAN AND HIS MEN.
YOU SURE IT'S GOING TO WORK AGAINST HIM?
YOU SAW HOW THEY WORKED AGAINST THE MERMAIDS. WE'VE TESTED THEM AND THEY HAVE THE SAME EFFECT ON ALL THE BEINGS IN THIS WORLD.
WE WILL TAKE HIM BY SURPRISE. HE HAS NO IDEA THAT THESE TYPES OF WEAPONS CAN EXIST.
AND WE HAVE YOU AND YOUR POWER, AS WELL.
YOU KEEP TALKING ABOUT THIS POWER I HAVE BUT I HAVE NO CLUE HOW TO ACCESS IT, OR IF IT WILL EVER WORK AGAIN.
YOU KNOW HOW TO ACCESS IT... YOU'VE JUST FORGOTTEN.

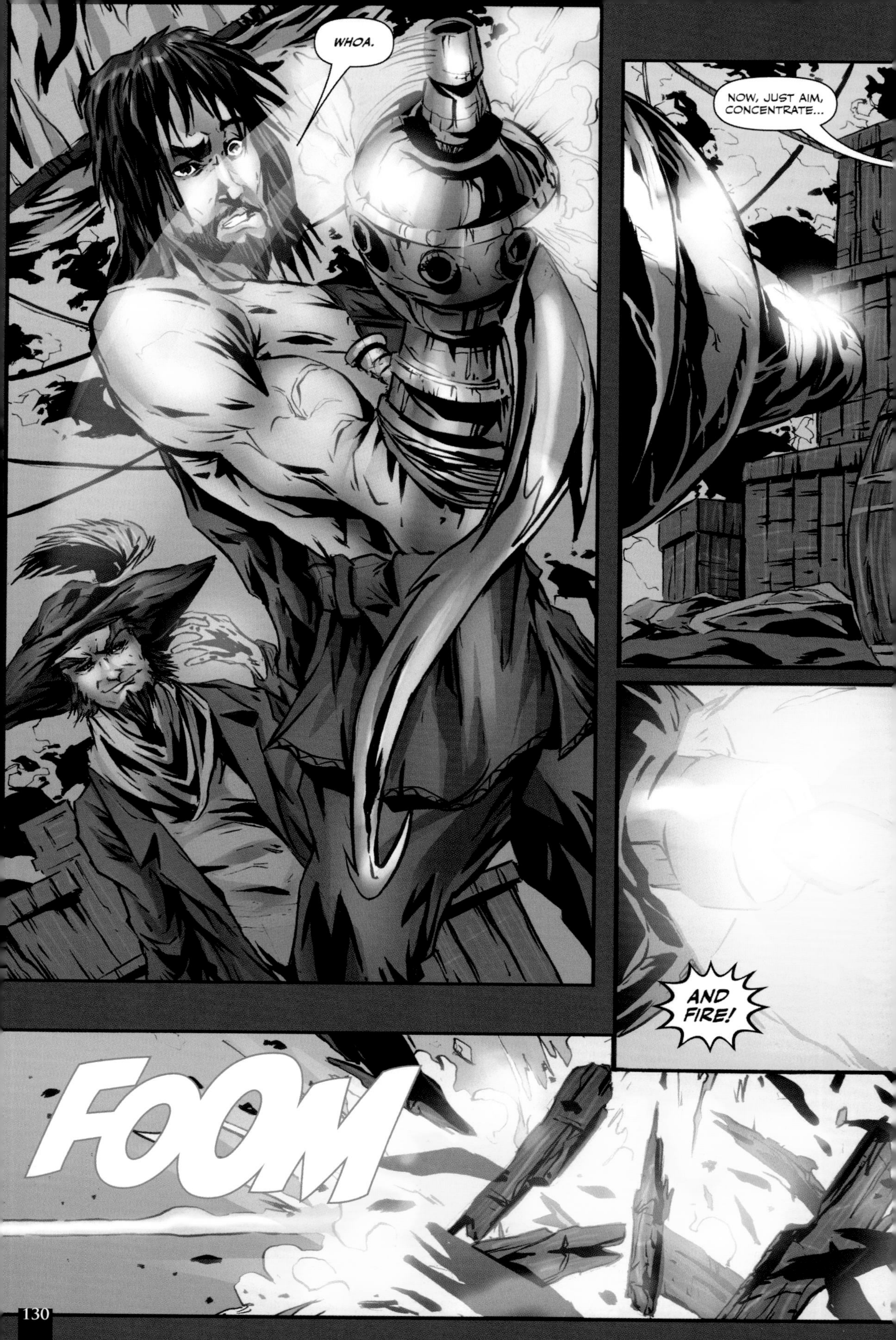
WHOA.
NOW, JUST AIM, CONCENTRATE...
AND FIRE!
FOOM

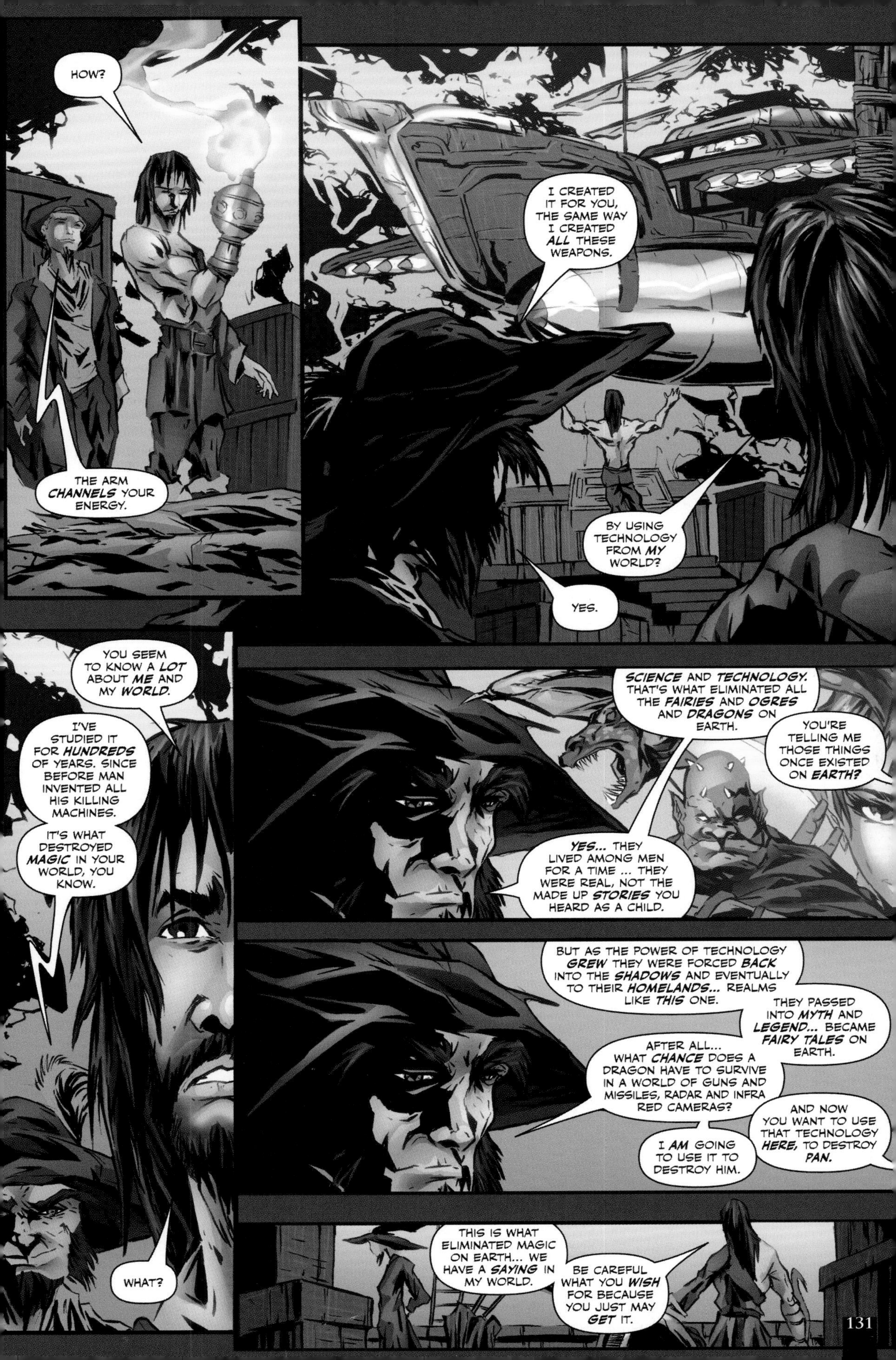
HOW?
THE ARM CHANNELS YOUR ENERGY.
I CREATED IT FOR YOU, THE SAME WAY I CREATED ALL THESE WEAPONS.
BY USING TECHNOLOGY FROM MY WORLD?
YES.
YOU SEEM TO KNOW A LOT ABOUT ME AND MY WORLD.
I'VE STUDIED IT FOR HUNDREDS OF YEARS. SINCE BEFORE MAN INVENTED ALL HIS KILLING MACHINES.
IT'S WHAT DESTROYED MAGIC IN YOUR WORLD, YOU KNOW.
WHAT?
SCIENCE AND TECHNOLOGY. THAT'S WHAT ELIMINATED ALL THE FAIRIES AND OGRES AND DRAGONS ON EARTH.
YOU'RE TELLING ME THOSE THINGS ONCE EXISTED ON EARTH?
YES... THEY LIVED AMONG MEN FOR A TIME ... THEY WERE REAL, NOT THE MADE UP STORIES YOU HEARD AS A CHILD.
BUT AS THE POWER OF TECHNOLOGY GREW THEY WERE FORCED BACK INTO THE SHADOWS AND EVENTUALLY TO THEIR HOMELANDS... REALMS LIKE THIS ONE.
THEY PASSED INTO MYTH AND LEGEND... BECAME FAIRY TALES ON EARTH.
AFTER ALL... WHAT CHANCE DOES A DRAGON HAVE TO SURVIVE IN A WORLD OF GUNS AND MISSILES, RADAR AND INFRA RED CAMERAS?
AND NOW YOU WANT TO USE THAT TECHNOLOGY HERE, TO DESTROY PAN.
I AM GOING TO USE IT TO DESTROY HIM.
THIS IS WHAT ELIMINATED MAGIC ON EARTH... WE HAVE A SAYING IN MY WORLD.
BE CAREFUL WHAT YOU WISH FOR BECAUSE YOU JUST MAY GET IT.

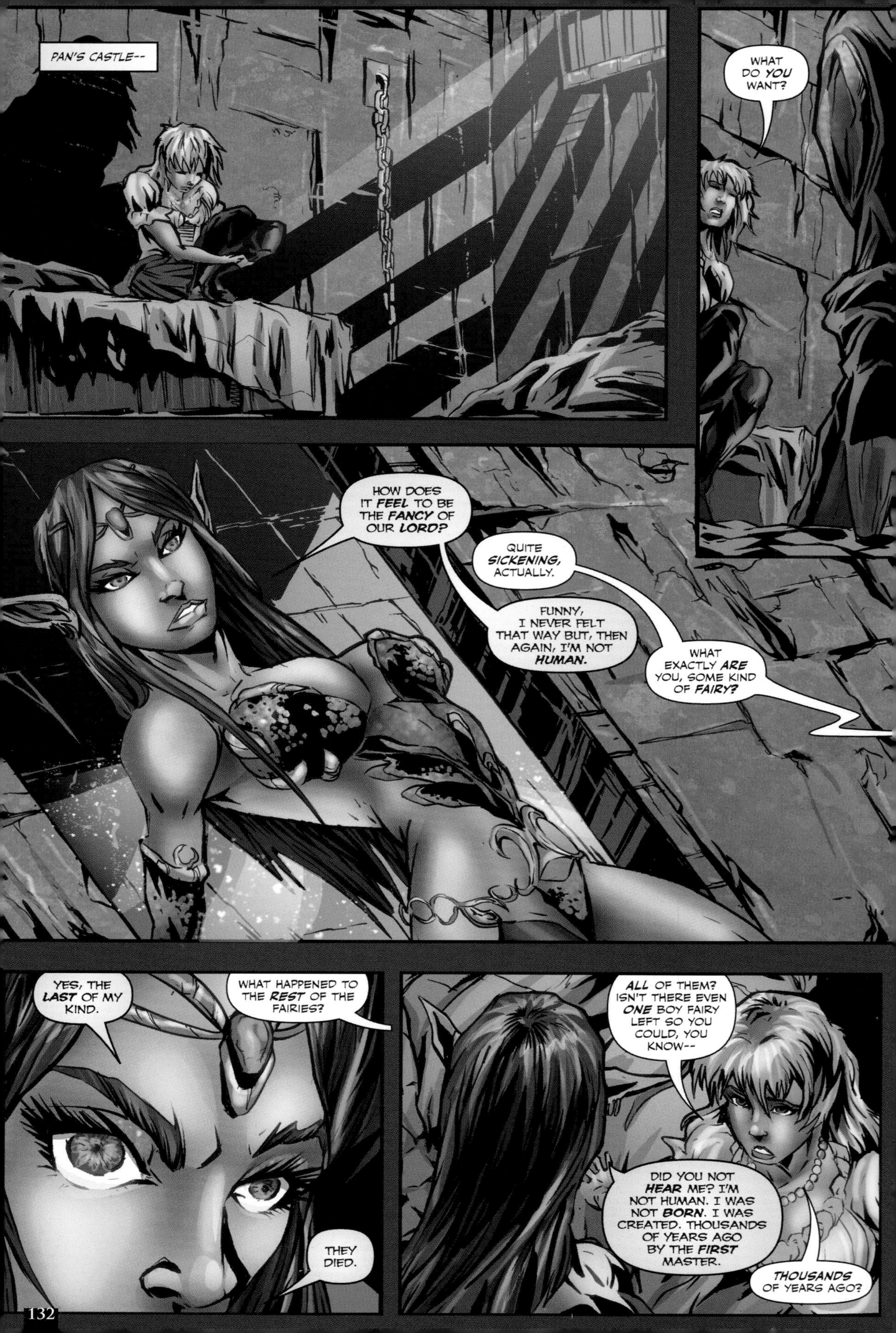

PAN'S CASTLE--
WHAT DO YOU WANT?
HOW DOES IT FEEL TO BE THE FANCY OF OUR LORD?
QUITE SICKENING, ACTUALLY.
FUNNY, I NEVER FELT THAT WAY BUT, THEN AGAIN, I'M NOT HUMAN.
WHAT EXACTLY ARE YOU, SOME KIND OF FAIRY?
YES, THE LAST OF MY KIND.
WHAT HAPPENED TO THE REST OF THE FAIRIES?
THEY DIED.
ALL OF THEM? ISN'T THERE EVEN ONE BOY FAIRY LEFT SO YOU COULD, YOU KNOW--
DID YOU NOT HEAR ME? I'M NOT HUMAN. I WAS NOT BORN. I WAS CREATED. THOUSANDS OF YEARS AGO BY THE FIRST MASTER.
THOUSANDS OF YEARS AGO?

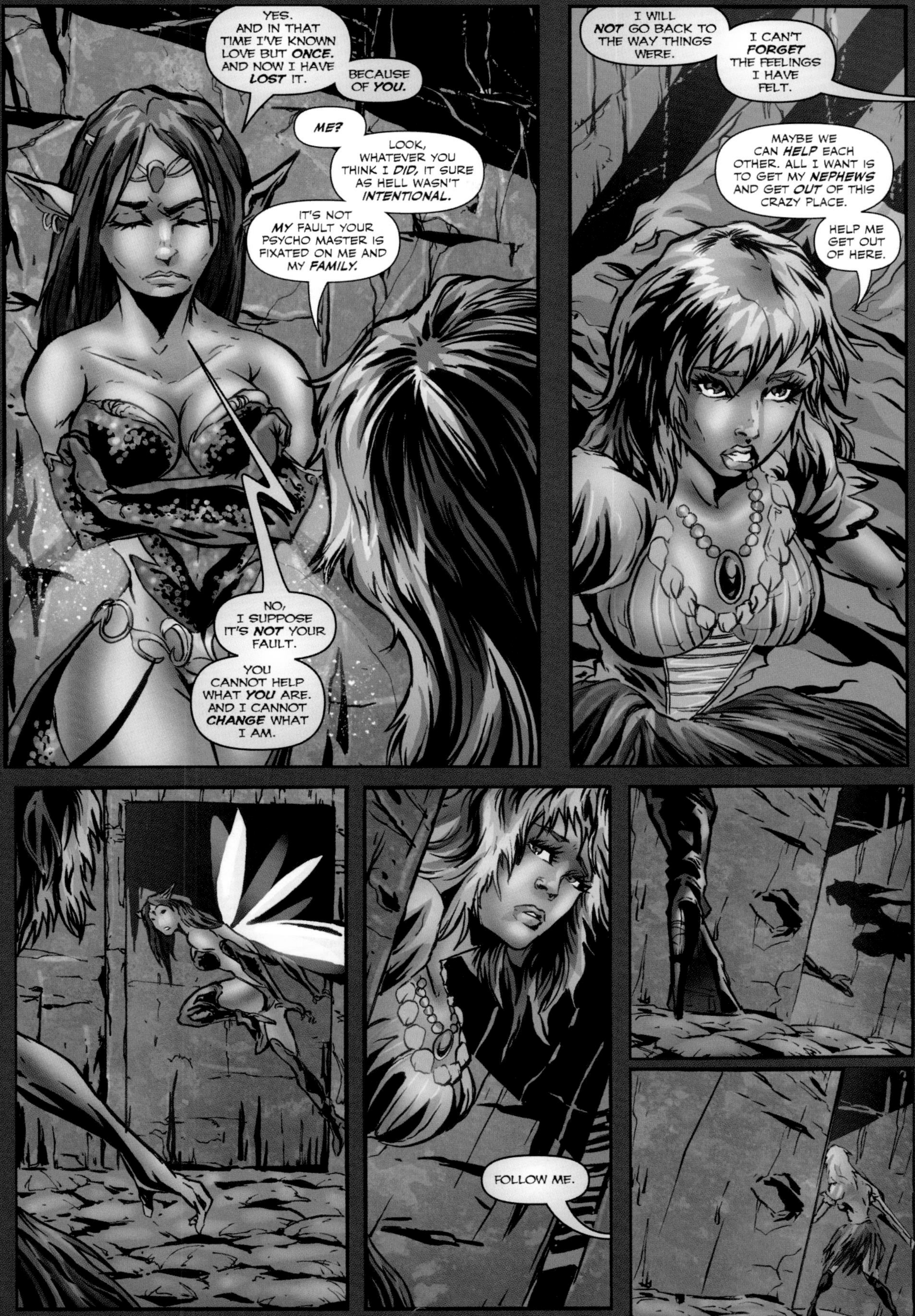
YES. AND IN THAT TIME I'VE KNOWN LOVE BUT ONCE. AND NOW I HAVE LOST IT.
BECAUSE OF YOU.
ME?
LOOK, WHATEVER YOU THINK I DID, IT SURE AS HELL WASN'T INTENTIONAL.
IT'S NOT MY FAULT YOUR PSYCHO MASTER IS FIXATED ON ME AND MY FAMILY.
NO, I SUPPOSE IT'S NOT YOUR FAULT.
YOU CANNOT HELP WHAT YOU ARE. AND I CANNOT CHANGE WHAT I AM.
I WILL NOT GO BACK TO THE WAY THINGS WERE.
I CAN'T FORGET THE FEELINGS I HAVE FELT.
MAYBE WE CAN HELP EACH OTHER. ALL I WANT IS TO GET MY NEPHEWS AND GET OUT OF THIS CRAZY PLACE.
HELP ME GET OUT OF HERE.
FOLLOW ME.

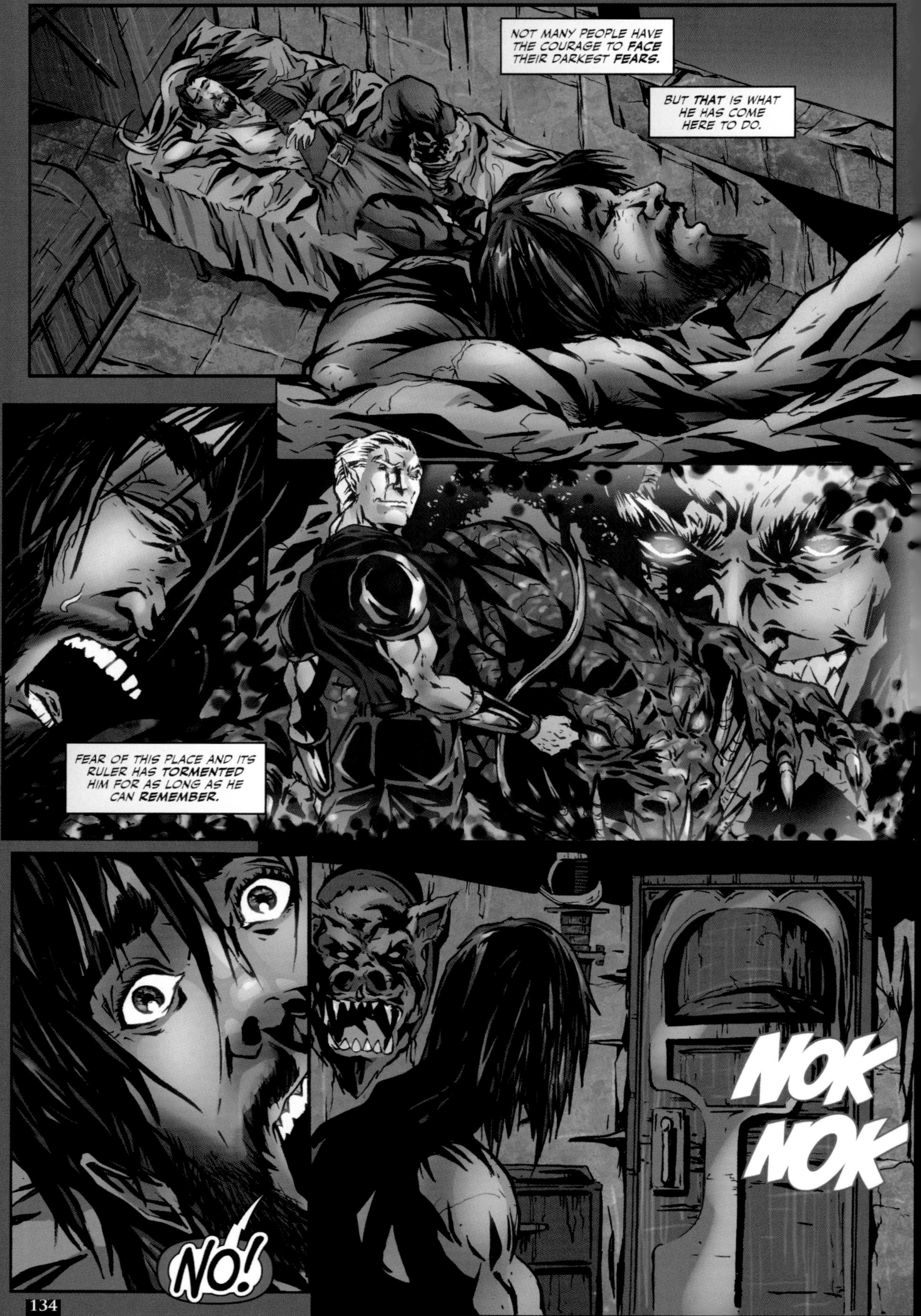
NOT MANY PEOPLE HAVE THE COURAGE TO FACE THEIR DARKEST FEARS.
BUT THAT IS WHAT HE HAS COME HERE TO DO.
FEAR OF THIS PLACE AND ITS RULER HAS TORMENTED HIM FOR AS LONG AS HE CAN REMEMBER.
NO!
NOK NOK

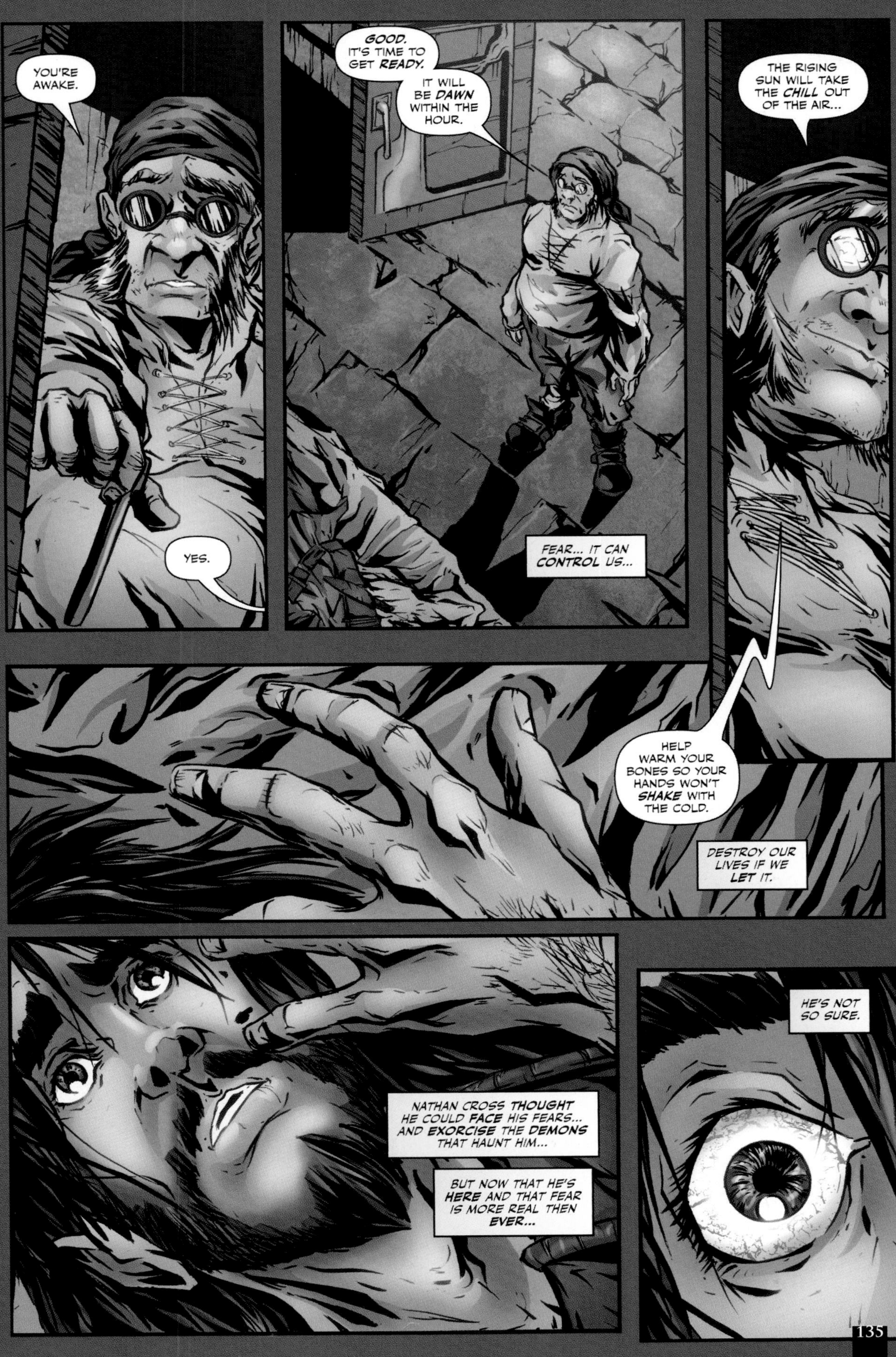
YOU'RE AWAKE.
YES.
GOOD. IT'S TIME TO GET READY.
IT WILL BE DAWN WITHIN THE HOUR.
FEAR... IT CAN CONTROL US...
THE RISING SUN WILL TAKE THE CHILL OUT OF THE AIR...
HELP WARM YOUR BONES SO YOUR HANDS WON'T SHAKE WITH THE COLD.
DESTROY OUR LIVES IF WE LET IT.
NATHAN CROSS THOUGHT HE COULD FACE HIS FEARS... AND EXORCISE THE DEMONS THAT HAUNT HIM...
BUT NOW THAT HE'S HERE AND THAT FEAR IS MORE REAL THEN EVER...
HE'S NOT SO SURE.

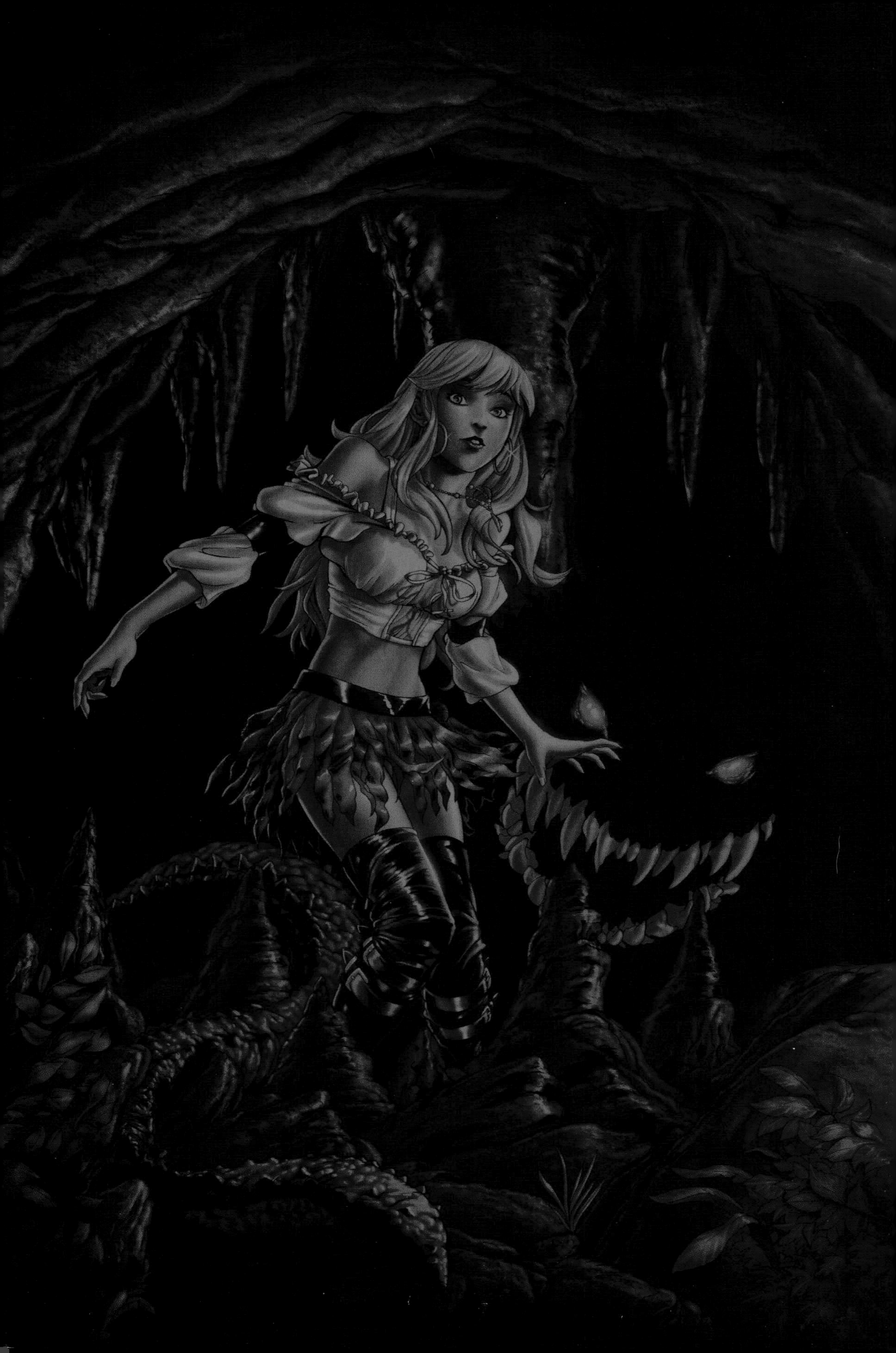

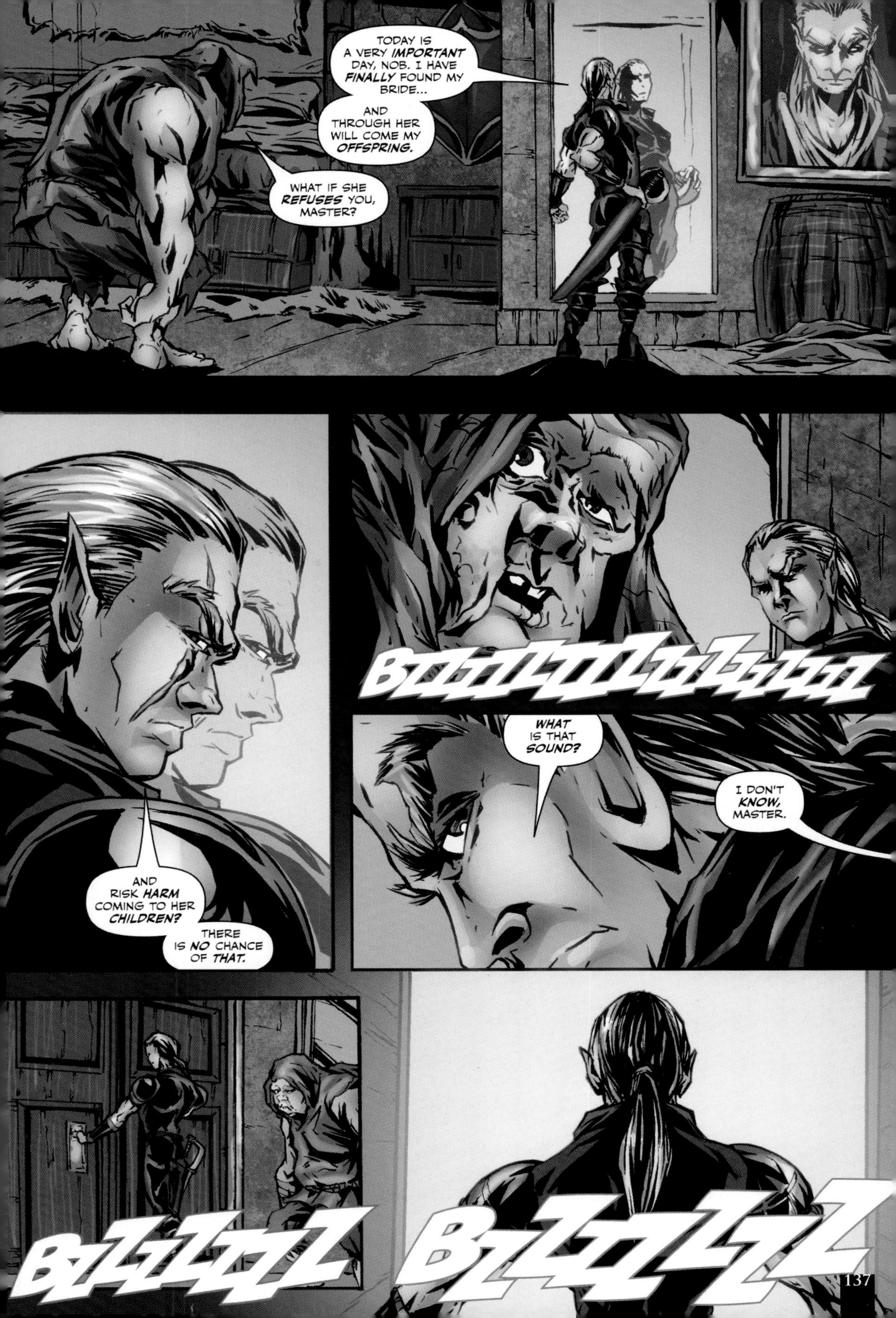
TODAY IS A VERY IMPORTANT DAY, NOB. I HAVE FINALLY FOUND MY BRIDE...
AND THROUGH HER WILL COME MY OFFSPRING.
WHAT IF SHE REFUSES YOU, MASTER?
AND RISK HARM COMING TO HER CHILDREN?
THERE IS NO CHANCE OF THAT.
BZZZZZZZZZZ
WHAT IS THAT SOUND?
I DON'T KNOW, MASTER.
BZZZZZ
BZZZZZ

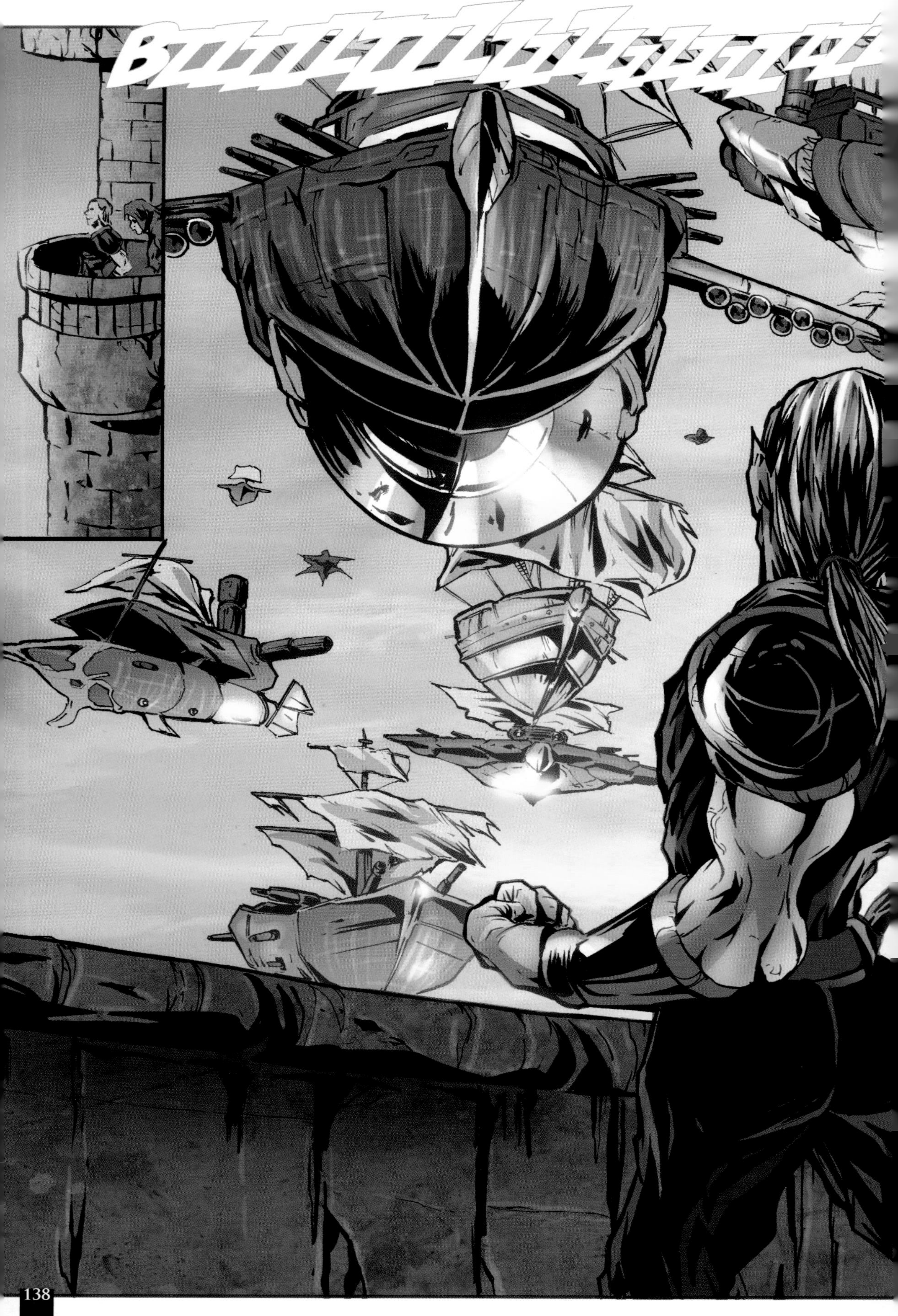

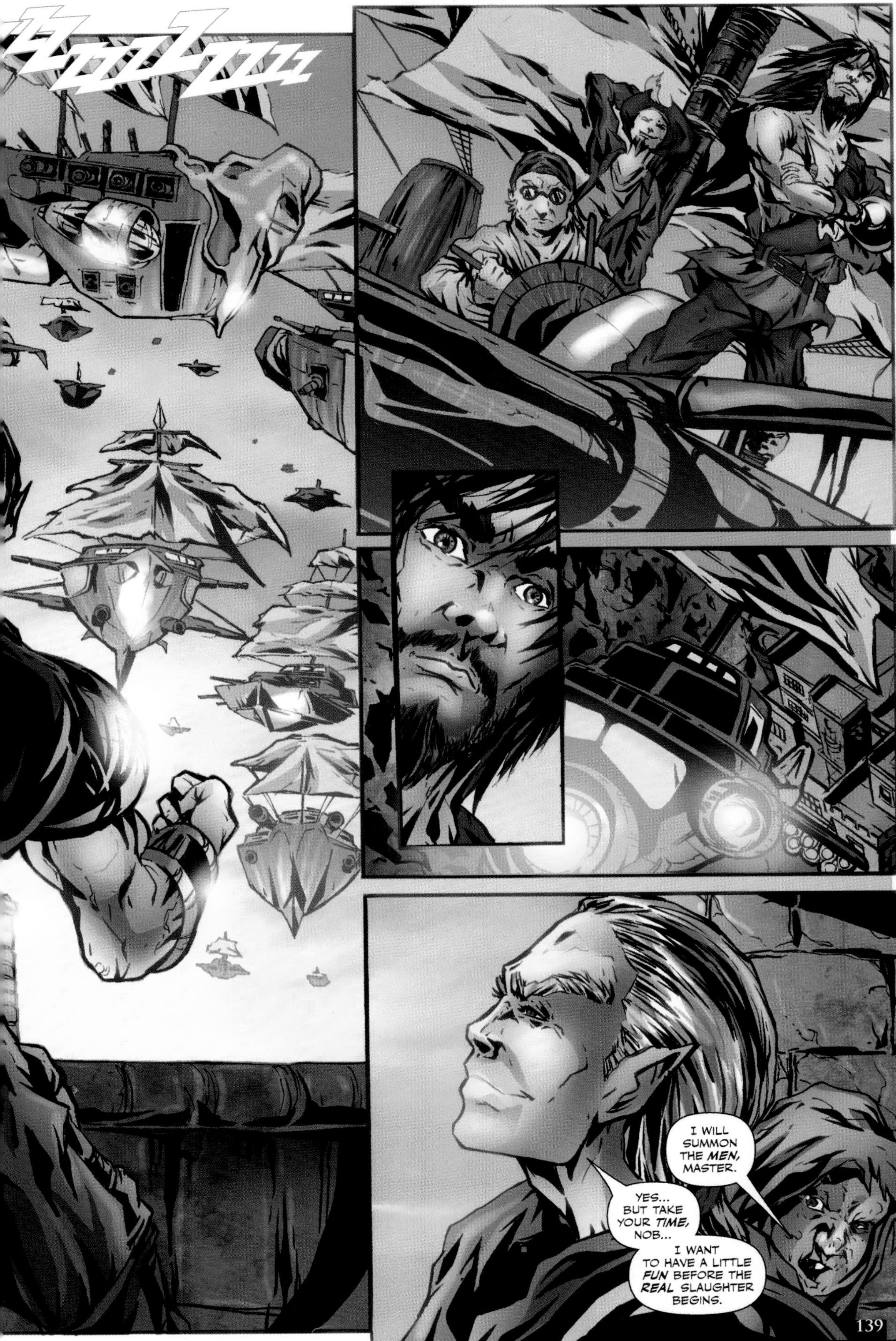

ZZZZZZZ
I WILL SUMMON THE MEN, MASTER.
YES... BUT TAKE YOUR TIME, NOB...
I WANT TO HAVE A LITTLE FUN BEFORE THE REAL SLAUGHTER BEGINS.

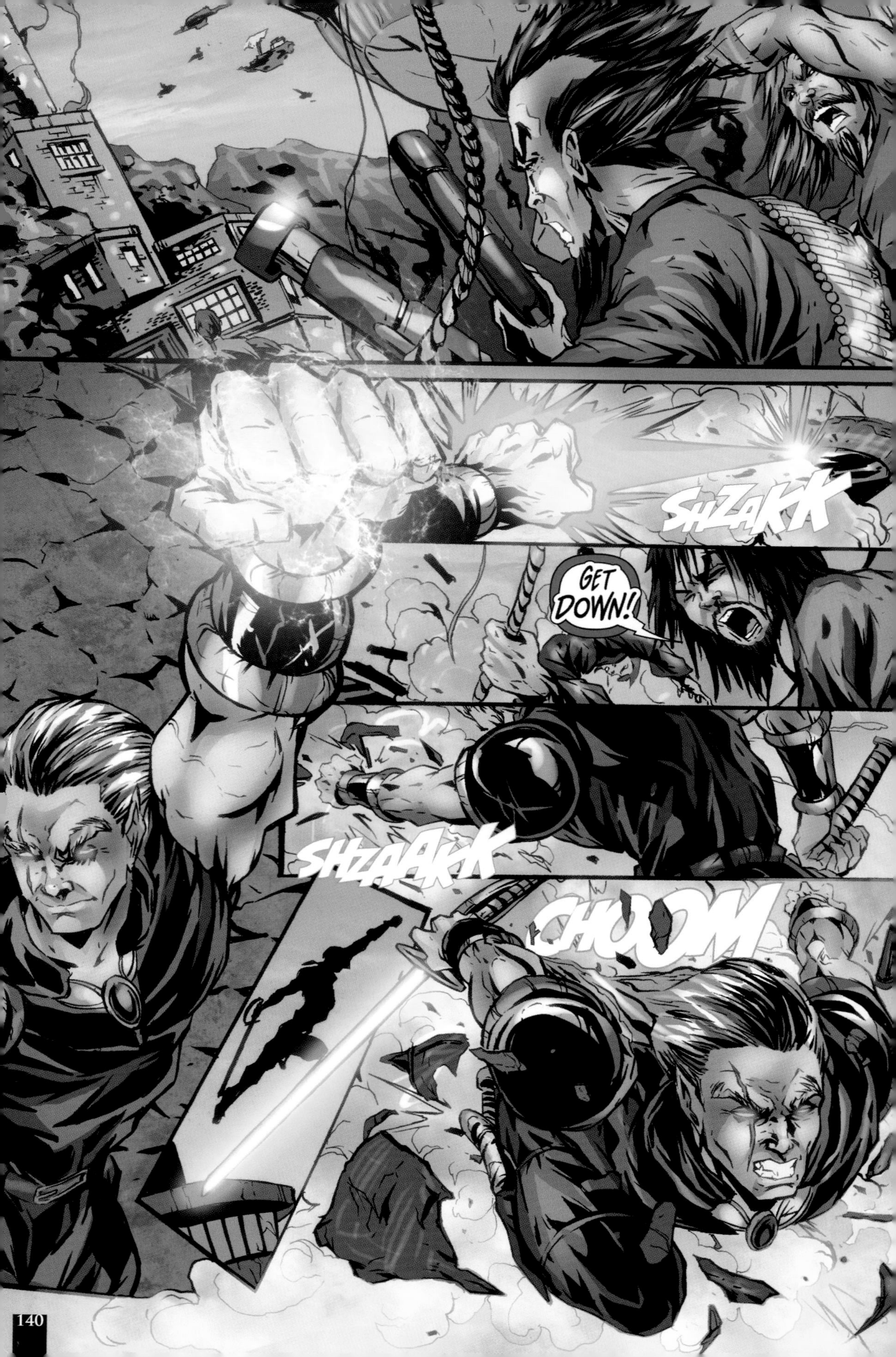
SHZAKK
GET DOWN!
SHZAAKK
CHOOOM

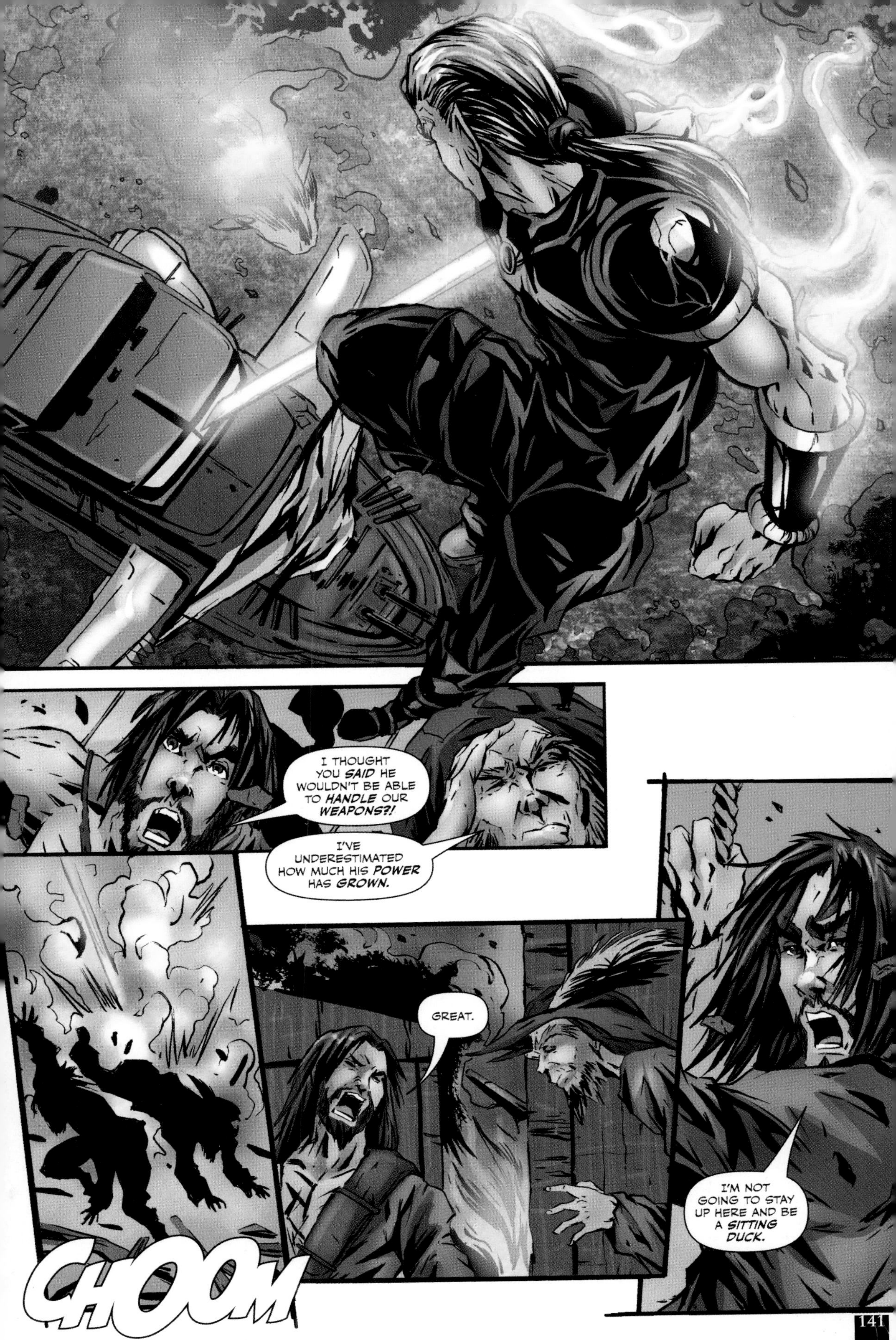
I THOUGHT YOU SAID HE WOULDN'T BE ABLE TO HANDLE OUR WEAPONS?!
I'VE UNDERESTIMATED HOW MUCH HIS POWER HAS GROWN.
CHOOM
GREAT.
I'M NOT GOING TO STAY UP HERE AND BE A SITTING DUCK.

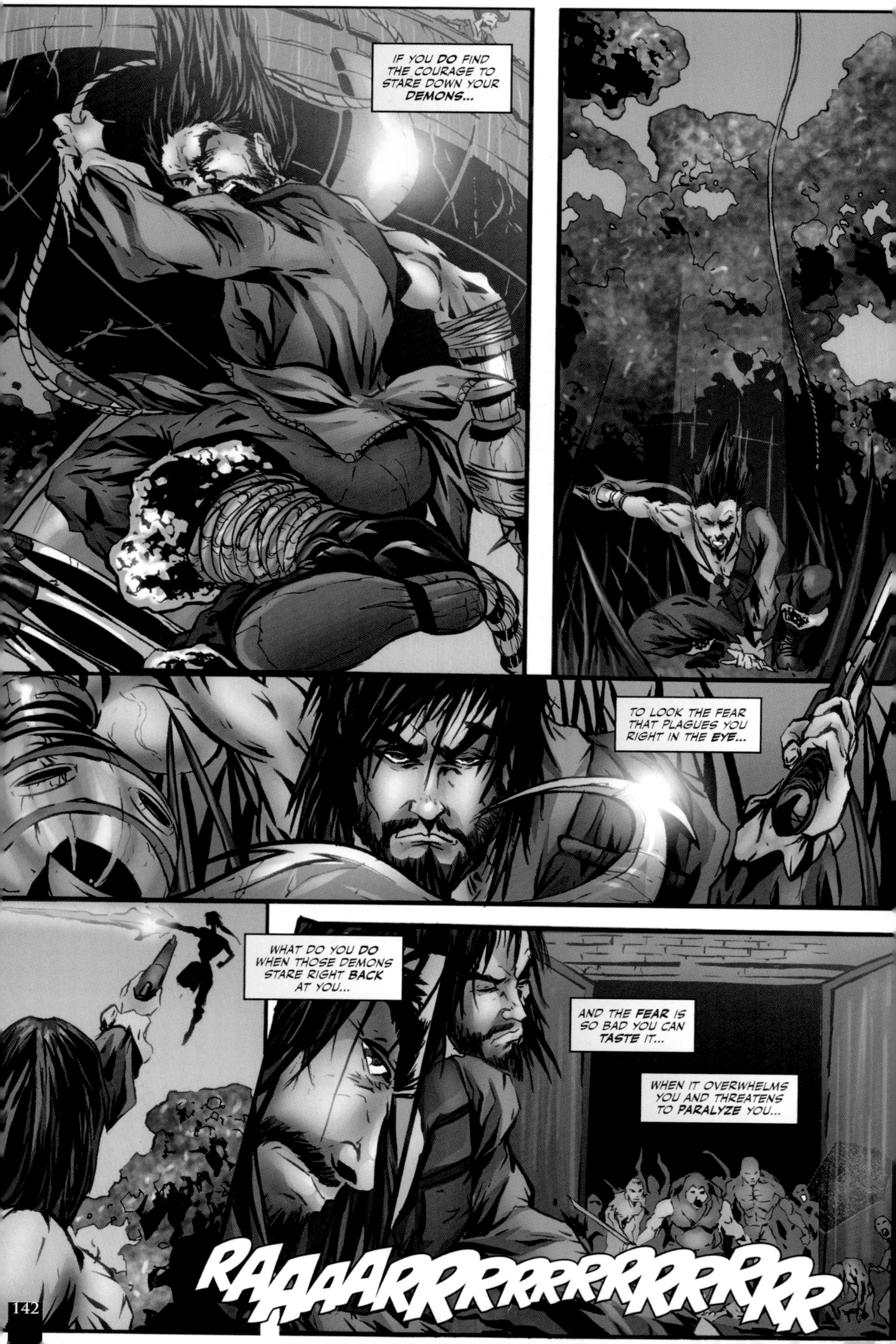
IF YOU DO FIND THE COURAGE TO STARE DOWN YOUR DEMONS...
TO LOOK THE FEAR THAT PLAGUES YOU RIGHT IN THE EYE...
WHAT DO YOU DO WHEN THOSE DEMONS STARE RIGHT BACK AT YOU...
AND THE FEAR IS SO BAD YOU CAN TASTE IT...
WHEN IT OVERWHELMS YOU AND THREATENS TO PARALYZE YOU...
RAAAARRRRRRRRRRRRRRR

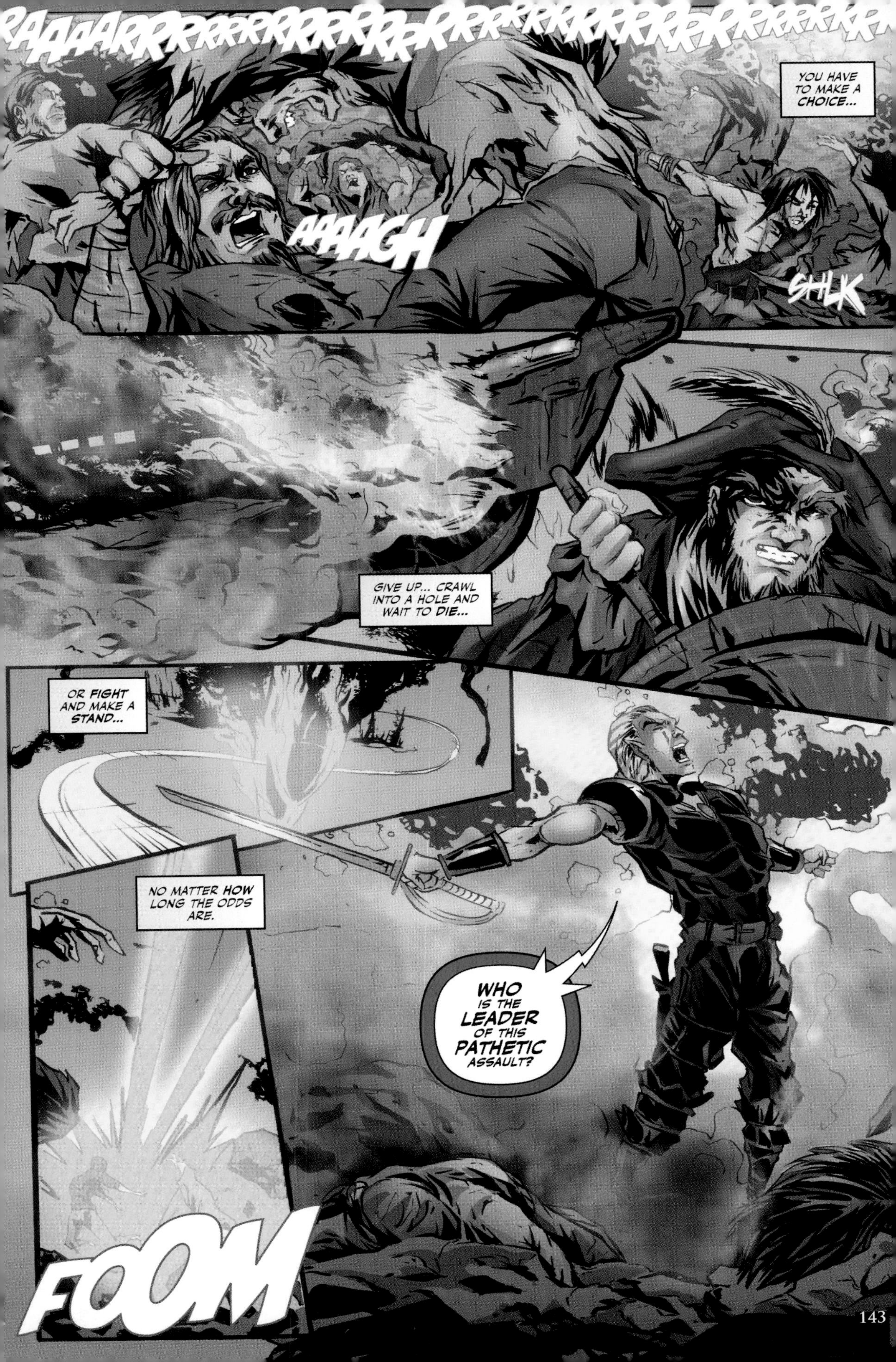
RAAAARRRRRRRRRRRRRRRRRRRRRRRRRRRRRRRRR
YOU HAVE TO MAKE A CHOICE...
AAAAGH
SHLK
GIVE UP... CRAWL INTO A HOLE AND WAIT TO DIE...
OR FIGHT AND MAKE A STAND...
NO MATTER HOW LONG THE ODDS ARE.
WHO IS THE LEADER OF THIS PATHETIC ASSAULT?
FOOM

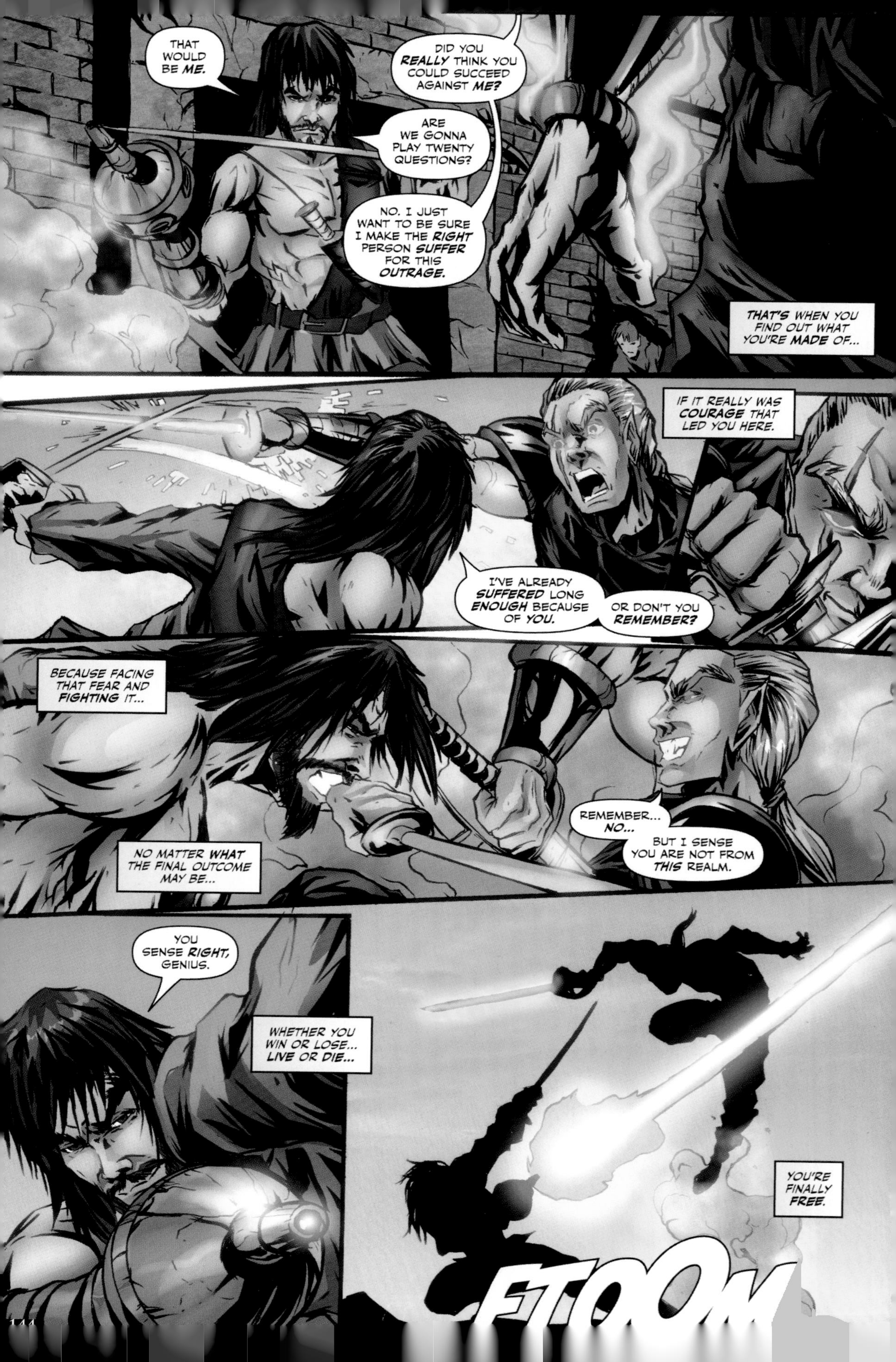
THAT WOULD BE ME.
DID YOU REALLY THINK YOU COULD SUCCEED AGAINST ME?
ARE WE GONNA PLAY TWENTY QUESTIONS?
NO. I JUST WANT TO BE SURE I MAKE THE RIGHT PERSON SUFFER FOR THIS OUTRAGE.
THAT'S WHEN YOU FIND OUT WHAT YOU'RE MADE OF...
IF IT REALLY WAS COURAGE THAT LED YOU HERE.
I'VE ALREADY SUFFERED LONG ENOUGH BECAUSE OF YOU.
OR DON'T YOU REMEMBER?
BECAUSE FACING THAT FEAR AND FIGHTING IT...
NO MATTER WHAT THE FINAL OUTCOME MAY BE...
REMEMBER... NO...
BUT I SENSE YOU ARE NOT FROM THIS REALM.
YOU SENSE RIGHT, GENIUS.
WHETHER YOU WIN OR LOSE... LIVE OR DIE...
YOU'RE FINALLY FREE.
FTOOM

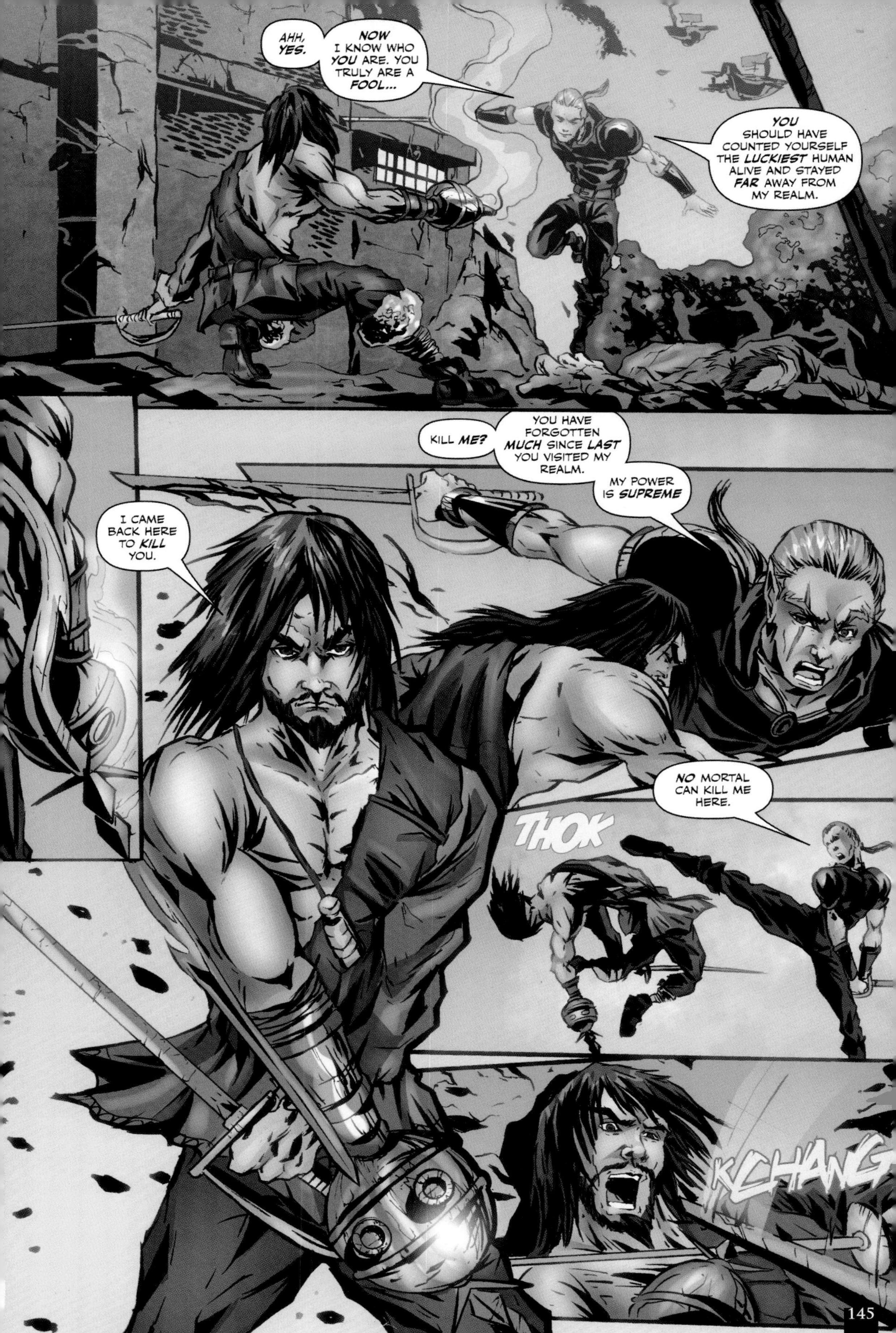

AHH, YES.
NOW I KNOW WHO YOU ARE. YOU TRULY ARE A FOOL...
YOU SHOULD HAVE COUNTED YOURSELF THE LUCKIEST HUMAN ALIVE AND STAYED FAR AWAY FROM MY REALM.
I CAME BACK HERE TO KILL YOU.
KILL ME?
YOU HAVE FORGOTTEN MUCH SINCE LAST YOU VISITED MY REALM.
MY POWER IS SUPREME
NO MORTAL CAN KILL ME HERE.
THOK
KCHANG

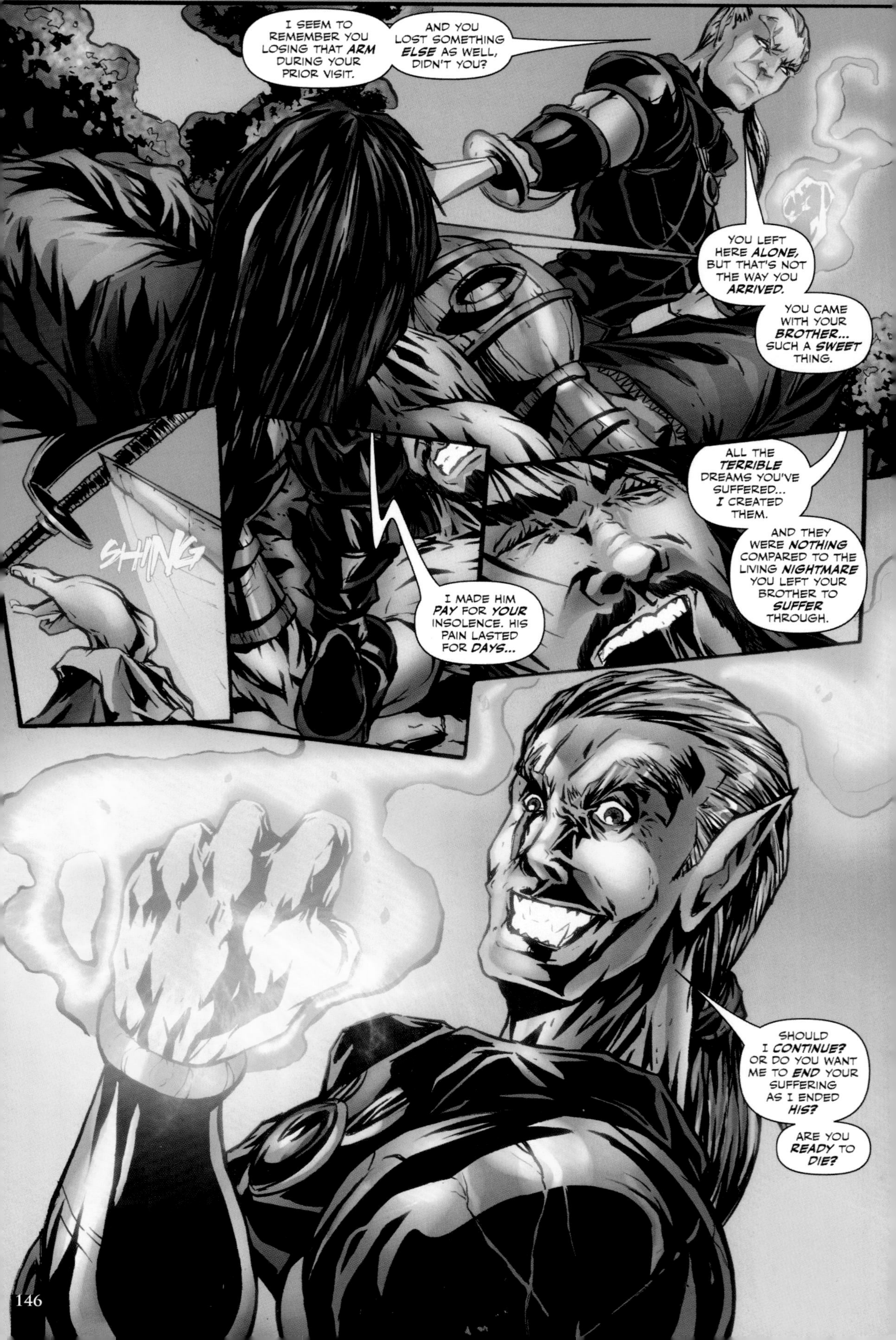
I SEEM TO REMEMBER YOU LOSING THAT ARM DURING YOUR PRIOR VISIT.
AND YOU LOST SOMETHING ELSE AS WELL, DIDN'T YOU?
YOU LEFT HERE ALONE, BUT THAT'S NOT THE WAY YOU ARRIVED.
YOU CAME WITH YOUR BROTHER... SUCH A SWEET THING.
SHING
I MADE HIM PAY FOR YOUR INSOLENCE. HIS PAIN LASTED FOR DAYS...
ALL THE TERRIBLE DREAMS YOU'VE SUFFERED... I CREATED THEM.
AND THEY WERE NOTHING COMPARED TO THE LIVING NIGHTMARE YOU LEFT YOUR BROTHER TO SUFFER THROUGH.
SHOULD I CONTINUE? OR DO YOU WANT ME TO END YOUR SUFFERING AS I ENDED HIS?
ARE YOU READY TO DIE?

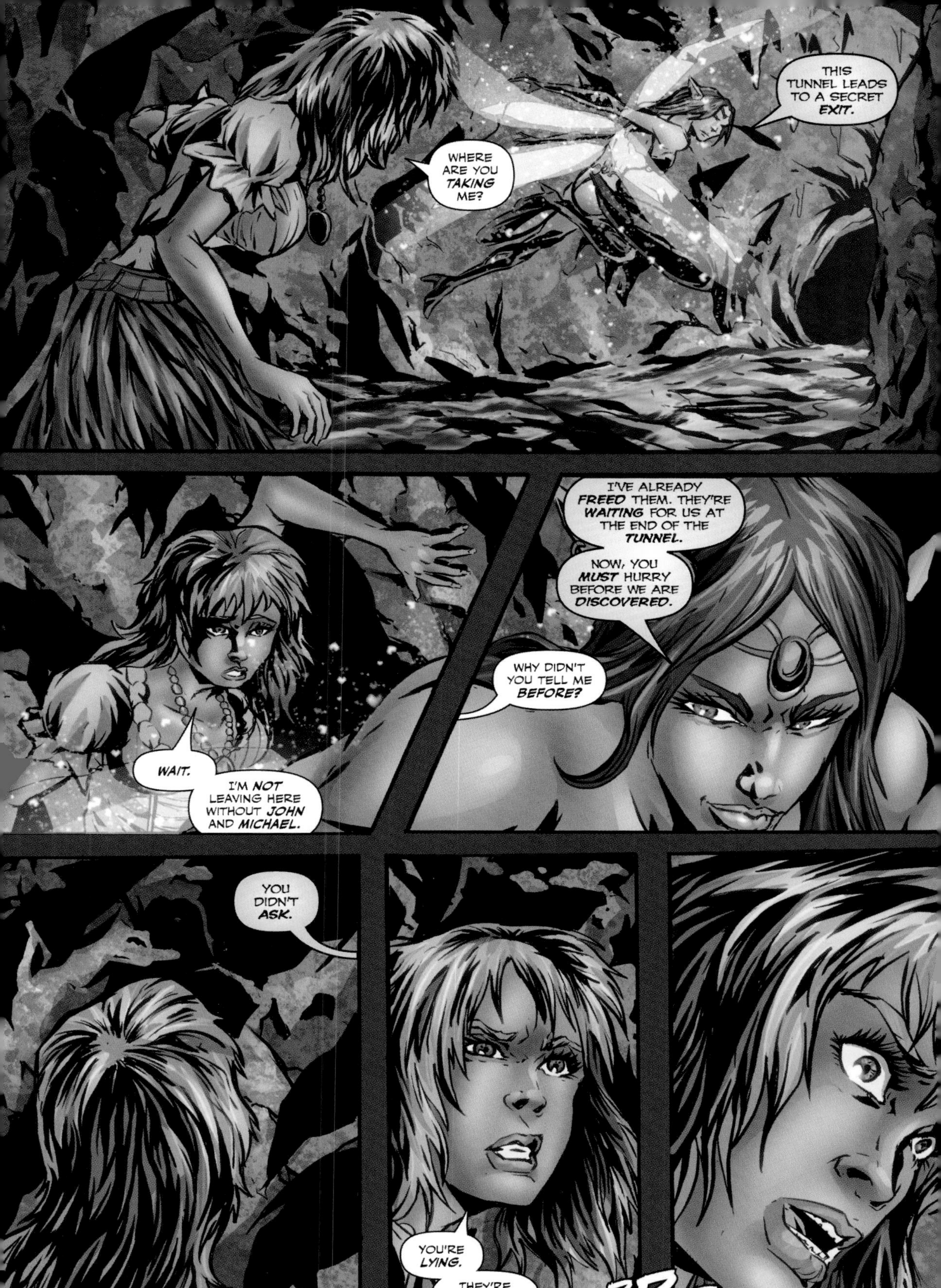

THIS TUNNEL LEADS TO A SECRET *EXIT*.
WHERE ARE YOU *TAKING* ME?
WAIT.
I'M *NOT* LEAVING HERE WITHOUT *JOHN* AND *MICHAEL*.
I'VE ALREADY *FREED* THEM. THEY'RE *WAITING* FOR US AT THE END OF THE *TUNNEL*.
NOW, YOU *MUST* HURRY BEFORE WE ARE *DISCOVERED*.
WHY DIDN'T YOU TELL ME *BEFORE?*
YOU DIDN'T *ASK*.
YOU'RE *LYING*.
THEY'RE *NOT* WAITING FOR US.
WHAT THE *HELL* IS GOING ON?
RRRRRRRR

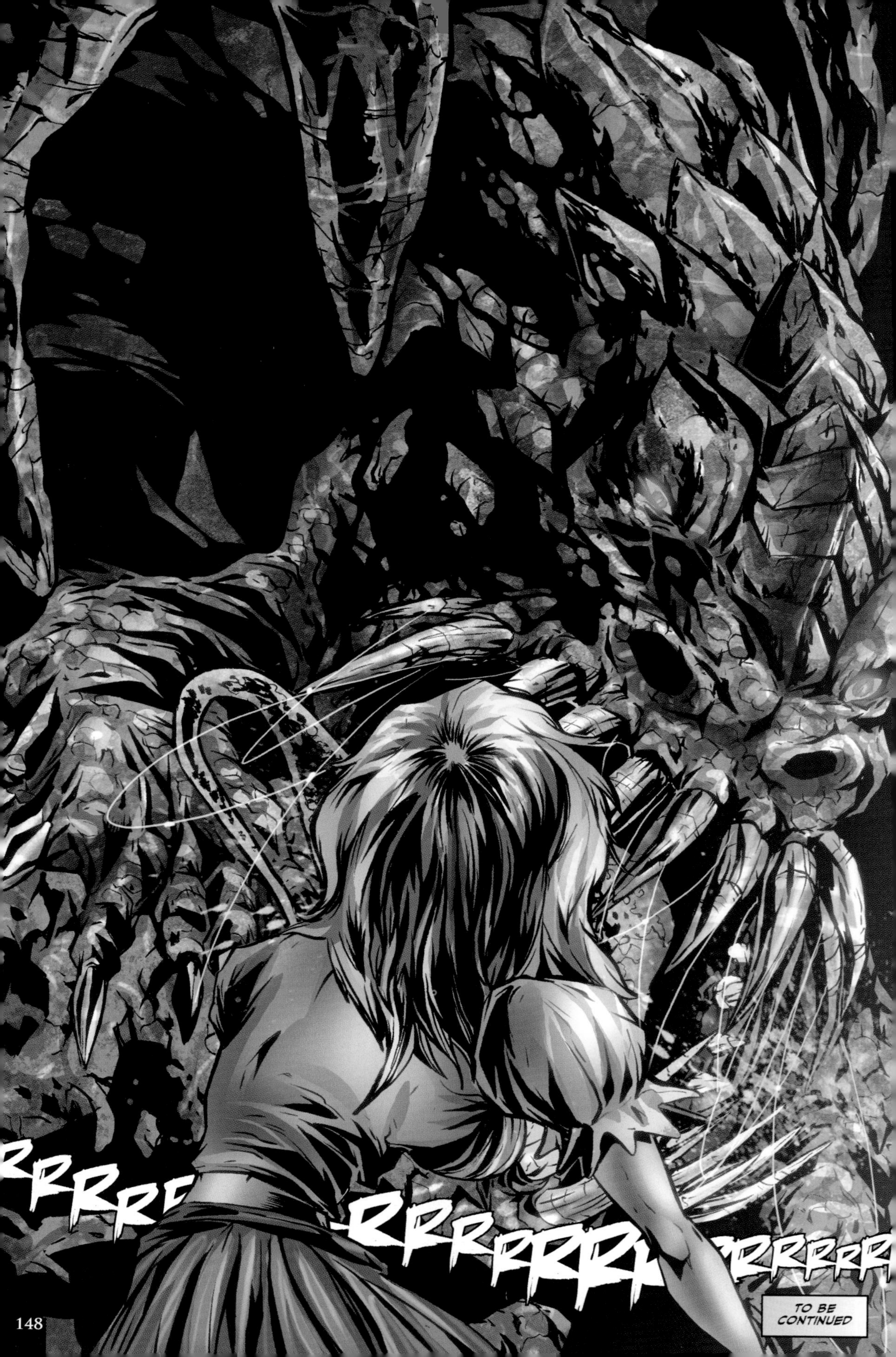
RRRRR
RRRRRRRRRRRRRRRRRR
TO BE CONTINUED

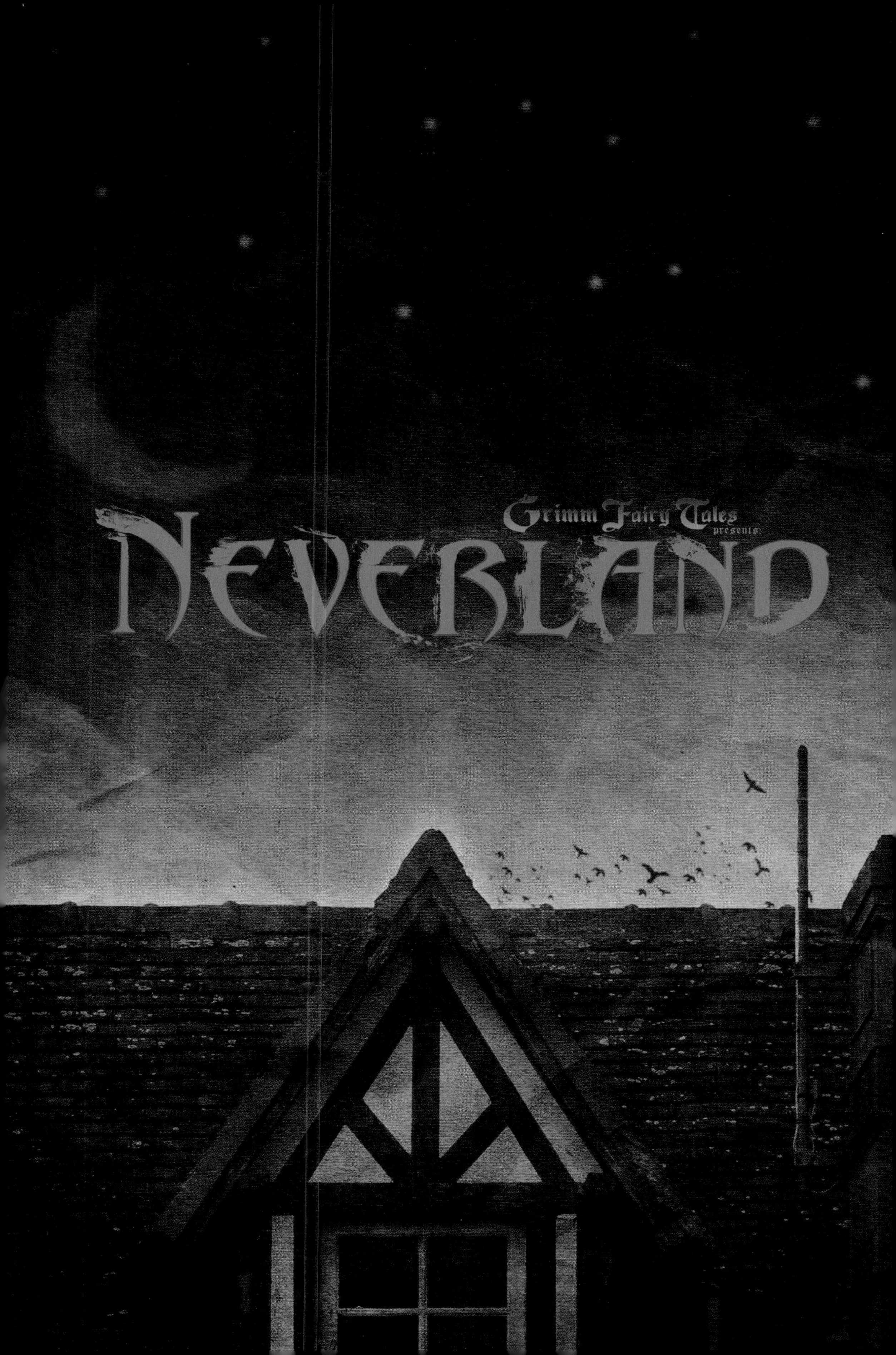
Grimm Fairy Tales presents:
NEVERLAND

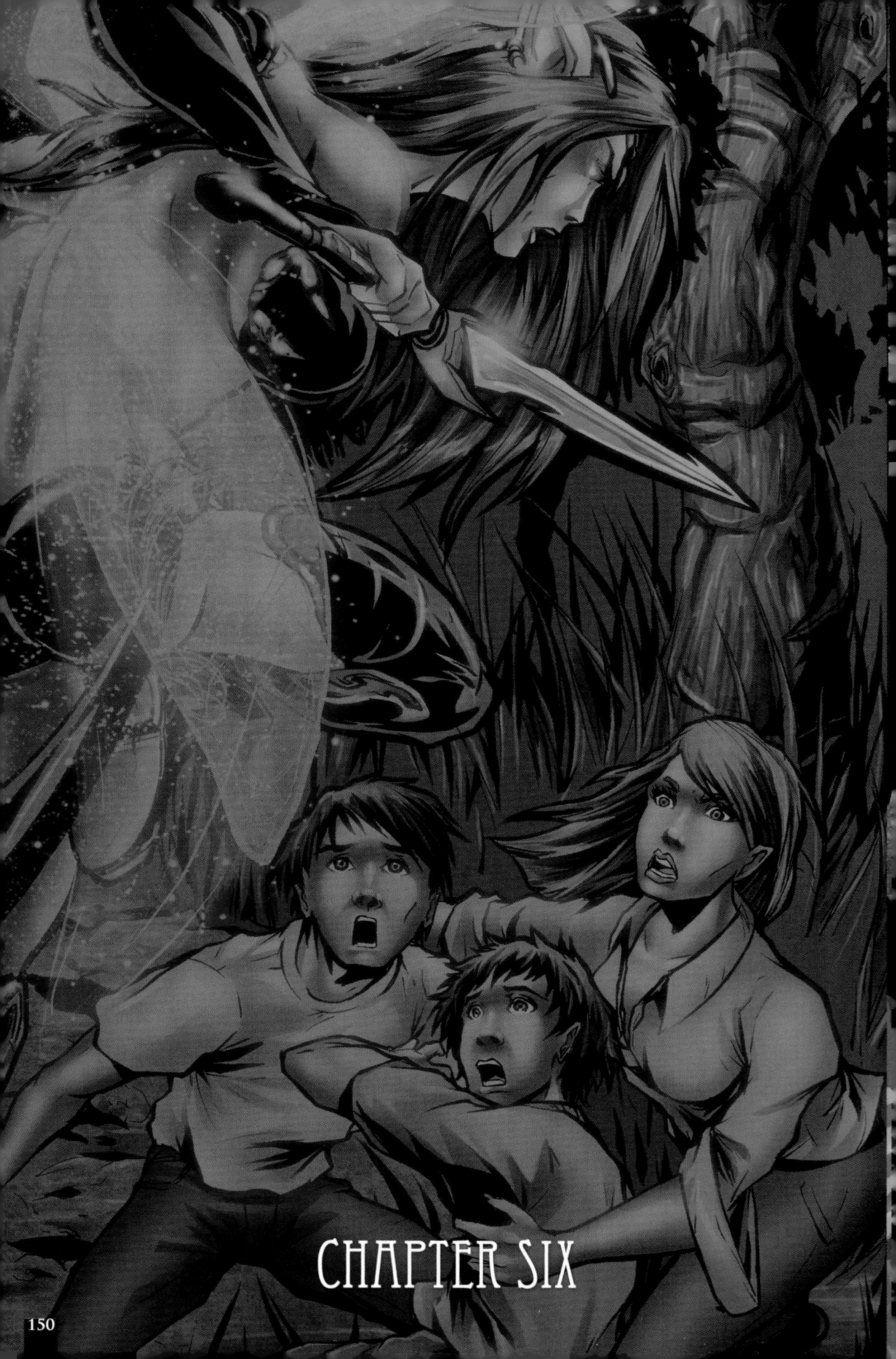

CHAPTER SIX

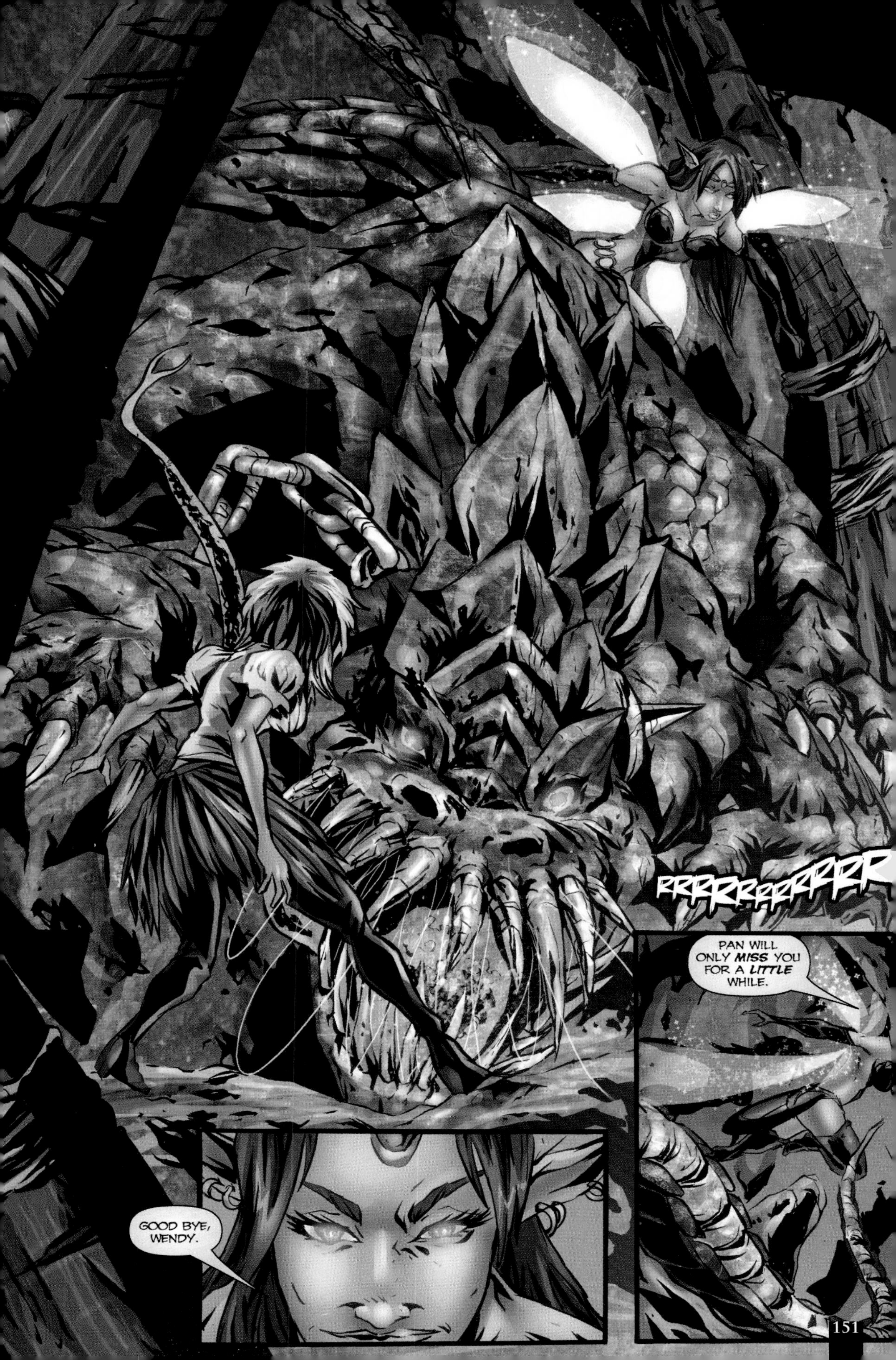
RRRRRRRRRRRRR
GOOD BYE, WENDY.
PAN WILL ONLY MISS YOU FOR A LITTLE WHILE.

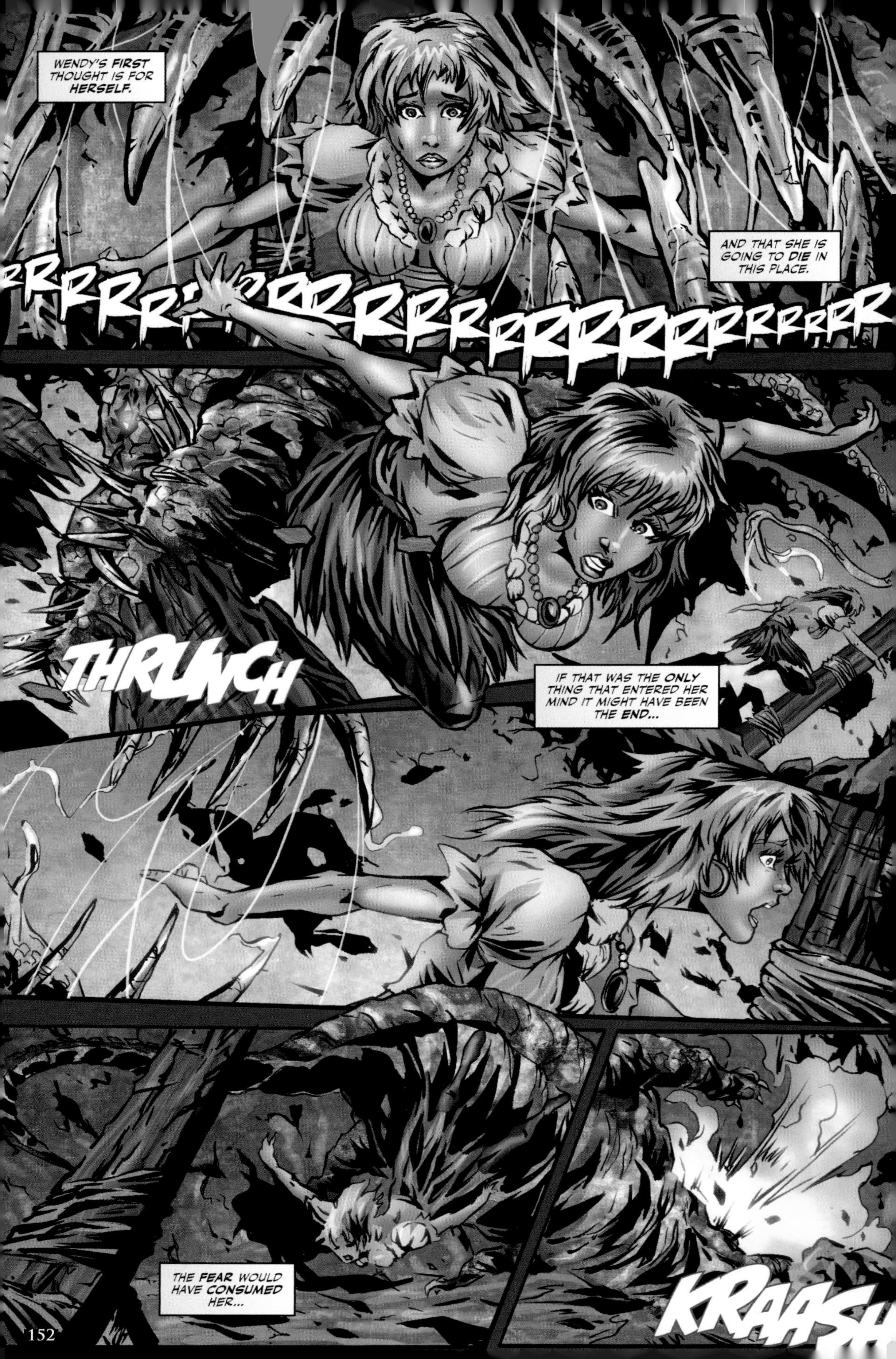
WENDY'S FIRST THOUGHT IS FOR HERSELF.
AND THAT SHE IS GOING TO DIE IN THIS PLACE.
RRRRRRRRRRRRRRRRRRRRRRRRRR
THRUNCH
IF THAT WAS THE ONLY THING THAT ENTERED HER MIND IT MIGHT HAVE BEEN THE END...
THE FEAR WOULD HAVE CONSUMED HER...
KRAASH

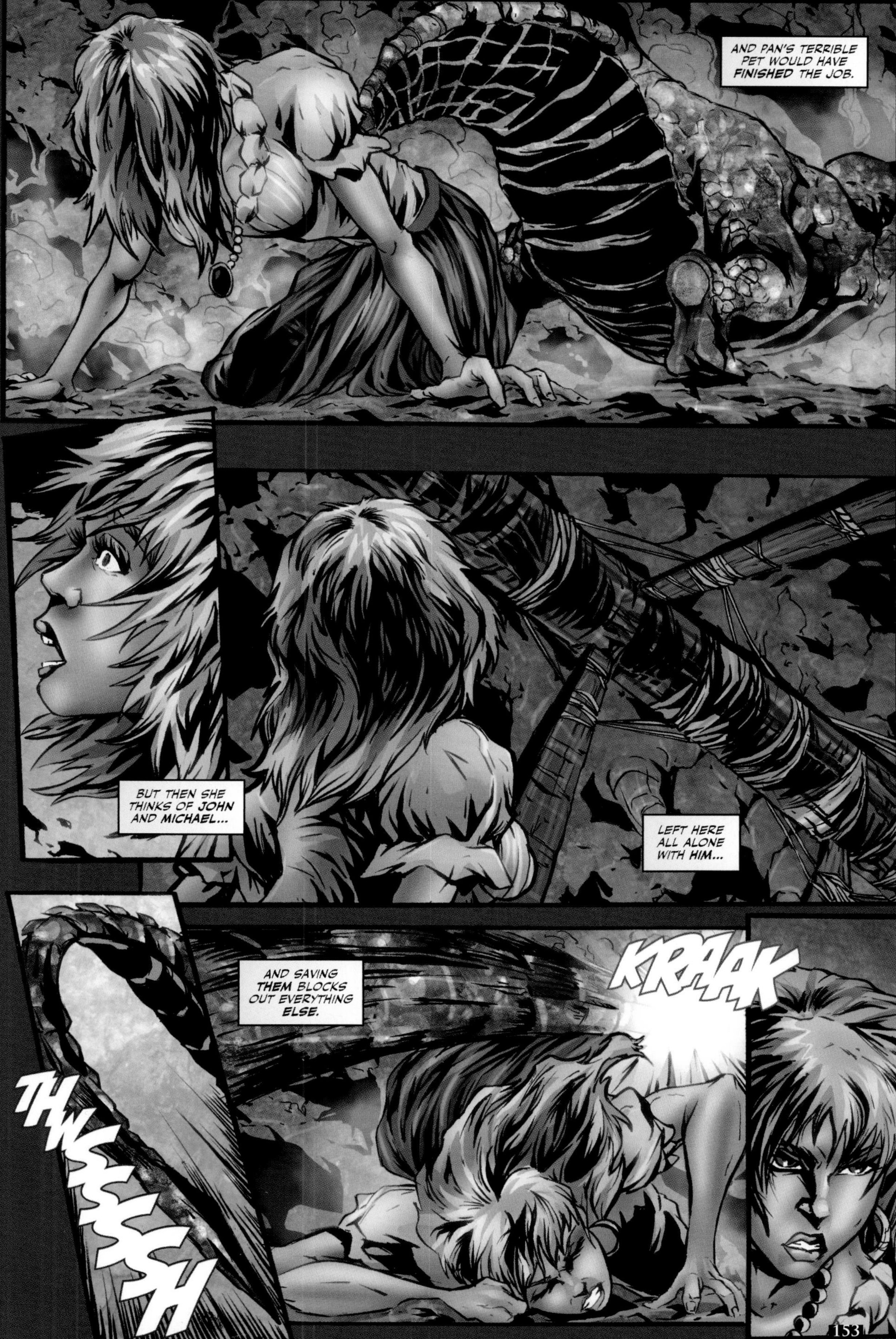
AND PAN'S TERRIBLE PET WOULD HAVE FINISHED THE JOB.
BUT THEN SHE THINKS OF JOHN AND MICHAEL...
LEFT HERE ALL ALONE WITH HIM...
AND SAVING THEM BLOCKS OUT EVERYTHING ELSE.
KRAAK
THWSSSSH

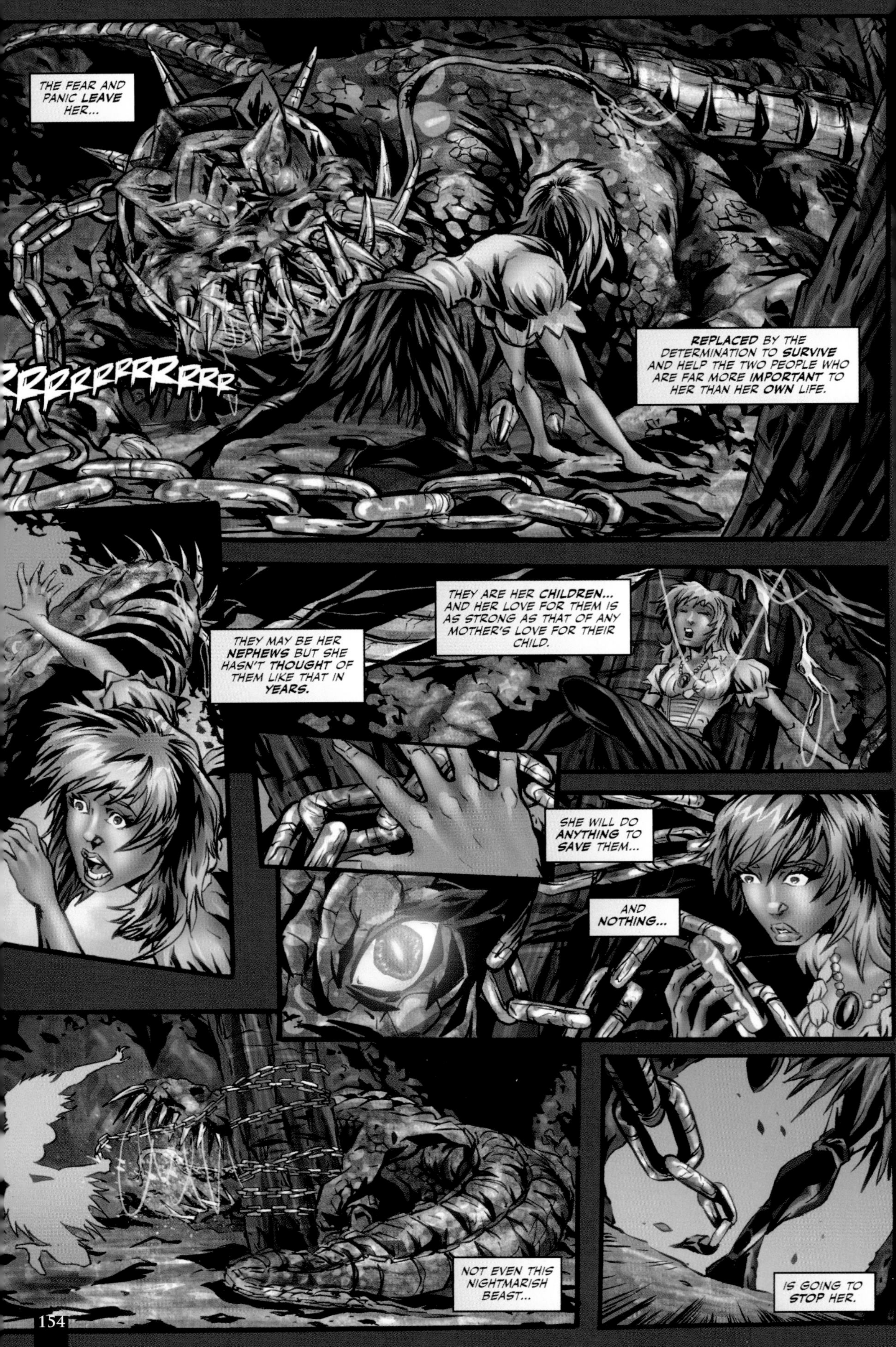
THE FEAR AND PANIC LEAVE HER...
RRRRRRRRRrrr
REPLACED BY THE DETERMINATION TO SURVIVE AND HELP THE TWO PEOPLE WHO ARE FAR MORE IMPORTANT TO HER THAN HER OWN LIFE.
THEY MAY BE HER NEPHEWS BUT SHE HASN'T THOUGHT OF THEM LIKE THAT IN YEARS.
THEY ARE HER CHILDREN... AND HER LOVE FOR THEM IS AS STRONG AS THAT OF ANY MOTHER'S LOVE FOR THEIR CHILD.
SHE WILL DO ANYTHING TO SAVE THEM...
AND NOTHING...
NOT EVEN THIS NIGHTMARISH BEAST...
IS GOING TO STOP HER.

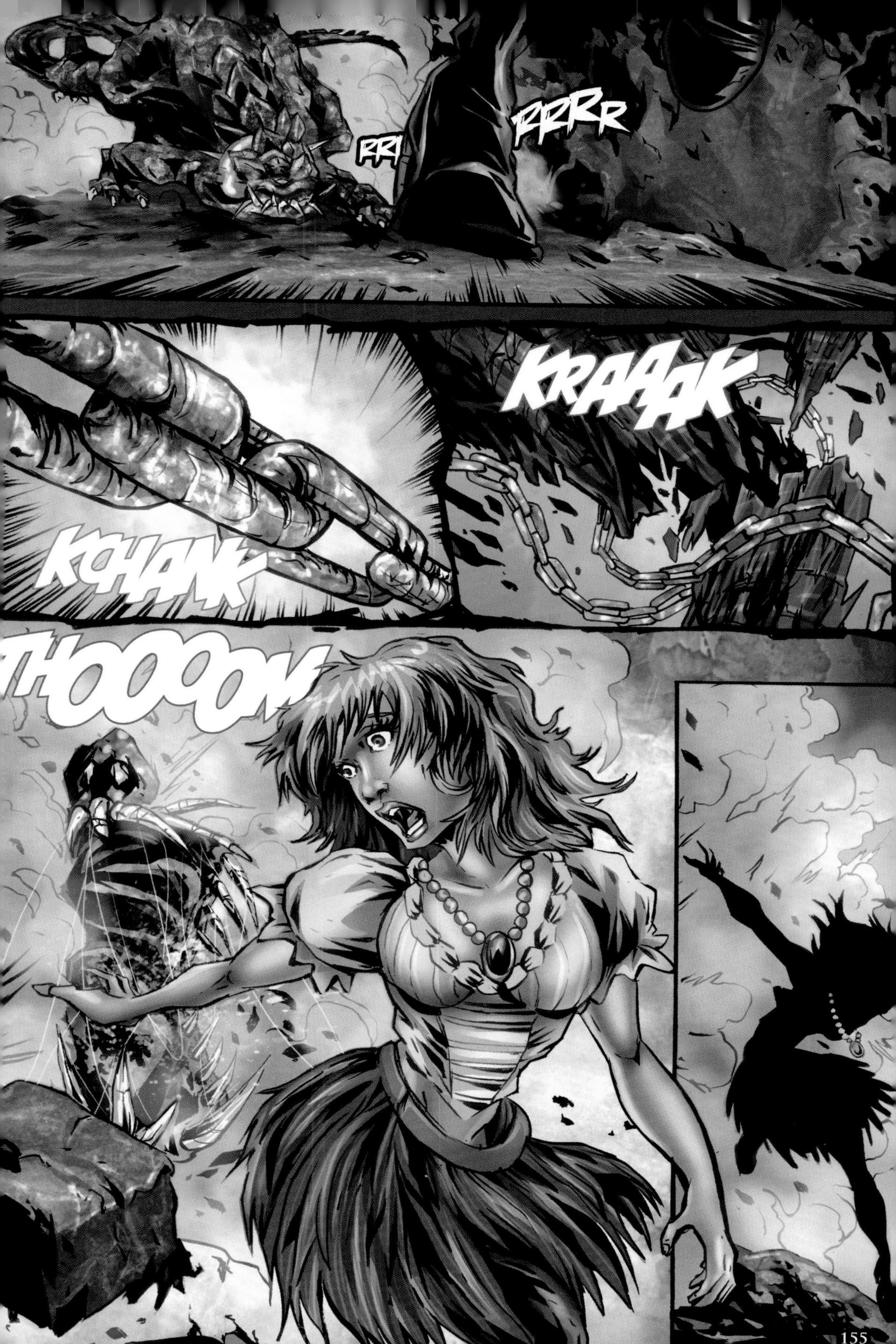
RRR
RRRR
KRAAAK
KCHANK
THOOOOM

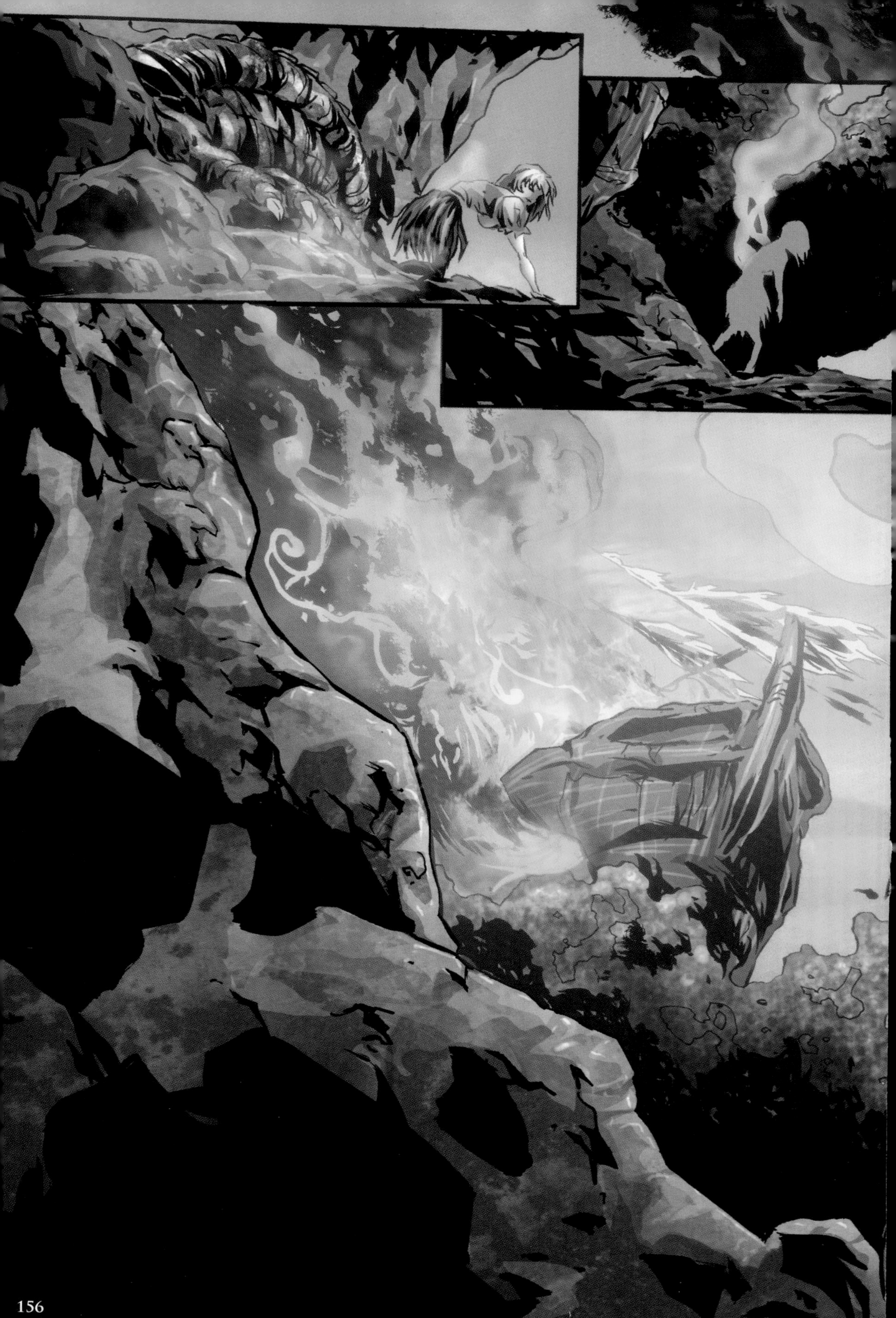

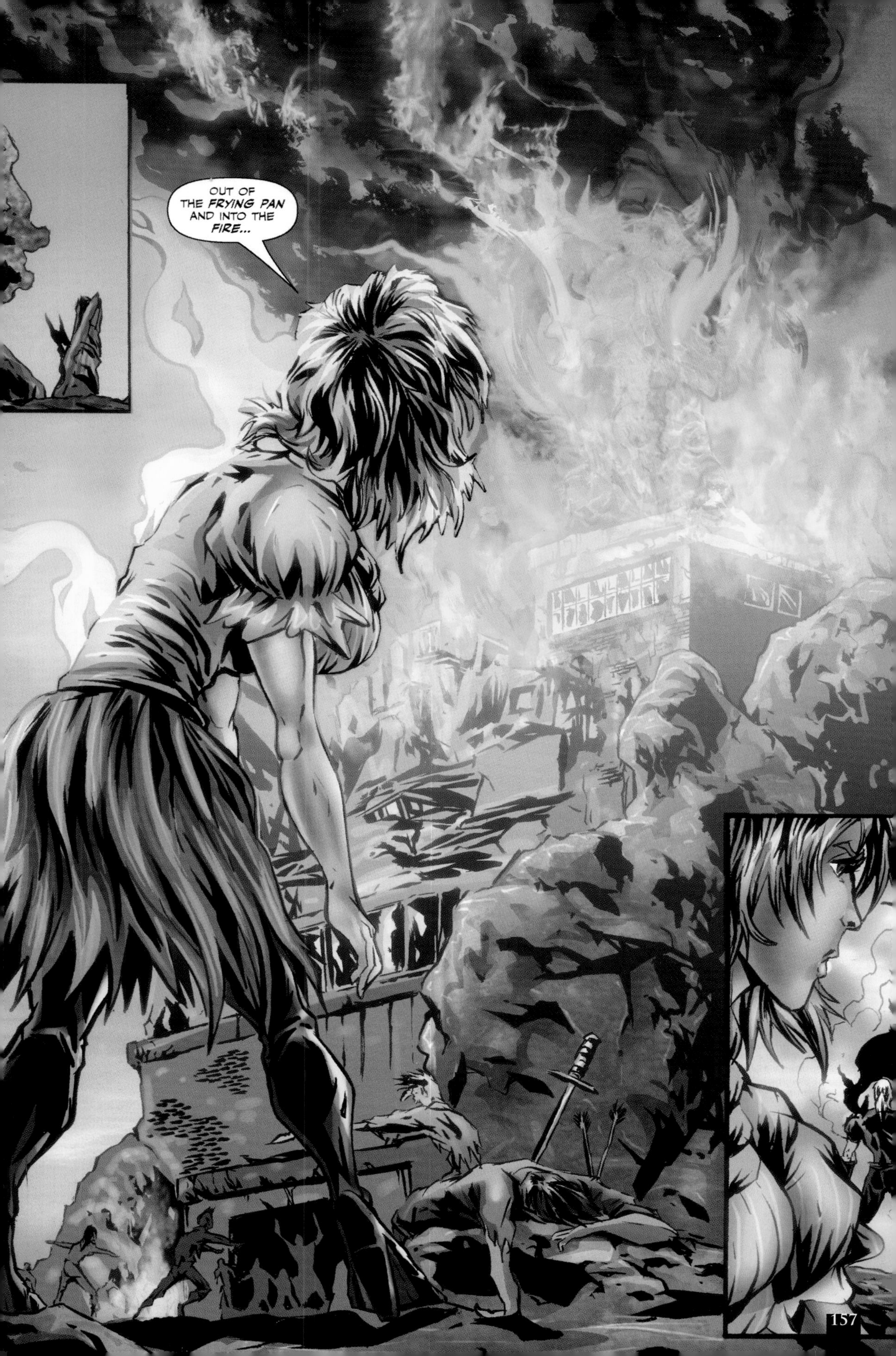
OUT OF THE *FRYING PAN* AND INTO THE *FIRE*...

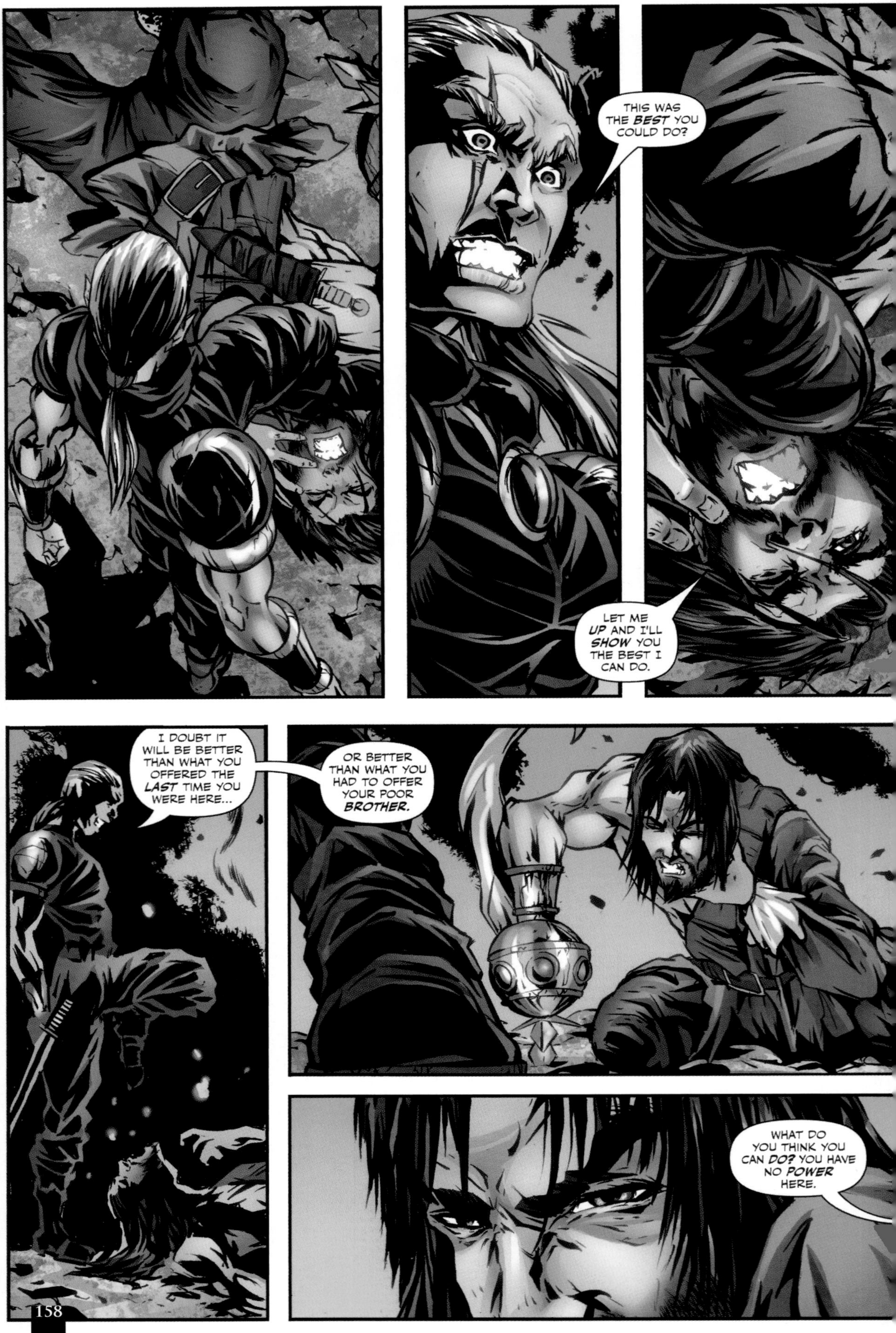
THIS WAS THE BEST YOU COULD DO?
LET ME UP AND I'LL SHOW YOU THE BEST I CAN DO.
I DOUBT IT WILL BE BETTER THAN WHAT YOU OFFERED THE LAST TIME YOU WERE HERE...
OR BETTER THAN WHAT YOU HAD TO OFFER YOUR POOR BROTHER.
WHAT DO YOU THINK YOU CAN DO? YOU HAVE NO POWER HERE.

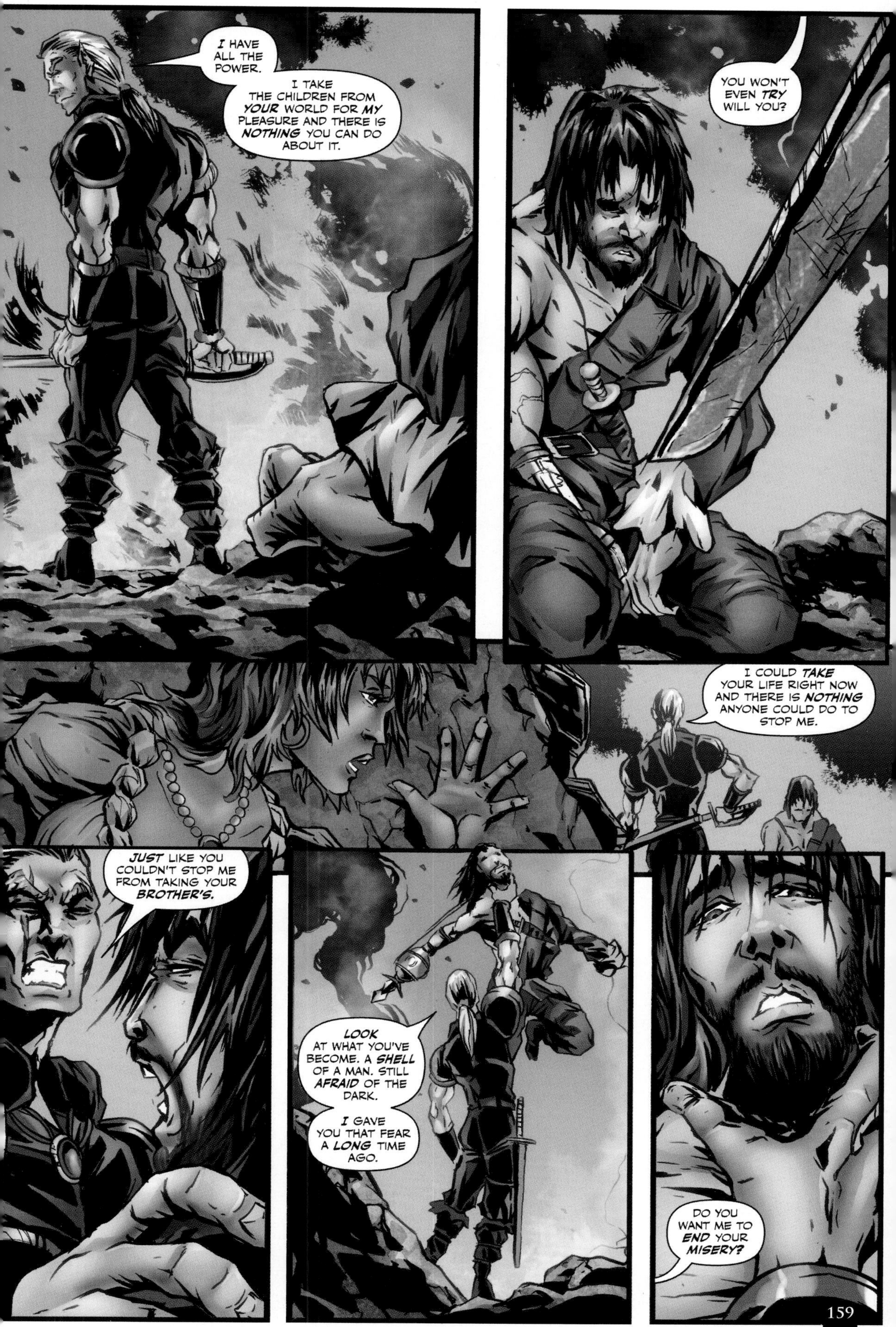
I HAVE ALL THE POWER.
I TAKE THE CHILDREN FROM YOUR WORLD FOR MY PLEASURE AND THERE IS NOTHING YOU CAN DO ABOUT IT.
YOU WON'T EVEN TRY WILL YOU?
I COULD TAKE YOUR LIFE RIGHT NOW AND THERE IS NOTHING ANYONE COULD STOP ME DO TO STOP ME.
JUST LIKE YOU COULDN'T STOP ME FROM TAKING YOUR BROTHER'S.
LOOK AT WHAT YOU'VE BECOME. A SHELL OF A MAN. STILL AFRAID OF THE DARK.
I GAVE YOU THAT FEAR A LONG TIME AGO.
DO YOU WANT ME TO END YOUR MISERY?

YOU'RE NOT WORTH THE *EFFORT.*

YOU'LL SUFFER *MORE* BEING *ALIVE,* THINKING OF THE HORRIBLE THINGS THAT I DID TO THE PERSON YOU LOVED *MOST.*

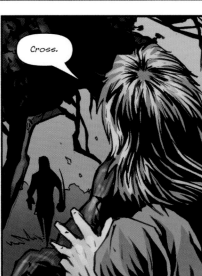

Cross.

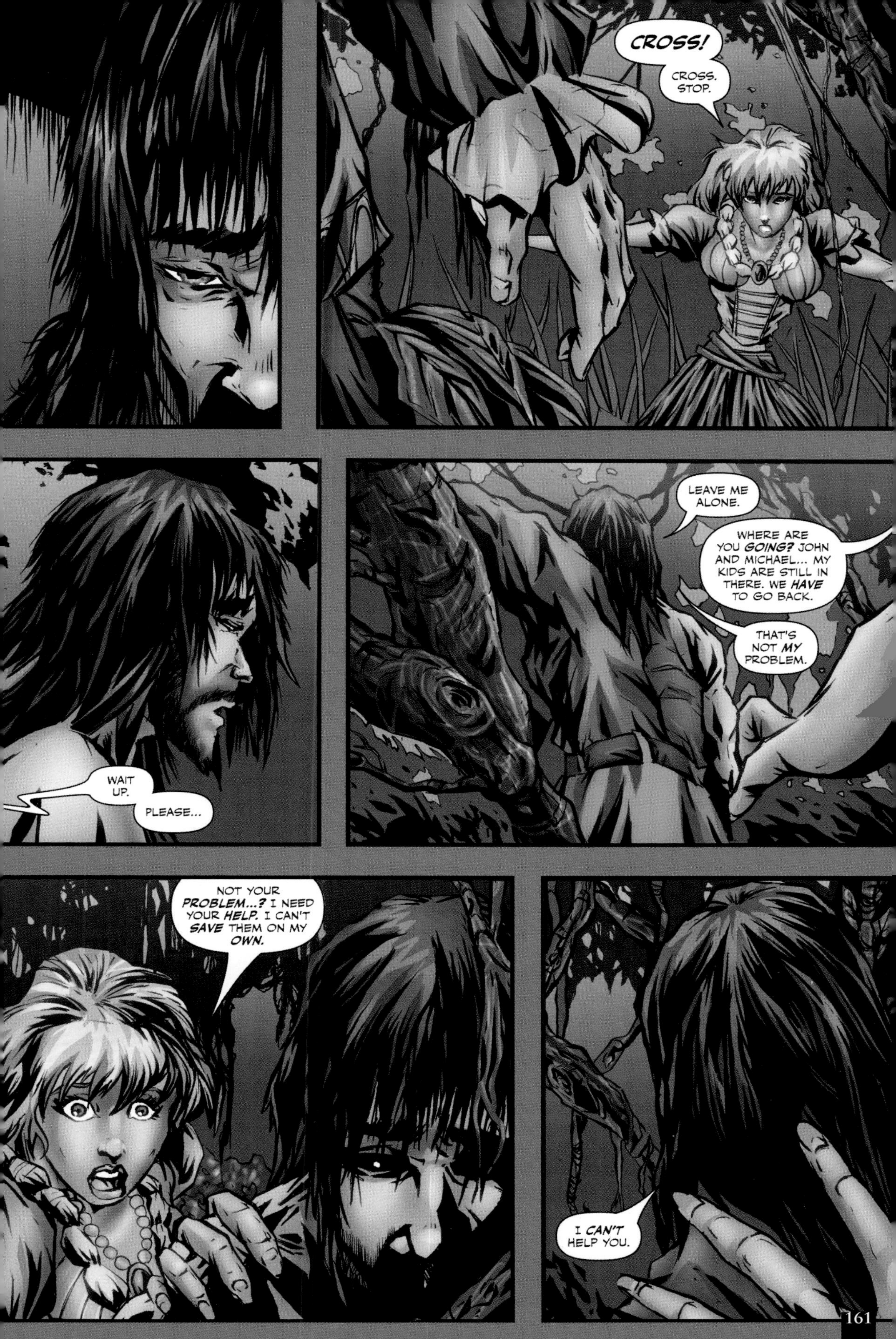
CROSS!
CROSS. STOP.
WAIT UP.
PLEASE...
LEAVE ME ALONE.
WHERE ARE YOU GOING? JOHN AND MICHAEL... MY KIDS ARE STILL IN THERE. WE HAVE TO GO BACK.
THAT'S NOT MY PROBLEM.
NOT YOUR PROBLEM...? I NEED YOUR HELP. I CAN'T SAVE THEM ON MY OWN.
I CAN'T HELP YOU.

TIME FOR A LITTLE AFTER-BATTLE *FUN*... NOT THAT SUCH A SLAUGHTER *WASN'T* FUN BUT I NEED A *DIFFERENT* SORT OF ENTERTAINMENT.

NOB, BRING ME THE *GIRL*.

SHE'S *GONE*.

WHAT DO YOU *MEAN* SHE'S *GONE?*

SHE ESCAPED.

IMPOSSIBLE! HOW COULD THIS HAPPEN?

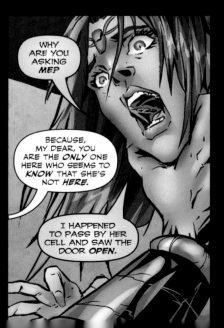

WHY ARE YOU ASKING *ME?*

BECAUSE, MY DEAR, YOU ARE THE *ONLY* ONE HERE WHO SEEMS TO *KNOW* THAT SHE'S NOT *HERE.*

I HAPPENED TO PASS BY HER CELL AND SAW THE DOOR *OPEN.*

NOB, *CHECK* HER ROOM AND *SEARCH* THE CASTLE GROUNDS. I WANT HER *FOUND.*

AND BRING HER TWO *BRATS* TO *ME.*

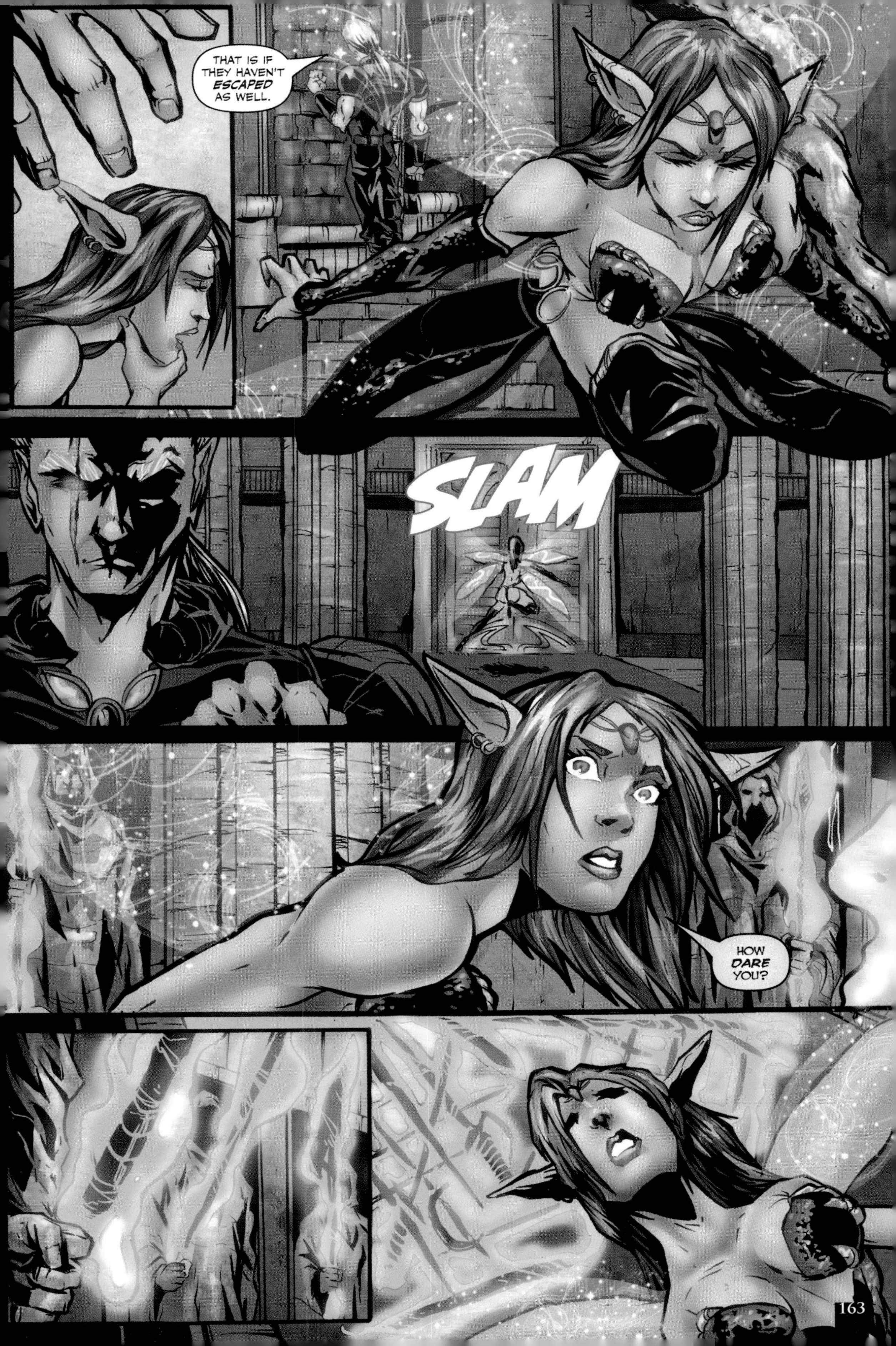
THAT IS IF THEY HAVEN'T ESCAPED AS WELL.
SLAM
HOW DARE YOU?

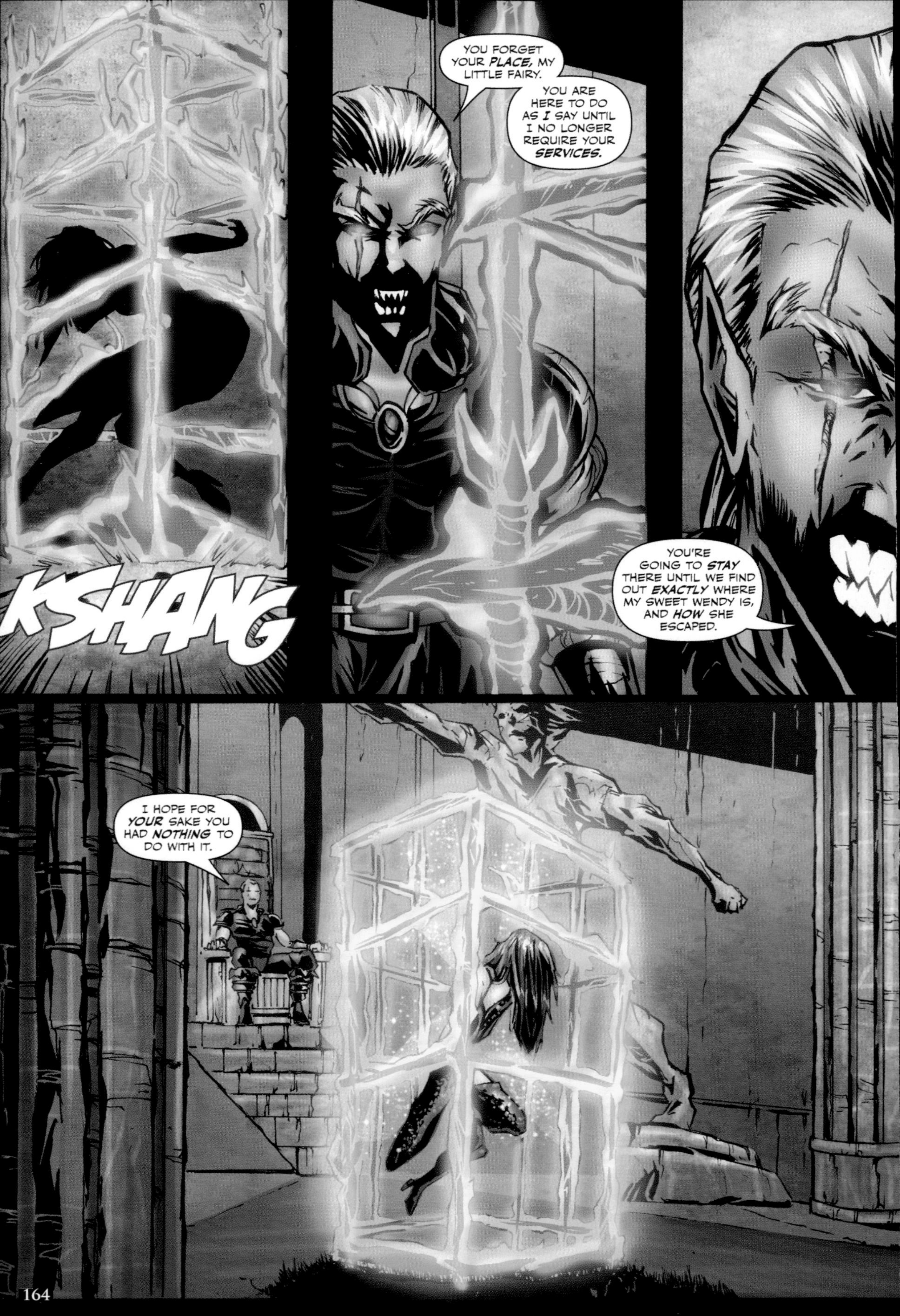
KSHANG
YOU FORGET YOUR PLACE, MY LITTLE FAIRY.
YOU ARE HERE TO DO AS I SAY UNTIL I NO LONGER REQUIRE YOUR SERVICES.
YOU'RE GOING TO STAY THERE UNTIL WE FIND OUT EXACTLY WHERE MY SWEET WENDY IS, AND HOW SHE ESCAPED.
I HOPE FOR YOUR SAKE YOU HAD NOTHING TO DO WITH IT.

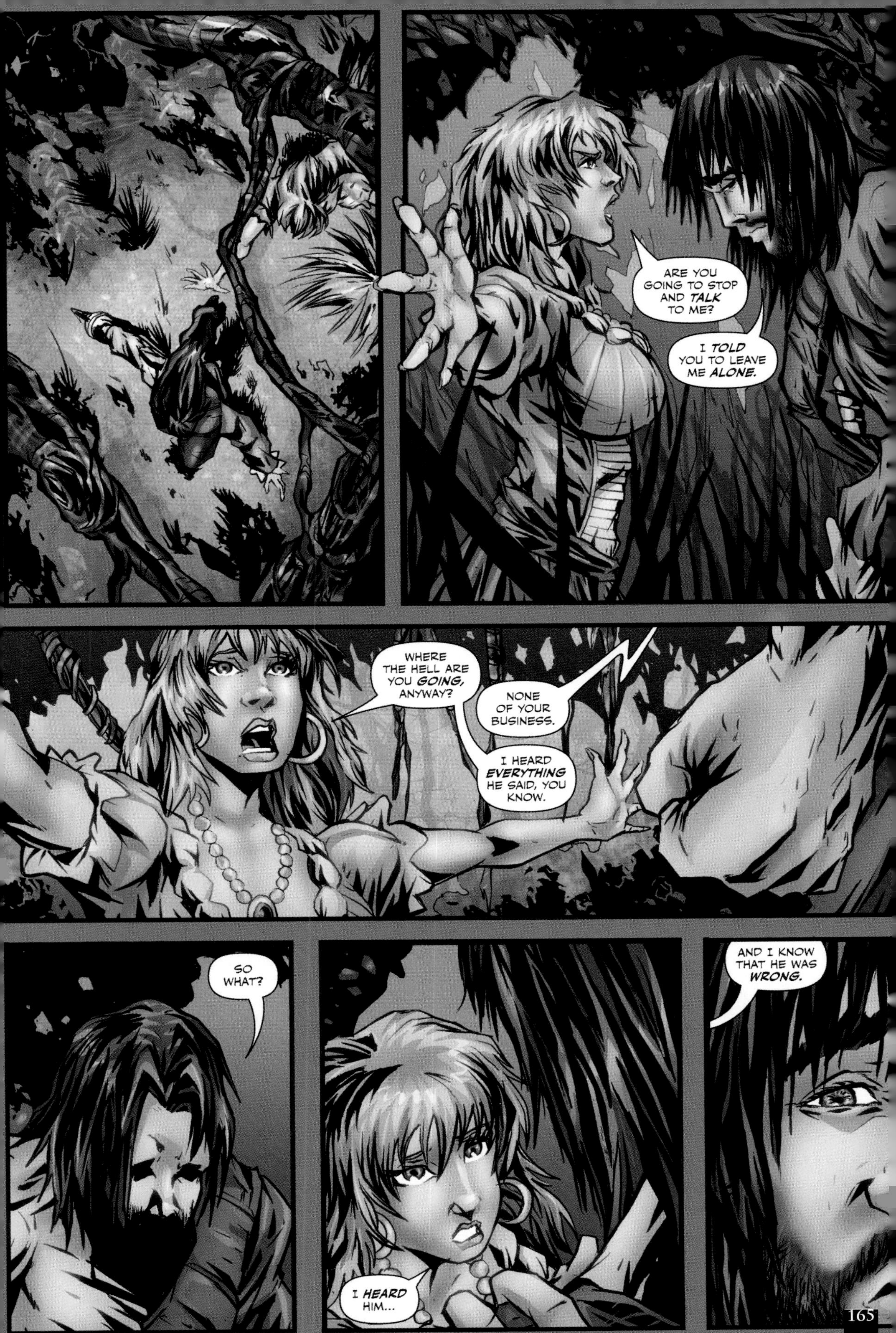

ARE YOU GOING TO STOP AND TALK TO ME?
I TOLD YOU TO LEAVE ME ALONE.
WHERE THE HELL ARE YOU GOING, ANYWAY?
NONE OF YOUR BUSINESS.
I HEARD EVERYTHING HE SAID, YOU KNOW.
SO WHAT?
I HEARD HIM...
AND I KNOW THAT HE WAS WRONG.

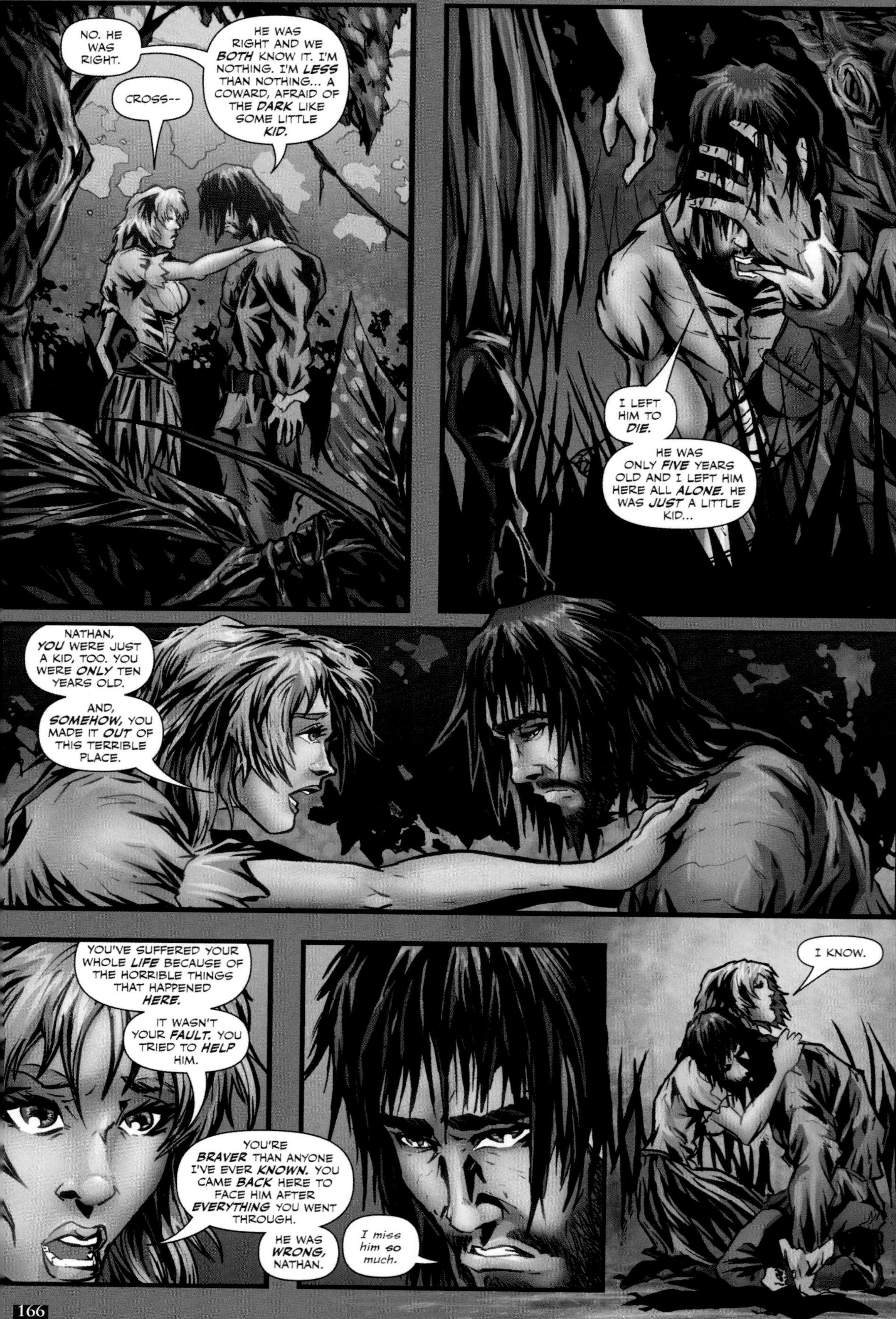
NO. HE WAS RIGHT.
CROSS--
HE WAS RIGHT AND WE BOTH KNOW IT. I'M NOTHING. I'M LESS THAN NOTHING... A COWARD, AFRAID OF THE DARK LIKE SOME LITTLE KID.
I LEFT HIM TO DIE.
HE WAS ONLY FIVE YEARS OLD AND I LEFT HIM HERE ALL ALONE. HE WAS JUST A LITTLE KID...
NATHAN, YOU WERE JUST A KID, TOO. YOU WERE ONLY TEN YEARS OLD.
AND, SOMEHOW, YOU MADE IT OUT OF THIS TERRIBLE PLACE.
YOU'VE SUFFERED YOUR WHOLE LIFE BECAUSE OF THE HORRIBLE THINGS THAT HAPPENED HERE.
IT WASN'T YOUR FAULT. YOU TRIED TO HELP HIM.
YOU'RE BRAVER THAN ANYONE I'VE EVER KNOWN. YOU CAME BACK HERE TO FACE HIM AFTER EVERYTHING YOU WENT THROUGH.
HE WAS WRONG, NATHAN.
I miss him so much.
I KNOW.

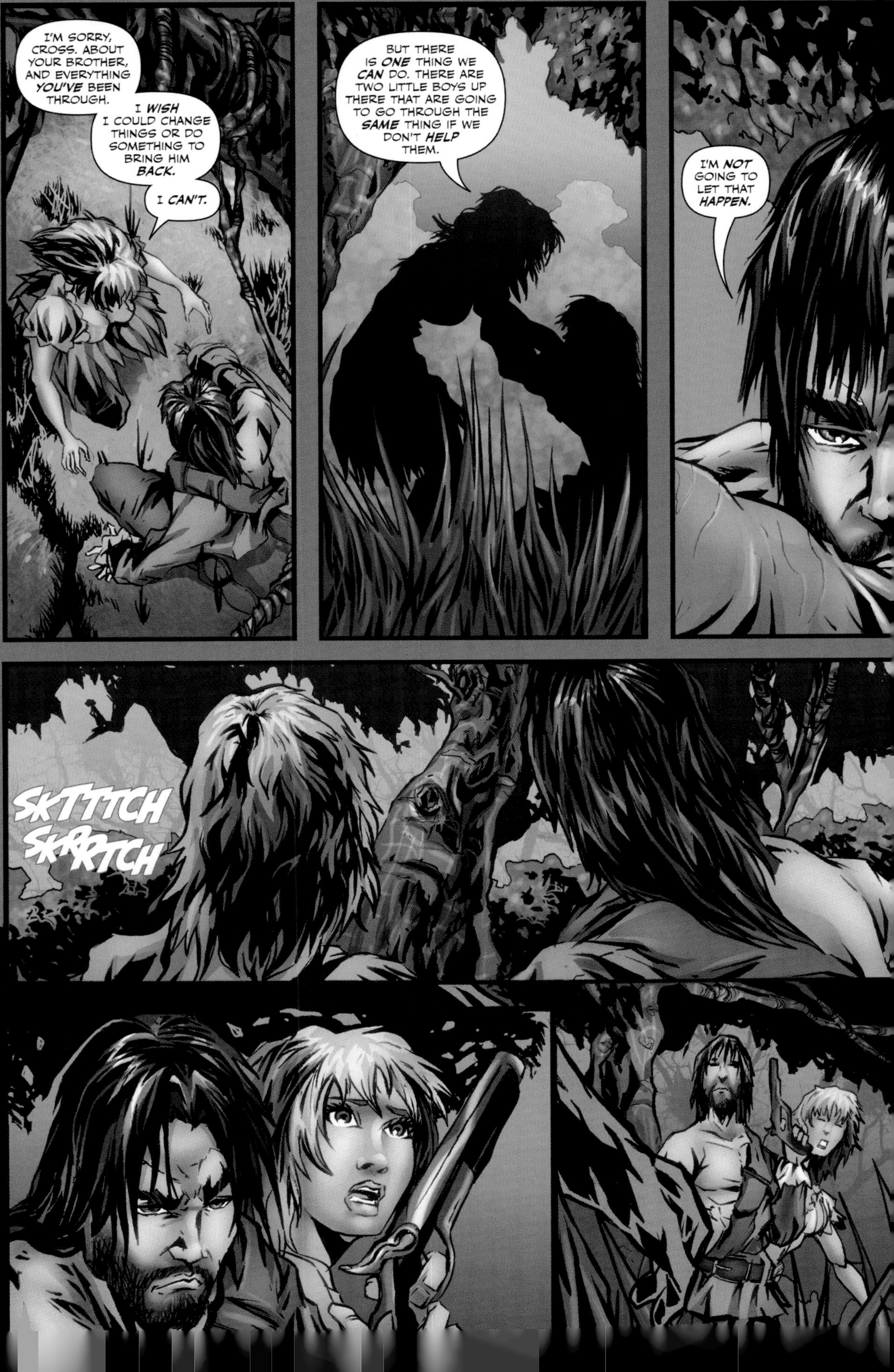

I'M SORRY, CROSS. ABOUT YOUR BROTHER, AND EVERYTHING YOU'VE BEEN THROUGH.
I WISH I COULD CHANGE THINGS OR DO SOMETHING TO BRING HIM BACK.
I CAN'T.
BUT THERE IS ONE THING WE CAN DO. THERE ARE TWO LITTLE BOYS UP THERE THAT ARE GOING TO GO THROUGH THE SAME THING IF WE DON'T HELP THEM.
I'M NOT GOING TO LET THAT HAPPEN.
SKTTTCH
SKRRTCH

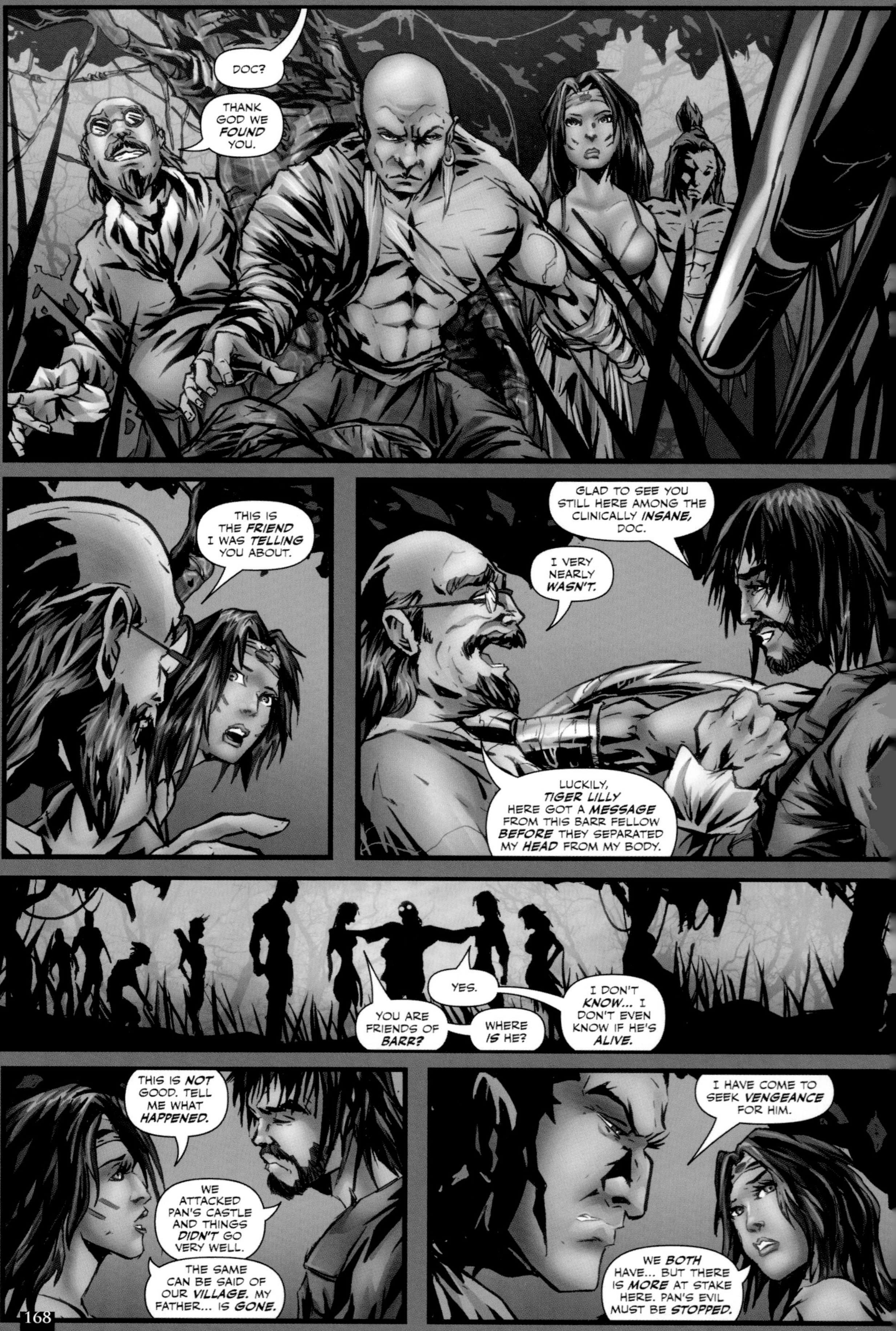

DOC?
THANK GOD WE FOUND YOU.
THIS IS THE FRIEND I WAS TELLING YOU ABOUT.
GLAD TO SEE YOU STILL HERE AMONG THE CLINICALLY INSANE, DOC.
I VERY NEARLY WASN'T.
LUCKILY, TIGER LILLY HERE GOT A MESSAGE FROM THIS BARR FELLOW BEFORE THEY SEPARATED MY HEAD FROM MY BODY.
YOU ARE FRIENDS OF BARR?
YES.
WHERE IS HE?
I DON'T KNOW... I DON'T EVEN KNOW IF HE'S ALIVE.
THIS IS NOT GOOD. TELL ME WHAT HAPPENED.
WE ATTACKED PAN'S CASTLE AND THINGS DIDN'T GO VERY WELL.
THE SAME CAN BE SAID OF OUR VILLAGE. MY FATHER... IS GONE.
I HAVE COME TO SEEK VENGEANCE FOR HIM.
WE BOTH HAVE... BUT THERE IS MORE AT STAKE HERE. PAN'S EVIL MUST BE STOPPED.

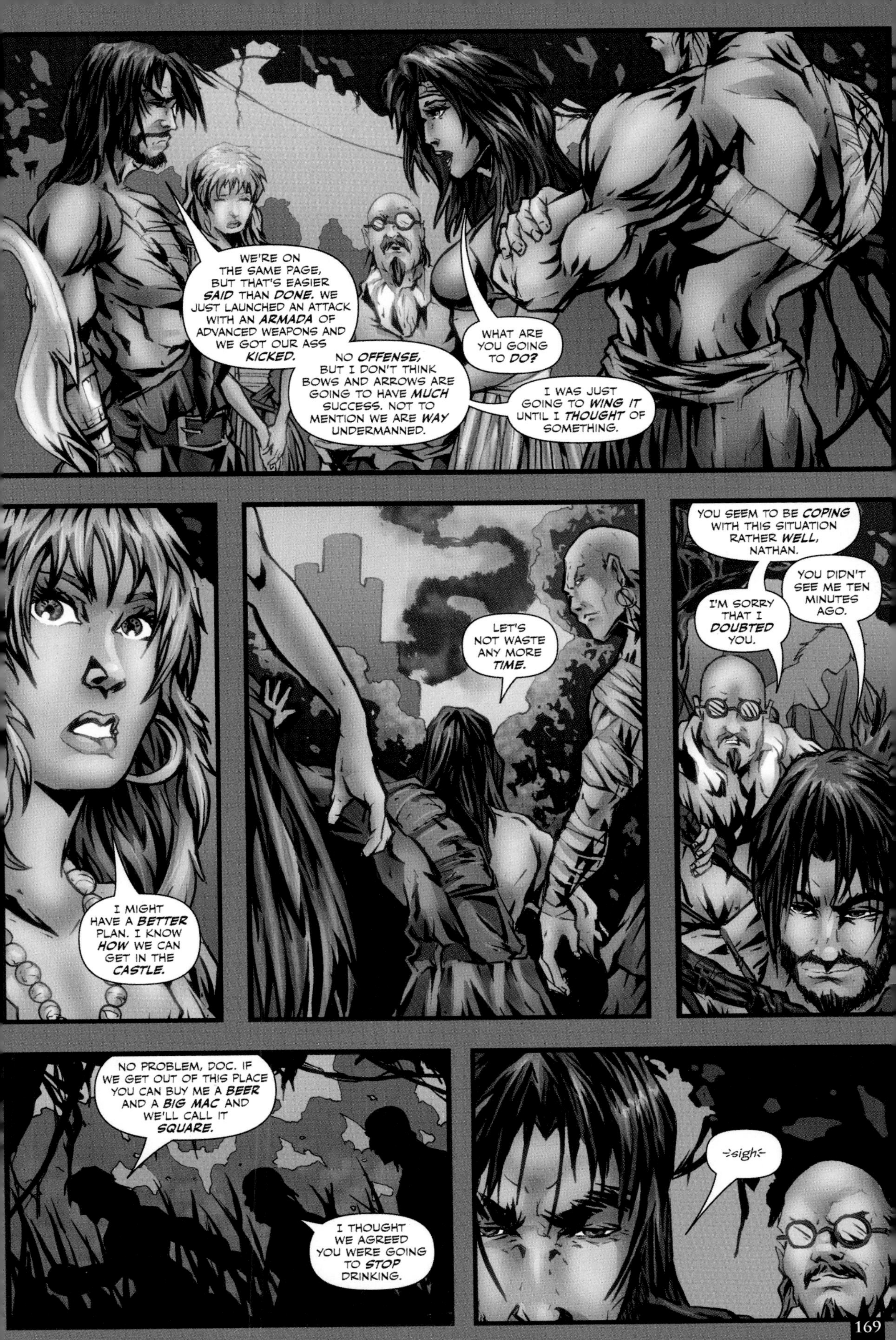
WE'RE ON THE SAME PAGE, BUT THAT'S EASIER SAID THAN DONE. WE JUST LAUNCHED AN ATTACK WITH AN ARMADA OF ADVANCED WEAPONS AND WE GOT OUR ASS KICKED.
WHAT ARE YOU GOING TO DO?
NO OFFENSE, BUT I DON'T THINK BOWS AND ARROWS ARE GOING TO HAVE MUCH SUCCESS. NOT TO MENTION WE ARE WAY UNDERMANNED.
I WAS JUST GOING TO WING IT UNTIL I THOUGHT OF SOMETHING.
I MIGHT HAVE A BETTER PLAN. I KNOW HOW WE CAN GET IN THE CASTLE.
LET'S NOT WASTE ANY MORE TIME.
YOU SEEM TO BE COPING WITH THIS SITUATION RATHER WELL, NATHAN.
YOU DIDN'T SEE ME TEN MINUTES AGO.
I'M SORRY THAT I DOUBTED YOU.
NO PROBLEM, DOC. IF WE GET OUT OF THIS PLACE YOU CAN BUY ME A BEER AND A BIG MAC AND WE'LL CALL IT SQUARE.
I THOUGHT WE AGREED YOU WERE GOING TO STOP DRINKING.
sigh

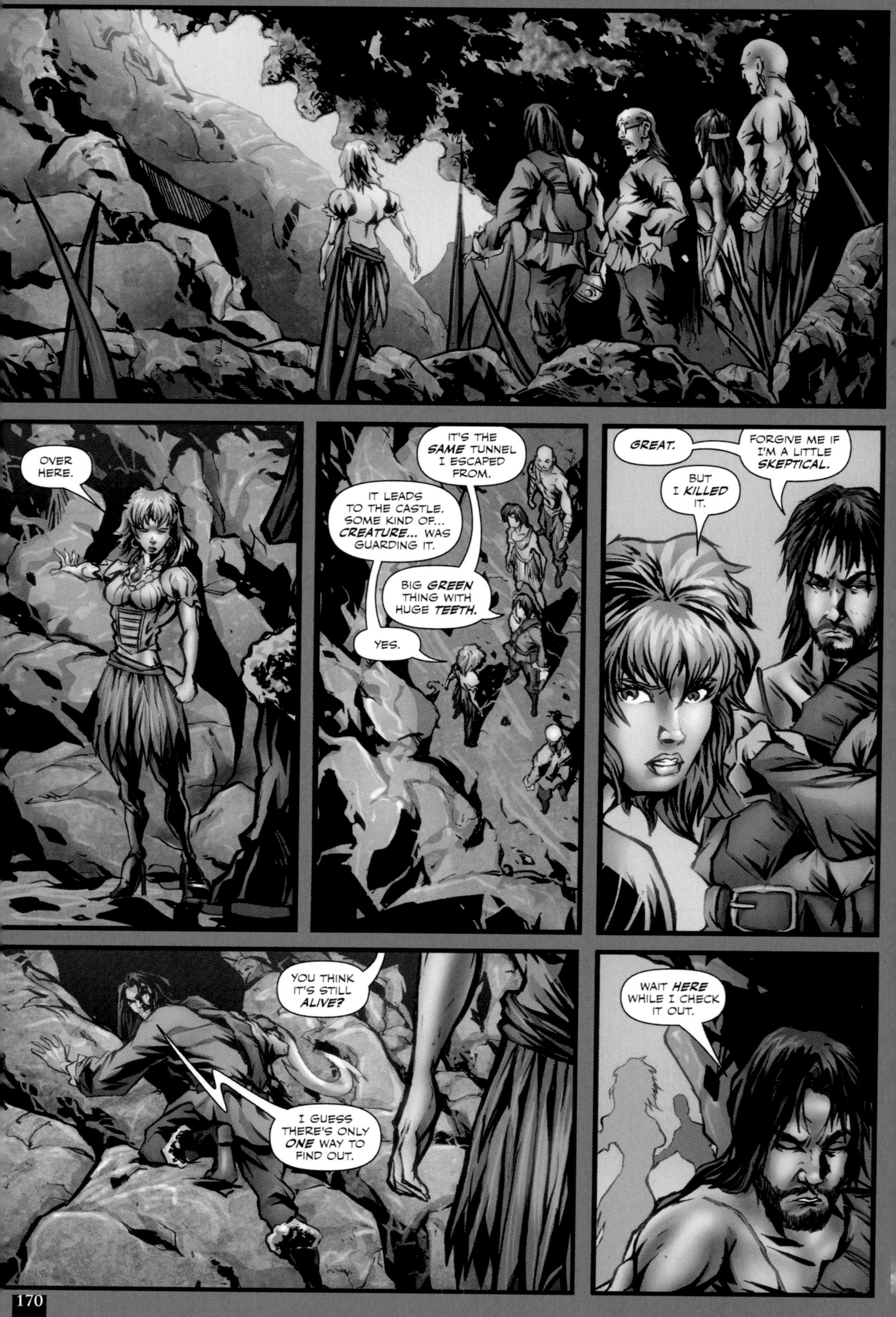
OVER HERE.
IT'S THE SAME TUNNEL I ESCAPED FROM.
IT LEADS TO THE CASTLE. SOME KIND OF... CREATURE... WAS GUARDING IT.
BIG GREEN THING WITH HUGE TEETH.
YES.
GREAT.
FORGIVE ME IF I'M A LITTLE SKEPTICAL.
BUT I KILLED IT.
YOU THINK IT'S STILL ALIVE?
I GUESS THERE'S ONLY ONE WAY TO FIND OUT.
WAIT HERE WHILE I CHECK IT OUT.

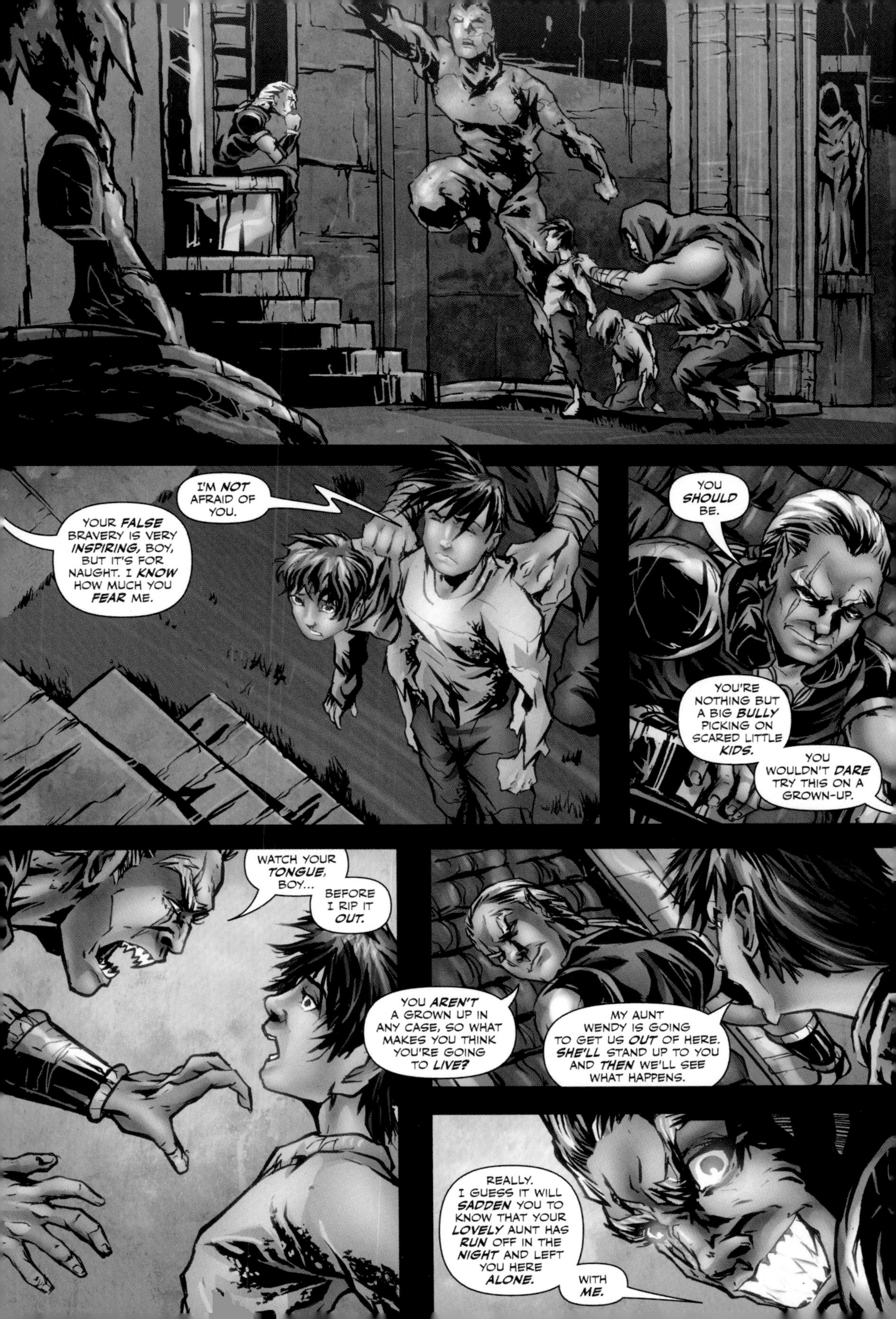
I'M NOT AFRAID OF YOU.
YOUR FALSE BRAVERY IS VERY INSPIRING, BOY, BUT IT'S FOR NAUGHT. I KNOW HOW MUCH YOU FEAR ME.
YOU SHOULD BE.
YOU'RE NOTHING BUT A BIG BULLY PICKING ON SCARED LITTLE KIDS.
YOU WOULDN'T DARE TRY THIS ON A GROWN-UP.
WATCH YOUR TONGUE, BOY...
BEFORE I RIP IT OUT.
YOU AREN'T A GROWN UP IN ANY CASE, SO WHAT MAKES YOU THINK YOU'RE GOING TO LIVE?
MY AUNT WENDY IS GOING TO GET US OUT OF HERE. SHE'LL STAND UP TO YOU AND THEN WE'LL SEE WHAT HAPPENS.
REALLY. I GUESS IT WILL SADDEN YOU TO KNOW THAT YOUR LOVELY AUNT HAS RUN OFF IN THE NIGHT AND LEFT YOU HERE ALONE.
WITH ME.

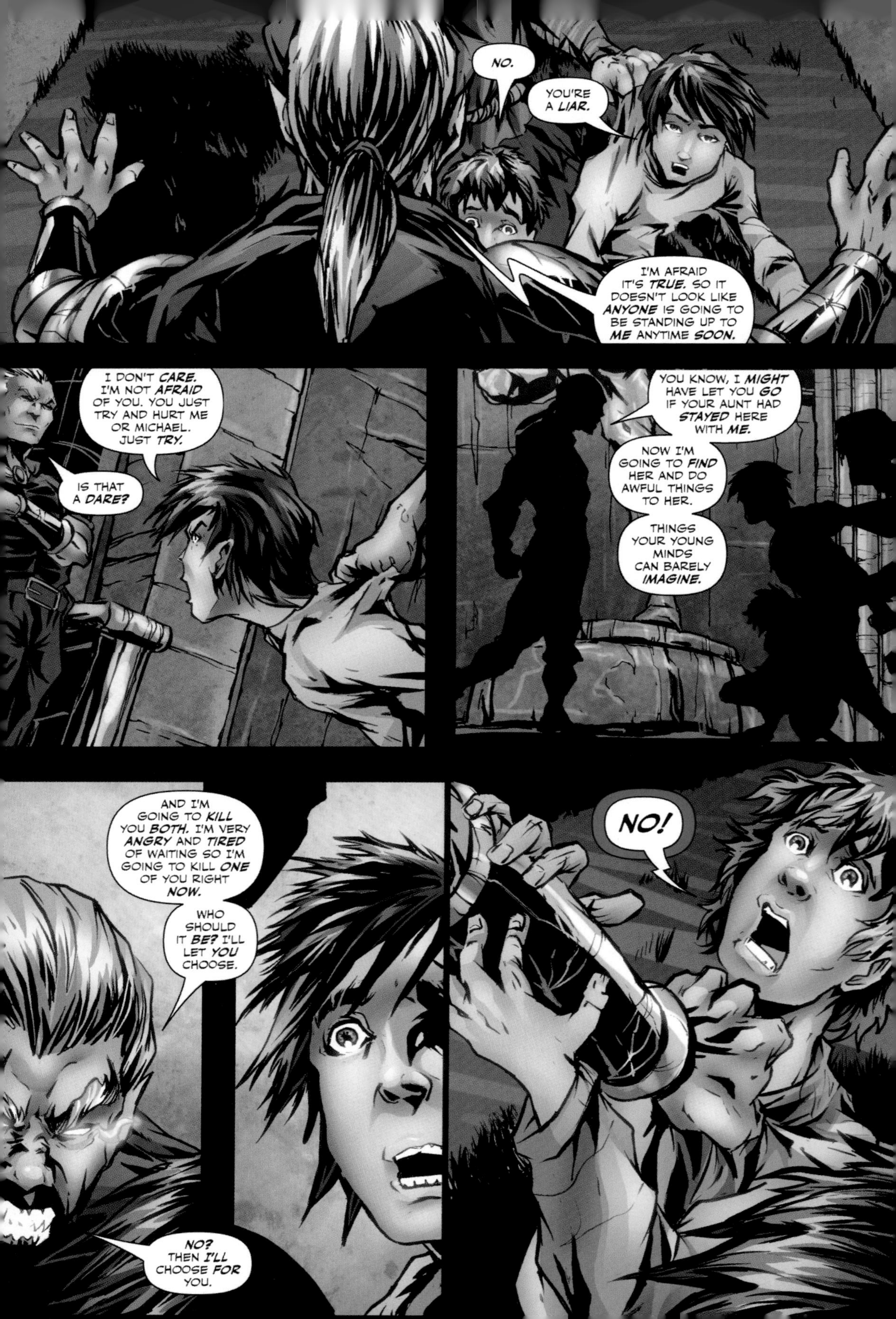
NO.
YOU'RE A LIAR.
I'M AFRAID IT'S TRUE. SO IT DOESN'T LOOK LIKE ANYONE IS GOING TO BE STANDING UP TO ME ANYTIME SOON.
I DON'T CARE. I'M NOT AFRAID OF YOU. YOU JUST TRY AND HURT ME OR MICHAEL. JUST TRY.
IS THAT A DARE?
YOU KNOW, I MIGHT HAVE LET YOU GO IF YOUR AUNT HAD STAYED HERE WITH ME.
NOW I'M GOING TO FIND HER AND DO AWFUL THINGS TO HER.
THINGS YOUR YOUNG MINDS CAN BARELY IMAGINE.
AND I'M GOING TO KILL YOU BOTH. I'M VERY ANGRY AND TIRED OF WAITING SO I'M GOING TO KILL ONE OF YOU RIGHT NOW.
WHO SHOULD IT BE? I'LL LET YOU CHOOSE.
NO? THEN I'LL CHOOSE FOR YOU.
NO!

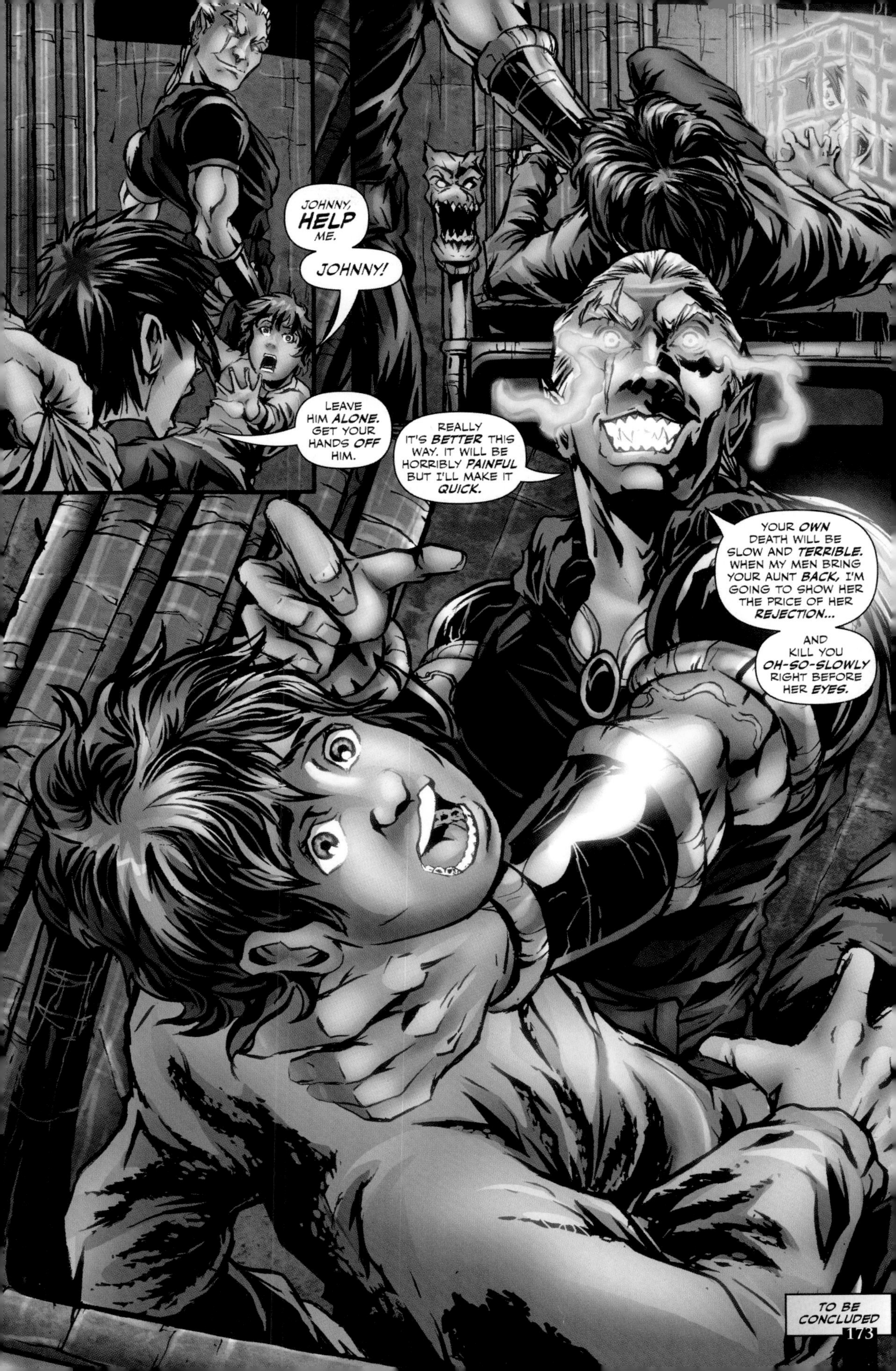

JOHNNY, HELP ME.
JOHNNY!
LEAVE HIM ALONE. GET YOUR HANDS OFF HIM.
REALLY IT'S BETTER THIS WAY. IT WILL BE HORRIBLY PAINFUL BUT I'LL MAKE IT QUICK.
YOUR OWN DEATH WILL BE SLOW AND TERRIBLE. WHEN MY MEN BRING YOUR AUNT BACK, I'M GOING TO SHOW HER THE PRICE OF HER REJECTION...
AND KILL YOU OH-SO-SLOWLY RIGHT BEFORE HER EYES.
TO BE CONCLUDED
173

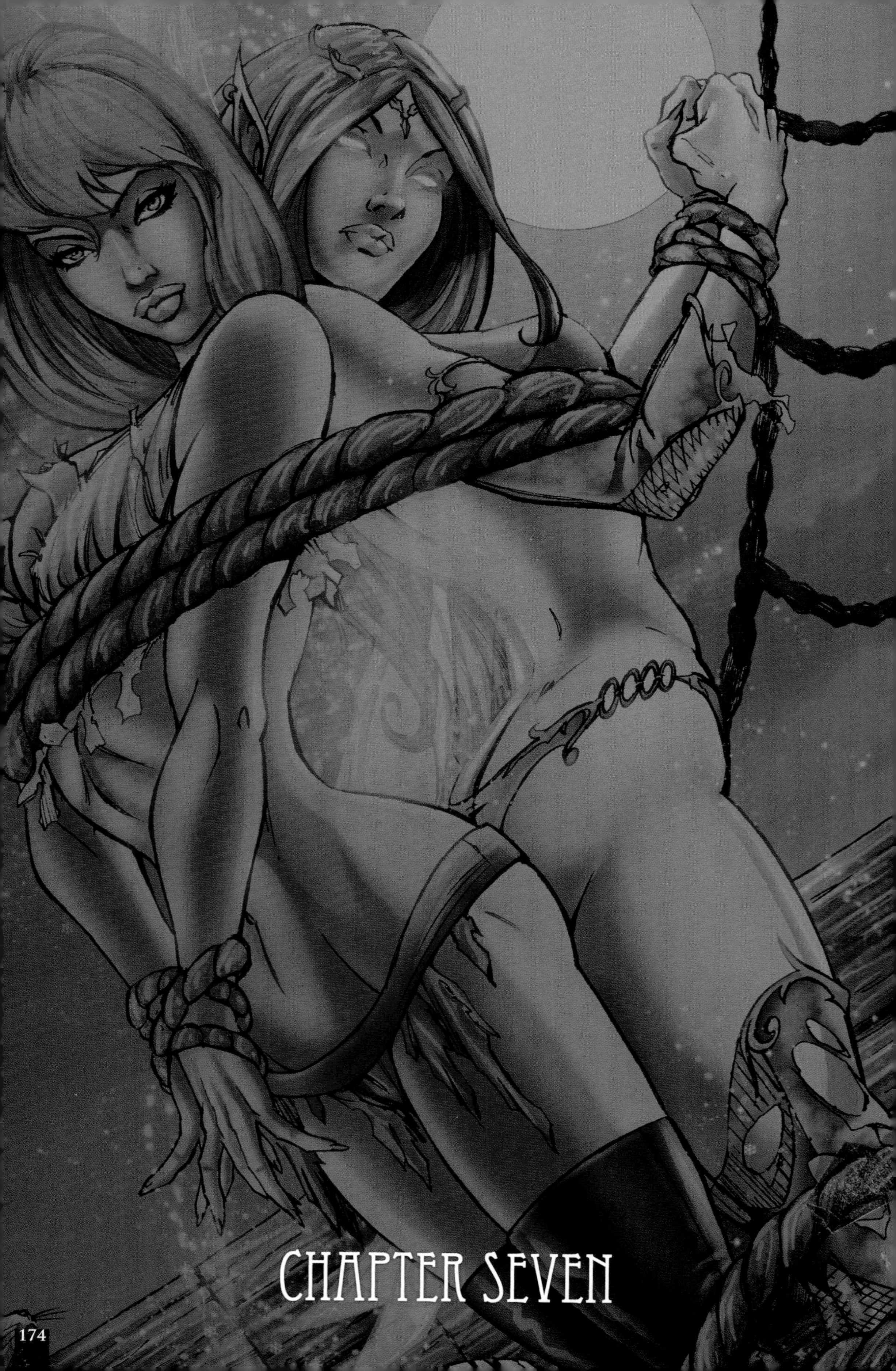

CHAPTER SEVEN

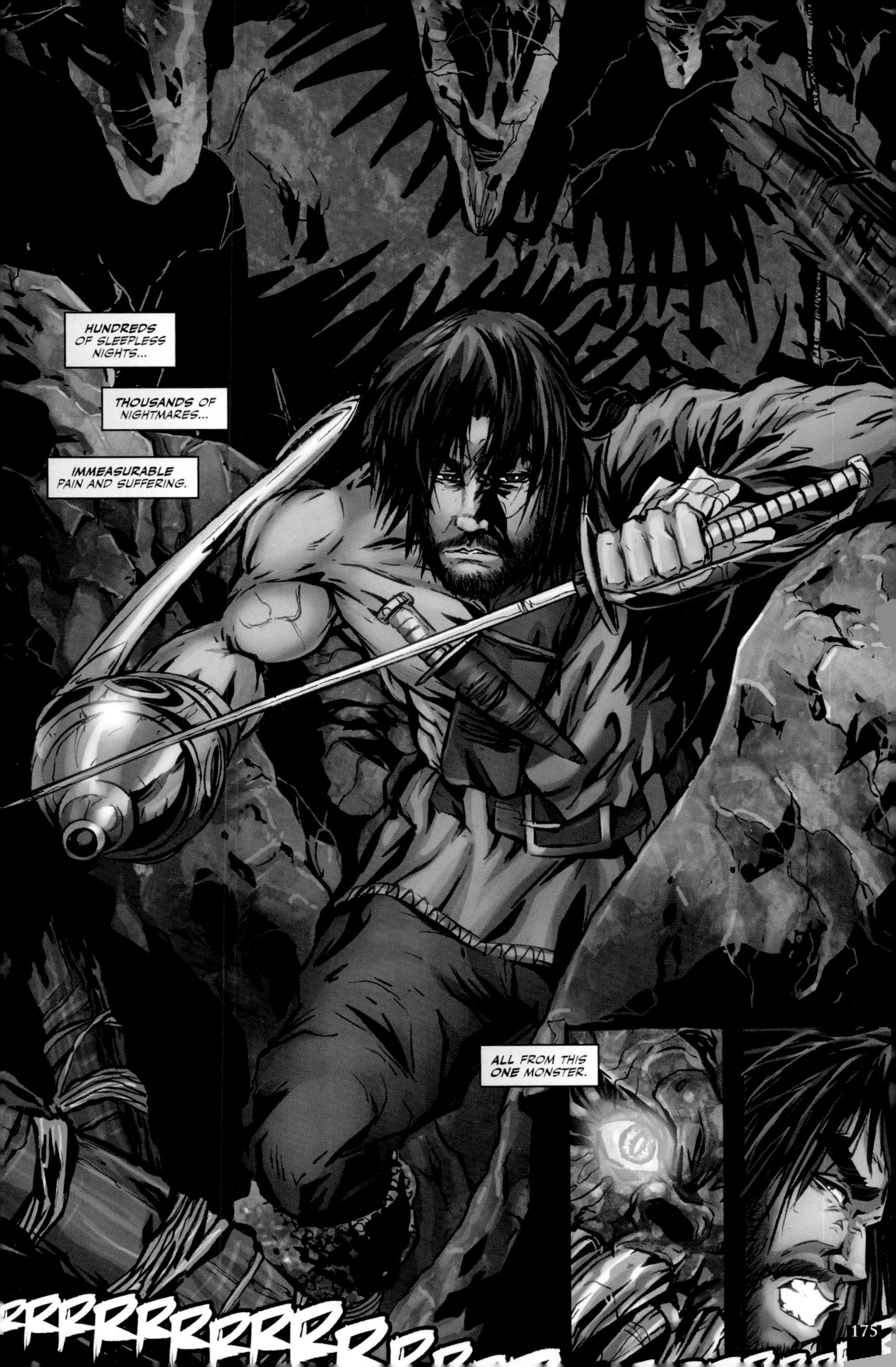
HUNDREDS OF SLEEPLESS NIGHTS...
THOUSANDS OF NIGHTMARES...
IMMEASURABLE PAIN AND SUFFERING.
ALL FROM THIS ONE MONSTER.
RRRRRRRRRRRR

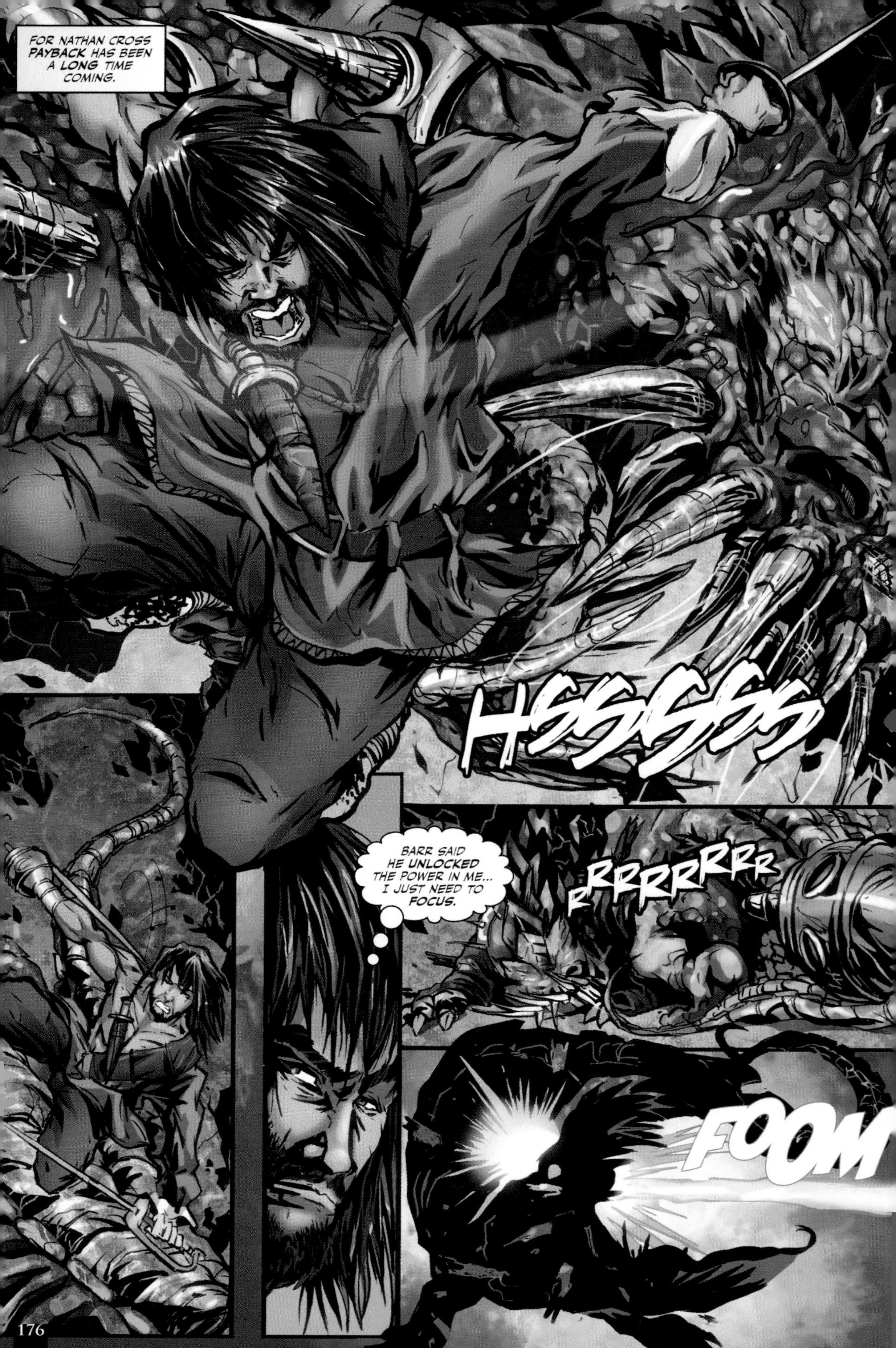
FOR NATHAN CROSS PAYBACK HAS BEEN A LONG TIME COMING.
HSSSSS
BARR SAID HE UNLOCKED THE POWER IN ME... I JUST NEED TO FOCUS.
RRRRRRRRR
FOOM

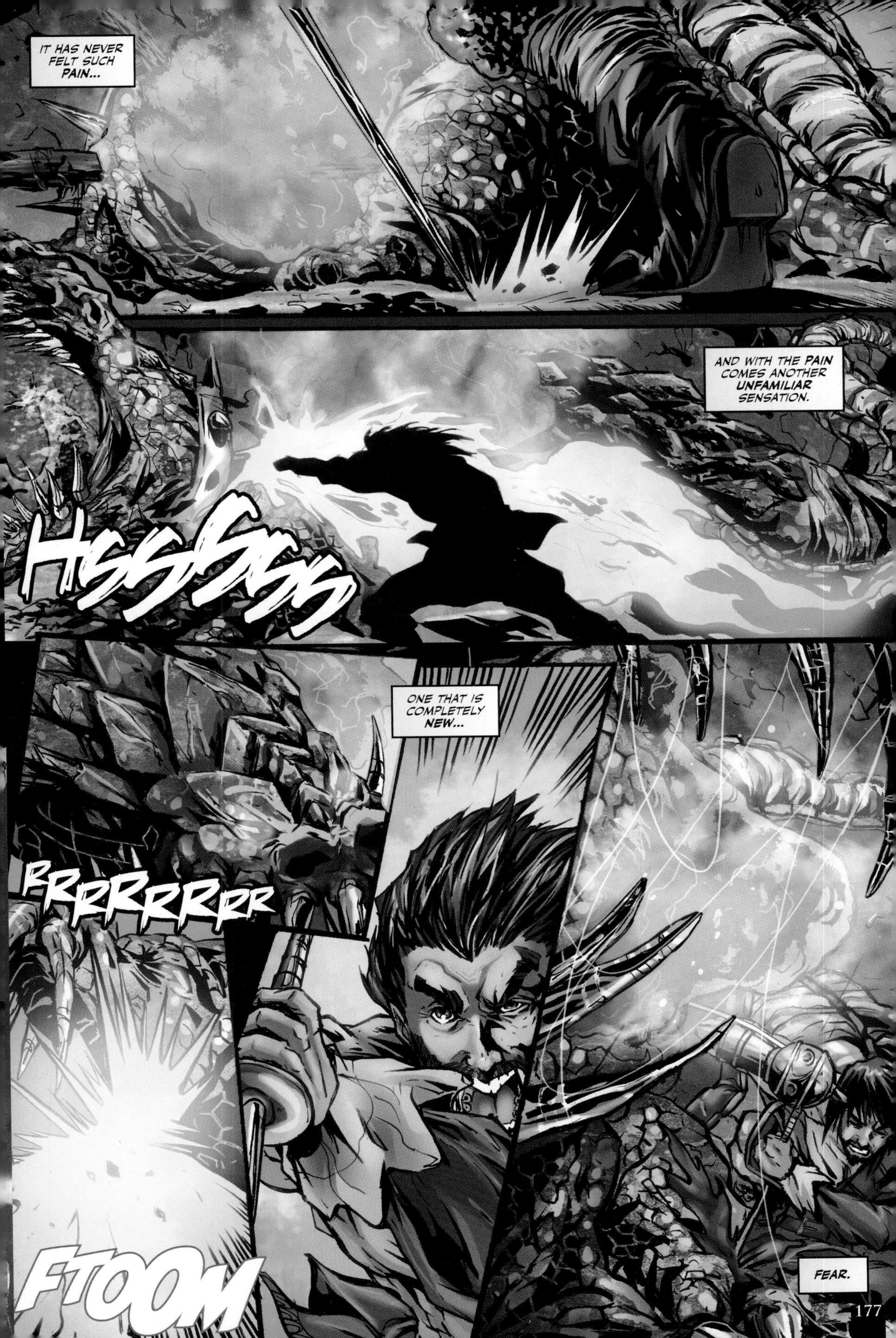
IT HAS NEVER FELT SUCH PAIN...
AND WITH THE PAIN COMES ANOTHER UNFAMILIAR SENSATION.
HSSSSSS
ONE THAT IS COMPLETELY NEW...
RRRRRRRRR
FTOOM
FEAR.

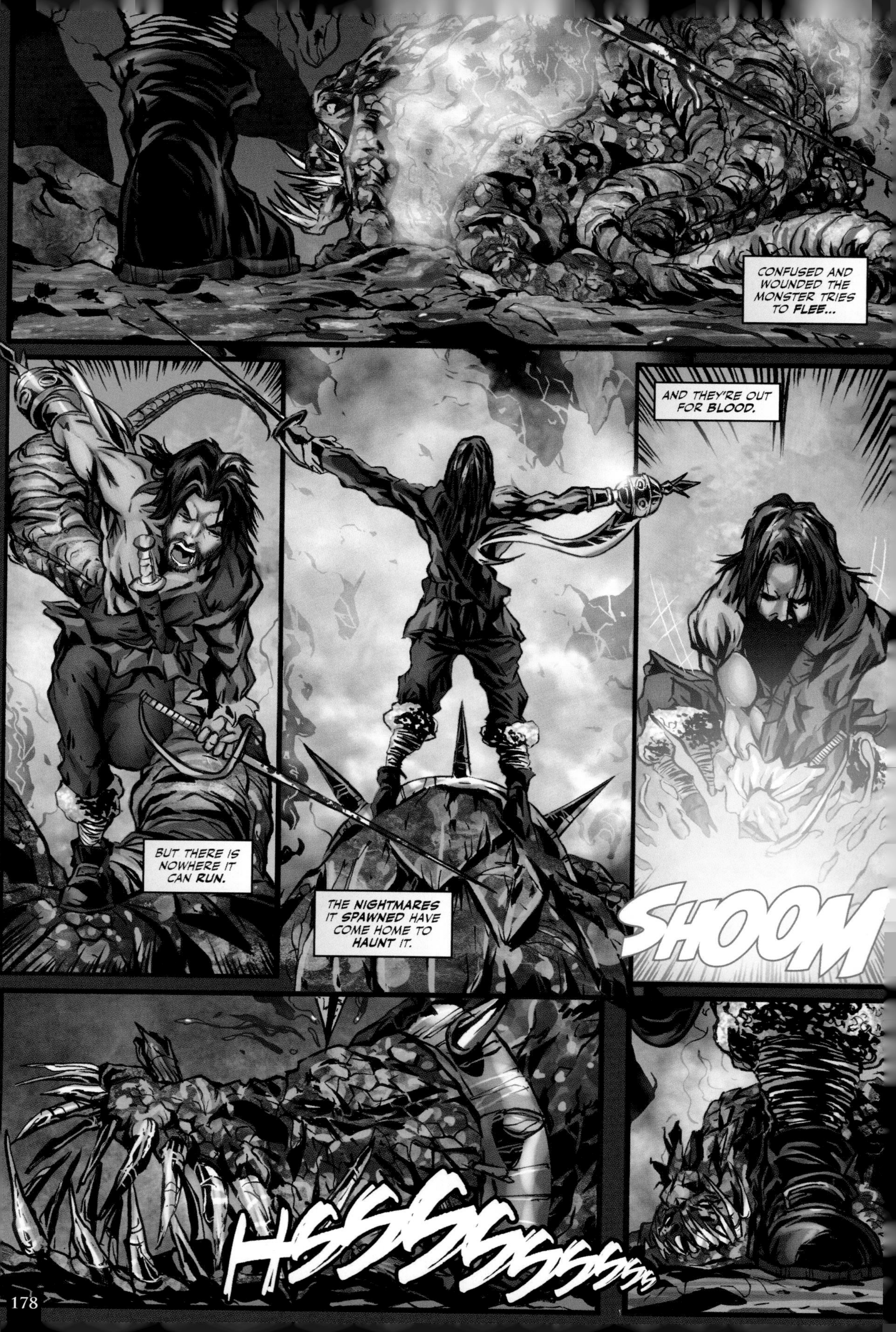
CONFUSED AND WOUNDED THE MONSTER TRIES TO FLEE...
BUT THERE IS NOWHERE IT CAN RUN.
THE NIGHTMARES IT SPAWNED HAVE COME HOME TO HAUNT IT.
AND THEY'RE OUT FOR BLOOD.
SHOOM
HSSSSSSSSSS

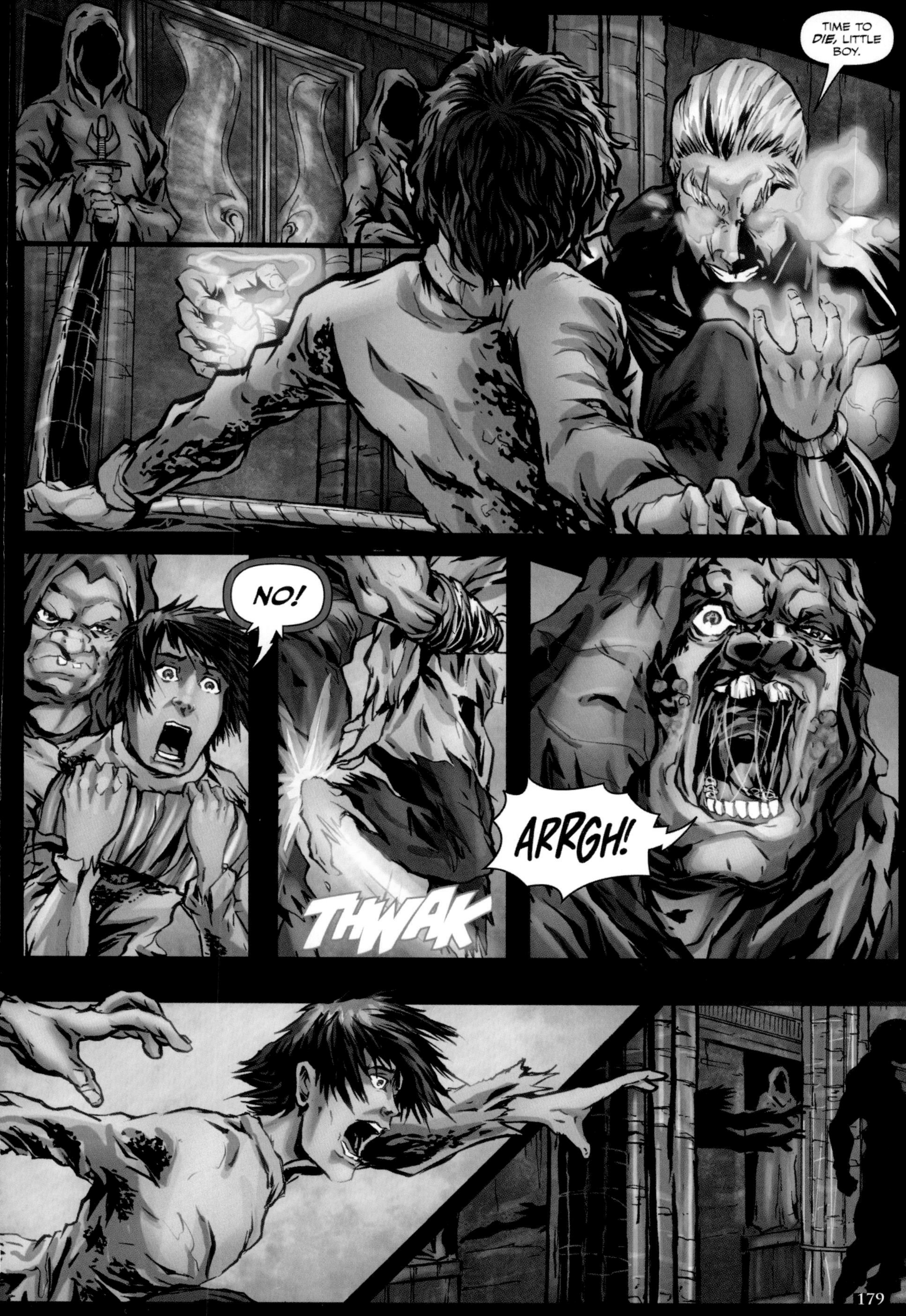
TIME TO DIE, LITTLE BOY.
NO!
THWAK
ARRGH!

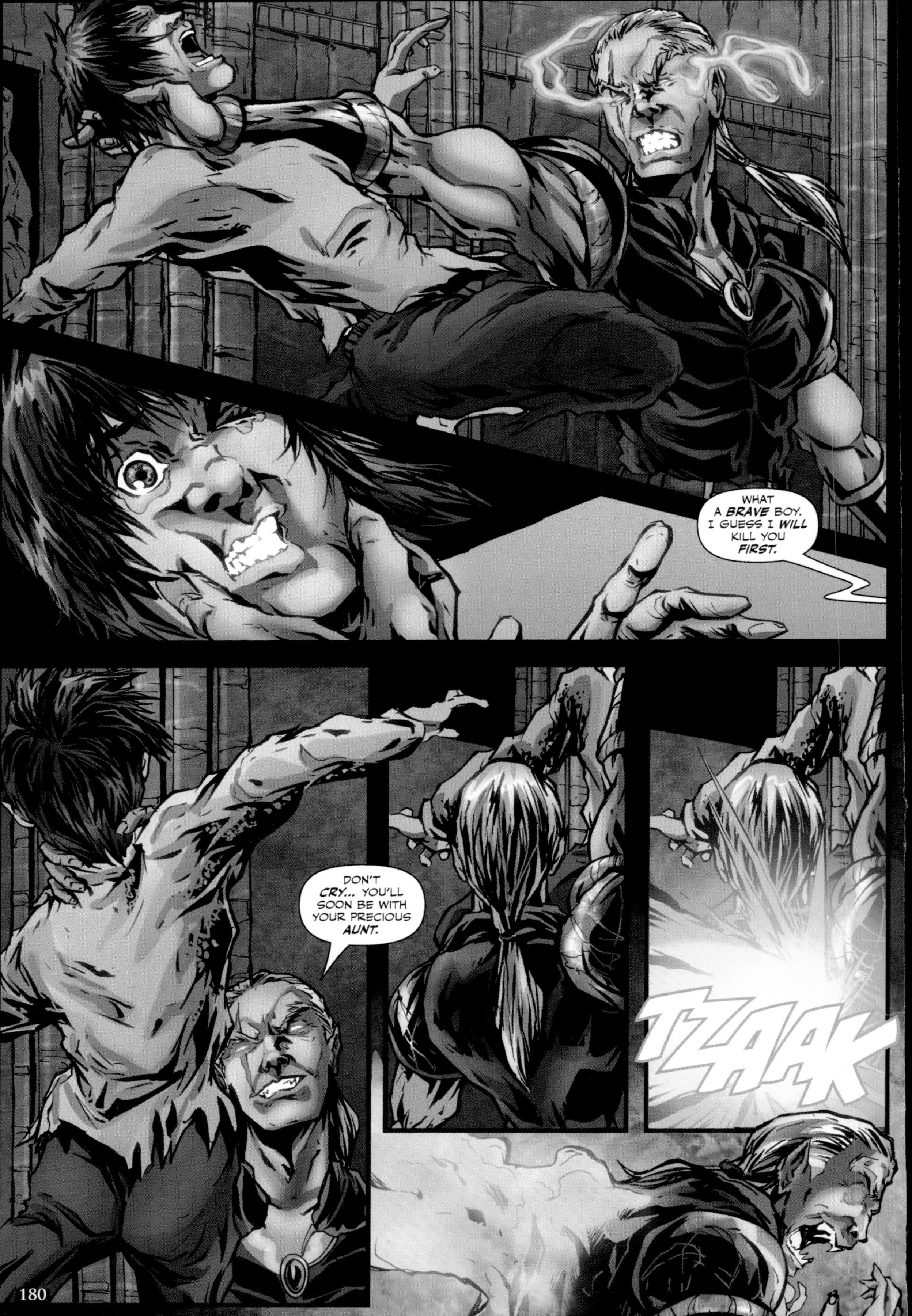
WHAT A BRAVE BOY. I GUESS I WILL KILL YOU FIRST.
DON'T CRY... YOU'LL SOON BE WITH YOUR PRECIOUS AUNT.
TZAAK

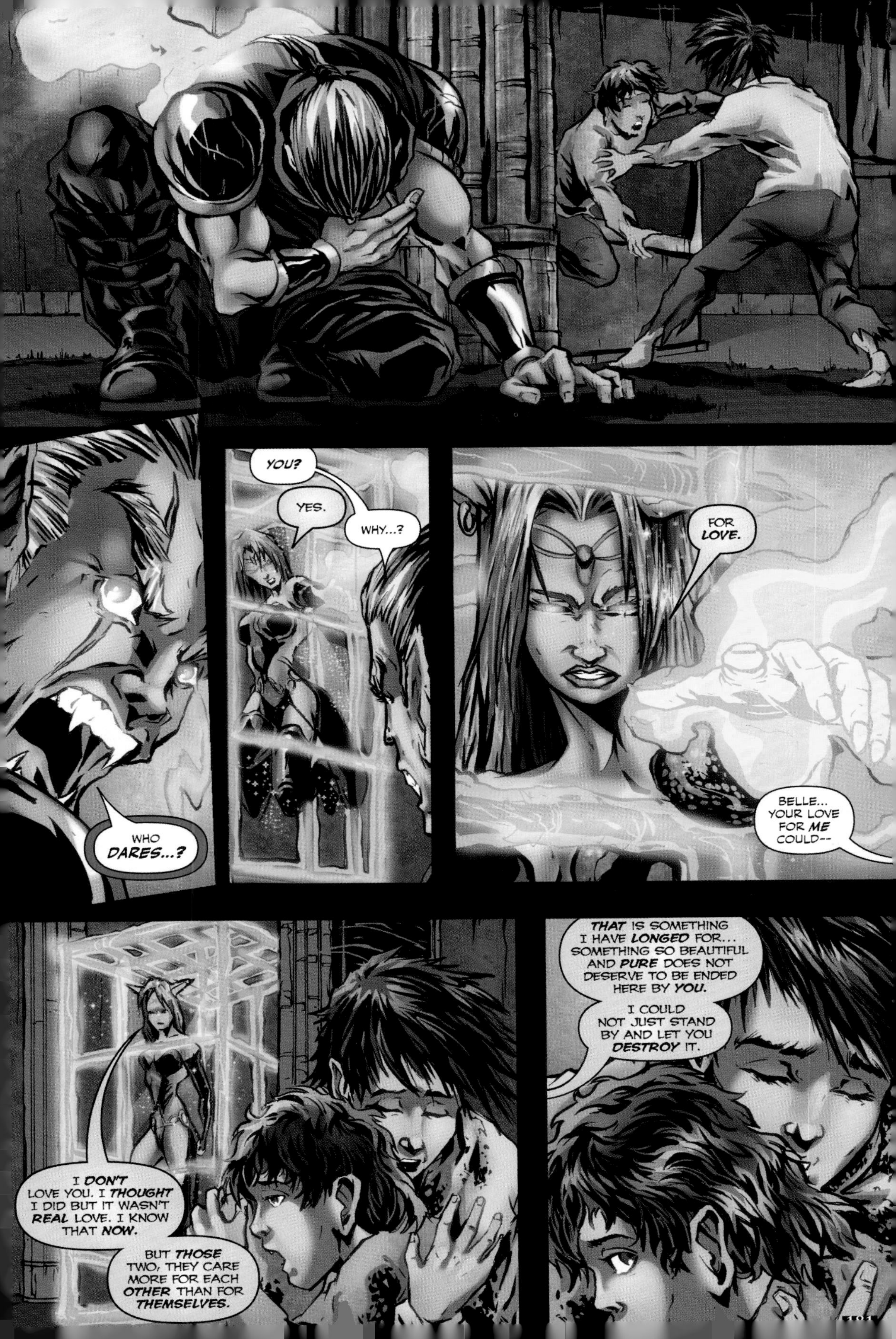
WHO DARES...?
YOU?
YES.
WHY...?
FOR LOVE.
BELLE... YOUR LOVE FOR ME COULD--
I DON'T LOVE YOU. I THOUGHT I DID BUT IT WASN'T REAL LOVE. I KNOW THAT NOW.
BUT THOSE TWO, THEY CARE MORE FOR EACH OTHER THAN FOR THEMSELVES.
THAT IS SOMETHING I HAVE LONGED FOR... SOMETHING SO BEAUTIFUL AND PURE DOES NOT DESERVE TO BE ENDED HERE BY YOU.
I COULD NOT JUST STAND BY AND LET YOU DESTROY IT.

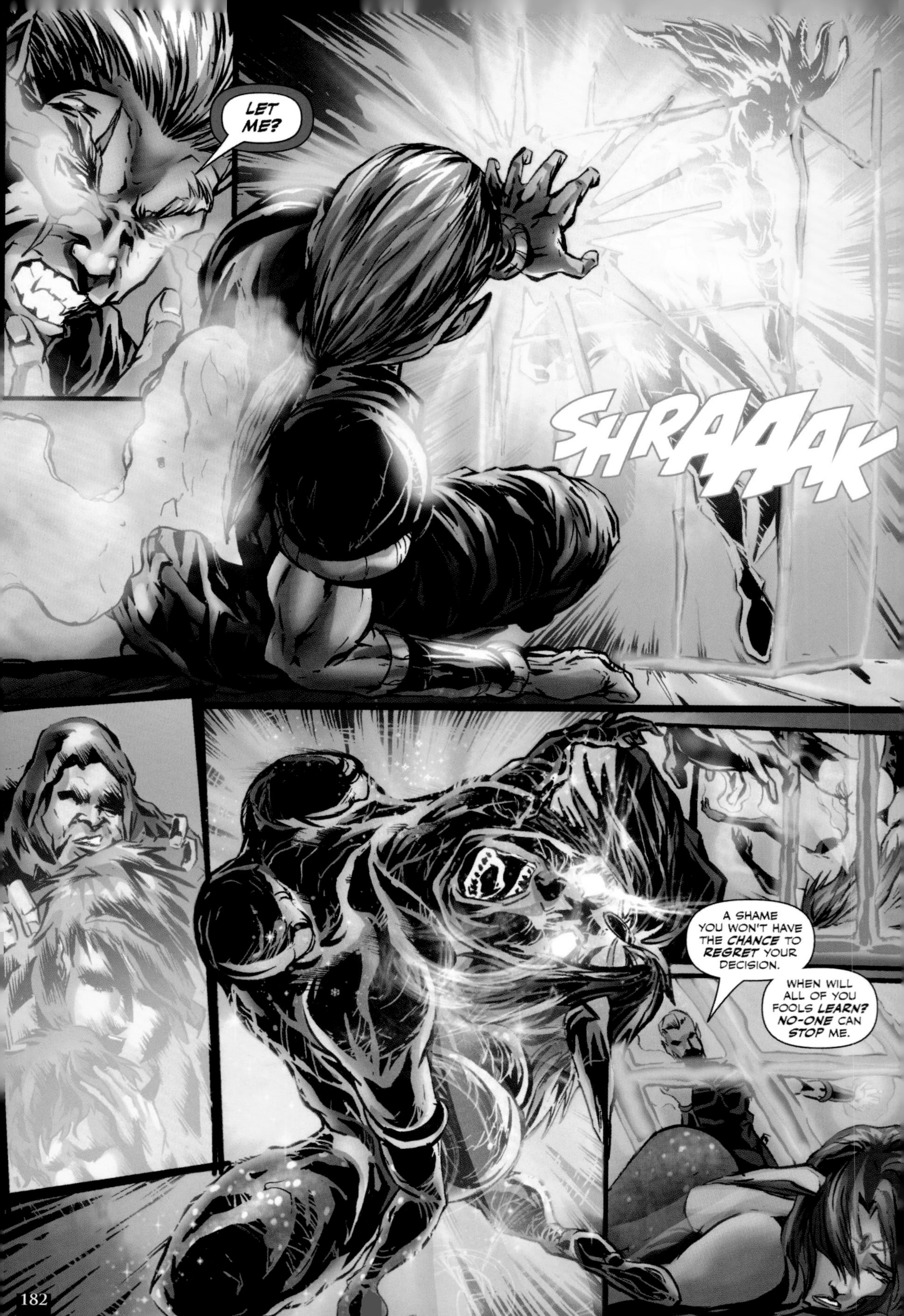
LET ME?
SHRAAAK
A SHAME YOU WON'T HAVE THE CHANCE TO REGRET YOUR DECISION.
WHEN WILL ALL OF YOU FOOLS LEARN? NO-ONE CAN STOP ME.

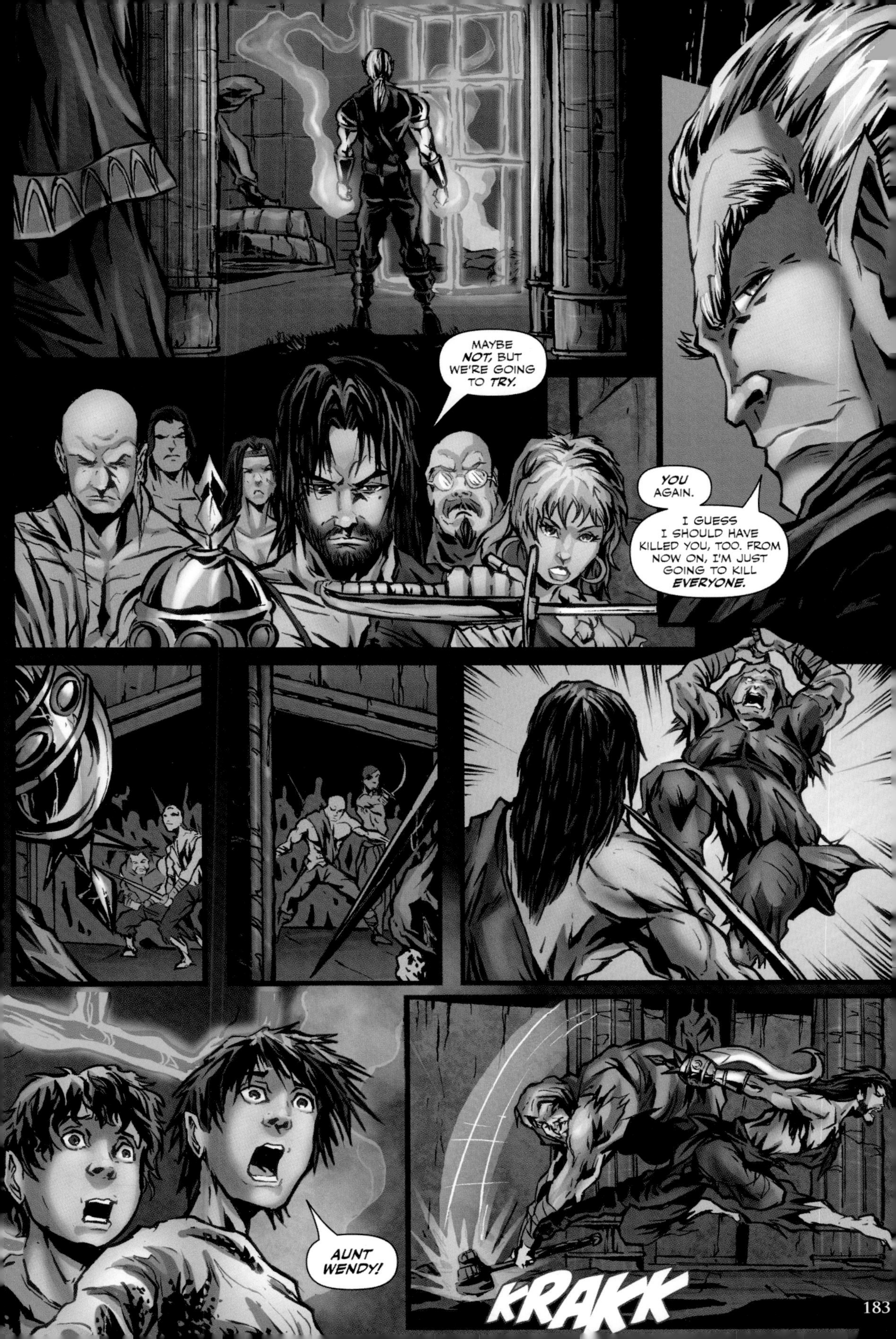
MAYBE NOT, BUT WE'RE GOING TO TRY.
YOU AGAIN.
I GUESS I SHOULD HAVE KILLED YOU, TOO. FROM NOW ON, I'M JUST GOING TO KILL EVERYONE.
AUNT WENDY!
KRAKK

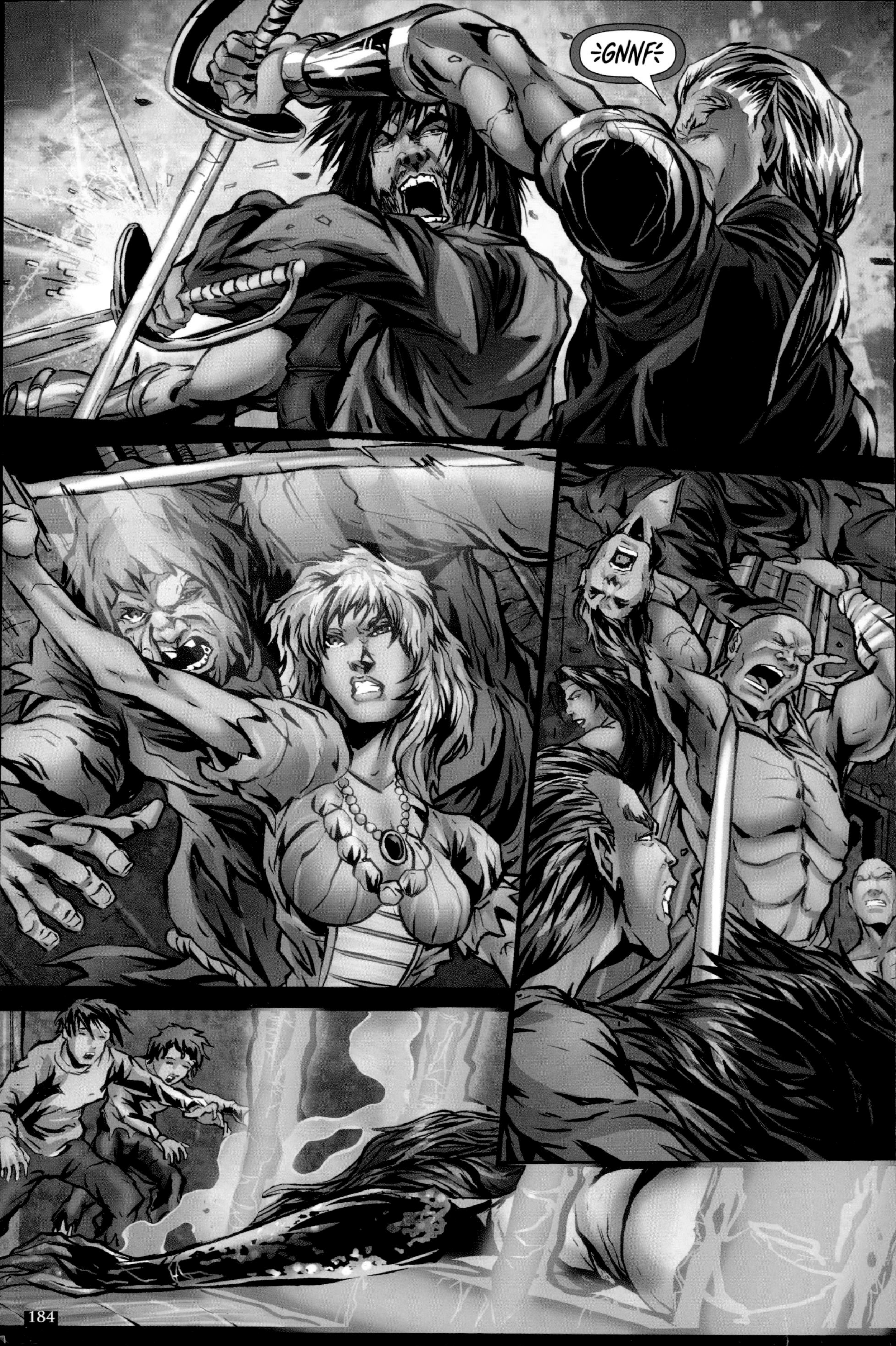
GNNF

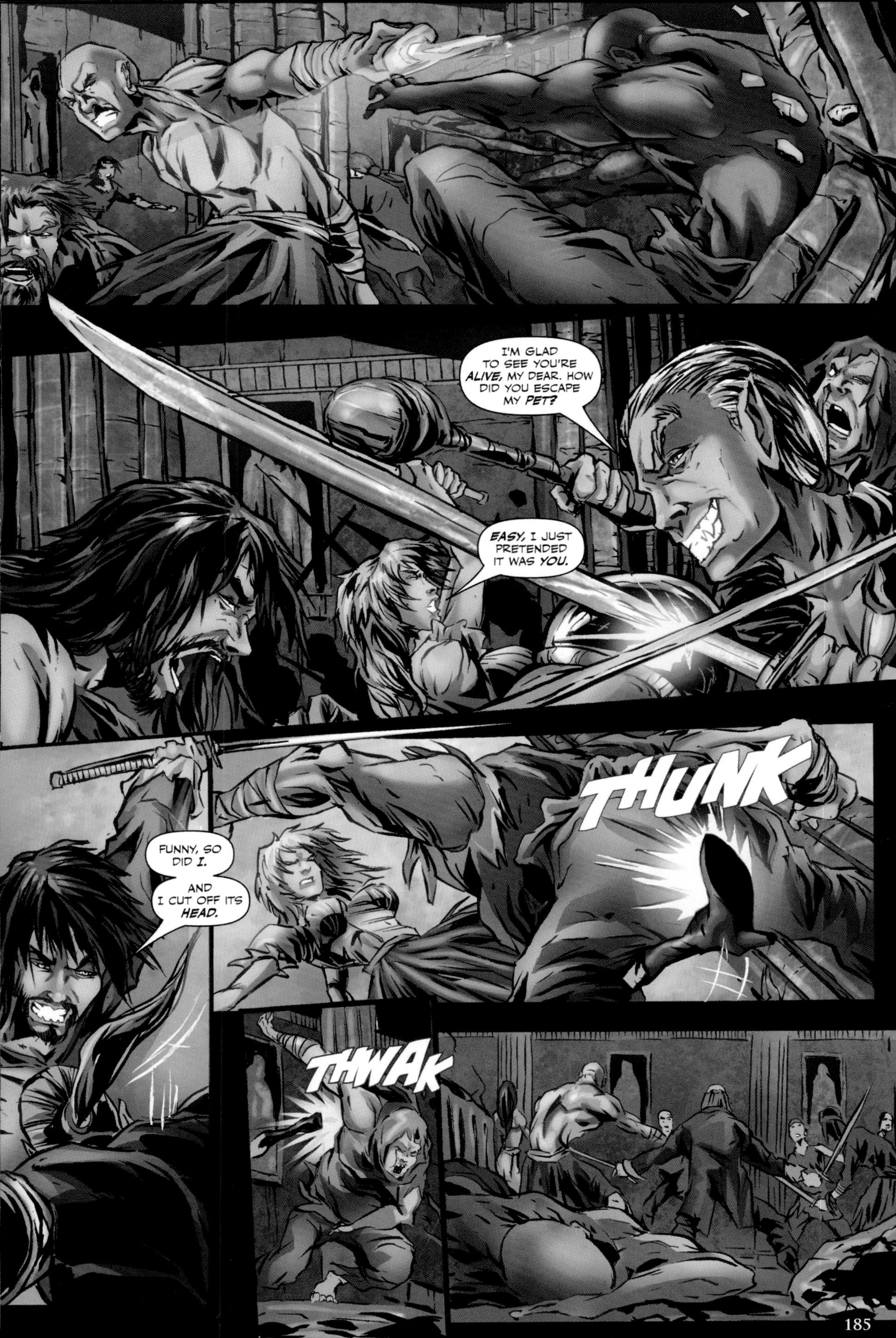
I'M GLAD TO SEE YOU'RE ALIVE, MY DEAR. HOW DID YOU ESCAPE MY PET?
EASY, I JUST PRETENDED IT WAS YOU.
FUNNY, SO DID I.
AND I CUT OFF ITS HEAD.
THUNK
THWAK

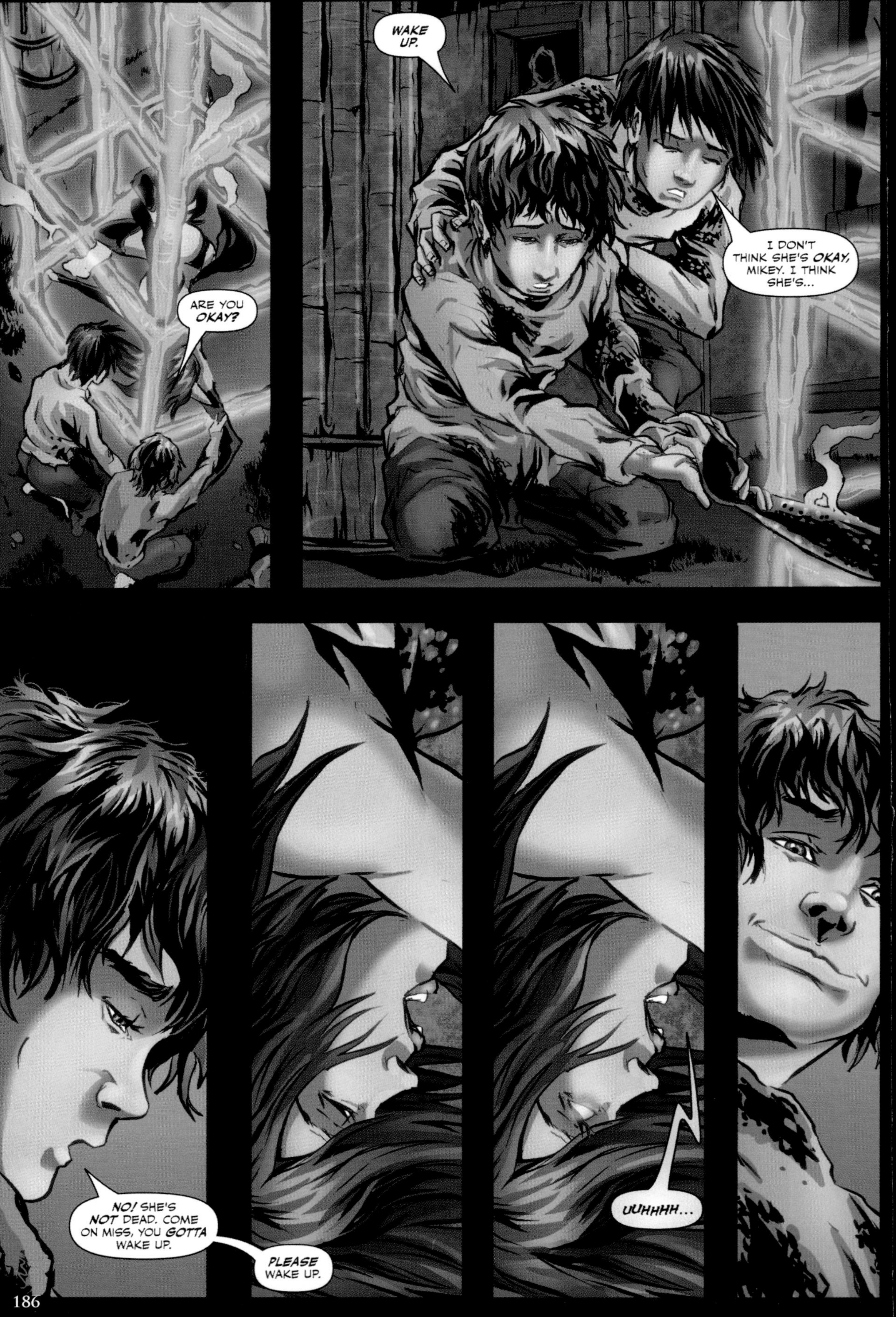
ARE YOU OKAY?
WAKE UP.
I DON'T THINK SHE'S OKAY, MIKEY. I THINK SHE'S...
NO! SHE'S NOT DEAD. COME ON MISS, YOU GOTTA WAKE UP.
PLEASE WAKE UP.
UUHHHH...

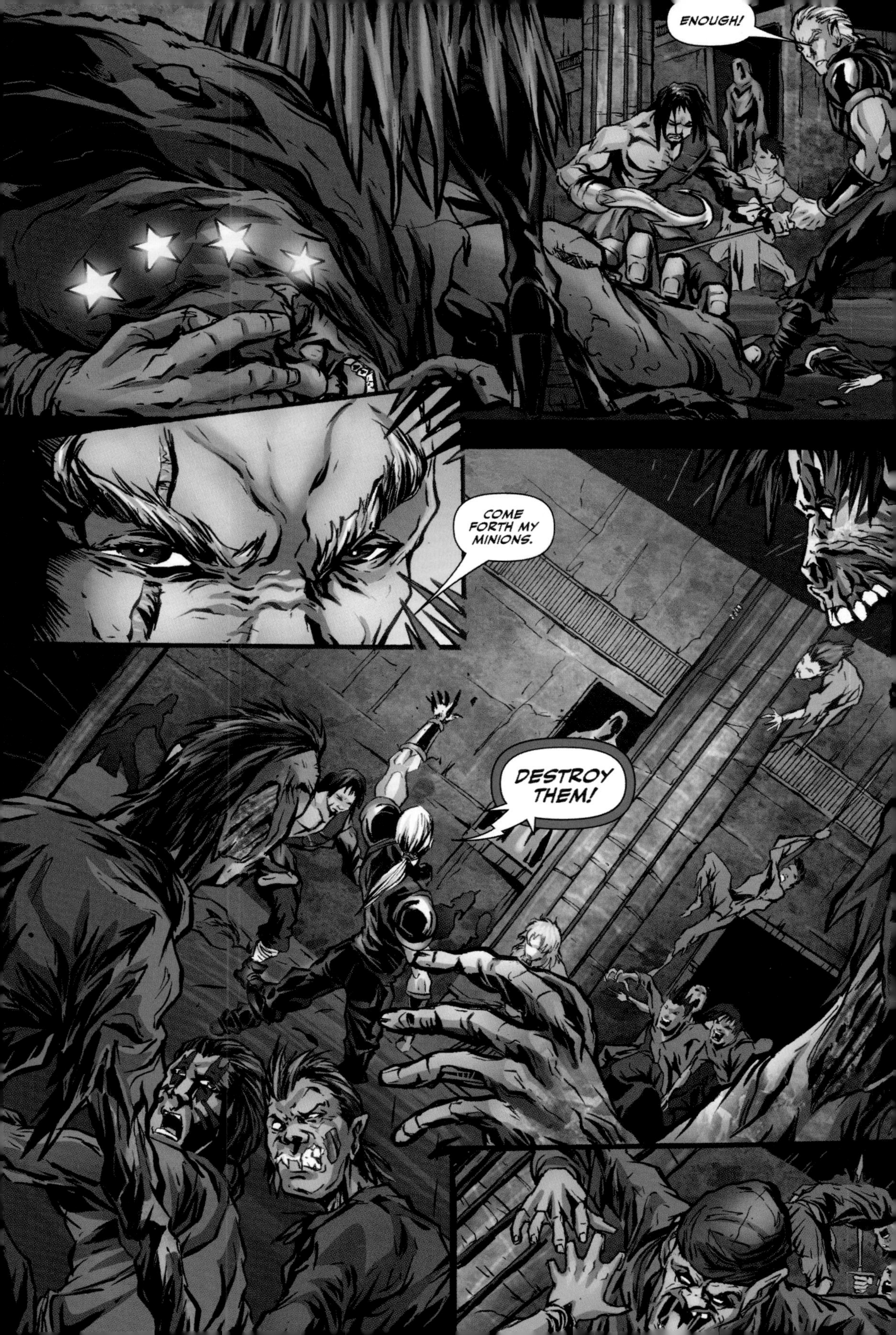
ENOUGH!
COME FORTH MY MINIONS.
DESTROY THEM!

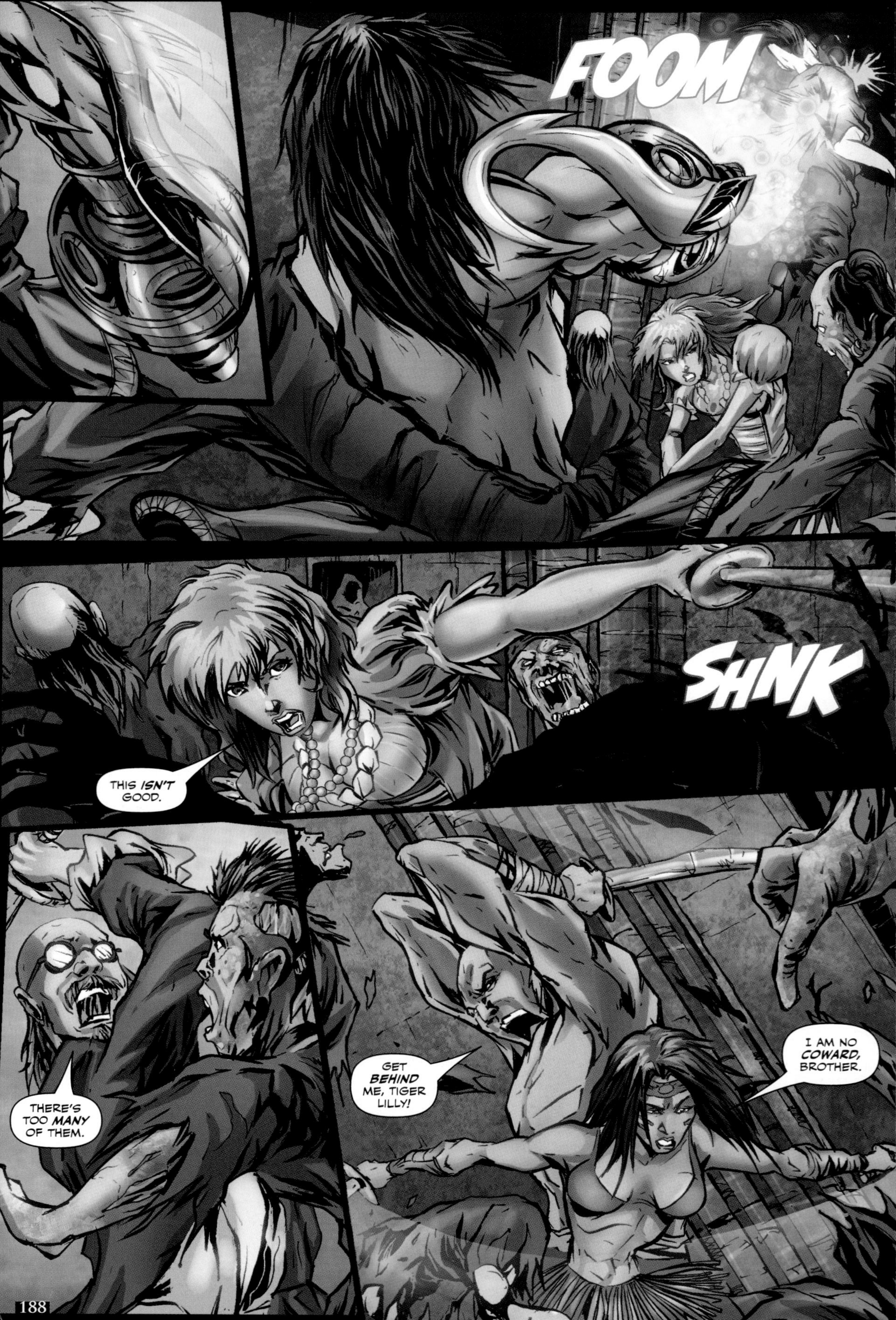
FOOM
SHNK
THIS ISN'T GOOD.
THERE'S TOO MANY OF THEM.
GET BEHIND ME, TIGER LILLY!
I AM NO COWARD, BROTHER.

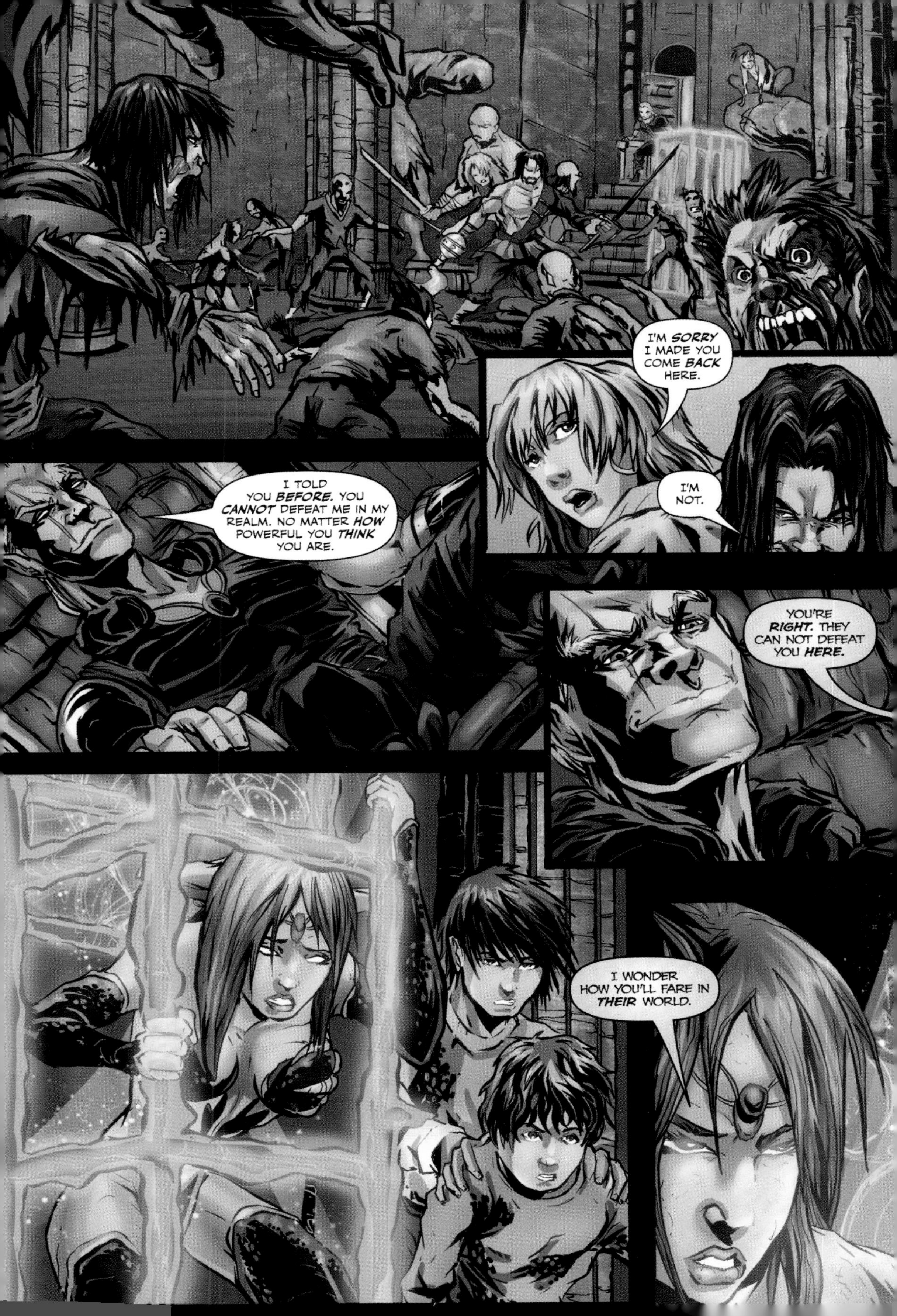

I'M *SORRY* I MADE YOU COME *BACK* HERE.
I'M NOT.
I TOLD YOU *BEFORE.* YOU *CANNOT* DEFEAT ME IN MY REALM. NO MATTER *HOW* POWERFUL YOU *THINK* YOU ARE.
YOU'RE *RIGHT.* THEY CAN NOT DEFEAT YOU *HERE.*
I WONDER HOW YOU'LL FARE IN *THEIR* WORLD.

WHAT ARE YOU **DOING?**

PUTTING THINGS *RIGHT.*

NO...

I COMMAND YOU TO STOP!

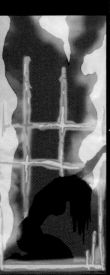

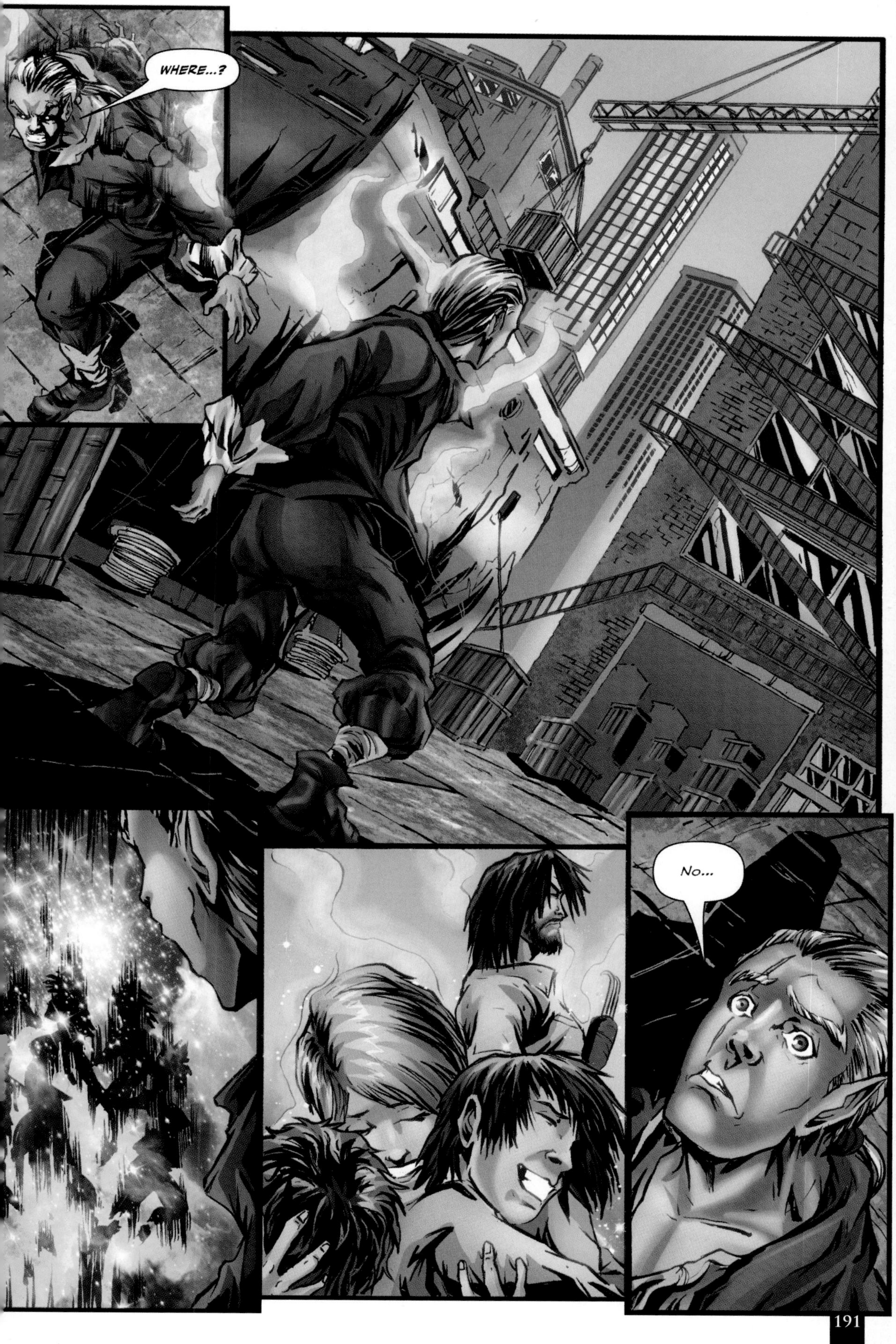
WHERE...?
No...

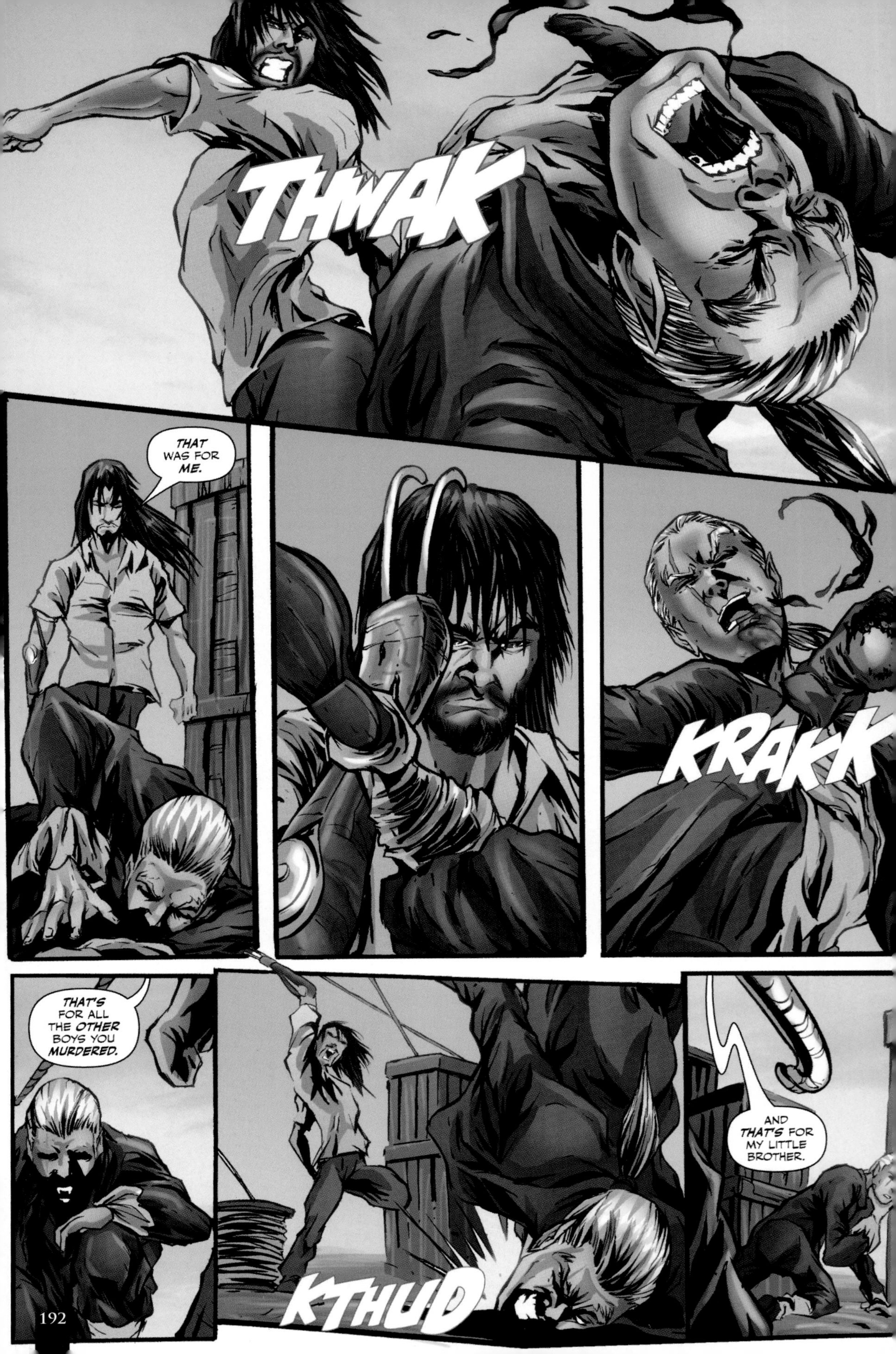
THWAK
THAT WAS FOR ME.
KRAKK
THAT'S FOR ALL THE OTHER BOYS YOU MURDERED.
KTHUD
AND THAT'S FOR MY LITTLE BROTHER.

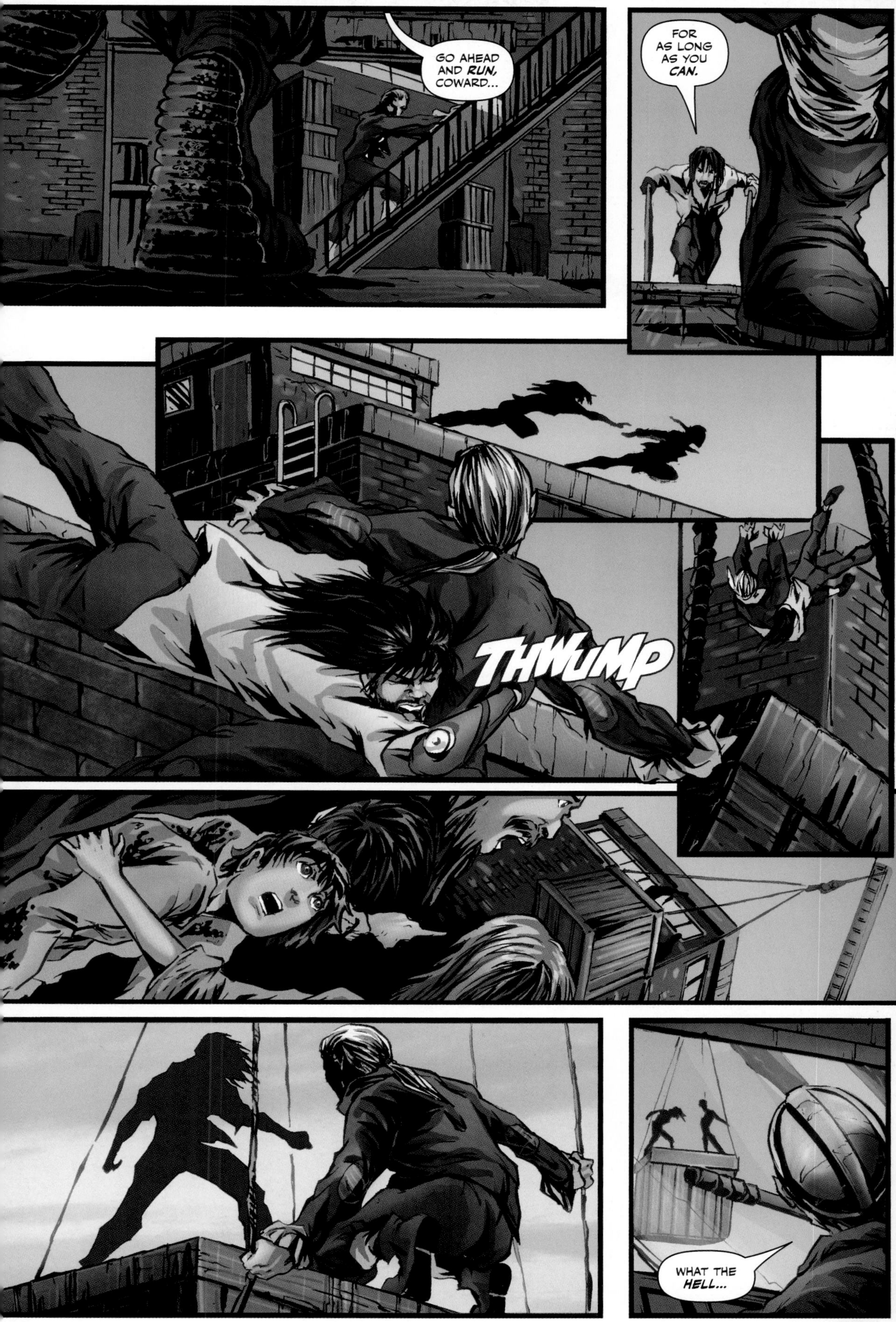
GO AHEAD AND RUN, COWARD...
FOR AS LONG AS YOU CAN.
THWUMP
WHAT THE HELL...

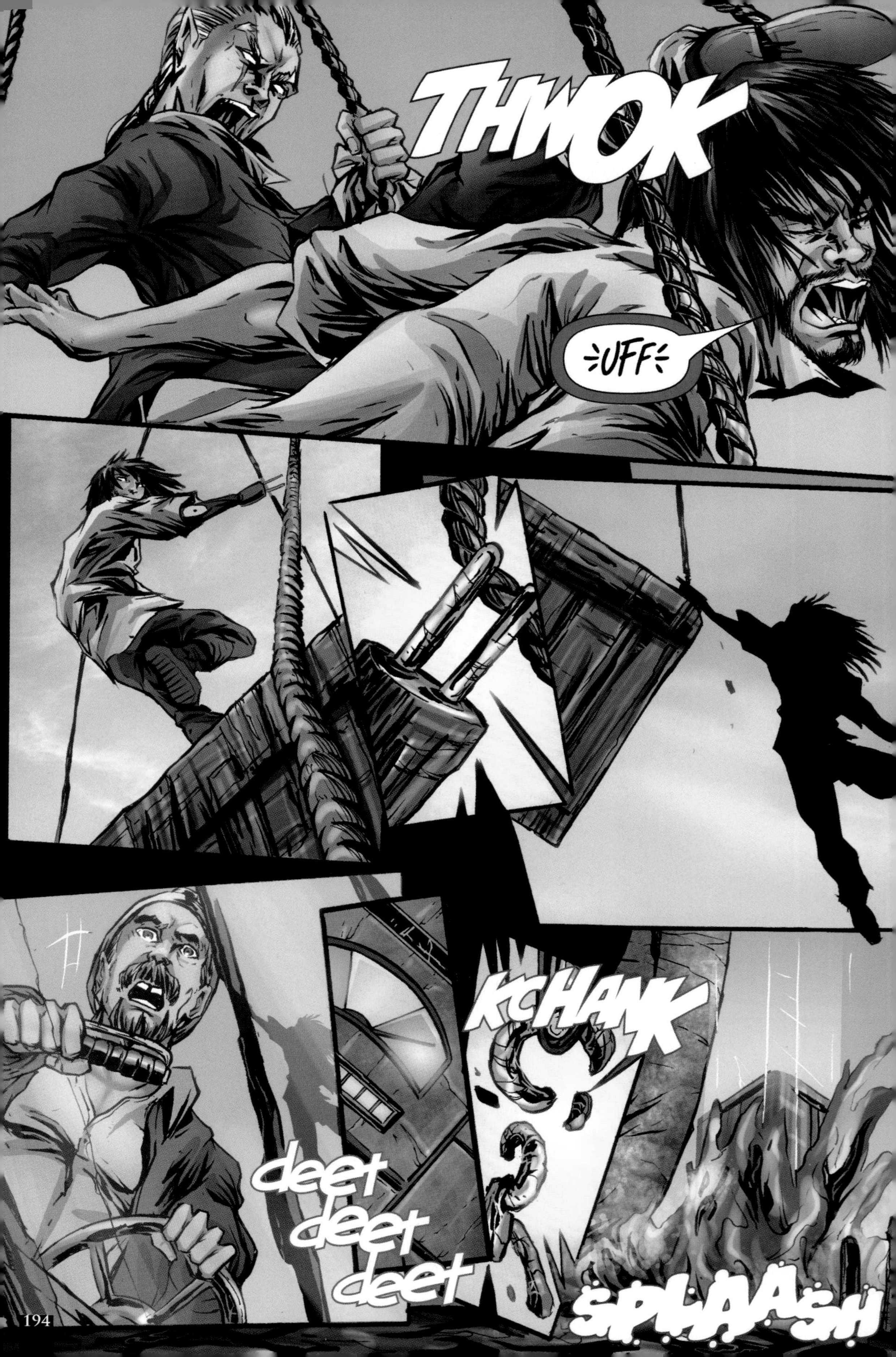
THWOK
UFF
KCHANK
deet
deet
deet
SPLAASH

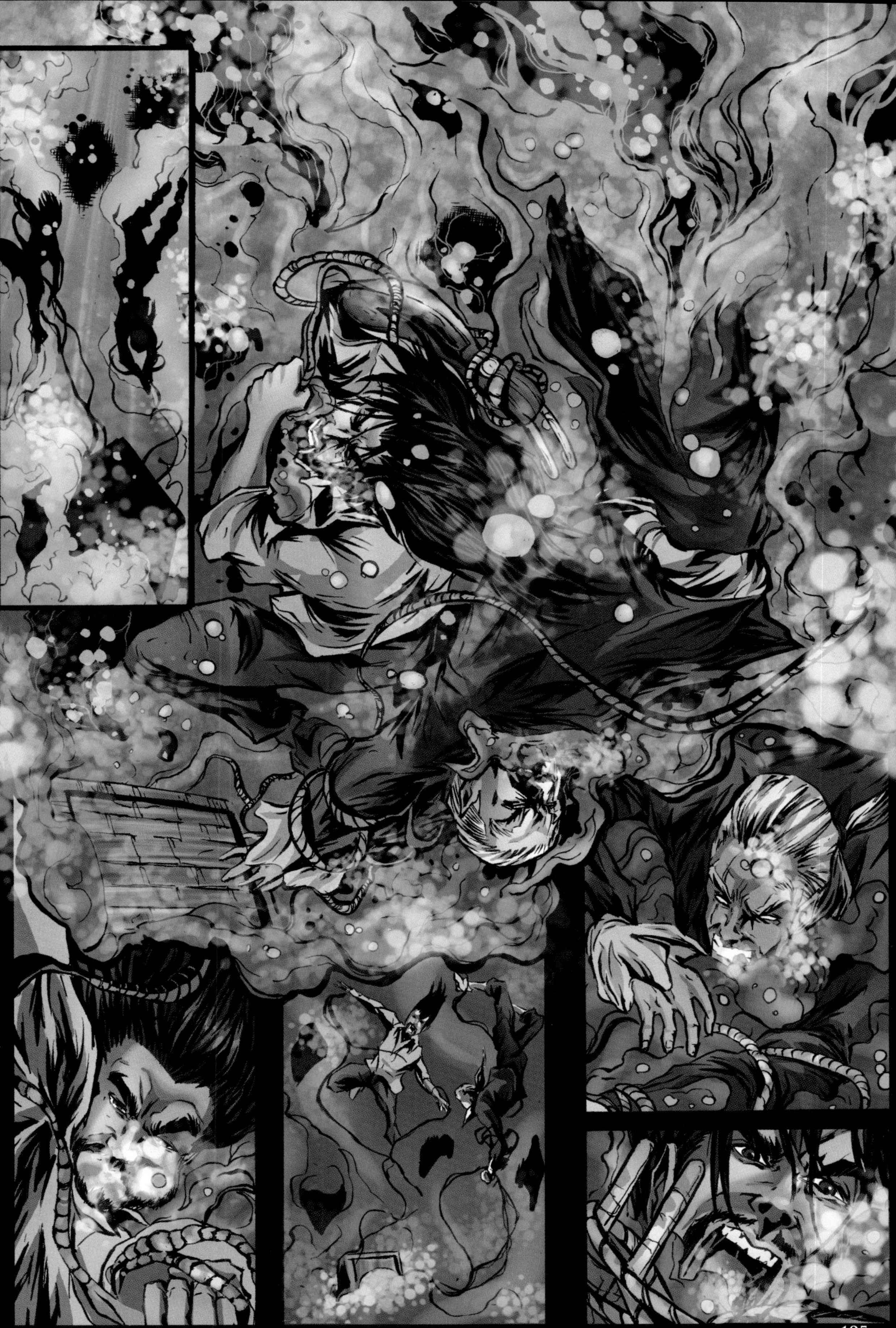

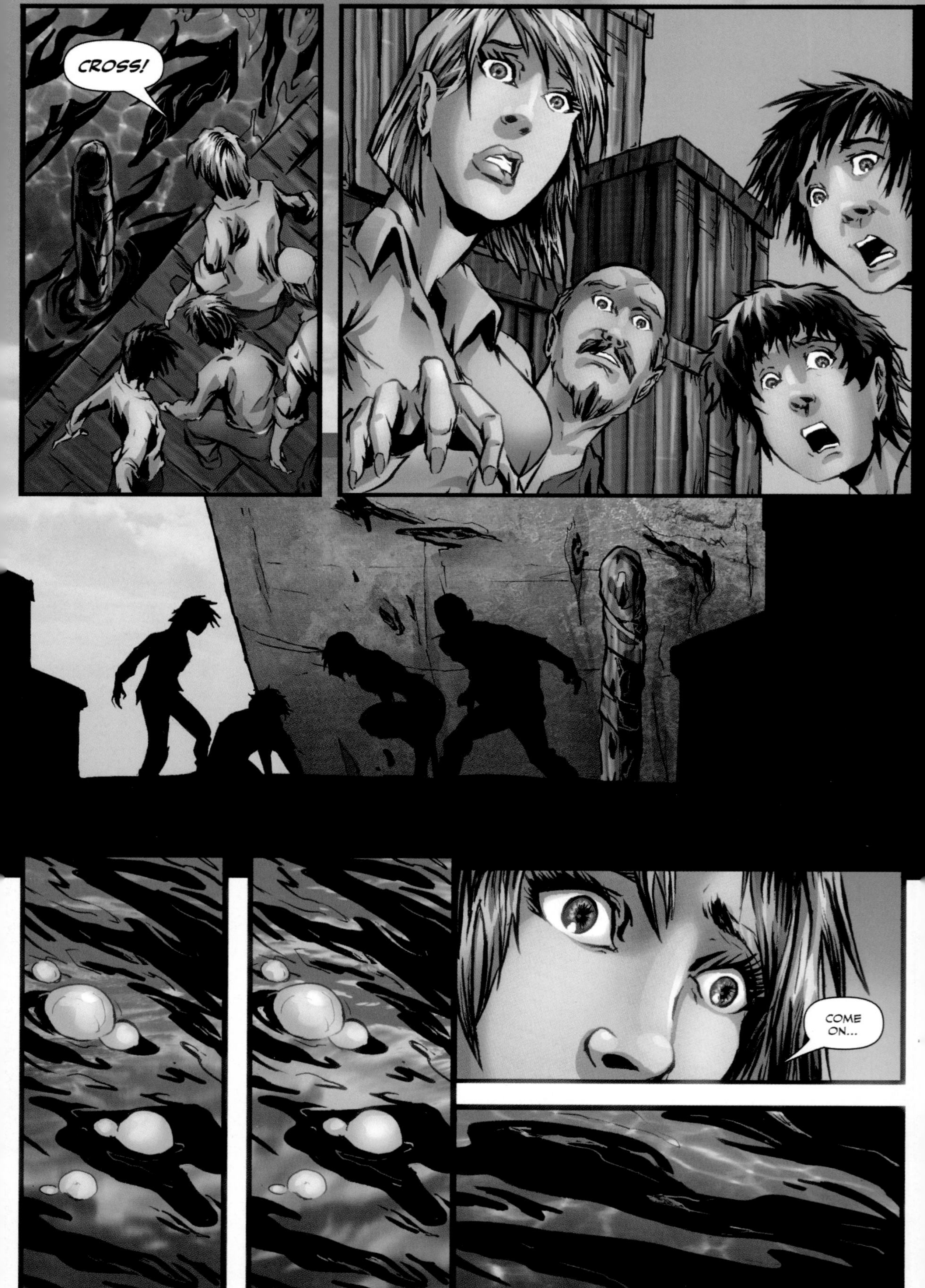
CROSS!
COME ON...

GASP

THANKS, DOC.

NATHAN!

THANK YOU.

THANK YOU FOR *SAVING* MY KIDS.

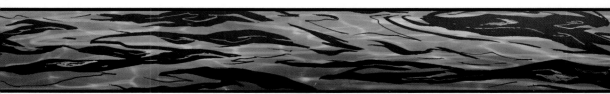

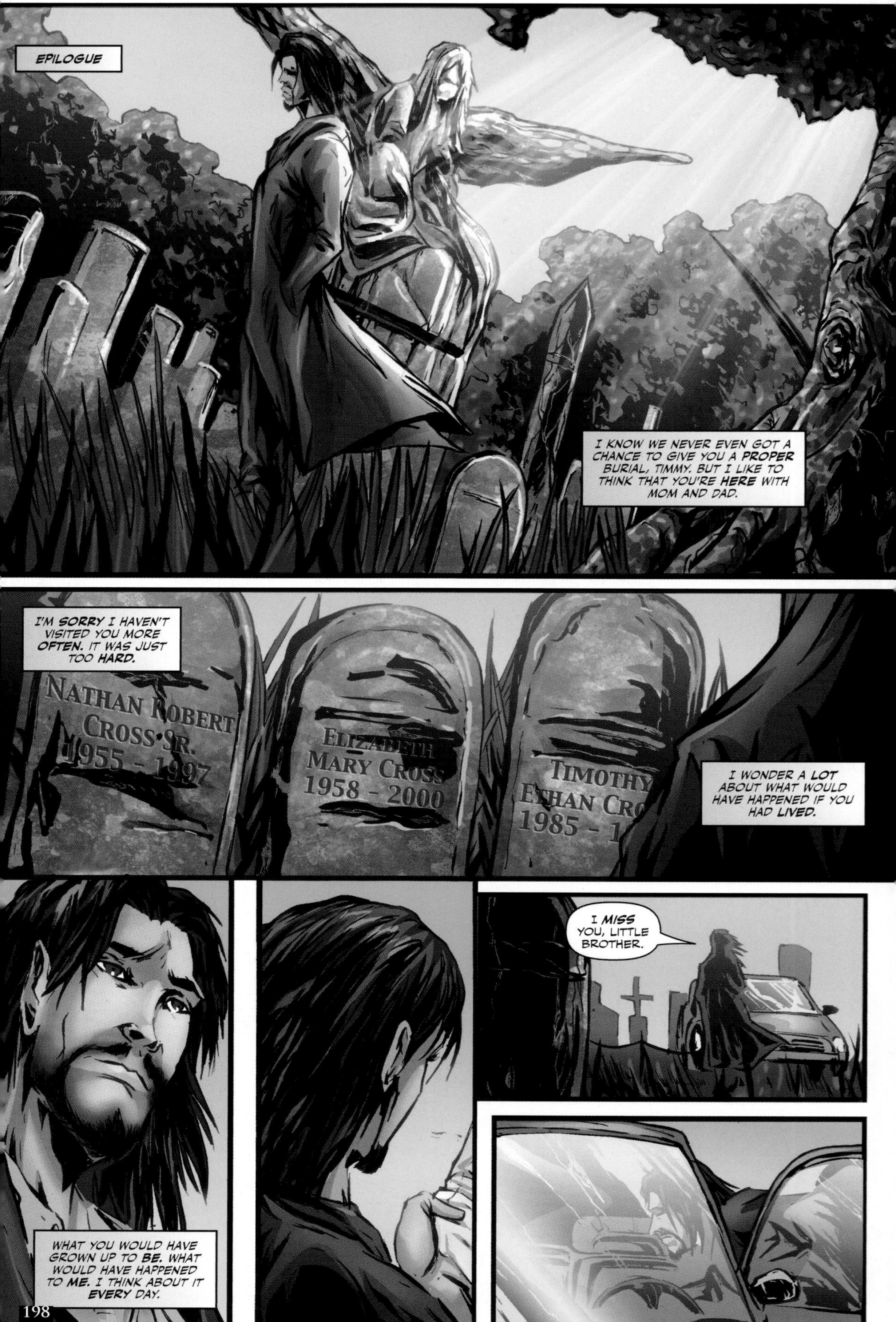
EPILOGUE
I KNOW WE NEVER EVEN GOT A CHANCE TO GIVE YOU A PROPER BURIAL, TIMMY. BUT I LIKE TO THINK THAT YOU'RE HERE WITH MOM AND DAD.
I'M SORRY I HAVEN'T VISITED YOU MORE OFTEN. IT WAS JUST TOO HARD.
NATHAN ROBERT
CROSS·SR.
1955 – 1997
ELIZABETH
MARY CROSS
1958 – 2000
TIMOTHY
I WONDER A LOT ABOUT WHAT WOULD HAVE HAPPENED IF YOU HAD LIVED.
WHAT YOU WOULD HAVE GROWN UP TO BE. WHAT WOULD HAVE HAPPENED TO ME. I THINK ABOUT IT EVERY DAY.
I MISS YOU, LITTLE BROTHER.

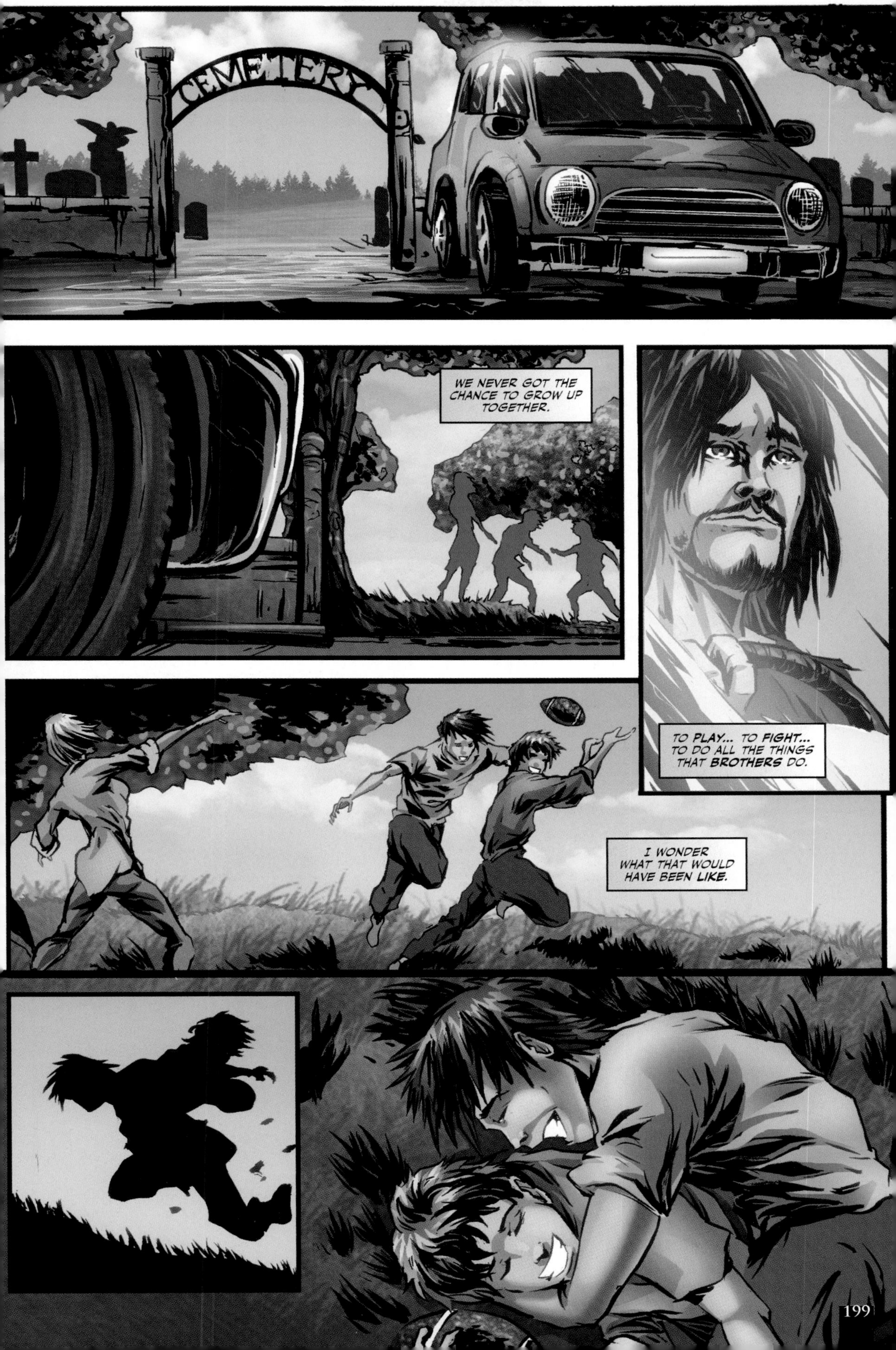
CEMETERY
WE NEVER GOT THE CHANCE TO GROW UP TOGETHER.
TO PLAY... TO FIGHT... TO DO ALL THE THINGS THAT BROTHERS DO.
I WONDER WHAT THAT WOULD HAVE BEEN LIKE.

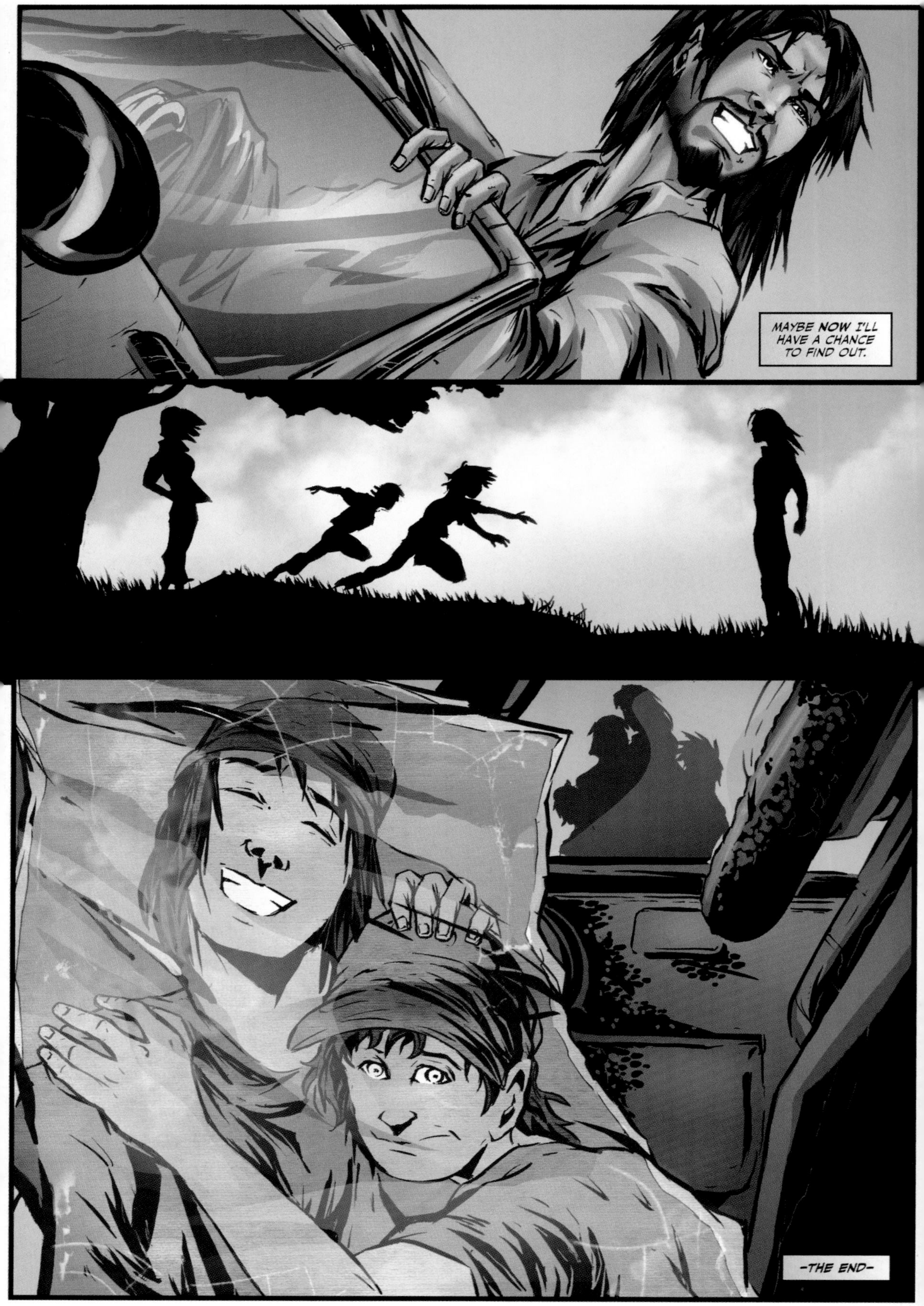
MAYBE NOW I'LL HAVE A CHANCE TO FIND OUT.
-THE END-

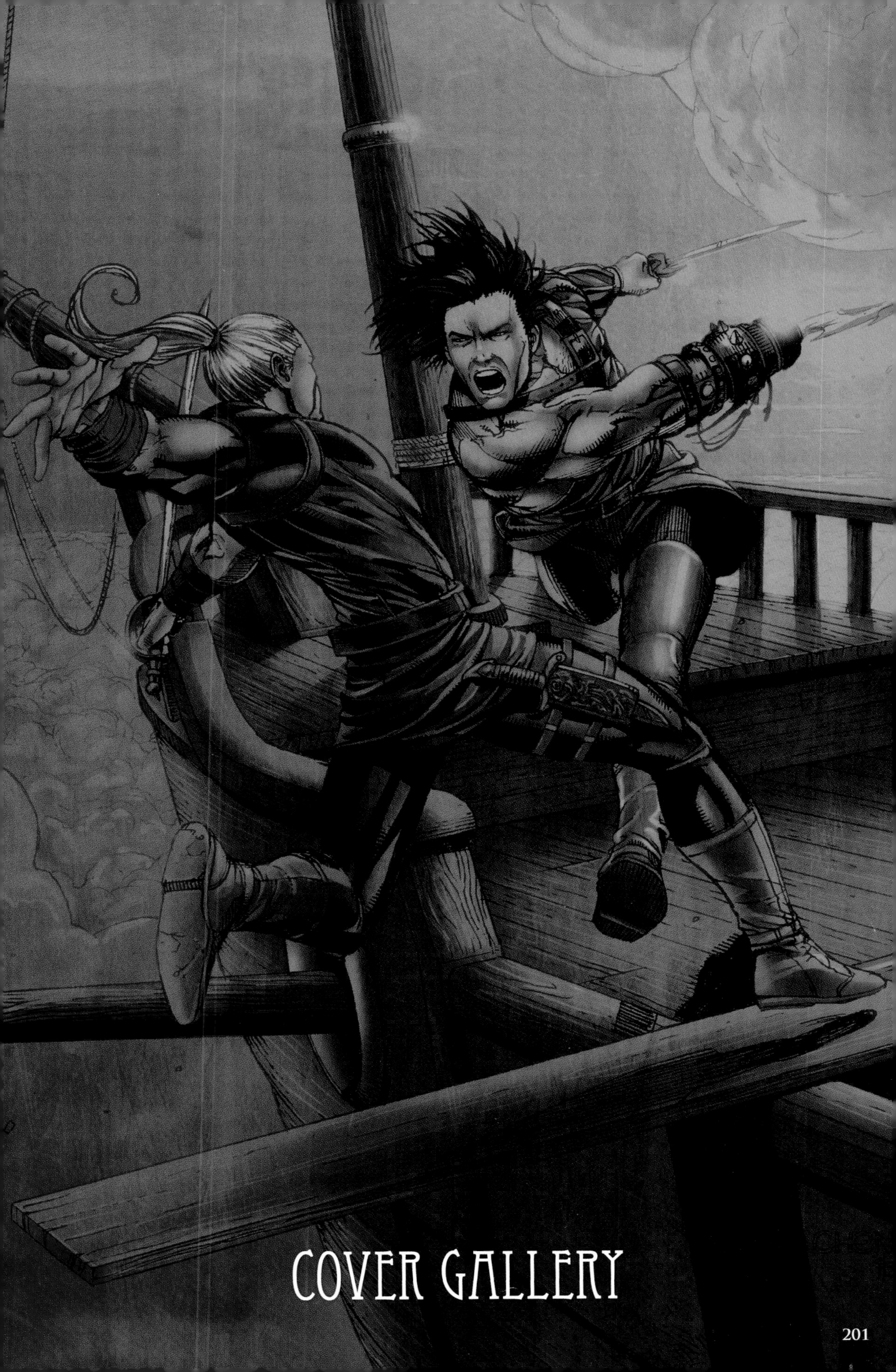

COVER GALLERY

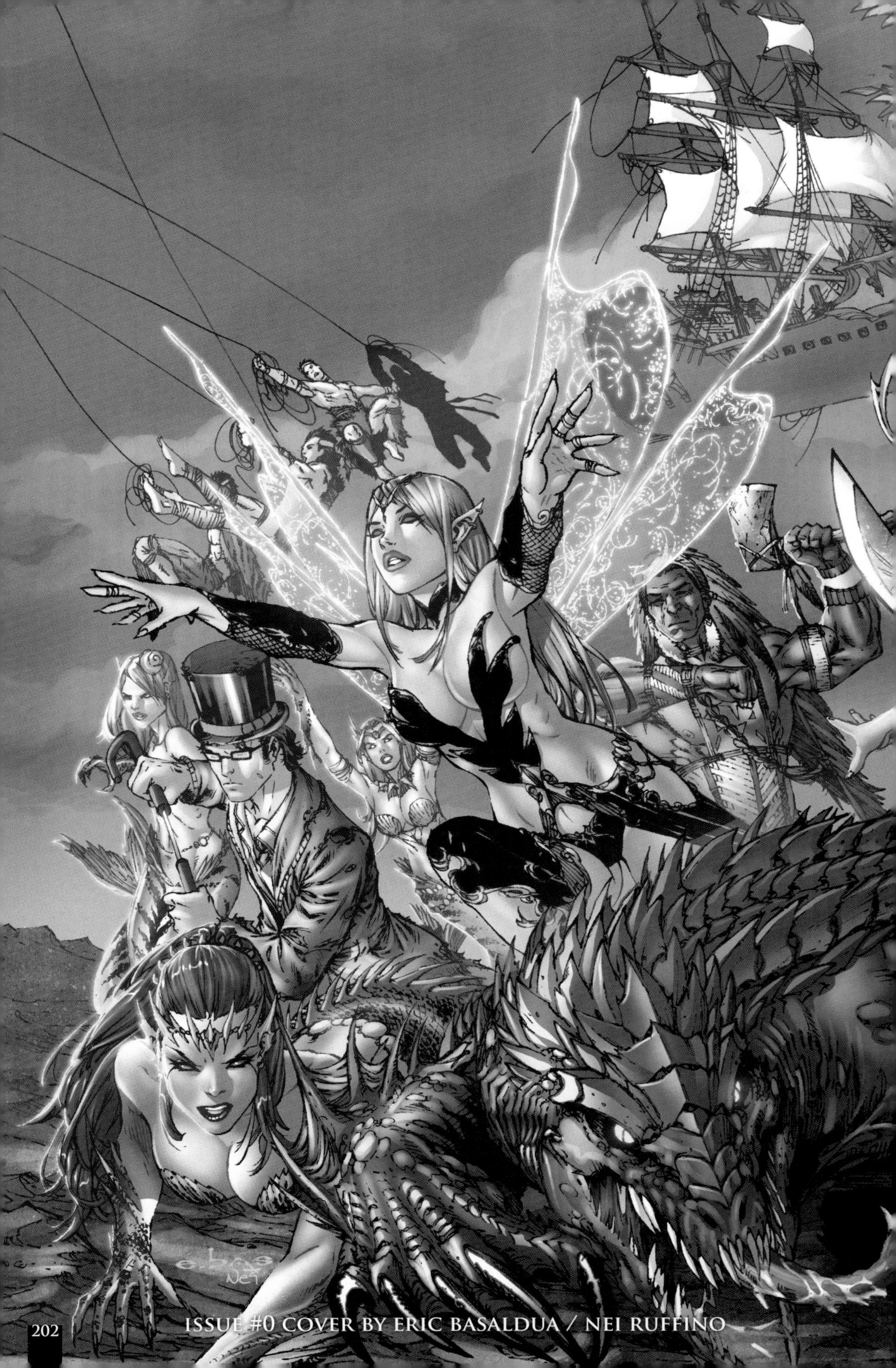

ISSUE #0 COVER BY ERIC BASALDUA / NEI RUFFINO

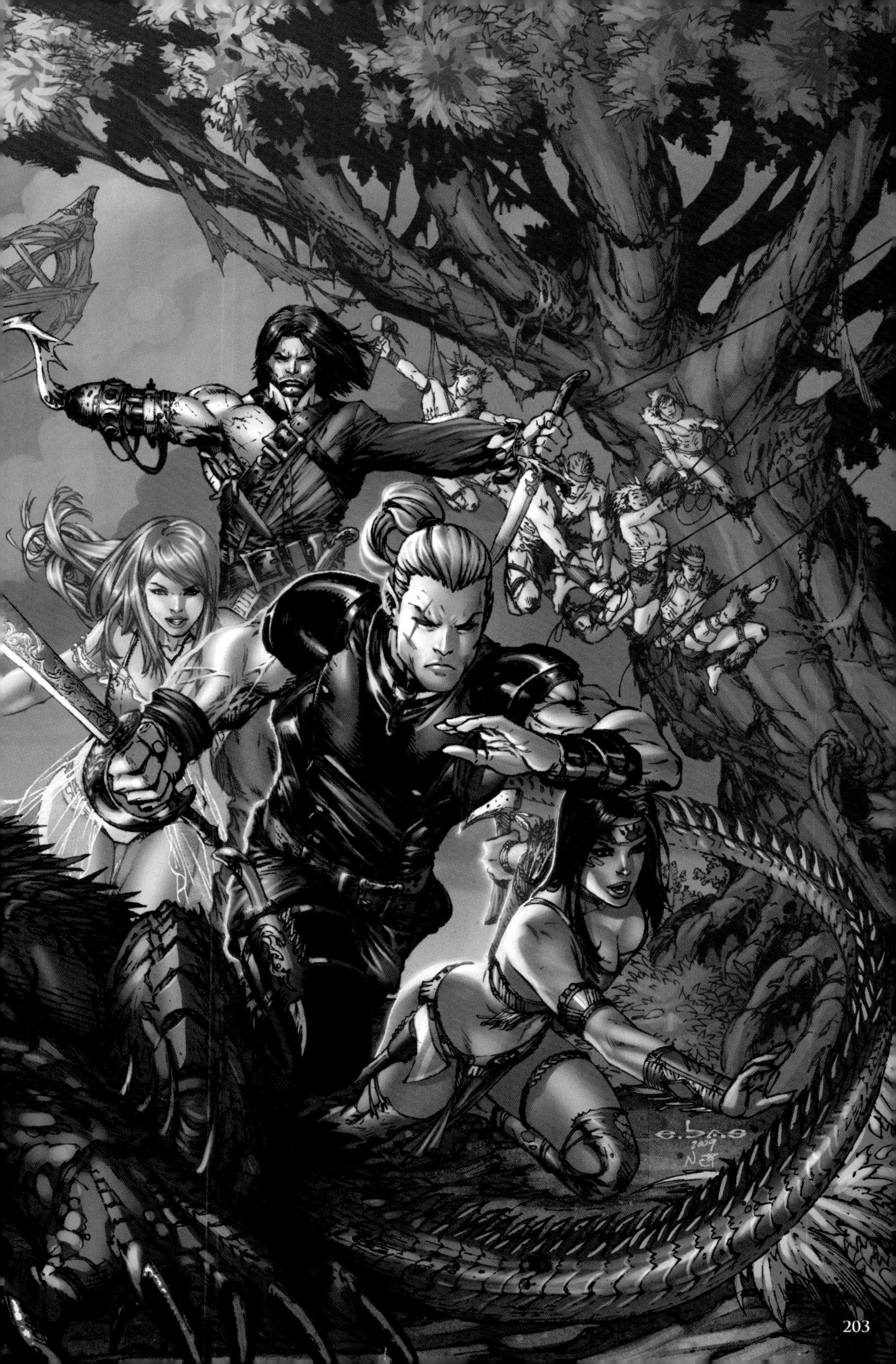

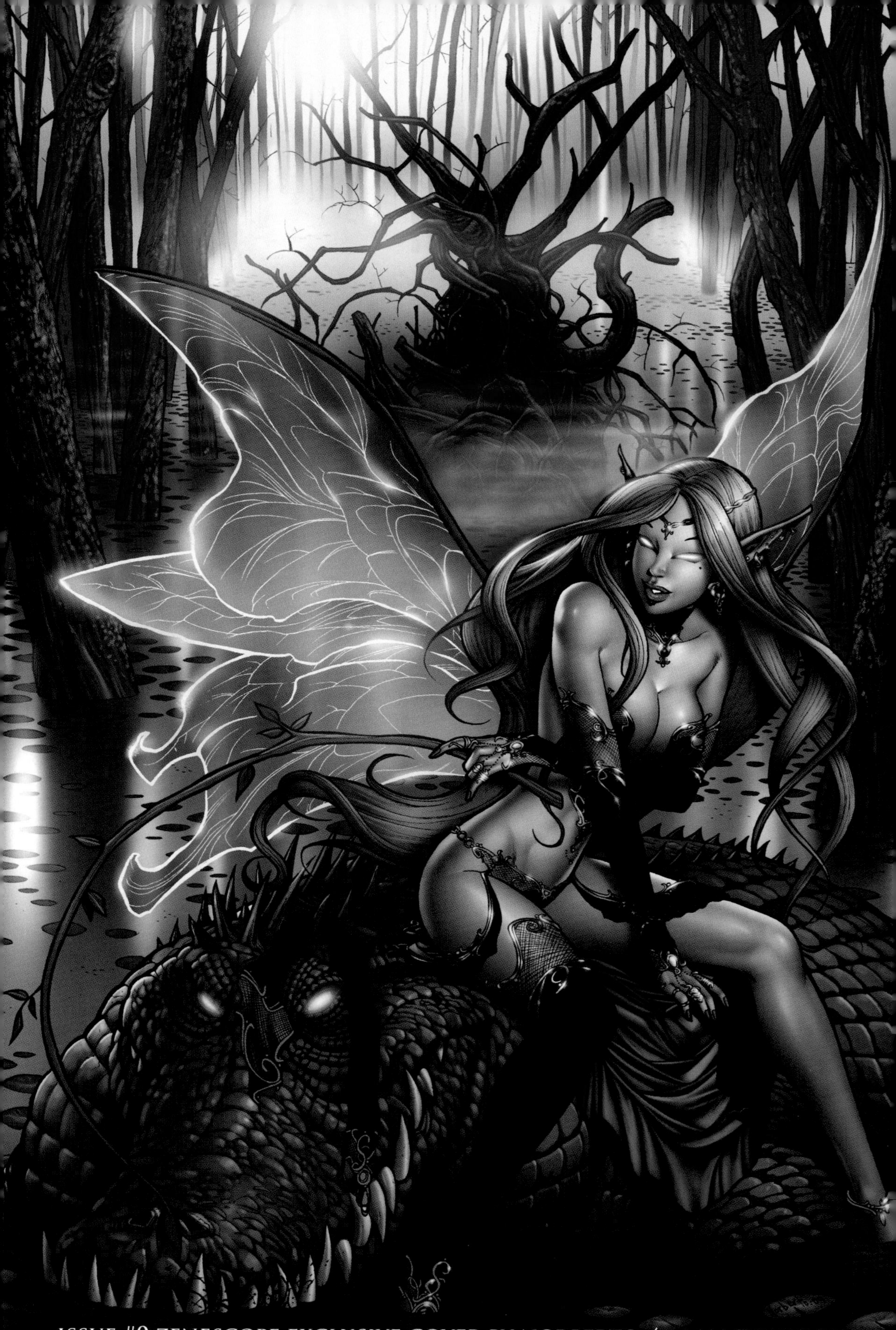

ISSUE #0 ZENESCOPE EXCLUSIVE COVER BY NORBERTO / DJ MACKINNION

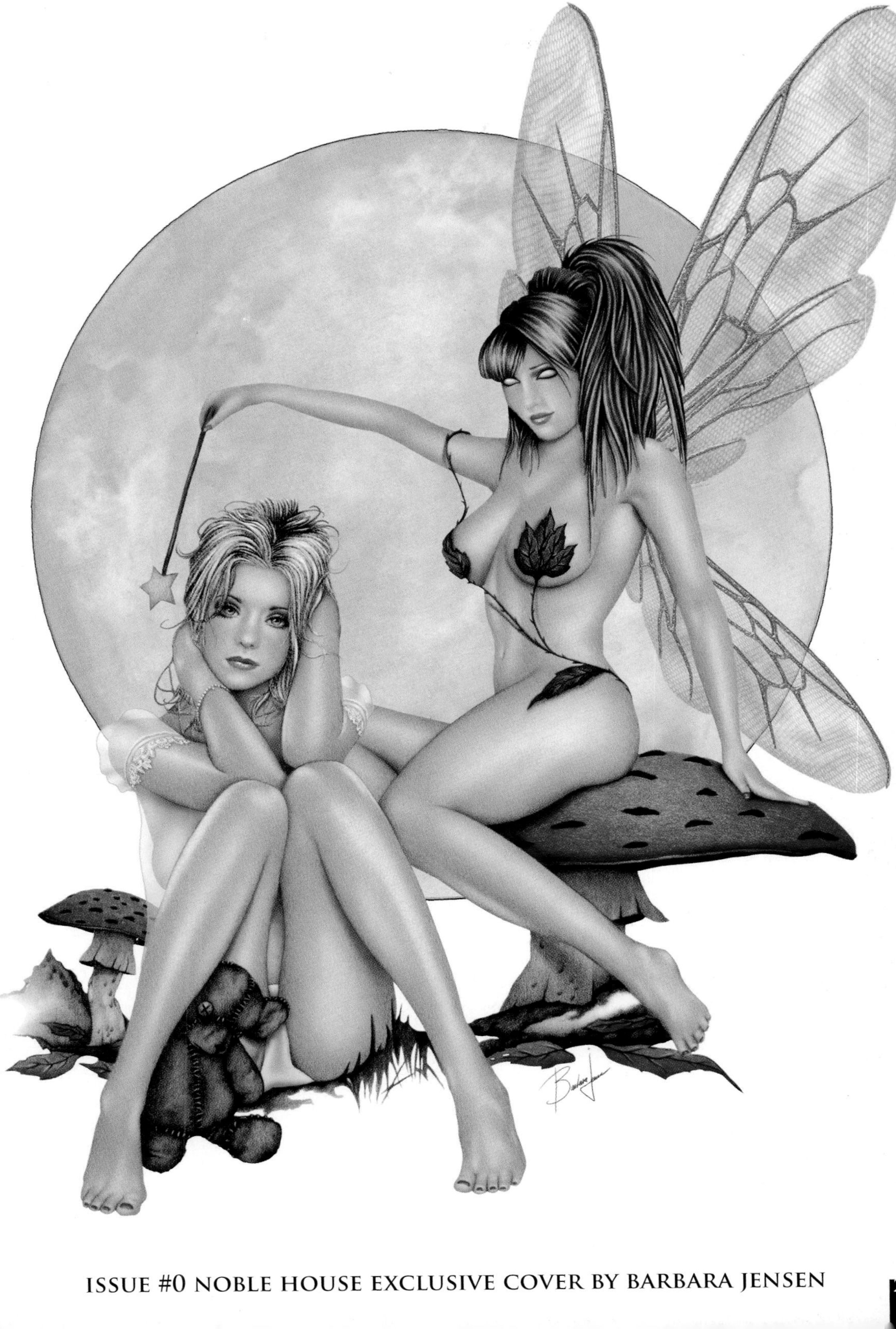

ISSUE #0 NOBLE HOUSE EXCLUSIVE COVER BY BARBARA JENSEN

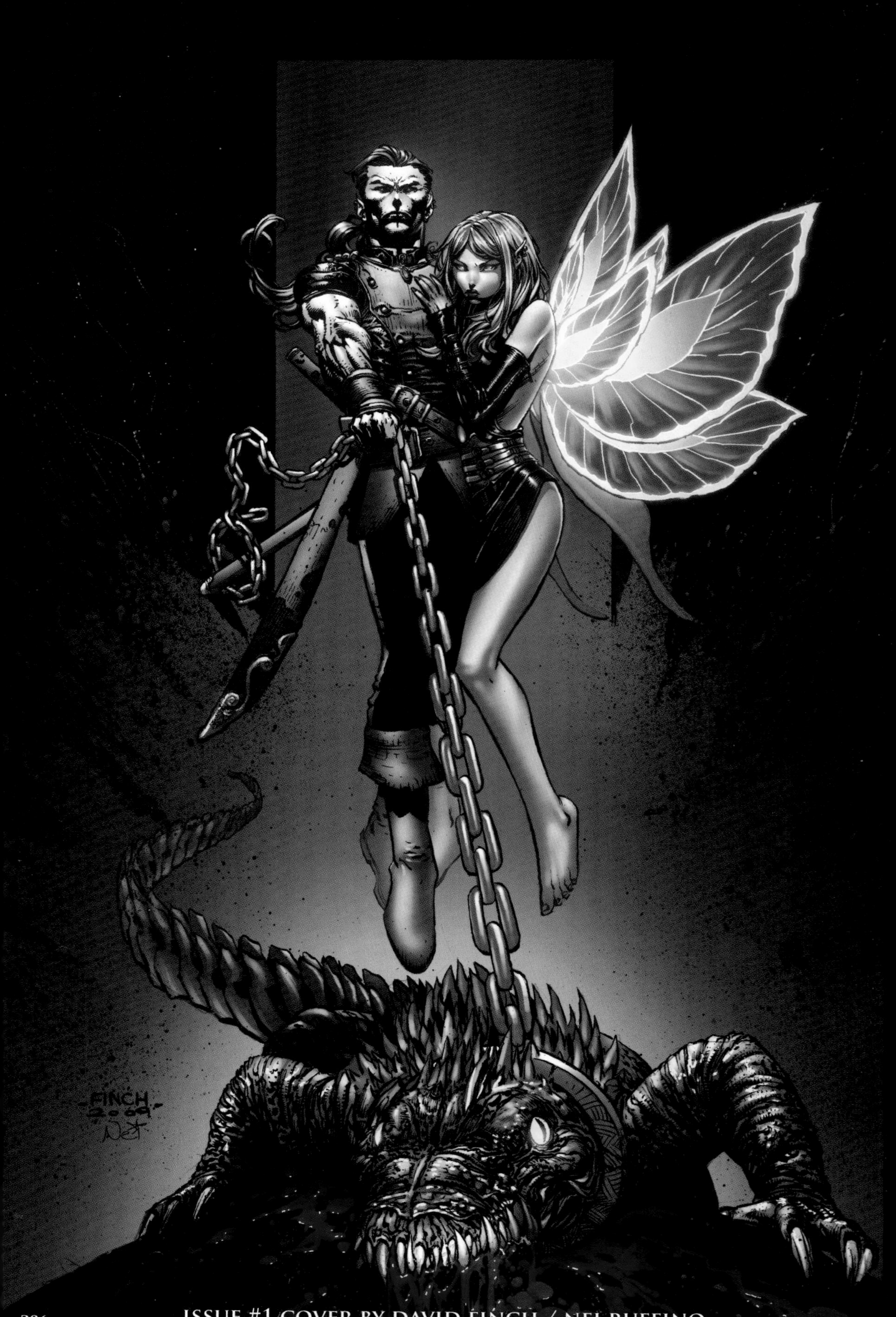
FINCH
2009

ISSUE #1 COVER BY DAVID FINCH / NEI RUFFINO

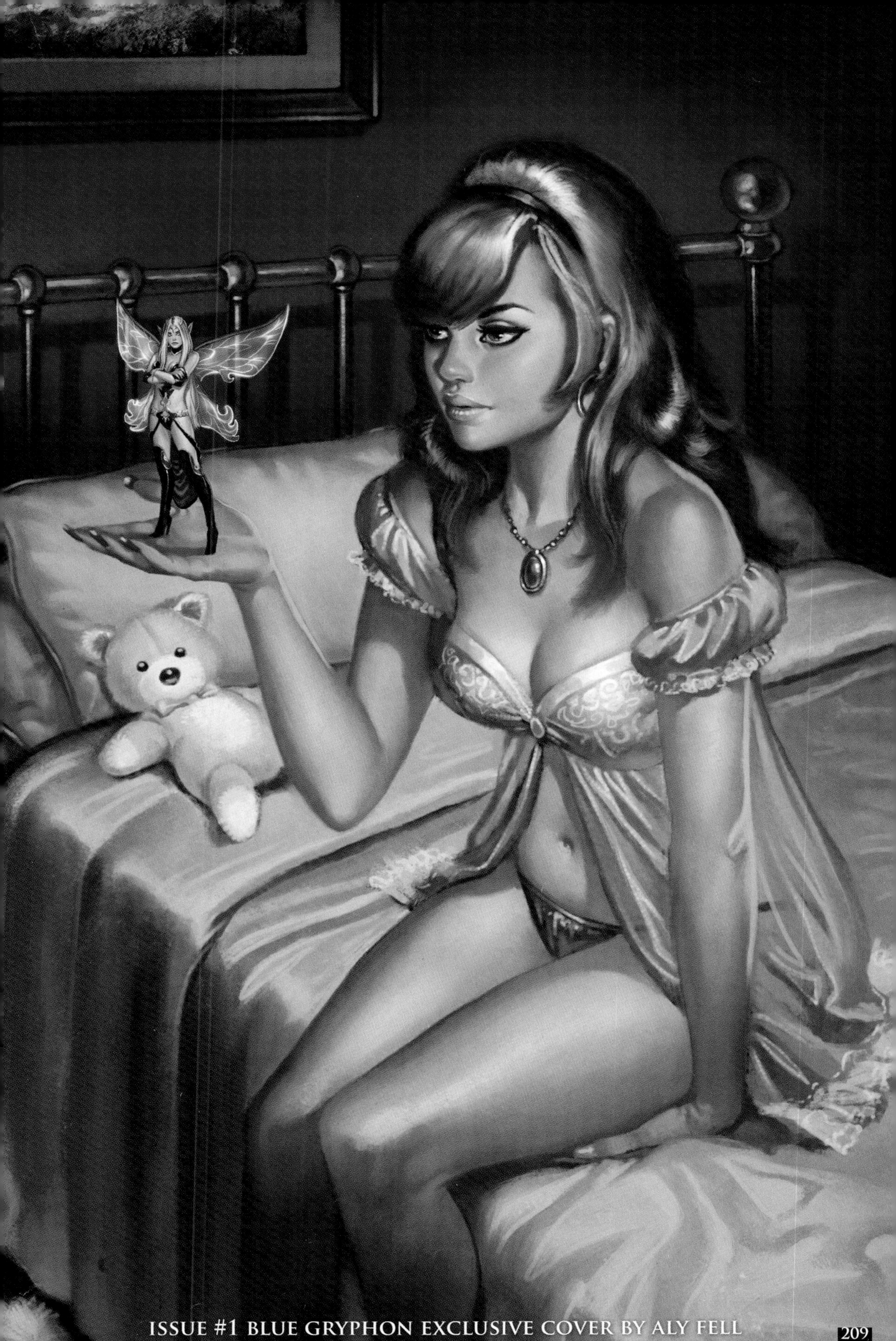

ISSUE #1 BLUE GRYPHON EXCLUSIVE COVER BY ALY FELL

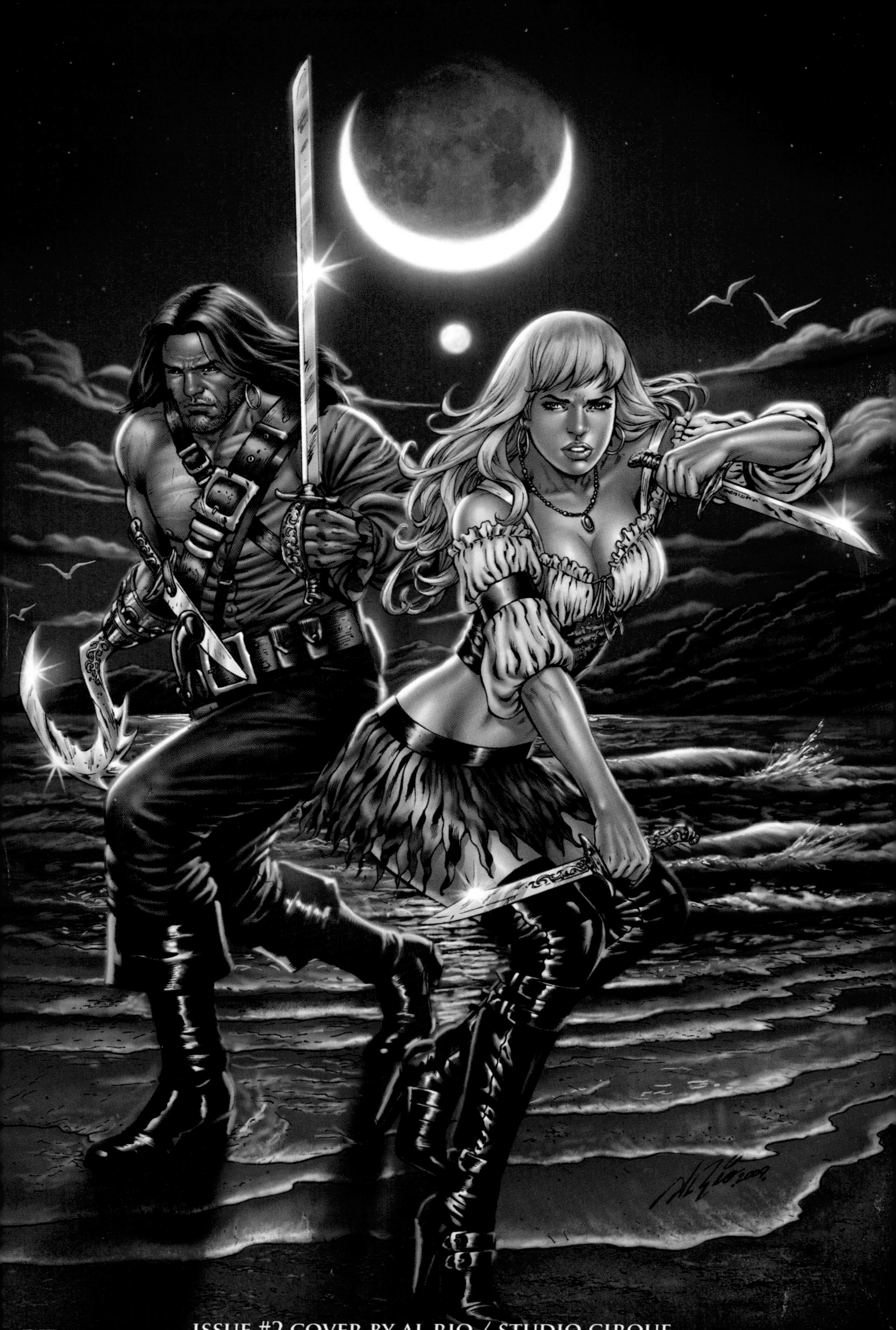

ISSUE #2 COVER BY AL RIO / STUDIO CIRQUE

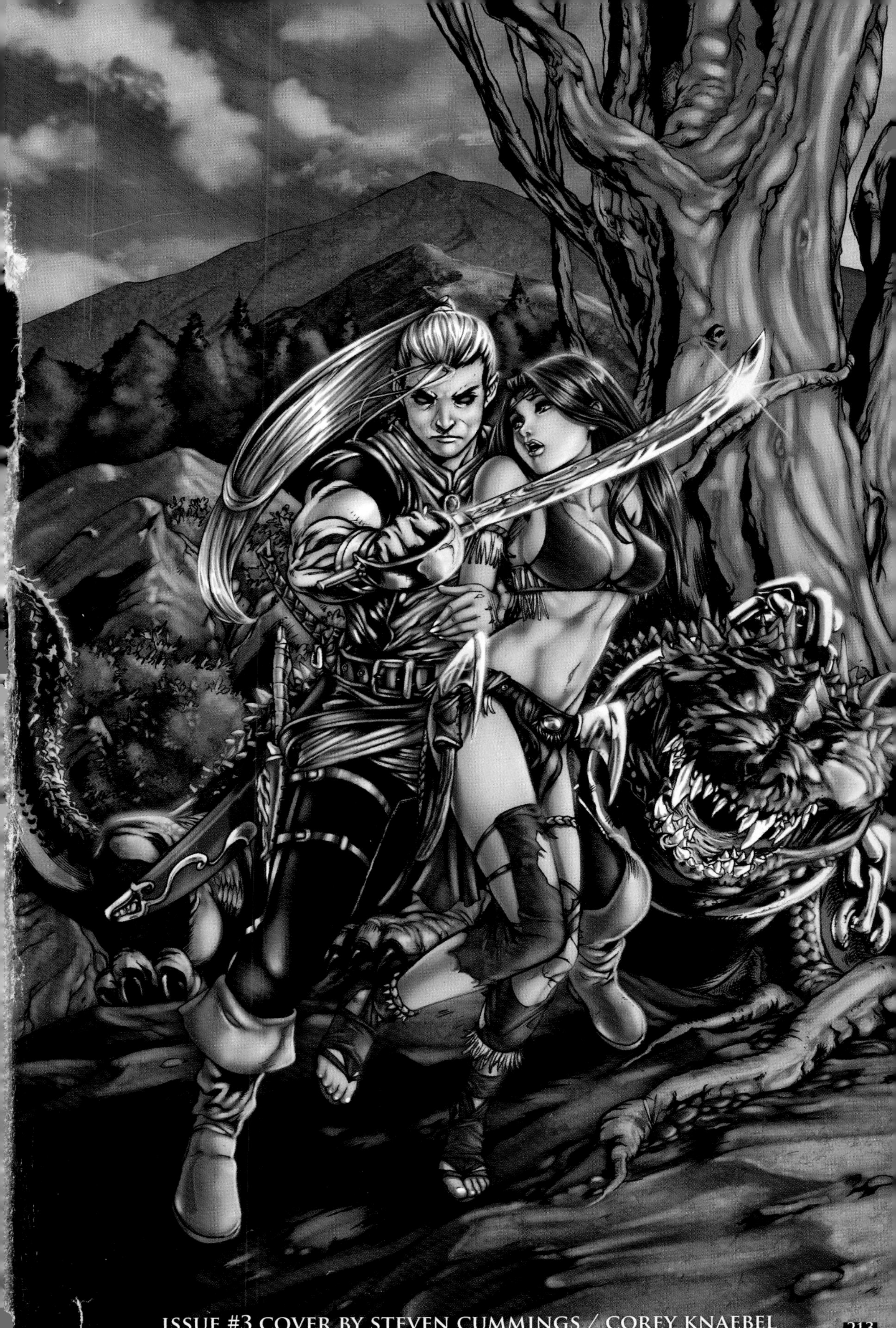

ISSUE #3 COVER BY STEVEN CUMMINGS / COREY KNAEBEL

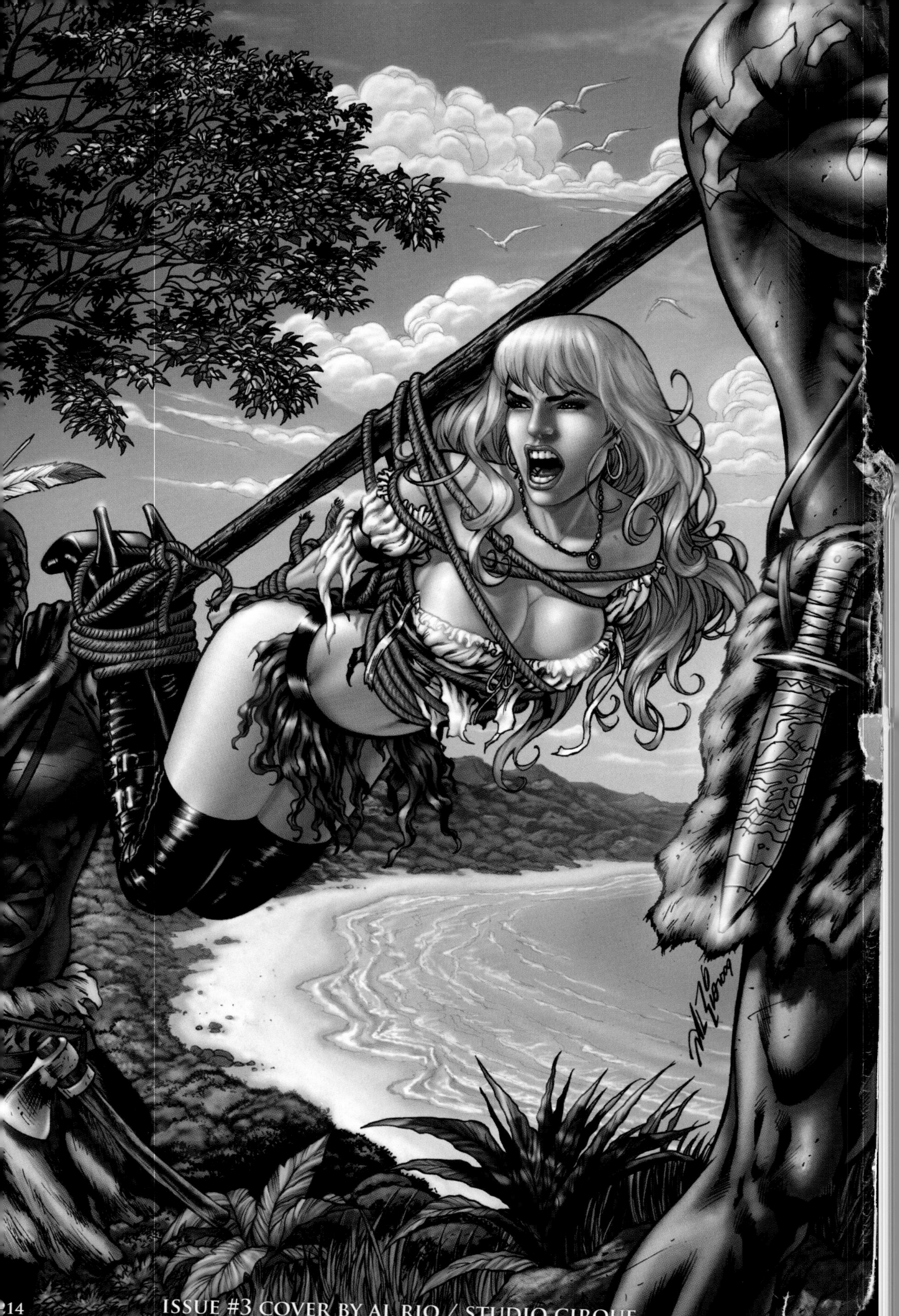
ISSUE #3 COVER BY AL RIO / STUDIO CIRQUE

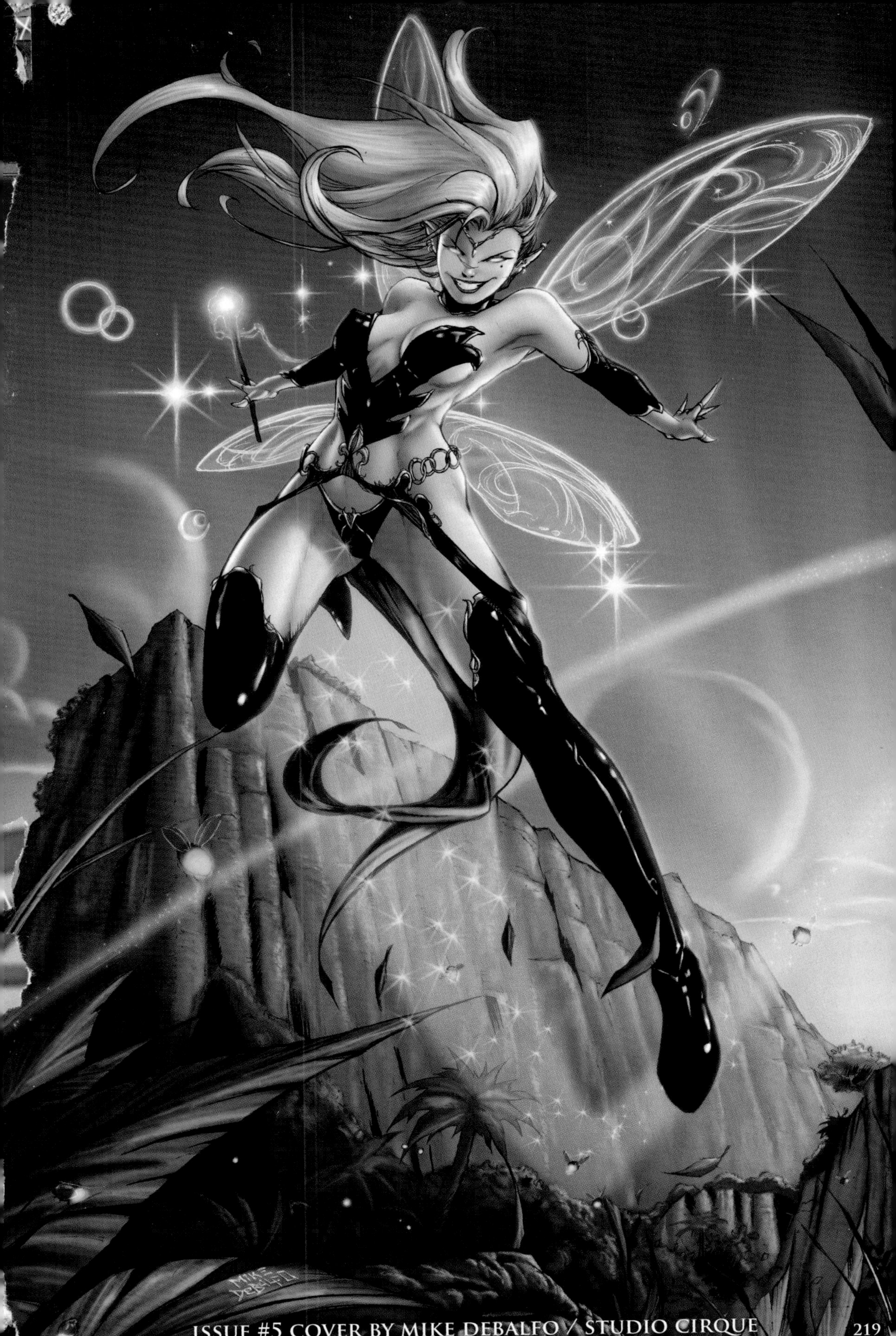

ISSUE #5 COVER BY MIKE DEBALFO / STUDIO CIRQUE

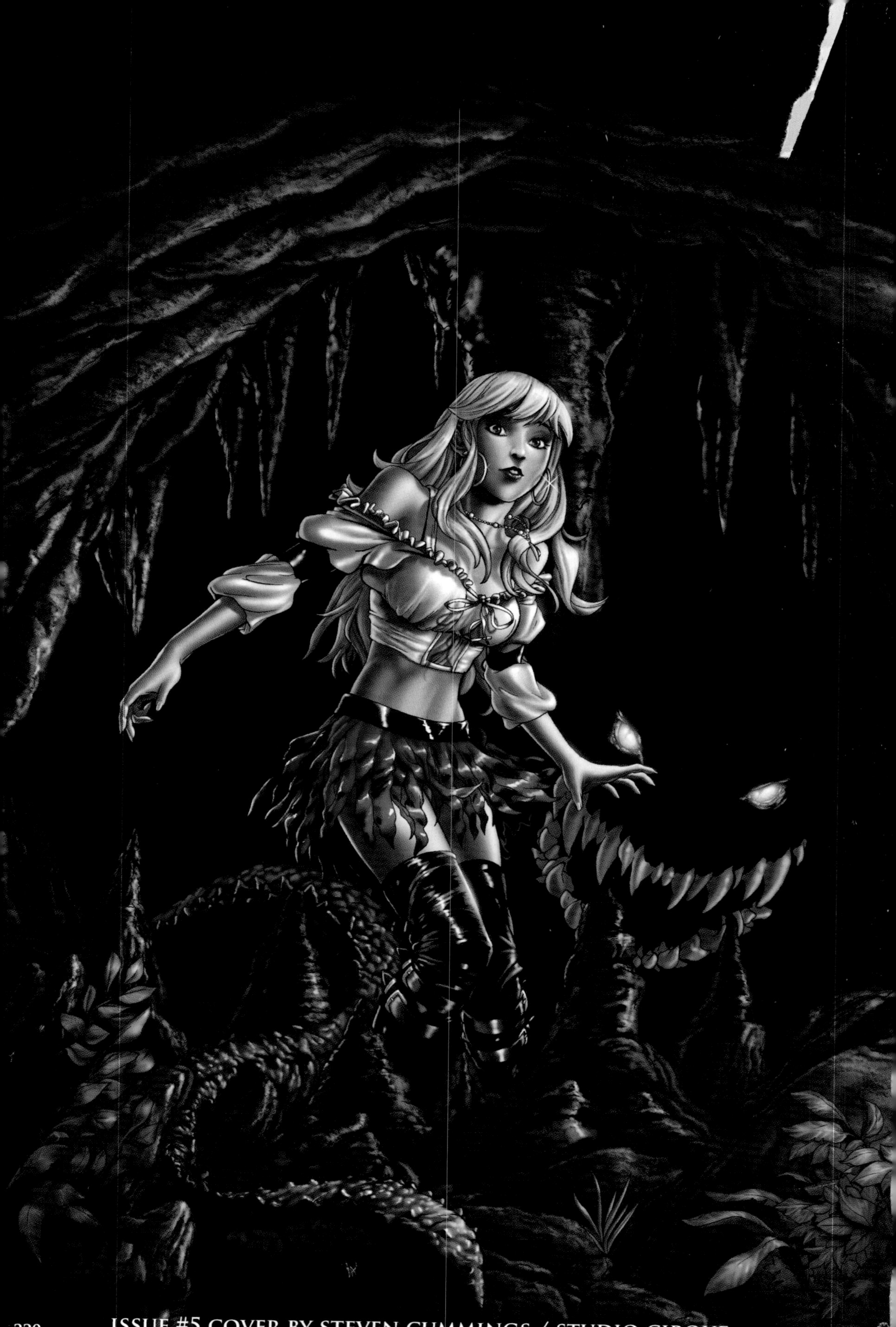

ISSUE #5 COVER BY STEVEN CUMMINGS / STUDIO CIRQUE

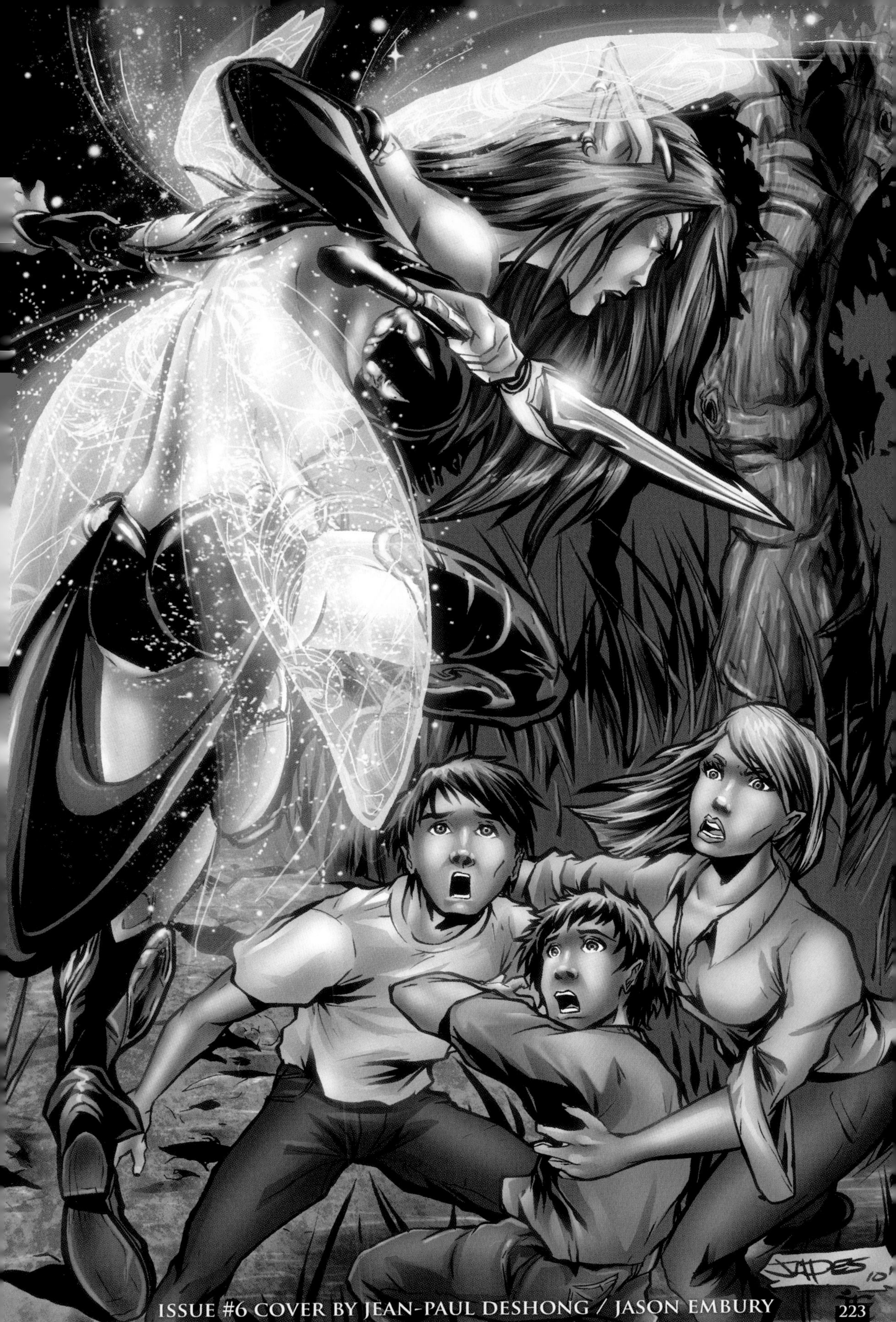

ISSUE #6 COVER BY JEAN-PAUL DESHONG / JASON EMBURY

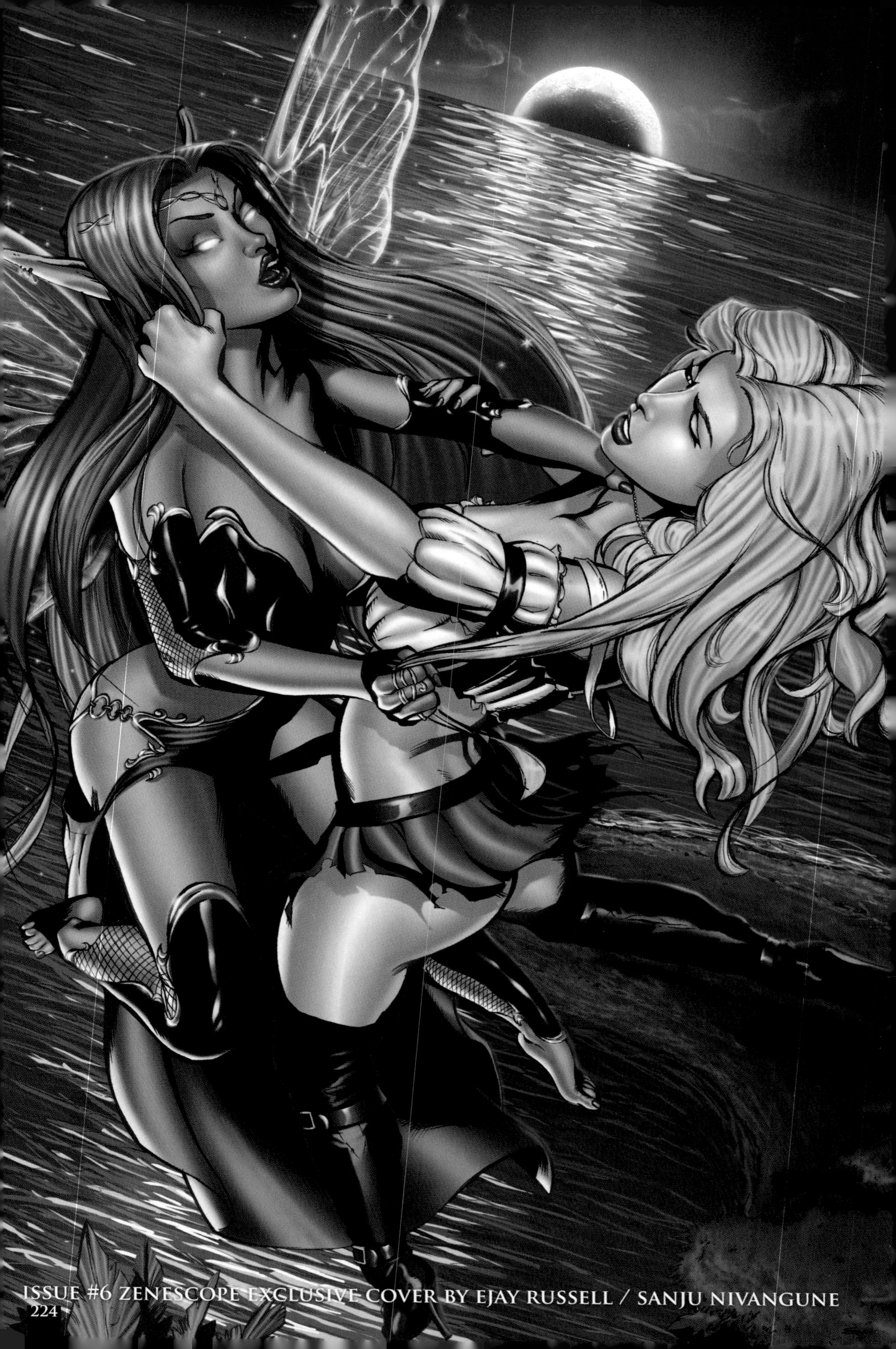

ISSUE #6 ZENESCOPE EXCLUSIVE COVER BY EJAY RUSSELL / SANJU NIVANGUNE

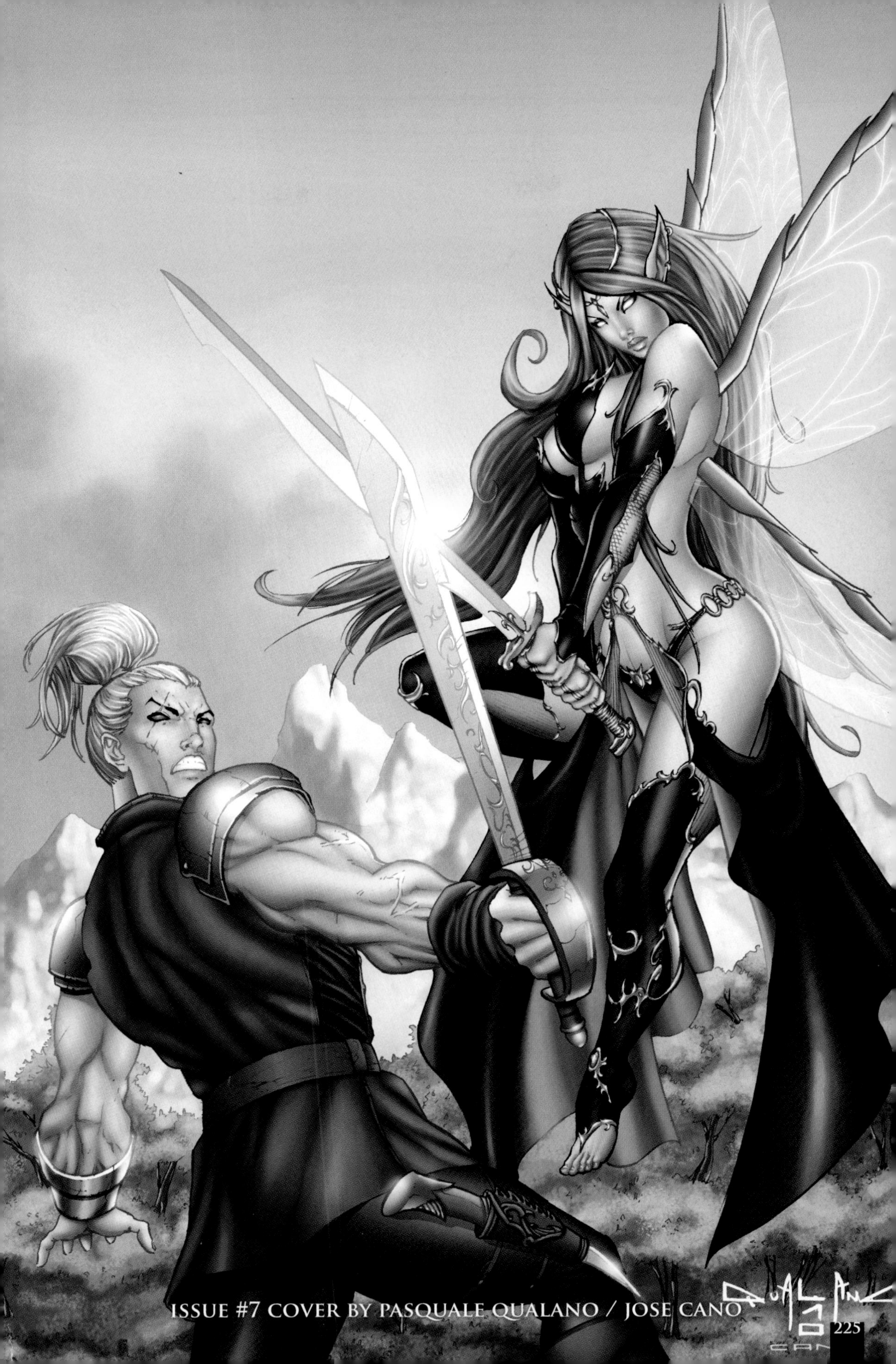

ISSUE #7 COVER BY PASQUALE QUALANO / JOSE CANO

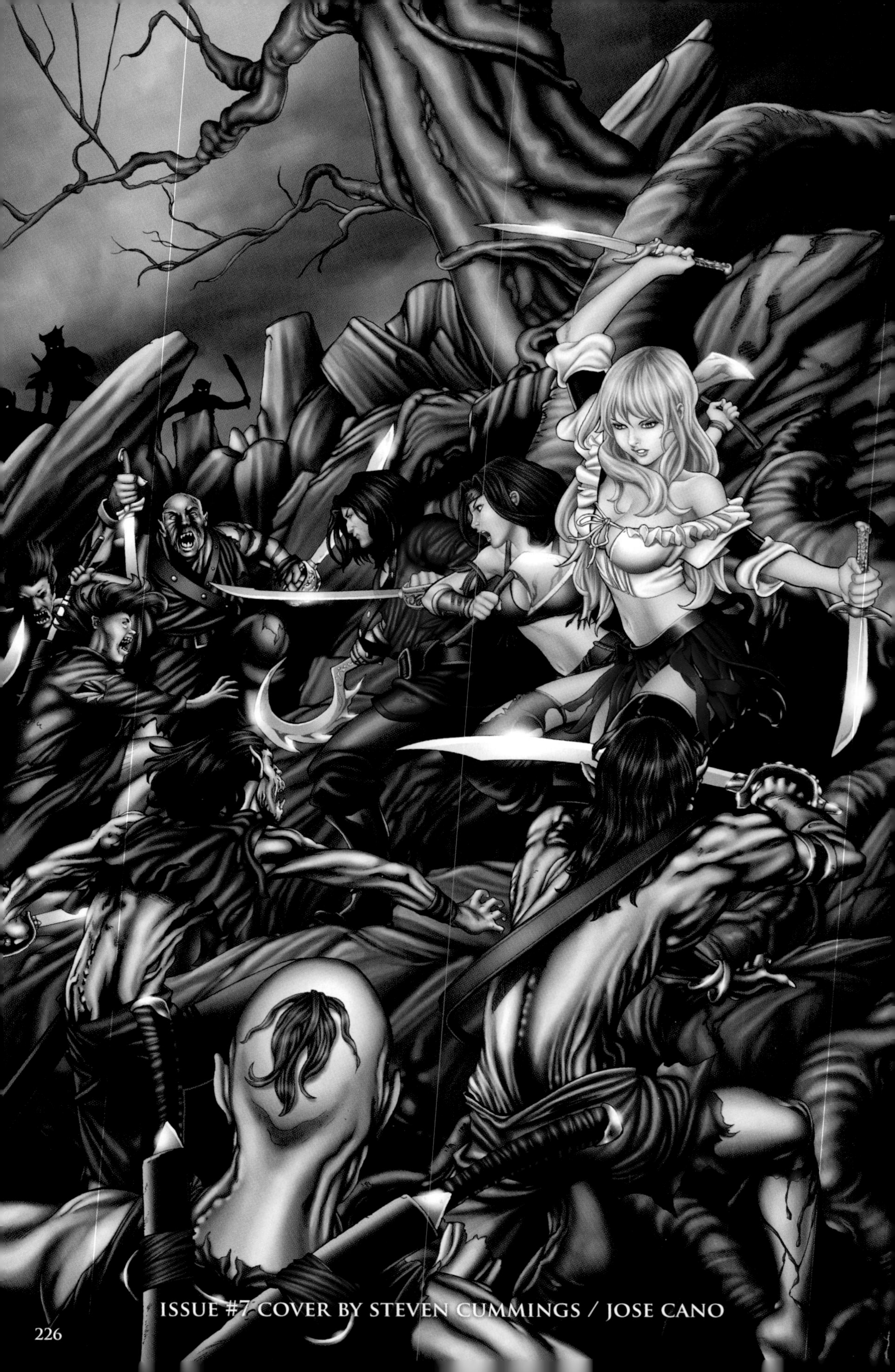

ISSUE #7 COVER BY STEVEN CUMMINGS / JOSE CANO